OXFORD MEDICAL PUBLICATIONS

CUNNINGHAM'S
MANUAL OF
PRACTICAL
ANATOMY

CUNNINGHAM'S MANUAL OF PRACTICAL ANATOMY

THIRTEENTH EDITION

REVISED BY

G. J. ROMANES, *C.B.E.*

B.A., Ph.D., M.B., Ch.B., F.R.C.S.Ed., F.R.S.E.

Professor of Anatomy in the University of Edinburgh

VOLUME III
HEAD AND NECK AND BRAIN

LONDON
OXFORD UNIVERSITY PRESS
NEW YORK   BOMBAY

Oxford University Press, Ely House, London W. 1

GLASGOW NEW YORK TORONTO MELBOURNE WELLINGTON
CAPE TOWN IBADAN NAIROBI DAR ES SALAAM LUSAKA ADDIS ABABA
DELHI BOMBAY CALCUTTA MADRAS KARACHI LAHORE DACCA
KUALA LUMPUR SINGAPORE HONG KONG TOKYO

ISBN 0 19 263120 9

New material in this edition
© Oxford University Press 1966

Dissector's Guide, 1879
Manual of Practical Anatomy, 1889
Present Series
First Edition, 1893
Thirteenth Edition, 1966
Reprinted 1968, 1971, 1973 and 1975

*Printed in Great Britain
at the University Press, Oxford
by Vivian Ridler
Printer to the University*

CONTENTS

THE HEAD AND NECK

THE BRAIN

PREFACE
TO THE THIRTEENTH EDITION

THIS volume has been modified in keeping with the general principles set out in the Preface to Volume I. The text has been rewritten mainly with the aim of reducing the over-all length. This has been achieved by the removal of unessential detail, but new material has been added where the earlier edition failed to meet the needs of the present-day student.

The total number of alterations is considerable, and only the major changes are noted here. New procedures have been designed to allow the dissection of the pharynx, larynx, and paranasal sinuses from the medial side. Together with the appropriate new illustrations, the dissections should give the student a better appreciation of the position and functions of the major structures in the walls of these cavities, which are of particular importance because they are readily inspected in the living patient, but which are difficult for the student to understand when dissected in the conventional manner from the lateral side.

A new method for removal of the brain is described. This is intended to stress the relation of the brain and the cranial nerves to the skull and meninges, and should help to make a closer link between the study of the head and neck and the brain than is possible when the brain is removed in a single operation. An alternative dissection for the removal of the brain is described for those departments where it is necessary to use the brain from the cadaver for more detailed study.

Many new illustrations have been added in the section on the brain. Some of these are designed to assist with the more complex dissections of the central nervous system, and it is hoped that they will help the student to obtain a better understanding of this system in a shorter time, when taken in association with the new dissection instructions. Other new illustrations and additions to the text have increased the amount of information on those major tracts and nuclei in the central nervous system which can be demonstrated either by dissection, or by the study of stained sections of the brain stem under a hand lens or with the low power of the microscope.

All the illustrations in this and the other volumes have been redrawn, and a number have been replaced by photographs or drawings of new dissections, while illustrations of the bones have been introduced at appropriate points in the text. It is a pleasure to acknowledge the assistance given by the artists, Miss M. Benstead, Mrs. C. Clarke, and Mr. R. N. Lane, in the production of high-quality illustrations even in the face of repeated modifications.

I am grateful to a number of members of the Staff of this Department for suggestions and help ; more especially to Dr. H. S. Barrett who has borne the brunt of correcting the typescript and proofs, and who has made a number of valuable suggestions that have been incorporated.

Edinburgh
October, 1966

G. J. ROMANES

THE HEAD AND NECK

As a preliminary to the dissection of the head and neck, the dissectors should study the skull, relating its main features to the bony points which can be felt. They should realize that a sound knowledge of the skull and cervical vertebrae, and of the structures which pass through or are attached to them, is invaluable to an understanding of the anatomy of this region [see FIGS. 1, 2, 18, 39, 93, 101].

THE SCALP, THE TEMPLE, AND THE FACE

SURFACE ANATOMY

The dissectors should begin by examining the living head, and identifying the parts mentioned in the following paragraphs.

Auricle [Fig. 5]

It is nearer the back of the head than the front, and is at the level of the eye and nose. The concha is the 'well of the ear' and leads into the external acoustic meatus. The helix is the outer rim; it begins in the concha, and ends at the lobule, which is the soft, lower end of the auricle. The tragus is the small lid that overlaps the concha anteriorly; it carries hairs which project backwards and, to some extent, prevent small foreign bodies from entering the meatus; they become thicker after middle age.

Back and Side of the Head

The **external occipital protuberance** is the knob felt in the median line where the back of the head joins the neck. Feel for the **superior nuchal line**, an indistinct, curved ridge that extends laterally from the protuberance towards the mastoid process; it marks the boundary between the head and the neck posteriorly. The **mastoid process** is the smooth, rounded bone behind the lower part of the auricle. Press the finger tip into the hollow below the mastoid process, behind the jaw; the resistance felt is due to the transverse process of the atlas vertebra with the lower part of the parotid salivary gland, the anterior border of the sternocleidomastoid muscle, and the accessory nerve intervening.

Identify the **supramastoid crest** on the skull. It is a blunt ridge that begins immediately above the external acoustic meatus and curves posterosuperiorly for 2·5 cm. The **parietal tuber** is the most convex part of the parietal bone. The **frontal tuber** is situated where the front, top, and side of the head meet. On the side of the head, identify the curved **temporal line** that marks the upper limit of the temporal region. The only part of this line that can be felt distinctly begins at a prominence at the lateral end of the eyebrow. The line arches posterosuperiorly and, rapidly becoming impalpable, passes a little below the parietal eminence and turns downwards to join the supramastoid crest.

Face

External Nose. The term 'nose' also includes the paired cavities which extend posteriorly from the nostrils to open into the pharynx. The lower part of the external nose is composed of skin and cartilage and is movable; the upper part is bony and consists of: (1) the bridge of the nose, formed by the two **nasal bones**, and (2) postero-inferior to each

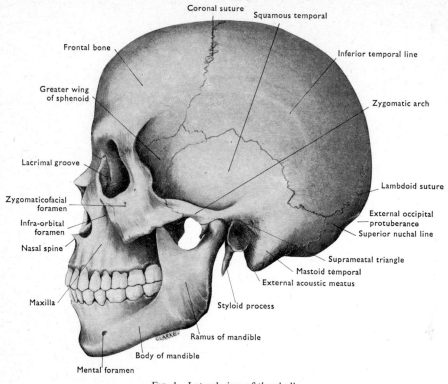

Coronal suture
Squamous temporal
Frontal bone
Inferior temporal line
Greater wing of sphenoid
Zygomatic arch
Lacrimal groove
Lambdoid suture
Zygomaticofacial foramen
External occipital protuberance
Infra-orbital foramen
Superior nuchal line
Nasal spine
Suprameatal triangle
Mastoid temporal
External acoustic meatus
Maxilla
Styloid process
Ramus of mandible
Body of mandible
Mental foramen

Fig. 1   Lateral view of the skull.

nasal bone the **frontal process of the maxilla.**
The skin is adherent to the cartilages, but is
mobile over the bones. The part of the cavity
of the nose immediately above each nostril is
the **vestibule of the nose.** The lateral wall of the
vestibule is slightly expanded; this is the **ala**
of the nose. The vestibule is lined by hairy
skin.

Lips, Cheeks, and Teeth

The lips and cheeks are composed chiefly of
muscle and fat covered with skin and lined
with mucous membrane. The space that separates the lips and cheeks from the teeth and
gums is the **vestibule of the mouth.** A full set
of adult teeth consists of 32 (milk dentition is
20), the 8 in each half jaw, counting from before backwards, are 2 incisors, 1 canine, 2
premolars, and 3 molars. The **oral fissure,**

between the lips, is opposite the upper teeth
near their biting edges, the corner or angle of
the mouth is opposite the first premolar tooth.
The **philtrum** is the median groove on the external surface of the upper lip. In the median
plane, the deep surface of each lip is attached
to the gum by a fold of mucous membrane,
the **frenulum of the lip.**

Mandible

Identify the horizontal **body** of the mandible
below the lower lip and the cheeks, and follow
its lower border posteriorly to the **angle** of the
mandible, a point often used as a landmark.
Find the **mental foramen** about 4 cm. from the
median plane, and half way between the gum
and the lower border of the mandible. It can
be felt as a slight depression in the living
person if the finger tip is pressed firmly over it.

2

The **oblique line** of the mandible is a blunt ridge that begins behind the mental foramen and passes posterosuperiorly to become continuous with the anterior border of the ramus. The ramus of the mandible is the wide, flat plate which extends superiorly from the posterior part of the body and ends above in the **condylar** and **coronoid** processes. Only its anterior and posterior borders can be felt, for it is covered by the thick masseter muscle that can be felt hardening when the jaws are clenched. The condylar process stands up from the posterior part of the ramus and forms the **head** and **neck** of the mandible. The neck lies immediately anterior to the lobule of the auricle; the head is in front of the tragus. Place your finger tip in front of your own tragus, and open your mouth; the head of the mandible is felt gliding downwards and forwards, leaving a fossa into which the finger slips. Note that the mouth cannot be shut while the finger lies in this fossa.

Zygomatic Arch

This is the bony bridge which spans the interval between the ear and the eye. The

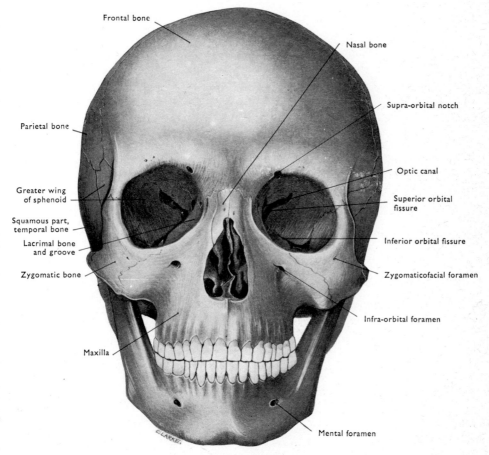

FIG. 2 Anterior view of the skull.

3

zygomatic process of the temporal bone forms its narrow posterior part, and begins at a **tubercle** which lies immediately anterior to the head of the mandible when the mouth is shut, and immediately above it when the mouth is open. The wide anterior part of the arch is the zygomatic bone, which is below and lateral to the eye, and forms the prominent part of the cheek. It extends vertically from the frontal bone to the maxilla.

Orbit

The orbit is the socket for the eyeball. Its facial opening is approximately square, and is slightly oblique. The **lower margin** is formed by the zygomatic bone and the maxilla, and has the **infra-orbital foramen** a few millimetres below it, a finger's breadth from the side of the nose. The **lateral margin** is formed by the frontal process of the zygomatic bone. The **medial margin** is chiefly the frontal process of the maxilla, which separates it from the nose. Immediately posterior to this, on the **medial wall** of the orbit, is the vertical lacrimal groove which accommodates the membranous lacrimal sac, and is continuous inferiorly with the nose through the nasolacrimal canal. The superior margin of the orbit is the **supra-orbital margin** of the frontal bone, which extends into the lateral and medial margins joining the zygomatic and maxillary bones. Its lateral end, the zygomatic process of the frontal bone, forms the prominence felt at the lateral end of the eyebrow, and there is a palpable notch posteriorly where it meets the zygomatic bone. Run your finger along the superior margin of the orbit, and feel the **supra-orbital notch** at the highest point. It is a small groove through which the supra-orbital nerve reaches the forehead. It may be converted into a foramen by a spicule of bone.

Eyebrow

This hairy fold of skin covers the supra-orbital margin; the hairs being longer and stronger in the elderly than in the young. Above its medial end is a curved ridge of bone, the **superciliary arch.** It is only well formed in

males, and is separated from its fellow by the smooth, median **glabella.**

Eye

The white of the eye is the **sclera,** the clear front, the **cornea.** Through the cornea can be seen a dark, circular aperture, the **pupil,** surrounded by the coloured **iris.** The visible part of the sclera is covered with a moist, transparent membrane, the **conjunctiva,** and this is reflected off the sclera on to the deep surfaces of the eyelids to become continuous with the skin at their margins. The angle of reflexion, above and below, is called the **fornix** of the conjunctiva, and the whole conjunctiva forms the **conjunctival sac.**

Eyelids

These folds or palpebrae protect the front of the eye, and join each other at the lateral and medial angles of the eye. The upper lid is larger and more movable than the lower, and the upper fornix is much deeper. When the eye is open, the eyelids overlap the cornea slightly and are separated by an elliptical **palpebral fissure.** When the eye is closed the fissure is nearly a horizontal line which lies opposite the lower margin of the cornea.

In the medial angle of the eye is a small, triangular space, the **lacus lacrimalis,** with a reddish, fleshy-looking elevation, the **lacrimal caruncle,** in its centre. The caruncle carries a

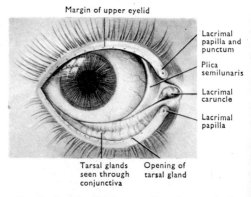

Margin of upper eyelid

Lacrimal papilla and punctum

Plica semilunaris

Lacrimal caruncle

Lacrimal papilla

Tarsal glands seen through conjunctiva

Opening of tarsal gland

FIG. 3 Eyelids slightly everted to show part of the conjunctival sac.

4

few fine hairs, and has a small, vertical, curved fold of conjunctiva, the **plica semilunaris,** immediately lateral to it [FIG. 3]. This fold slightly overlaps the eyeball, and is the rudimentary representative of the nictitating membrane possessed by some animals.

Evert the lids. The lower lid is easily turned inside out, and the lower fornix exposed by turning the eye up. The upper lid is difficult to evert because a rigid tarsal plate is buried in it, and once everted tends to remain so. Even when this is done the deep superior fornix is not exposed.

On the deep surface of the lids, note the **tarsal glands** which show through the conjunctiva as a number of yellowish, parallel streaks [FIG. 3]; their ducts open on the flat, free margin of the lid near the posterior edge, while the eyelashes **(cilia)** project from the anterior edge. The free margin of each lid which abuts on the caruncle is smooth and rounded, and where it joins the flat margin is a small **lacrimal papilla** surmounted by a tiny aperture, the **lacrimal punctum.** This is the open end of a slender tube, the **lacrimal canaliculus,** which carries the lacrimal fluid (tears) to the lacrimal sac, whence it is conducted to the nose through the nasolacrimal duct. Note that the puncta face posteriorly into the conjunctival sac, and that the eyelids move medially when the eye is forcibly closed, thus moving the lacrimal fluid towards the medial angle and the openings of the lacrimal canaliculi.

Press the finger tip on the skin between the nose and the medial angle of the eye; a rounded, horizontal cord will be felt. This is the **medial palpebral ligament** which connects both eyelids and their muscle to the medial margin of the orbit. If the eyelids are drawn gently in a lateral direction, it may raise a small skin ridge.

THE SCALP AND SUPERFICIAL PARTS OF THE TEMPLE

The scalp covers the vault of the skull and extends between the right and left temporal lines, and the eyebrows and the superior nuchal lines. Essentially it consists of a flat aponeurotic sheet, the **epicranial aponeurosis,** which is the tendon of the two frontal and the two occipital bellies of the occipitofrontalis muscle. To this the skin is bound by dense strands of fibrous tissue which traverse the subcutaneous tissue and split it into a large number of separate pockets filled with fat. It is in this superficial layer that the blood vessels and nerves of the scalp are found. Deep to the aponeurosis is a layer of loose connective tissue which allows it to slide freely on the periosteum (pericranium) covering the skull.

The **temple** is the area between the temporal line and the zygomatic arch. Here the skull is thin, and covered by the temporalis muscle, the temporal fascia, and an extension of the

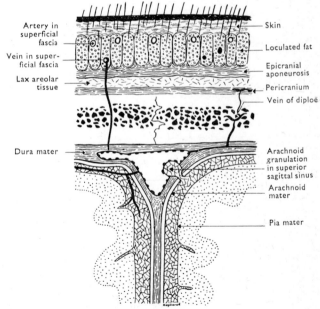

FIG. 4 Diagram of section through scalp, skull, and brain. Note venous connexions through the skull.

5

epicranial aponeurosis from which the extrinsic muscles of the auricle arise.

The blood vessels of the temple and scalp are very numerous and enter all round the periphery. Because of this, large pieces of the scalp may be torn from the skull, but they will survive and heal satisfactorily provided their peripheral attachments are intact.

DISSECTION. Place a block under the back of the head to raise it to a convenient angle. Make a median incision from the root of the nose to the external occipital protuberance, and a coronal incision from the middle of the first cut to the top of the root of the auricle. Carry it around each side of the auricle, to the mastoid process behind and the root of the zygoma in front. In making these incisions try not to cut deeper than the skin, and certainly do not cut the aponeurosis. Carefully reflect the skin flaps without cutting into the superficial fascia, and avoid dividing the vessels and nerves. During the reflexion of the skin, turn to Figures 10, 13, 26, and 27 to identify the position of the main structures in the scalp.

In FIGURE 26 note the position of the parotid salivary gland and the frontal belly of occipitofrontalis. The fibres of this muscle run upwards and backwards from the eyebrow where they are partly intermingled with, and overlapped by, the orbicularis oculi [FIG. 6].

DISSECTION. Clean the frontal belly from below upwards, and find the branches of the supratrochlear and supra-orbital vessels and nerves which pierce it. The supratrochlear is about a finger's breadth from the median line; the supra-orbital a further finger's breadth laterally where it runs superiorly from the supra-orbital notch. Clean the anterior part of the epicranial aponeurosis and note its extension downwards into the temple below the temporal line.

Now find two or more temporal branches of the facial nerve which cross the zygomatic arch 2 cm. or more in front of the auricle [Fig. 27] and trace them upwards. As the anterior part of the temporal fascia is exposed, look for the slender zygomaticotemporal nerve which pierces it a little behind the frontal process of the zygomatic bone.

Find the superficial temporal artery [Fig. 26], its middle temporal branch, the corresponding veins, and the auriculotemporal nerve, all of which cross the zygomatic arch immediately anterior to the auricle. The middle temporal artery pierces the temporal fascia almost at once; the others should be traced superiorly

into the scalp, though the auriculotemporal nerve may be so slender that it is difficult to identify. In following these, the remainder of the temporal fascia will be exposed together with the anterior and superior auricular muscles.

Posterior to the auricle, clean the branches of the great auricular and lesser occipital nerves which ascend from the neck [Fig. 10]; also the posterior auricular vessels and nerve which lie immediately behind the root of the auricle, and the small posterior auricular muscle.

AURICLE

The auricle consists of a thin plate of yellow, elastic, fibrocartilage covered with skin, though the cartilage is absent in the lobule and in the part between the tragus and the helix [FIG. 5].

The cartilage is continuous with that which forms the lateral part of the external acoustic meatus and is firmly fixed to the lateral end of the bony part of the meatus. The cartilage is incomplete above and in front, and the wall is completed by dense fibrous tissue which also stretches between the tragus and the beginning of the helix. For details of the auricular muscles and cartilage, see a larger textbook.

Vessels and Nerves. The muscles are supplied by the facial nerve which innervates the muscles of facial expression. The great auricular nerve is sensory to the lower third of the lateral surface and the lower two-thirds of the medial surface. The auriculotemporal supplies the remainder of the lateral surface, the lesser occipital the rest of the medial surface.

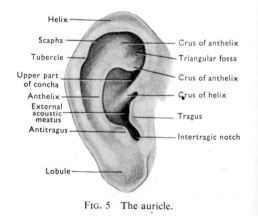

Helix —
Scapha —
Tubercle —
Upper part of concha —
Anthelix —
External acoustic meatus —
Antitragus —
Lobule —

Crus of anthelix
Triangular fossa
Crus of anthelix
Crus of helix
Tragus
Intertragic notch

FIG. 5   The auricle.

DISSECTION. Explore the superficial fascia over the external occipital protuberance for the slender terminal twigs of the third occipital nerve [Fig. 13]. Now cut through the dense, tough, superficial fascia over the superior nuchal line 2·5 cm. lateral to the occipital protuberance, and find the occipital vessels and the greater occipital nerve piercing the deep fascia. Trace them superiorly towards the vertex.

Clean the occipital belly of occipitofrontalis and the posterior part of the epicranial aponeurosis, avoiding injury to the vessels and nerves.

Occipitofrontalis Muscle

The **occipital bellies** are shorter and narrower than the frontal bellies, and are widely separated by the aponeurosis passing to the external occipital protuberance and the medial part of the superior nuchal line. Each arises from the lateral part of the superior nuchal line and is inserted into the aponeurosis.

Each **frontal belly** lies in the forehead and the adjoining part of the top of the head. It has no attachments to bone, but runs between the skin of the forehead and the epicranial aponeurosis, which it joins just anterior to the coronal suture. Because of these attachments it not only tenses the aponeurosis, but also raises the eyebrows (if the occipital belly contracts) or wrinkles the forehead (if the occipital belly does not contract). It is fused to its fellow for a short distance above the nose, and partly inserted into the skin of the nose (procerus) which it wrinkles. Nerve supply: the facial nerve.

Epicranial Aponeurosis. Most of the features of this sheet have been described above. In addition it should be noted that it is partly attached to the temporal lines and firmly attached to the superior nuchal lines. Elsewhere it slides freely on the pericranium; and thus traction injuries tend to tear it away from the skull through the loose connective tissue deep to it, carrying the skin and superficial fascia with it (scalping). Veins may cross this layer of loose tissue from the skull to the scalp, and if torn may lead to an extensive extravasation of blood which raises the scalp from the skull over a wide area.

DISSECTION. Introduce the handle of a scalpel through a median incision in the aponeurosis, and ascertain the looseness of the subjacent areolar tissue by pushing it in all directions. Note that the aponeurosis fuses with the periosteum at the temporal lines, at the supra-orbital margins, and at the nuchal lines.

NERVES OF THE SCALP AND SUPERFICIAL TEMPORAL REGION
[FIGS. 10, 13, 27]

The superficial structures of this region and of the face are innervated by motor branches from the facial nerve, and by sensory branches from the trigeminal and the second and third cervical spinal nerves. Anterior to a line extending from the ear to the vertex, the sensory supply is from the trigeminal nerve, except for the skin over the lower half of the ramus of the mandible and the lower half of the auricle which are supplied by the ventral rami of the second and third cervical nerves through the great auricular nerve. Posterior to that line the sensory supply is entirely from the cervical nerves; the antero-inferior part from the ventral rami (C. 2 and 3) through the great auricular and lesser occipital branches of the cervical plexus. The posterosuperior part is supplied by the dorsal rami of the second and, to a lesser extent, third cervical nerves, through the greater and third occipital nerves respectively.

Trigeminal Nerve

This is the fifth cranial nerve and it derives its name from the fact that it divides into three large nerves (ophthalmic, maxillary, and mandibular) which escape from the cranial cavity separately. Each of the three divisions supplies sensory branches to the skin of the face and anterior half of the head.

Facial Nerve

This is the seventh cranial nerve and it supplies the muscles of the face, scalp, and auricle. Its branches communicate freely with each other and with the branches of the trigeminal nerve, the latter conveying sensory fibres from the muscles of the face. The communications add greatly to the difficulty of dissecting the nerves in the face.

The individual branches supplying this region are:

Trigeminal Nerve (Sensory)

Ophthalmic Division. The **supratrochlear nerve** arises in the orbit and emerges at the supra-orbital margin a finger's breadth from the median plane. It supplies the forehead near the median plane, and gives a twig to the medial part of the upper eyelid. The **supra-orbital nerve** emerges through the supra-orbital notch, sends twigs to the upper eyelid, and then divides into lateral and medial branches. Each branch sends a twig through the bone to the mucous lining of the frontal sinus (the cavity in the frontal bone above the nose and the orbit) and together they supply the skin of the forehead and the top of the head as far as the vertex.

Maxillary Division. The **zygomaticotemporal** is a very slender nerve which arises from the zygomatic nerve in the orbit. It passes through the zygomatic bone, emerges from its temporal surface, and piercing the temporal fascia behind the frontal process of the zygomatic bone, supplies the skin of the anterior part of the temple.

Mandibular Division. The **auriculotemporal nerve** reaches the surface at the upper end of the parotid gland, close to the auricle, immediately below the root of the zygomatic arch. It supplies the upper part of the auricle and external acoustic meatus, and the skin of the side of the head.

Facial Nerve (Motor)

The **temporal branches** emerge from the anterosuperior part of the parotid gland, cross the zygomatic arch obliquely, and run upwards and forwards into the side of the head and the forehead. They supply the frontal belly of occipitofrontalis, the upper part of orbicularis oculi, and the anterior and superior auricular muscles.

The **posterior auricular nerve** leaves the facial nerve as it emerges from the stylomastoid foramen of the skull. It curves posterosuperiorly close to the root of the auricle, and supplies the occipital belly of occipitofrontalis and the posterior and superior auricular muscles.

Cervical Nerves (Sensory)

The ventral rami of cervical 2 and 3 give the great auricular and lesser occipital nerves. The **great auricular** [FIG. 10] supplies the postero-inferior part of the face, the lower part of the auricle, and a small area behind it. The **lesser occipital** (C. 2) supplies the upper part of the back of the auricle and a variable area of skin in the lateral part of the back of the head.

The dorsal rami of cervical 2 and 3 form the greater and third occipital nerves respectively. The **greater occipital nerve** pierces trapezius and the deep fascia at the superior nuchal line 2·5 cm. lateral to the median plane. Its branches communicate with the lesser occipital and great auricular nerves, and supply most of the skin of the back of the head up to the vertex. The **third occipital** is a very slender nerve which pierces trapezius to supply the skin adjacent to the median plane over the uppermost part of the neck and the external occipital protuberance.

ARTERIES OF THE SCALP AND SUPERFICIAL TEMPORAL REGION

This region is supplied by branches of the external carotid artery except for the medial part of the forehead which receives the supra-orbital and supratrochlear arteries. These run with the corresponding nerves, and originate in the orbit from the ophthalmic branch of the internal carotid artery.

Superficial Temporal Artery. This large vessel arises as a terminal branch of the external carotid behind the neck of the mandible, in, or deep to, the parotid gland. It leaves the upper end of that gland with the auriculo-temporal nerve, and piercing the deep fascia enters the temple over the zygomatic arch. About 2·5 cm. above the arch it divides into an **anterior** and a **posterior** branch, which course respectively towards the frontal and parietal eminences. The anterior branch can frequently be seen through the skin in elderly people, in whom its tortuosity is particularly marked.

8

Other Branches [FIG. 26]. The **transverse facial** runs forwards across the masseter muscle, below the zygomatic arch. The **middle temporal** crosses the root of the zygomatic arch, pierces the temporal fascia, and runs vertically upwards, grooving the skull above the external acoustic meatus. The **zygomatico-orbital** runs anteriorly above the zygomatic arch between the two layers of temporal fascia, and anastomoses with branches of the ophthalmic artery.

Posterior Auricular Artery. A small branch of the external carotid, it arises under cover of the parotid gland. It runs posterosuperiorly on the upper border of the posterior belly of the digastric muscle, and turns superiorly, behind the auricle, with the posterior auricular nerve.

Occipital Artery. This large branch arises from the external carotid in the front of the neck. It passes posteriorly and joins the greater occipital nerve as it pierces trapezius and the deep fascia [FIG. 13]. It supplies the back of the head.

All these arteries anastomose freely with each other and with the arteries of the opposite side. Because of this, wounds of the scalp bleed profusely, but heal rapidly.

VEINS OF THE SCALP AND SUPERFICIAL TEMPORAL REGION

Like the arteries, the veins anastomose freely and their main tributaries accompany the arteries in the scalp, but their proximal parts drain by different routes:

The **supratrochlear** and **supra-orbital** veins unite at the medial angle of the eye to form the **facial vein.** They communicate with the orbital veins.

The **superficial temporal vein** joins the middle temporal vein at the root of the zygomatic arch to form the retromandibular vein.

The **retromandibular vein** descends through the parotid gland and is joined by the transverse facial and maxillary veins. Inferiorly it divides into an anterior and a posterior branch. The **anterior branch** joins the facial vein which ends in the internal jugular vein. The **posterior branch** unites with the posterior auricular vein

on the surface of the sternocleidomastoid muscle, and forms the external jugular vein.

The **occipital veins** run downwards with the artery, but leave it at the back of the neck to join the suboccipital plexus deep to the semispinalis capitis muscle (q.v.)

Emissary veins pierce the skull and connect this system of veins with the venous sinuses inside it. One passes through the parietal foramen to the superior sagittal sinus; another through the mastoid foramen to the sigmoid sinus [FIG. 93]. These emissary veins, like the communications with the veins of the orbit, form routes along which infection may spread into the skull from without.

LYMPH VESSELS OF THE SCALP AND TEMPLE

Though these vessels cannot be displayed by ordinary dissection, the student should appreciate that those from the anterior area end in small lymph nodes buried in the surface of the parotid gland. Lymph vessels from the region behind the ear terminate in lymph nodes on the upper ends of trapezius and sternocleidomastoid, the **occipital** and **retroauricular nodes.**

THE SUPERFICIAL DISSECTION OF THE FACE

In this dissection it is helpful to stretch the eyelids and the cheeks by packing the conjunctival sacs and the vestibule of the mouth with strips of cloth or cotton wool soaked in preservative. It is an advantage too, for the later dissections, if the pharynx is similarly packed to prevent drying. Once dissection of the face has begun, it is essential to keep the surface moist and avoid drying.

The face extends from the margin of the hair to the chin, and from one auricle to the other. The forehead is therefore common to the face and scalp.

DISSECTION. In reflecting the skin there is inevitably some damage to the facial muscles which are attached to it, and to minimize this the knife should be kept as close to the skin as possible. Make a median

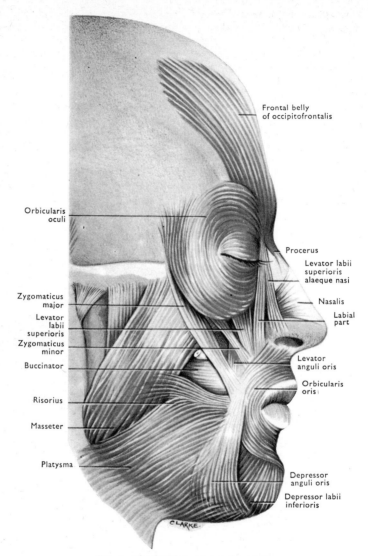

Orbicularis oculi

Zygomaticus major

Levator labii superioris

Zygomaticus minor

Buccinator

Risorius

Masseter

Platysma

Frontal belly of occipitofrontalis

Procerus

Levator labii superioris alaeque nasi

Nasalis

Labial part

Levator anguli oris

Orbicularis oris

Depressor anguli oris

Depressor labii inferioris

CLARKE.

FIG. 6   The facial muscles and masseter.

incision from the root of the nose to the point of the chin, and a horizontal incision from the angle of the mouth to the posterior border of the mandible. Reflect the lower flap downwards to the lower border of the mandible, and the upper flap backwards, together with the anterior flap of the scalp, and leave it attached at the auricle.

Proceed to clean the facial muscles, having identified their position in Figure 6.

Orbicularis oculi. Pull the eyelids laterally and identify the medial palpebral ligament, then clean the orbicularis, beginning with the part external to the eyelids. The part in the eyelids is very thin and pale and is easily removed with the fat. Look for the small palpebral branch of the lacrimal nerve entering the lateral part of the upper eyelid through the muscle.

Now clean the orbicularis oris. It has no well defined external margin because of the large number of other muscles which fuse with it, parts of which will be exposed as it is cleaned.

At the upper part of the side of the nose, find the levator labii superioris alaeque nasi, with the facial vein lying on its surface. Try to define compressor and dilator naris (nasalis), and two slender nerves which run downwards on the side of the nose; the infratrochlear in the upper half, and the external nasal in the lower half [Fig. 27].

Trace the facial vein downwards till it disappears under zygomaticus major. Clean that muscle, and then levator labii superioris, raising the lower part of orbicularis oculi to expose the upper part of the latter muscle.

At the lower border of the mandible clean the broad, thin sheet of muscle (platysma) which ascends over the mandible from the neck, and note that the posterior fibres curve forwards towards the angle of the mouth to form part of the risorius muscle. Next clean depressor anguli oris and depressor labii inferioris. The deeper muscles, especially buccinator which is continuous with the lateral part of orbicularis oris, will be dissected later.

FACIAL MUSCLES

These muscles, including buccinator, receive their motor supply from the facial nerve; sensory fibres from them, and from the skin which overlies them, reach the brain through the trigeminal nerve [FIG. 27].

The facial muscles are known collectively as the 'muscles of facial expression'; the actions of many of them are implied in their names; the actions of the others may be inferred from

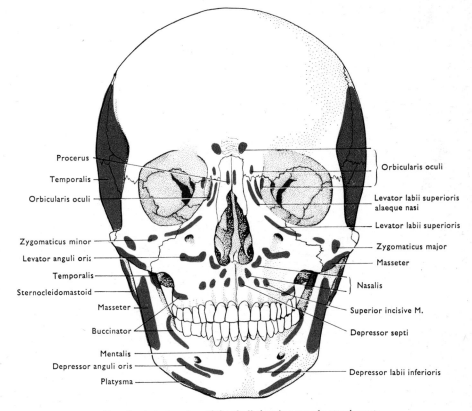

FIG. 7 Anterior view of the skull showing muscle attachments.

their positions. Because they are attached to the skin they tend to pull open wounds of the face which therefore require to be stitched, and though it is unnecessary for the student to burden his memory with the attachments of these muscles he should appreciate that a number of them have very important actions. Thus paralysis of the orbiculares muscles and the buccinator (q.v.) has serious consequences for the patient.

Orbicularis Oculi

Orbital Part. This is the widest and thickest part. Its dark, coarse fibres arise from the medial palpebral ligament and the adjacent part of the orbital margin. They form complete loops on and around the orbital margin, and return to the same point medially, having no attachment laterally except a loose connexion with the skin. Thus they sweep downwards into the cheek (overlapping some muscles of the upper lip), laterally into the temple, and superiorly into the forehead to mingle with the fibres of occipitofrontalis. A few fibres that arise from the bone superior to the medial palpebral ligament end in the skin of the eyebrow (corrugator supercilii).

Palpebral Part. These paler, thinner fibres also arise from the medial palpebral ligament and form similar loops, without lateral attachment, within the eyelids. At the periphery they are continuous with the orbital part; at the margin of the eyelid they form a small, partially isolated ciliary bundle immediately posterior to the roots of the eyelashes.

Lacrimal Part. This small sheet arises from the posterior margin of the lacrimal fossa and the sheath of the lacrimal sac. It curves round the lateral side of the sac, and divides into slips which pass laterally into the eyelids.

Actions. Because it is attached at the medial angle of the eye, it draws the skin and eyelids

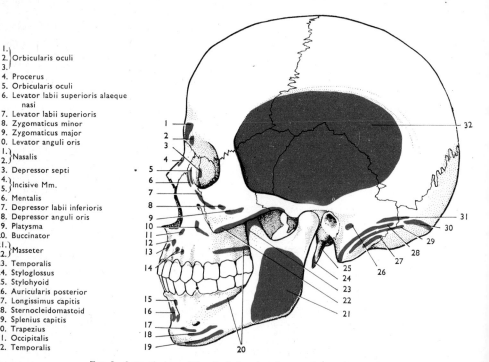

1.
2. }Orbicularis oculi
3.
4. Procerus
5. Orbicularis oculi
6. Levator labii superioris alaeque nasi
7. Levator labii superioris
8. Zygomaticus minor
9. Zygomaticus major
10. Levator anguli oris
11.
12. }Nasalis
13. Depressor septi
14.
15. }Incisive Mm.
16. Mentalis
17. Depressor labii inferioris
18. Depressor anguli oris
19. Platysma
20. Buccinator
21.
22. }Masseter
23. Temporalis
24. Styloglossus
25. Stylohyoid
26. Auricularis posterior
27. Longissimus capitis
28. Sternocleidomastoid
29. Splenius capitis
30. Trapezius
31. Occipitalis
32. Temporalis

Fig. 8   Lateral view of the skull showing the muscle attachments.

medially and promotes the flow of lacrimal fluid towards the lacrimal canaliculi. The lacrimal part not only draws the eyelids medially, but probably also dilates the lacrimal sac and promotes the flow of fluid through it. The palpebral part, acting alone, closes the eye lightly as in sleep or blinking. The orbital part screws up the eye to give partial protection from bright light, sun, or wind; the fibres passing to the eyebrows draw them together as in frowning. The orbital and palpebral parts contract together to protect the eye from sudden danger, and in strong expiratory efforts such as coughing, sneezing, or crying in a child. The latter action, by compressing the orbital contents, probably prevents over-distention of the orbital veins, and the tension of the palpebral part keeps the lower eyelid in contact with the eye.

Orbicularis Oris

This is the sphincter muscle of the mouth, and it forms the greater part of the lips. It is a complex muscle formed mainly of the inter-lacing fibres of the muscles which converge on the mouth. Intrinsic bundles pass obliquely between the skin and the mucous membrane. Incisive slips arise from the jaws opposite the roots of the incisor teeth, and pass laterally into the lips.

The fibres of the other muscles converging on the mouth mingle and sweep in curves through the lips. The buccinator (q.v.) plays a large part, but is a deep muscle of the cheek not yet dissected. Its decussating fibres sweep into the margins of the lips and form a marginal

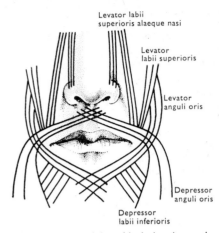

FIG. 9 Diagram of the orbicularis oris muscle.

bundle; its upper and lower fibres enter the corresponding lip and cross the midline to interdigitate with the corresponding fibres of the opposite muscle.

The variety of movements which the lips can execute is due to the large number of muscles entering them: the levator labii superioris alaeque nasi, the levator labii superioris, and the levator anguli oris, all raise the upper lip. Zygomaticus major draws the corner of the mouth upwards and laterally, while depressor anguli oris pulls it inferolaterally.

Platysma tenses the skin of the neck, while its posterior fibres curve forwards towards the lips and form the greater part of risorius which pulls the lips laterally and tightens them against the teeth.

THE SIDE OF THE NECK

The side of the neck is bounded below by the clavicle, above by the lower border of the mandible, the mastoid process of the temporal bone, and the superior nuchal line of the occipital bone. It extends posteriorly to the anterior border of trapezius, and is divided obliquely by the sternocleidomastoid muscle into the anterior and posterior triangles of the neck.

The sternocleidomastoid raises up a wide, low ridge that extends from the manubrium and the medial third of the clavicle to the skull behind the ear. It is made prominent when the face is turned to the opposite side, and the external jugular vein may be seen crossing its surface almost vertically from the region below the auricle to the clavicle [FIG. 10].

The lesser supraclavicular fossa is a shallow

13

depression between the sternal and clavicular parts of the sternocleidomastoid. It lies above the medial part of the clavicle and is opposite the internal jugular vein. The greater supra-clavicular fossa is the larger depression behind the intermediate third of the clavicle, between the lower parts of trapezius and sternocleido-mastoid. It overlies the cervical part of the brachial plexus and the third part of the sub-clavian artery.

THE POSTERIOR TRIANGLE

During the dissection of this triangle it is advisable for the dissectors of the head and neck to work at different times from the dis-sectors of the upper limb. This avoids any interference as it is advisable for the limb to be by the side and the shoulder depressed for this dissection.

GENERAL ARRANGEMENT OF THE NECK
[FIG. 98]

The major structures in the neck are sur-rounded by a layer of deep fascia which en-closes between its two laminae the sterno-cleidomastoid and trapezius muscles. Internal to this are two compartments. (1) The larger, posterior compartment consists of the verte-bral column and the muscles which immedia-tely surround it. This is enclosed in a sleeve of fascia which passes anterior to the vertebral bodies, and is known there as the **prevertebral fascia**. Lateral to this, the fascia forms the floor of the posterior triangle, and then covers the erector spinae muscles. (2) The smaller, anterior compartment is composed of the pharynx, larynx, oesophagus, trachea and their associated muscles, and on each side is the neurovascular bundle of the neck (the carotid sheath) containing the carotid artery, the internal jugular vein and the vagus nerve.

The ventral rami of the cervical nerves, which emerge between the vertebrae, pass anterolaterally and appear between the muscles attached to the anterior and posterior tubercles of the transverse processes: *i.e.*, be-tween scalenus anterior and scalenus medius. Since they arise within the layer of prevertebral

fascia, they tend either to carry a sheath of this outwards with them (*e.g.*, sheath of brachial plexus) or to remain within the fascia (phrenic nerve).

DISSECTION. In the reflexion of the skin take care to work superficially, to avoid damage to the supra-clavicular and accessory nerves. The former lie deep to the platysma in the lower part of the triangle, the latter lies deep to the deep fascia which forms the roof of the upper part of the triangle.

Make an incision through the skin from the mastoid process to the sternal end of the clavicle, along the middle of the sternocleidomastoid muscle. Take care not to cut through the fascia, or the transverse nerve of the neck may be destroyed. Extend the incision along the clavicle to its acromial end, and reflect the flap so formed to the anterior border of trapezius.

The skin is thickest in the posterosuperior part, and the thin superficial fascia contains relatively little fat, most of which tends to accumulate under the deep fascia, except in the greater supraclavicular fossa.

DISSECTION. Divide platysma along the line of the clavicle and turn it upwards and forwards; avoid injury to the supraclavicular nerves and the external jugular vein which lie deep to it [Fig. 10].

Find the external jugular vein, and trace it upwards till it is joined by the posterior auricular vein, and down-wards till it pierces the deep fascia.

Find the three cutaneous nerves which pierce the deep fascia at the middle of the posterior border of sternoclei-domastoid: (1) the lesser occipital which runs upwards along the posterior border of the muscle; (2) the great auricular which crosses the muscle obliquely towards the auricle; (3) the transverse nerve of the neck which crosses the muscle horizontally.

Identify the three supraclavicular nerves (medial, intermediate, and lateral).

DEEP FASCIA OF THE POSTERIOR TRIANGLE

The deep fascia of the roof of the triangle is part of the sheet of fascia which invests the whole neck and encloses the sternocleidomas-toid and trapezius muscles. It stretches from the intermediate third of the clavicle to the superior nuchal line of the occipital bone, and it is pierced by: (1) supraclavicular nerves; (2) the external jugular vein; (3) small cutaneous arteries. It is a thin layer which is single above, but splits inferiorly, the superficial layer passing to the clavicle and the deep layer passing down behind it to be attached to its lower part. The deep layer also forms the fascia on the inferior belly of the omohyoid muscle [Figs. 11, 98] and holds it in position. The space between the two layers of the fascia extends from the coracoid process laterally to pass deep to the sternocleidomastoid muscle medially, and this can be demonstrated by introducing a blunt instrument. Over the posterior triangle the space contains: (1) part of the external jugular vein; (2) the terminal part of the transverse cervical vein; (3) the suprascapular vessels behind the clavicle.

The accessory nerve emerges from the sternocleidomastoid, where the lesser occipital nerve appears at its posterior border, and runs postero-inferiorly across the middle of the triangle embedded in the deep fascia of the

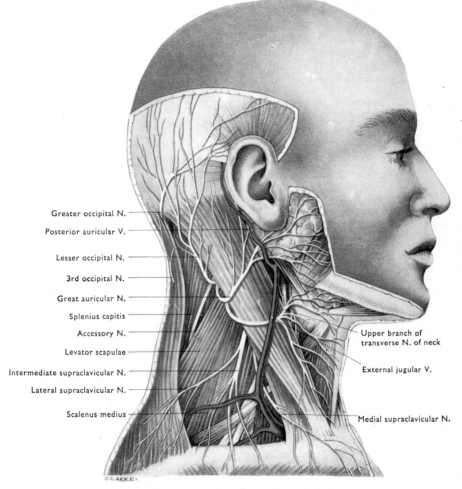

Greater occipital N.

Posterior auricular V.

Lesser occipital N.

3rd occipital N.

Great auricular N.

Splenius capitis

Accessory N.

Levator scapulae

Intermediate supraclavicular N.

Lateral supraclavicular N.

Scalenus medius

Upper branch of transverse N. of neck

External jugular V.

Medial supraclavicular N.

CLARKE

FIG. 10   The cutaneous branches of the cervical plexus.

15

roof. At the sternocleidomastoid it is closely related to the lymph nodes of the posterior triangle.

The deep fascia of the floor of the triangle encloses the deep muscles of the back of the neck, sweeps forwards over the scalene muscles, and passes between the muscles on the front of the cervical vertebrae and the pharynx. The cervical nerves emerge deep to this fascial layer which forms a sleeve around the nerves of the brachial plexus, and this is continuous laterally with the fascia of the cervico-axillary canal [FIG. 12].

DISSECTION. Trace the supraclavicular nerves upwards, through the deep fascia, to their common trunk. Pull them aside and cut through the superficial layer of the fascia of the roof immediately above the clavicle and along the posterior border of sternocleidomastoid; turn it upwards. Explore the space between the two layers of fascia, and clean the external jugular, transverse cervical, and suprascapular veins that lie in it, following the latter two to their entry into the external jugular.

Identify the nerve to subclavius, which descends on the lateral side of the external jugular vein; clean it upwards and downwards. An accessory branch to the phrenic nerve may be seen arising from it.

Pull the external jugular vein backwards and note the anterior jugular vein entering it. Identify the suprascapular vessels deep to the clavicle.

Follow the cutaneous nerves emerging at the middle of the posterior border of sternocleidomastoid, but take care not to injure the accessory nerve as the lesser occipital hooks round it.

CUTANEOUS BRANCHES OF THE CERVICAL PLEXUS
[FIG. 95]

The cervical plexus is formed from the ventral rami of the upper four cervical nerves. It lies under cover of the internal jugular vein and sternocleidomastoid muscle in the upper part of the neck, and its cutaneous branches emerge at the middle of the posterior border of the sternocleidomastoid muscle.

Lesser Occipital Nerve (C. 2). It ascends for a short distance along the posterior border of sternocleidomastoid, and gives small branches to the skin of the neck. Piercing the deep fascia, it divides into branches which supply the upper third of the cranial surface of the auricle, and a portion of the skin behind the auricle. Here it may communicate with the greater occipital nerve.

Great Auricular Nerve (C. 2, 3). It turns round the posterior border of sternocleidomastoid, pierces the deep fascia and runs over that muscle towards the parotid gland, lying a little posterior and parallel to the external jugular vein. It gives small branches to the skin of the neck, and breaks into two sets of branches. The **posterior branches** supply skin over the mastoid process and the lower part of both surfaces of the auricle. The **anterior** set ramify over the lower surface of the masseter and the parotid gland; some filaments enter the parotid gland and communicate with the facial and auriculotemporal nerves.

Transverse Nerve of the Neck (C. 2, 3). It emerges with the great auricular, curves round the posterior border of sternocleidomastoid, and entering the superficial fascia, passes forwards either superficial or deep to the external jugular vein, under cover of platysma. It divides into **upper** and **lower branches**, which supply most of the skin of the side and front of the neck. The upper branch communicates with the cervical branch of the facial nerve.

Supraclavicular Nerves (C. 3, 4). These arise as a single trunk which divides into the **medial, intermediate,** and **lateral** supraclavicular nerves. They diverge, send small branches to the skin of the neck, and pierce the deep fascia a little above the clavicle. The nerves pass over the corresponding thirds of the clavicle. The medial and intermediate supply skin over the front of the chest down to the level of the sternal angle, the lateral supplies skin over the upper half of the deltoid muscle.

EXTERNAL JUGULAR VEIN

This is a fairly large vein that lies in the superficial fascia for most of its course, and is often conspicuous in the living neck.

It begins on the surface of the sternocleidomastoid by the union of the posterior auricular vein and the posterior branch of the retromandibular vein, at a point behind the angle of the mandible and just inferior to the parotid gland. It passes vertically downwards between platysma and the deep fascia, usually crosses the transverse nerve of the neck [FIGS. 10, 11] and pierces the fascial roof of the posterior triangle at the posterior border of sternocleidomastoid, about 2·5 cm. above the clavicle. In the posterior triangle it receives the transverse cervical, suprascapular, and anterior jugular veins, and passing close to sternocleidomastoid, crosses the lower roots of the brachial plexus and the third part of the subclavian artery. It ends behind the clavicle by entering the subclavian vein; the entry is guarded by a valve.

DISSECTION. To clean the contents of the posterior triangle, begin at the apex. Clean the occipital artery as it crosses the apex, and then remove the fat and fascia in the upper half of the floor [Fig. 11].

Pick up the accessory nerve at the posterior border of sternocleidomastoid and trace it across the triangle to trapezius. Find also the branches of the third and fourth cervical nerves which pass to trapezius adjacent to the accessory nerve; one of them may be mistaken for it. Two other small nerves arise from the same spinal nerves and pass into levator scapulae.

Cut through the fascia along the upper border of the inferior belly of omohyoid, and reflect the fascia downwards. Turn the upper border of the muscle towards you and find its nerve; this enters its deep surface near the sternocleidomastoid.

Clean the upper part of the brachial plexus, but take care of the nerves which arise from it: (1) the suprascapular nerve that runs postero-inferiorly immediately above the plexus, and is partly under cover of the omohyoid; (2) slightly above (1) the slender dorsal scapular nerve (C. 5) runs postero-inferiorly to disappear through the floor of the triangle; (3) turn the upper part of the brachial plexus forwards and find the upper roots of the long thoracic nerve. These spring from the back of the roots of the plexus and run down posterior to it; the upper two pierce the scalenus medius muscle which lies immediately behind the plexus.

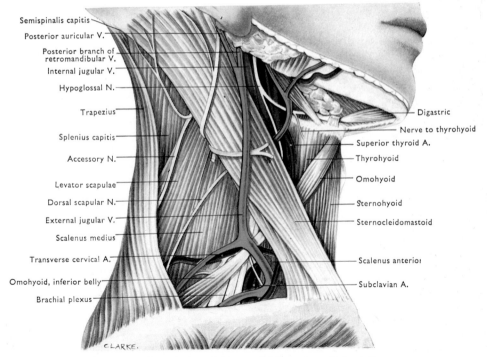

FIG. 11 Lateral view of the superficial structures in the neck.

Semispinalis capitis
Posterior auricular V.
Posterior branch of retromandibular V.
Internal jugular V.
Hypoglossal N.
Trapezius
Splenius capitis
Accessory N.
Levator scapulae
Dorsal scapular N.
External jugular V.
Scalenus medius
Transverse cervical A.
Omohyoid, inferior belly
Brachial plexus

Digastric
Nerve to thyrohyoid
Superior thyroid A.
Thyrohyoid
Omohyoid
Sternohyoid
Sternocleidomastoid
Scalenus anterior
Subclavian A.

CLARKE.

Find the transverse cervical artery at the upper border of omohyoid, and follow it across the posterior triangle.

Remove the terminal parts of the suprascapular and transverse cervical veins if they are in the way, and clean the suprascapular artery behind the clavicle. Remove the second layer of deep fascia and follow the proximal part of the transverse cervical artery towards its origin.

Find the nerve to subclavius again, and follow it to its termination. Clean the subclavian vessels and the brachial plexus that lies adjacent to them. Find the long thoracic nerve on the scalenus medius and trace it upwards and downwards.

BOUNDARIES AND CONTENTS OF THE POSTERIOR TRIANGLE

The boundaries are the adjacent margins of the sternocleidomastoid and trapezius muscles, and the intermediate third of the clavicle.

The deep fascia forming its roof is pierced by: (1) the external jugular vein, antero-inferiorly; (2) the supraclavicular nerves, just above the clavicle; (3) lymph vessels passing from the superficial structures to the nodes in the triangle.

The floor is formed from above downwards by the splenius capitis, the levator scapulae, and the scalenus medius, covered by the lateral extension of the prevertebral fascia.

Accessory Nerve (Eleventh Cranial)

The part of the accessory nerve in the posterior triangle is composed of fibres which arise from the cervical part of the spinal medulla. These fibres pass upwards beside the spinal medulla, and enter the cranial cavity through the foramen magnum. Here they join fibres of the nerve which arise from the medulla oblongata, and together escape from the skull through the jugular foramen with the vagus (tenth cranial) nerve. The spinal part immediately separates from the remainder, and passing postero-inferiorly across the transverse process of the atlas vertebra, pierces the deeper fibres of sternocleidomastoid and supplies it.

Leaving the sternocleidomastoid a little above the middle of its posterior border, the accessory nerve continues postero-inferiorly in the fascial roof of the posterior triangle (parallel to levator scapulae) and disappears beneath trapezius about 5 cm. above the clavicle. It ramifies on the deep surface of the muscle and forms its only motor supply; the other branches from the cervical plexus appear to be sensory in nature.

Branches of the Cervical Plexus

Apart from the cutaneous nerves already described [p. 16] there are: (1) two small branches to levator scapulae from the third and fourth cervical nerves. They enter the muscle opposite the middle of the posterior border of sternocleidomastoid; (2) branches from the third and fourth cervical nerves to trapezius. These communicate with the accessory nerve in the triangle and under cover of the trapezius.

DISSECTION. Cut through the clavicular attachment of sternocleidomastoid and reflect this part of the muscle forwards. Remove the underlying fat and expose scalenus anterior. Define the borders of this muscle and clean the following structures which lie on its surface: omohyoid, transverse cervical artery, anterior jugular vein, subclavian vein, and phrenic nerve. Depress the clavicle to reach the subclavian vein.

Scalenus Anterior [FIG. 99]

This muscle has important relations and is a clue to the anatomy of the lower part of the neck. It arises from the anterior tubercles of the third to sixth cervical transverse processes, and descends to be inserted into the first rib. It lies anterior to the ventral rami of the fourth to eighth cervical nerves, the cervical pleura, and the second part of the subclavian artery, and is concealed by the sternocleidomastoid. The phrenic nerve descends obliquely over the front of the muscle from lateral to medial border, posterolateral to the internal jugular vein. Superficial to these structures the muscle is crossed by the inferior belly of omohyoid, the transverse cervical artery, the suprascapular artery, the anterior jugular vein, and the subclavian vein [FIG. 87].

Nerve supply: the **ventral rami** of adjacent spinal nerves. Action: it raises the first rib and produces lateral flexion of the neck.

Inferior Belly of Omohyoid

This slender muscle springs from the upper border of the scapula and the superior transverse scapular ligament under cover of trapezius. It passes anterosuperiorly across the posterior triangle a short distance above the clavicle, and coursing over the brachial plexus runs deep to the sternocleidomastoid; here it joins the tendon which links it to the superior belly. The muscle can be palpated in a living person by moving the finger up and down a little above the clavicle, and its twitching can be seen in a thin person who is talking.

Nerve supply: a branch from the **ansa cervicalis** enters its deep surface. Action: it helps to steady or depress the hyoid bone.

Third Part of the Subclavian Artery

The right subclavian springs from the brachiocephalic trunk behind the right sternoclavicular joint. The left arises from the arch of the aorta, and enters the neck behind the left sternoclavicular joint. On each side, it arches laterally in the root of the neck across the front of the cervical pleura, and becomes the axillary artery at the outer border of the first rib. The scalenus anterior descends in front of the highest part of the arch, and use is made of this fact to divide the artery (for descriptive purposes) into three parts; the first medial to scalenus anterior, the second behind it, and the third lateral to it.

The third part begins about a finger's breadth above the clavicle opposite the posterior border of sternocleidomastoid. It lies on the cervical pleura and the apex of the lung, but slopes rapidly downwards to enter the subclavian groove on the first rib, and ends behind the middle of the clavicle. In the groove it is separated from the inferior part of scalenus medius by the lowest trunk of the brachial plexus. Between the artery and the clavicle lie the suprascapular artery and the veins in relation to it. These veins unite with each other and with the external jugular vein to form a complicated network in front of the artery.

Subclavian Vein

This vein begins at the outer border of the first rib as the continuation of the axillary vein. It passes medially and slightly upwards behind the clavicle and in front of the second and third parts of the artery, but on a lower plane, owing to the slope of the first rib. Scalenus anterior separates it from the second part of the artery, and it joins the internal jugular vein to form the brachiocephalic vein at the medial border of that muscle. Its only tributary, the external jugular vein, joins it at the lateral border of scalenus anterior. It has one valve just before the external jugular joins it.

Suprascapular and Transverse Cervical Vessels

The two arteries arise from a short, wide branch of the first part of the subclavian artery, the **thyrocervical trunk,** which also gives off the inferior thyroid artery.

The transverse cervical artery crosses scalenus anterior and the posterior triangle, running over the phrenic nerve, the upper trunks of the brachial plexus, and the suprascapular nerve. It splits around the anterior border of levator scapulae, the superficial branch ramifying on the deep surface of trapezius, while the deep branch runs inferiorly, deep to levator scapulae and the rhomboids, along the medial margin of the scapula. The artery may arise from the third part of the subclavian.

The suprascapular artery passes inferolaterally across scalenus anterior, and, passing behind the intermediate third of the clavicle in front of the subclavian artery, joins the suprascapular nerve near the postero-inferior angle of the posterior triangle. Together they descend to the scapular notch. The corresponding veins end in the external jugular.

THE BRACHIAL PLEXUS

The brachial plexus should be dissected in conjunction with the dissectors of the upper limb. Its full exposure will require either the dissection and disarticulation of the sternoclavicular joint [VOL. 1, p. 30], or the clavicle may be divided between drill holes placed in its intermediate third, thus allowing the

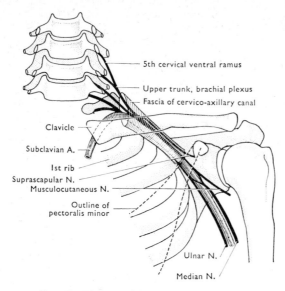

Labels on figure:
- 5th cervical ventral ramus
- Upper trunk, brachial plexus
- Fascia of cervico-axillary canal
- Clavicle
- Subclavian A.
- 1st rib
- Suprascapular N.
- Musculocutaneous N.
- Outline of pectoralis minor
- Ulnar N.
- Median N.

FIG. 12   Diagram of the cervico-axillary canal.

shoulder to fall backwards and opening the cervico-axillary canal. The latter method has the advantage of leaving the sternocleido-mastoid undisturbed and of allowing the replacement of the parts by wiring the cut ends of the clavicle together through the drill holes.

The brachial plexus lies in the lower part of the posterior triangle, behind the clavicle, and in the upper part of the axilla. The part that lies behind the clavicle varies with the position of the shoulder; thus in standing and sitting the clavicle is nearly horizontal in position, but its lateral end is considerably raised in the recumbent position, as it is in shrugging the shoulders. The plexus is formed by the union of ventral rami at the lateral margin of scalenus anterior, opposite the lower third of the posterior border of sternocleidomastoid. It ends in the axilla by breaking up into the large nerves of the limb.

PARTS OF THE BRACHIAL PLEXUS

Roots. These are the ventral rami of the lower four cervical and the first thoracic nerves with a small contribution from the

fourth cervical and the second thoracic. In addition, the ventral ramus of the first thoracic nerve gives the first inter-costal nerve.

Trunks. The fifth and sixth cervical ventral rami, with the twig from the fourth, join to form the superior trunk. The seventh cervical ventral ramus forms the middle trunk. The eighth cervical and first thoracic ventral rami join to form the inferior trunk which contains the twig from the second thoracic ventral ramus.

Divisions. Each trunk divides into an anterior and a posterior division. The three posterior divisions combine to form the **posterior cord,** while the upper two anterior divisions unite to form the **lateral cord,** and the lower anterior division forms the **medial cord.** The divisions are not equal, and very few of the fibres of the first thoracic nerve enter the posterior cord.

POSITION

In the neck (supraclavicular part) the plexus lies immediately anterior to the scalenus medius, the lower trunk lying above the first rib between this muscle and the subclavian artery. Between the plexus and the muscle lie the roots of the long thoracic nerve. Anterior to it lie: (1) the clavicle; (2) the suprascapular vessels and the inferior belly of omohyoid; (3) the external jugular vein and transverse cervical vessels; (4) the nerve to subclavius and the third part of the subclavian artery.

In the axilla (infraclavicular part) the cords lie close together, above, lateral, and pos-terior to the first part of the axillary artery. Around the second part of the artery they are grouped in positions indicated by their names; lateral, posterior, medial.

BRANCHES

The roots of the plexus receive grey rami communicantes from the ganglia of the sym-pathetic trunk; C. 5 and C. 6 from the middle cervical ganglion, the others from the cervico-thoracic ganglion.

Muscular branches are: (1) twigs to the scalene muscles and longus cervicis; (2) the lowest root of the phrenic nerve from C. 5; (3) the dorsal scapular, suprascapular, long thoracic, and nerve to subclavius—all nerves of the upper limb.

The **dorsal scapular nerve** arises from the back of the fifth cervical ventral´ ramus, pierces scalenus medius, runs inferolaterally a little superior to the plexus, and turns downwards anterior to the levator scapulae and the two rhomboids, supplying all three.

The **nerve to subclavius** is a slender nerve that arises at the union of the fifth and sixth cervical ventral rami. It descends close to scalenus anterior, crosses the brachial plexus and subclavian vessels, and enters the posterior surface of subclavius. It often sends a branch to the phrenic nerve which replaces the contribution from C. 5 to that nerve.

The **suprascapular nerve** arises from the fifth and sixth cervical ventral rami at their junction. It runs postero-inferiorly on scalenus medius lateral to the brachial plexus, and meeting the suprascapular artery [p. 19], descends with it over the scapula to supply supraspinatus, infraspinatus, and the shoulder joint.

The **long thoracic nerve** arises by three roots from the back of the fifth to seventh cervical ventral rami. The upper two roots pierce scalenus medius, unite on its surface, and descend into the axilla over the lateral aspect of the first digitation of serratus anterior on the first rib. The lower root runs over the surface of scalenus medius, enters the axilla separately, and joins the first part there.

THE DISSECTION OF THE BACK

Begin by studying the **surface anatomy** of the back with the dissectors of the upper limb [VOL. 1, p. 36].

DISSECTION. Make a vertical, median incision through the skin from the external occipital protuberance to the seventh cervical spine, and a horizontal incision laterally from this to the acromion. Reflect the skin flap and examine the posterior triangle from behind.

Clean the occipital belly of occipitofrontalis, and look for the cutaneous nerves over the upper part of trapezius. Trace the greater occipital nerve from the scalp downwards to the point where it pierces the deep fascia 2·5 cm. lateral to the external occipital protuberance. Clean the branches of the occipital artery. Find the third occipital nerve in the superficial fascia between the greater occipital nerve and the median plane; follow it upwards to its termination and down to the point where it pierces the deep fascia. Look for the cutaneous branches of the dorsal rami of the other cervical nerves in the superficial fascia. They are small and variable in position, but they pierce the deep fascia close to the midline.

Clean the surface of trapezius.

The portions of the occipital artery and nerves found here are described on pages 8, 9.

FIRST LAYER OF MUSCLES

This consists of trapezius and latissimus dorsi.

Trapezius [FIGS. 13, 15]

The lower part of this muscle and the latissimus dorsi will be dissected by the dissectors of the upper limb, but the head and neck dissectors should study its whole extent.

The trapezius arises from the medial third of the superior nuchal line, the external occipital protuberance, the ligamentum nuchae, and the spines of the seventh cervical and all the thoracic vertebrae. At the cervicothoracic junction the origin is aponeurotic, and this tendinous area spreads out into the muscle forming an ovoid area some 5 cm. in length.

The upper fibres sweep downwards to the lateral third of the clavicle and form the curve of the shoulder. The middle fibres run horizontally towards the shoulder, and are inserted into the medial edge of the acromion and the superior margin of the crest of the spine of the scapula. The lower fibres ascend, and terminate in a small flat tendon which slides on a bursa separating it from the root

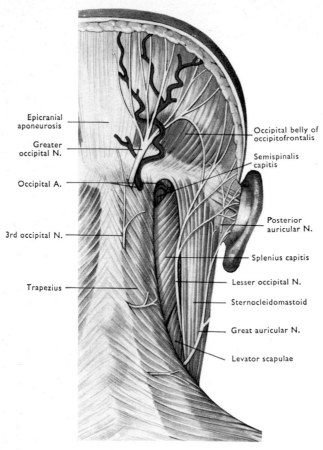

Epicranial
aponeurosis

Greater
occipital N.

Occipital A.

3rd occipital N.

Trapezius

Occipital belly of
occipitofrontalis

Semispinalis
capitis

Posterior
auricular N.

Splenius capitis

Lesser occipital N.

Sternocleidomastoid

Great auricular N.

Levator scapulae

FIG. 13   Superficial structures of the back of the neck.

of the scapular spine, and is inserted into the medial part of the upper margin of its crest.

Nerve supply: the accessory with a supplementary sensory supply from the third and fourth cervical nerves. Action: the middle fibres draw the scapula medially and brace the shoulder backwards. The upper fibres elevate the tip of the shoulder, while the lower fibres depress the medial part of the spine of the scapula. Acting together these two parts rotate the scapula so that the glenoid cavity is turned upwards in the movement of raising the arm above the head.

DISSECTION. Reflexion of trapezius. Separate the muscle from the occipital bone, and divide it vertically 1 cm. from the vertebral spines. Reflect the muscle laterally, and identify the accessory nerve, the branches from the third and fourth cervical nerves, and the superficial branch of the transverse cervical artery on its deep surface.

Define the attachments of the levator scapulae. Find the deep branch of the transverse cervical artery and the dorsal scapular nerve running on to its deep surface, and the branches passing into the muscle. Examine the origin of the inferior belly of the omohyoid, and note the relation of the superior transverse scapular ligament to the suprascapular artery and nerve.

SECOND LAYER OF MUSCLES

This consists of the levator scapulae, the rhomboids, the two serratus posterior muscles, and splenius.

Levator Scapulae

The levator scapulae arises by one slip from each of the transverse processes of the upper four cervical vertebrae. The muscle is cleft lengthwise into two parts, and extends downwards and backwards to be inserted into the medial border of the scapula from the upper angle to the spine; the uppermost fibres of origin are inserted lowest down.

Nerve supply: the ventral rami of the third and fourth cervical nerves, and the fifth through the dorsal scapular nerve. Action: it assists in elevation and rotation of the scapula, helping to hold it steady in active movements of the upper limb.

DISSECTION. When the dissectors of the upper limb have completed their dissection of the muscles of the second layer, clean the superior and inferior posterior serrate muscles. The superior is exposed by the removal of the trapezius and the rhomboids, the inferior by the removal of latissimus dorsi.

Posterior Serrate Muscles

These are two thin, partly fleshy, partly aponeurotic sheets that lie on the back of the thorax, and run from the spines of the vertebrae to the uppermost and lowermost ribs respectively.

Serratus posterior superior runs infero-laterally from the seventh cervical and the upper two or three thoracic spines to the second to fifth ribs.

Nerve supply: second to fourth inter-costal nerves. Action: it raises these ribs.

Serratus posterior inferior passes superolaterally from the lumbar fascia and the lower two thoracic spines to the last four ribs.

Nerve supply: the lower intercostal and subcostal nerves. Action: it is a respiratory muscle which helps to hold down the last four ribs when the dia-phragm contracts.

Thoracolumbar Fascia

The study of this fascia should be under-taken in conjunction with the dissectors of the abdomen.

This fascia is a strong aponeurotic layer which extends from the dorsal surface of the sacrum to the upper thoracic region. It is particularly thick in the lumbar and sacral regions, and binds down the erector spinae group of muscles throughout its extent.

The **thoracic part** is relatively thin and transparent, and extends from the tips of the spines and supraspinous ligaments to the angles of the ribs. Superiorly it passes deep to serratus posterior superior and fades out into the neck. Inferiorly it is continuous with the posterior layer of the lumbar part of this fascia deep to the serratus posterior inferior.

The **lumbar part** consists of three layers: (1) a **posterior layer,** which is continuous with the thoracic part, covers erector spinae, and is attached to the spines and supraspinous liga-ments. (2) A **middle layer** in the plane of the

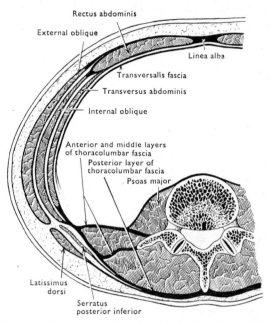

Rectus abdominis

External oblique

Linea alba

Transversalis fascia

Transversus abdominis

Internal oblique

Anterior and middle layers of thoracolumbar fascia

Posterior layer of thoracolumbar fascia

Psoas major

Latissimus dorsi

Serratus posterior inferior

FIG. 14   Diagram of a section through the abdominal wall at the level of the second lumbar vertebra to show the arrange-ment of the thoracolumbar fascia.

ribs. This passes between erector spinae and quadratus lumborum, and is attached to the tips of the lumbar transverse processes. (3) A thin, **anterior layer** which passes in front of quadratus lumborum and is attached to the anterior surfaces of the lumbar transverse processes medial to that muscle [FIG. 14]. The posterior layer fuses with the middle layer at the lateral edge of erector spinae, and this common layer fuses with the anterior layer at the lateral edge of quadratus lumborum. The internal oblique and transversus abdominis muscles arise from its lateral edge.

DISSECTION. Reflect the serratus posterior su-perior, and find its nerves entering its deep surface. Remove the thoracic part of the thoracolumbar fascia. and study splenius.

Splenius

The splenius has a continuous origin from the lower part of the ligamentum nuchae and the spines of the seventh cervical and upper

23

six thoracic vertebrae. Its fibres pass supero-laterally as a thick sheet of muscle which divides into cervical and cranial parts.

Splenius cervicis is the lateral part which curves forwards and is inserted into the transverse processes of the upper two or three cervical vertebrae, deep to levator scapulae.

Splenius capitis is inserted into the lower part of the mastoid process of the temporal bone and the lateral part of the superior nuchal line, under cover of sternocleidomastoid. Separate the sternocleidomastoid from the superior nuchal line and turn it forwards to see this insertion.

Nerve supply: the dorsal rami of the cervical nerves, the cutaneous branches of which pierce it. Action: it bends the head and neck backwards and turns the face towards its own side.

DISSECTION. **Detach the splenius from its origin and turn it towards its insertion; retain the cutaneous branches of the cervical nerves which pierce it.**

Reflexion of the splenius and removal of the underlying fat exposes a number of structures. (1) The cervical part of erector spinae. (2) Two small muscles (obliquus capitis superior and inferior) attached to the transverse process of the atlas, and forming part of the suboccipital group. (3) Part of the occipital artery. (4) Branches of the dorsal rami of the cervical nerves. Identify these.

DEEP MUSCLES OF THE BACK

Erector Spinae

The major part of this muscle begins on the sacrum and passes up into the loin. Here it thickens to form the mass of muscle, lying against the spines of the lumbar vertebrae, which divides into three columns to pass

up over the back of the thorax. Each column is inserted either into the ribs or the vertebrae, but is maintained by fresh slips which arise from the same situations and continue upwards. From lateral to medial the three columns are: **iliocostalis, longissimus,** and **spinalis.**

Semispinalis. The semispinalis is made up of a succession of deep slips that arise from the thoracic transverse processes, and are inserted into the upper thoracic spines (semispinalis thoracis) into the cervical spines (semispinalis cervicis) and into the skull (semispinalis capitis). Deeper still are the muscles which connect the back of the sacrum with the transverse processes, laminae, and spines. They are classified with semispinalis under the general name of transversospinal muscle, and are multifidus, rotatores, interspinales, and intertransversarii. The details of these muscles may be found in the larger textbooks, but their general arrangement should be studied as they are muscles of considerable importance in strains of the back.

Nerve supply: dorsal rami of spinal nerves. Actions: these are numerous, but on the whole the erector spinae extends the vertebral

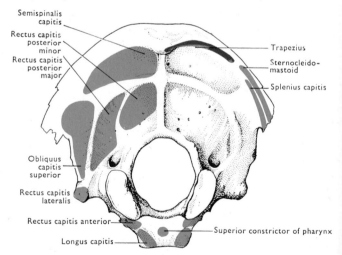

Fig. 15 Muscle attachments to the occipital bone. Origin, red; insertions, blue.

24

column, produces rotation and lateral flexion between the various vertebrae (oblique muscles such as multifidus and semispinalis) and movements of the pelvis.

Levatores Costarum. Deep to all these are twelve small muscles which radiate from the transverse process of the seventh cervical and first eleven thoracic vertebrae to the posterior parts of the shafts of the ribs. Nerve supply: ventral rami of the thoracic nerves, the intercostal nerves.

DISSECTION. Clean the semispinalis and longissimus capitis, taking care not to damage the dorsal rami of the spinal nerves which emerge close to the medial border of the semispinalis.

Clean the occipital artery and its branches. Follow the artery deep to the mastoid process by reflecting longissimus. Then clean the parts of the suboccipital muscles that are exposed.

Longissimus Capitis. This is a long slender muscle that lies under cover of the splenius immediately posterior to the transverse processes [FIG. 17]. It arises from the transverse processes of the upper four thoracic vertebrae, and passes upwards to be inserted into the back of the mastoid process under cover of splenius and sternocleidomastoid.

OCCIPITAL ARTERY

This artery arises from the external carotid in the front of the neck. It runs postero-superiorly deep to the posterior belly of the digastric muscle to reach and groove the skull deep to the mastoid process and the groove for attachment of the digastric. It then courses posteriorly immediately deep to the muscles attached to the superior nuchal line, crosses the apex of the posterior triangle, and pierces trapezius 2·5 cm. from the midline to ramify on the back of the head.

Branches. In this region these are **muscular** and **mastoid.** The latter enters the mastoid foramen to supply the bone and dura mater. One of the muscular branches descends among the muscles of the back of the neck (**descending branch**).

Semispinalis Capitis. This long, thick muscle produces a rounded ridge at the side of the median furrow of the back of the neck, despite the fact that it is deep to trapezius and splenius. It has the same origin as longissimus capitis, and is inserted into the medial half of the area between the superior and inferior nuchal lines [FIG. 15]. It is separated from its fellow by the ligamentum nuchae.

Nerve supply: dorsal rami of the upper cervical nerves. Action: it extends the neck and the head on the neck.

DISSECTION. Detach the semispinalis capitis from the occiput and turn it laterally. Find the deep cervical artery in the dense fascia beneath it, and take care not to injure the nerves piercing the muscle; a twig may be found entering it from the first cervical dorsal ramus, and a larger branch from the greater occipital nerve (C. 2).

If the twig from the first nerve is found, cut out a small piece of the muscle to which that nerve goes, to act as a guide to it when the rest of the nerve is dissected with the suboccipital triangle (now exposed).

The semispinalis cervicis lies deep to the lower part of semispinalis capitis, and is now partly exposed. Define its attachments, but preserve the dorsal rami running on it.

LIGAMENTUM NUCHAE
[FIG. 16]

This is a strong, median, fibrous septum between the muscles of the two sides of the back of the neck. It represents a powerful elastic structure in quadrupeds which helps to sustain the weight of the dependent head. In Man there is little elastic tissue in it, and it is a continuation of the supraspinous and interspinous ligaments from the spine of the seventh cervical vertebra to the external occipital protuberance. It is attached to the external occipital crest, to the posterior tubercle of the atlas, and to the spines of the other cervical vertebrae.

Deep Cervical Artery [FIG. 86]

This vessel springs from the costocervical trunk of the subclavian, and passes into the back of the neck between the seventh cervical transverse process and the neck of the first rib. It ascends deep to semispinalis capitis and anastomoses with the descending branch of the occipital artery.

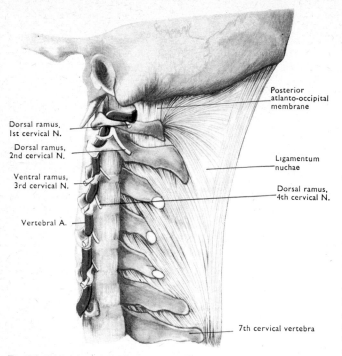

Dorsal ramus,
1st cervical N.

Dorsal ramus,
2nd cervical N.

Ventral ramus,
3rd cervical N.

Vertebral A.

Posterior
atlanto-occipital
membrane

Ligamentum
nuchae

Dorsal ramus,
4th cervical N.

7th cervical vertebra

FIG. 16 Dissection of the ligamentum nuchae and of the vertebral artery in the neck. The neck is slightly flexed.

Semispinalis Cervicis

This is a bulky muscle which lies deep to semispinalis capitis and has the same origin. It passes superomedially to be inserted into the spines of the second to fifth cervical vertebrae, principally the second. It is because of this large insertion that the spine of the second cervical vertebra is so thick and strong.

SUBOCCIPITAL TRIANGLE
[FIG. 17]

This small triangular area is bounded by three muscles: (1) the rectus capitis posterior major forms its superomedial boundary; (2) the obliquus inferior limits it below; (3) the obliquus superior bounds it superolaterally. It is crossed by the greater occipital nerve which hooks round the inferior border of obliquus inferior, and is under cover of semispinalis capitis. In its floor lie the posterior

arch of the atlas, the posterior atlanto-occipital membrane, and on top of the arch a part of the vertebral artery. The triangle contains the posterior ramus of the first cervical nerve and the suboccipital plexus of veins embedded in dense fascia. The suboccipital plexus drains into the deep cervical vein, a large vessel which joins the vertebral vein.

DISSECTION. Dissection of the suboccipital triangle is difficult because of the dense fibrous tissue, but this is greatly helped if the branch of the first cervical dorsal ramus to semispinalis capitis has been retained, as this may be followed into the triangle to the ramus. This ramus emerges between the posterior arch of the atlas and the vertebral artery, and when it is found its branches can be traced with ease. Now clean the muscles which surround the triangle, and uncover the structures in its floor.

Dorsal Ramus of First Cervical (Suboccipital) Nerve

This nerve enters the suboccipital triangle between the posterior arch of the atlas and the vertebral artery. Near the roof of the triangle it breaks up into branches which supply: (1) the muscles of the suboccipital triangle and part of semispinalis capitis; (2) communicating fibres to the greater occipital nerve which pass over the inferior oblique; (3) rarely a direct cutaneous branch which accompanies the occipital artery.

Vertebral Artery [FIGS. 86, 100]

Only the third part of this artery is in the suboccipital triangle. It emerges from the foramen in the transverse process of the atlas, and hooks posteromedially around the pos-

26

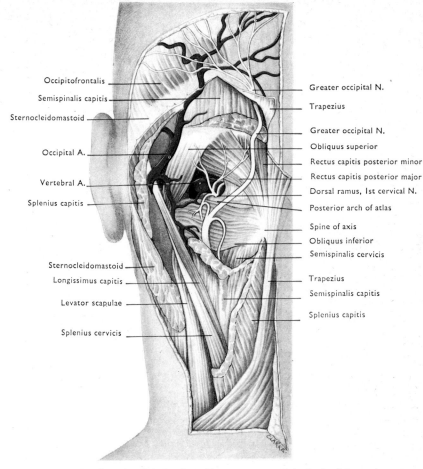

Occipitofrontalis

Semispinalis capitis

Sternocleidomastoid

Occipital A.

Vertebral A.

Splenius capitis

Greater occipital N.

Trapezius

Greater occipital N.

Obliquus superior

Rectus capitis posterior minor

Rectus capitis posterior major

Dorsal ramus, 1st cervical N.

Posterior arch of atlas

Spine of axis

Obliquus inferior

Semispinalis cervicis

Sternocleidomastoid

Longissimus capitis

Levator scapulae

Splenius cervicis

Trapezius

Semispinalis capitis

Splenius capitis

FIG 17 The suboccipital region. Deep structures of the back of the neck.

terior surface of the lateral mass of the atlas, grooving it and the adjacent part of the posterior arch from which it is partly separated by the first cervical nerve. It leaves the triangle by passing anteromedially in front of the thickened lateral edge of the posterior atlanto-occipital membrane. The lateral edge of the membrane arches over the artery from the posterior arch of the atlas to its lateral mass, and may be replaced by a bar of bone. Immediately beyond this the artery pierces

the dura mater and enters the vertebral canal.

Suboccipital Plexus of Veins

This network lies in and around the triangle, and drains a number of veins: (1) from adjacent muscles; (2) occipital veins; (3) internal vertebral venous plexuses; (4) the emissary vein which traverses the condylar canal from the sigmoid sinus. It drains into the deep cervical vein and also into the

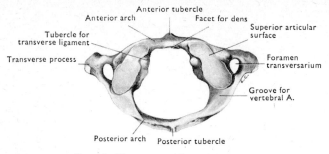

Anterior tubercle

Anterior arch

Facet for dens

Tubercle for transverse ligament

Superior articular surface

Transverse process

Foramen transversarium

Groove for vertebral A.

Posterior arch   Posterior tubercle

FIG. 18   The upper surface of the atlas.

vertebral venous plexus around the vertebral artery.

Suboccipital Muscles [FIG. 17]

The bony attachments of these muscles are to the occiput, the transverse process of the atlas, the spine of the axis, and the posterior arch of the atlas.

Rectus capitis posterior major passes supero-laterally from the spine of the axis to the lateral half of the area below the inferior nuchal line of the occiput [FIG. 15].

Obliquus capitis inferior extends from the spine of the axis to the transverse process of the atlas.

Obliquus capitis superior runs postero-superiorly from the transverse process of the atlas to the lateral half of the area between the nuchal lines.

Rectus capitis posterior minor is a small muscle under cover of the rectus major. It passes from the tubercle on the posterior arch of the atlas to the medial part of the area below the inferior nuchal line.

Nerve supply: dorsal ramus of C. 1. Actions: although it is possible to ascribe specific actions to each of these little muscles, their primary function is to stabilize the head on the atlas and the atlas on the axis, and to act as ligaments of variable length and tension.

GREATER OCCIPITAL NERVE

It is the medial branch of the dorsal ramus of the second cervical nerve, and the thickest cutaneous nerve in the body. It appears at the middle of the lower border of the inferior

oblique muscle, and curving superomedially across the suboccipital triangle [FIG. 17] pierces semispinalis capitis. It runs superiorly on that muscle, pierces trapezius about 2 cm. lateral to the occipital protuberance, and ramifies on the back of the head, ascending as far as the vertex [p. 8]. In addition to its cutaneous supply it gives branches to semispinalis capitis.

THIRD OCCIPITAL NERVE

This slender cutaneous nerve springs from the medial branch of the dorsal ramus of the third cervical nerve. It pierces semispinalis capitis and trapezius to supply the skin of the nape of the neck up to the external occipital protuberance.

DORSAL RAMI OF SPINAL NERVES

The nerves of the back are the dorsal rami of the spinal nerves. With the exception of the first cervical, fourth and fifth sacral, and the coccygeal, each dorsal ramus divides into a lateral and a medial branch. Both these branches supply the intervertebral joints and the muscles of the back (but not the muscles of the upper limb which extend over the back, *e.g.*, trapezius, latissimus dorsi, rhomboids) and one of them usually gives off a cutaneous branch. The cutaneous branches have already been seen, and partly destroyed when the superficial muscles were reflected, but look for the proximal parts that remain.

The general arrangement and distribution of these nerves follow the pattern shown in FIGURE 19, with the following exceptions:

1. The dorsal rami of the first and last two cervical and the last two lumbar nerves do not have cutaneous branches, but end in the muscles of the back.

2. The cutaneous branches of the dorsal rami down to the level of the sixth or seventh thoracic nerve arise from the medial branches, and emerge close to the midline (2–3 cm.). Below this level it is the lateral branches which

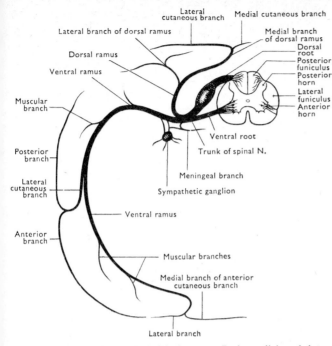

Lateral cutaneous branch

Medial cutaneous branch

Lateral branch of dorsal ramus

Medial branch of dorsal ramus

Dorsal ramus

Dorsal root

Ventral ramus

Posterior funiculus

Posterior horn

Muscular branch

Lateral funiculus

Anterior horn

Ventral root

Posterior branch

Trunk of spinal N.

Lateral cutaneous branch

Meningeal branch

Sympathetic ganglion

Ventral ramus

Anterior branch

Muscular branches

Medial branch of anterior cutaneous branch

Lateral branch

FIG. 19 Diagram of a typical spinal nerve. Both medial and lateral branches of the dorsal ramus supply muscles; the medial branch supplies skin in the upper half of the body, the lateral branch supplies it in the lower half.

become cutaneous, and these emerge 8–9 cm. from the midline in line with the angles of the ribs. The small dorsal rami of the sacral nerves have cutaneous branches which emerge on a line between the posterior superior iliac spine and the tip of the coccyx.

The medial branch of the second cervical dorsal ramus forms the greater occipital nerve. The cutaneous branches of the second thoracic, and sometimes adjacent nerves, are larger and extend further laterally over the scapula than the adjoining nerves. The same branches of the upper three lumbar nerves are also larger and extend out over the buttock to the level of the greater trochanter.

3. The medial branches of the dorsal rami of the second to sixth cervical nerves, and the lateral branches of the sacral dorsal rami communicate to form a simple looped plexus, the former deep to semi-spinalis, the latter deep to gluteus maximus.

4. The dorsal rami of the fourth and fifth sacral nerves join with the dorsal ramus of the coccygeal nerve to supply the skin and ligaments on the back of the coccyx.

BLOOD VESSELS OF THE BACK

Arteries

Cervical Region. In addition to the deep cervical artery, the descending branch of the occipital artery, and the third part of the vertebral artery, which have been seen already; minute twigs of the second part of the vertebral artery pass posteriorly between the transverse processes into the muscles of the back of the neck.

Thoracic Region. Posterior branches of the intercostal arteries pass backwards medial to the costotransverse ligaments, and are distributed to the muscles and skin.

Lumbar Region. Similar branches are derived from the lumbar arteries.

Veins

These follow the corresponding arteries and drain into the vertebral veins in the neck, and the intercostal and lumbar veins in the thorax and lumbar regions. These veins communicate with the posterior vertebral and the internal vertebral venous plexuses.

Posterior Vertebral Venous Plexus. This extensive plexus lies posterior to the vertebral arches under cover of multifidus. It drains the veins of the back into the vessels indicated above.

DISSECTION. Remove all the muscles of the back and clean the laminae and spines of the vertebrae and

29

the dorsum of the sacrum. Retain the dorsal rami of the spinal nerves as far as possible. Remove the posterior wall of the vertebral canal in one piece by sawing through the lateral parts of the laminae and dividing the ligamenta flava in a coronal plane. Take care not to cut completely through the laminae, but complete the division by levering up the laminae and spines, or cutting through the laminae with bone forceps. The spinal medulla and its coverings (meninges) lie deep to this and should not be injured. In the cervical region it is helpful to flex the neck as far as possible, while in the lumbar region the same result may be obtained by putting blocks under the abdomen. The laminae should be removed from the third cervical to the lower opening of the sacral canal.

In this way the laminae and spines should be removed in one piece with the elastic ligamenta flava holding them together. Test the elasticity of these ligaments by stretching the specimen, and then store it in a moist place until the joints of the neck can be examined.

THE CONTENTS OF THE VERTEBRAL CANAL

EPIDURAL SPACE

This is the interval which separates the walls of the vertebral canal and the spinal dura mater, the outer sheath of the spinal medulla. It is filled with loose areolar tissue and semi-liquid fat, among which is to be found a network of veins. These veins lie between the dura mater and the periosteum lining the vertebral canal in a position corresponding to that of the venous sinuses of the dura mater in the cranium. It contains also the arteries which supply the structures in the vertebral canal.

Spinal Arteries

These minute arteries arise from the vertebral arteries, the posterior branches of the intercostal and lumbar arteries, and from the lateral sacral ar-

teries. They enter the vertebral canal through the intervertebral foramina, and they supply the spinal medulla, its nerve roots and meninges, the periosteum, and the ligaments.

Internal Vertebral Venous Plexus [FIG. 20]

This plexus extends throughout the length of the vertebral canal and is divisible into four subordinate longitudinal channels: two anterior and two posterior.

The posterior plexuses lie on the deep surfaces of the laminae and ligamenta flava; the anterior plexuses are placed on the posterior surfaces of the vertebral bodies near the edges of the posterior longitudinal ligament. They are united by many transverse branches, and receive the veins from the walls and contents

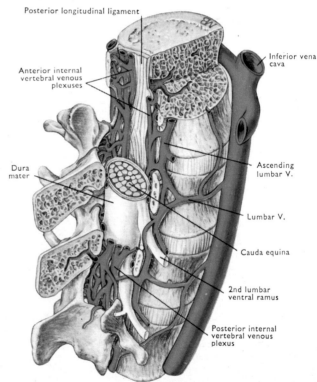

Posterior longitudinal ligament

Anterior internal vertebral venous plexuses

Dura mater

Inferior vena cava

Ascending lumbar V.

Lumbar V.

Cauda equina

2nd lumbar ventral ramus

Posterior internal vertebral venous plexus

FIG. 20 Dissection of the upper four lumbar vertebrae to show the internal vertebral venous plexuses and their communications with the inferior vena cava.

of the vertebral canal, the basivertebral veins which emerge from the back of the vertebral bodies being especially large. The plexuses communicate: (1) with each other; (2) with the posterior vertebral and suboccipital plexuses; (3) with the occipital sinus and basilar plexuses inside the skull, through the foramen magnum. They drain into the posterior tributaries of the intercostal and lumbar veins through the intervertebral foramina, and communicate with the pelvic veins through the anterior sacral foramina, and with the vertebral veins running in the foramina transversaria. These veins are without valves, and are capable of considerable distention. When the intrathoracic or intra-abdominal pressures are raised, blood tends to flow backwards into these plexuses, and since they form a direct channel of communication between the tributaries of the superior and inferior venae cavae, they are able to transmit blood from one territory to the other without passage through the lungs.

MENINGES OF THE SPINAL MEDULLA
[Fig. 21]

The entire central nervous system, comprising the brain and spinal medulla, is enclosed in three membranes or meninges which are separated from each other by two fluid-filled spaces. The meninges extend down the vertebral canal as tubular sheaths surrounding the spinal medulla. From without inwards they are: (1) the dura mater; (2) the subdural capillary space; (3) the delicate arachnoid mater; (4) the wider subarachnoid space which contains the cerebrospinal fluid; (5) the pia mater which is applied to the surface of the central nervous system.

DISSECTION. Clean the outer surface of the dura mater, and the lateral prolongations which it sends as sheaths over the spinal nerves.

Spinal Dura Mater [Fig. 21]

The external sheath is the loose sleeve of tough, fibrous dura mater which extends from the foramen magnum to the second piece of the sacrum. It is widest in the cervical and lumbar regions, fuses with the cranial periosteum at the foramen magnum, and at the second piece of the sacrum closes onto the central filum terminale with which it is attached to the coccyx. It is separated from the walls of the vertebral canal by the contents of the epidural space, is firmly adherent to the bodies of the second and third cervical vertebrae, and is loosely attached: (1) to the posterior longitudinal ligament (which covers the posterior surfaces of the vertebral bodies and intervertebral discs) especially in the cervical and lumbar regions; (2) to the intervertebral foramina by the sleeves which it sends out over the roots of the spinal nerves. These attachments hold the tube of dura mater close to the vertebral bodies and away from the laminae and ligamenta flava; thus the spinal medulla

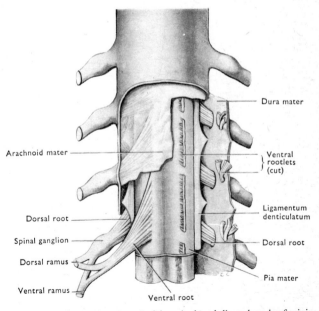

FIG. 21 Membranes (meninges) of the spinal medulla and mode of origin of spinal nerves. The contribution of each root to both rami is shown diagrammatically in the lowest spinal nerve on the left.

31

is close to the axis of movement of the vertebrae, and is only minimally affected by their movements.

The spinal medulla extends from the foramen magnum to the lower border of the first lumbar vertebra, and inferior to that, is continued as the thread-like filum terminale in the dural tube which also encloses the roots of the lower nerves descending in a leash (cauda equina) to their various levels of exit [Fig. 20].

Subdural Space. The deep surface of the dura mater is moist and smooth, and is separated from the equally smooth external surface of the arachnoid mater by a capillary interval, the subdural space. This space surrounds the entire central nervous system, and is only absent where structures entering or leaving the central nervous system pierce the dura mater. The space acts as a bursa and hence allows movement between the dura and the structures it contains; thus movements of the dural tube are not immediately transmitted to the spinal medulla.

Spinal Arachnoid Mater [Fig. 21]

The arachnoid mater lines the dura mater throughout its extent, except where the arachnoid forms finger-like extensions (arachnoid villi and granulations) which pierce the cranial dura mater to enter some of the venous sinuses of the skull. Apart from these it has the same shape, and is almost of the same size as the dural sheath. It differs from the dura in being extremely thin and transparent, and in forming the external limiting membrane of the subarachnoid space. It is adherent to the dura only where structures pierce that membrane, and where the ligamenta denticulata are attached to the dura through it.

32

Subarachnoid Space [Fig. 21]

This is the wide interval between the arachnoid and pia mater which contains the cerebrospinal fluid. Like the subdural space it surrounds the entire central nervous system, but unlike it, the subarachnoid space varies considerably in depth, particularly within the skull. Here the shape of the dural sheath is different from that of the brain it encloses, and the distance between the arachnoid (which lines the dura) and the pia mater (which covers the surface of the brain) alters with the closeness of fit.

Developed from a single mass of loose connective tissue into which the cerebrospinal fluid percolates, the arachnoid and pia form the outer and inner limits of the subarachnoid space, and are joined together by a variable number of strands of connective tissue which cross it. The number of these strands tends to be inversely proportional to the depth of the space.

The spinal subarachnoid space is relatively wide and the number of connecting strands relatively few; they are present mainly on the posterior surface of the spinal medulla, but the space is also crossed by the ligamenta denticulata (q.v.).

Cerebrospinal Fluid. This clear fluid is derived from special vascular tufts (choroid plexuses) in the cavities (ventricles) of the brain and from other sources. In addition to its metabolic function, it affords mechanical protection to the brain and spinal medulla as a kind of water bath.

Spinal Pia Mater

This is thicker than the pia mater of most of the brain. It is a firm vascular membrane which adheres closely to the spinal medulla, and is continued at the lower end of the spinal medulla into the filum terminale. The posterior median septum of the spinal medulla [Fig. 25] is firmly adherent to its deep surface. It passes into the anterior median fissure of the spinal medulla, and is thickened to form a median, longitudinal, glistening band (called the linea splendens) at the mouth of the fissure.

The blood vessels of the spinal medulla ramify in the pia mater before they enter its substance, and each rootlet of every nerve entering or leaving the central nervous system is covered by a sheath of pia mater as it crosses the subarachnoid space. Each blood vessel passing into the substance of the central nervous system carries a sheath of pia mater with it. This sheath is separated from the blood vessel by a narrow sleeve of subarachnoid space which accompanies the vessel for a short distance; this is the perivascular space.

Ligamenta Denticulata [Fig. 21]. These toothed ligaments appear as a thin ridge that stands out from the pia mater on each side of the spinal medulla midway between the ventral and dorsal nerve roots. It extends from the level of the foramen magnum to the level of the first lumbar vertebra. Twenty-one pointed processes project from its free edge, and each is attached through the arachnoid to the dura in the interval between the exits of two spinal nerves. The highest 'tooth' is at the level of the foramen magnum; the lowest between the twelfth thoracic and first lumbar nerves. The ligamenta denticulata suspend the spinal medulla in the subarachnoid space, yet allow some movement of the dural sheath without a corresponding movement of the spinal medulla.

Filum Terminale. This delicate, thread-like filament is about 15 cm. long. It lies among the roots of the lumbar and sacral nerves (cauda equina) but can readily be distinguished from them by its silvery appearance, and by its continuity with the tapering end of the spinal medulla [Fig. 22].

It is composed chiefly of pia mater, although the central canal of the spinal medulla and some nervous elements can be traced in it for nearly half its length. At the level of the second sacral vertebra it pierces the ends of the tubes of arachnoid and dura mater, receives an investment from them, and traversing the sacral canal, terminates by blending with the periosteum on the back of the coccyx or the last piece of the sacrum.

THE SPINAL MEDULLA

The spinal medulla begins at the foramen magnum as the inferior continuation of the medulla oblongata of the brain. It ends opposite the intervertebral disc between the first and second lumbar vertebrae. The point of termination is variable and is altered by the position of the trunk, thus it rises with flexion of the vertebral column and descends with extension.

The average length is approximately 45 cm. It is nearly cylindrical in shape though its girth increases considerably in the regions giving rise to the large nerves of the limbs. These enlargements are known as the cervical and lumbar swellings, and they extend respectively from the foramen magnum to the first thoracic vertebra (maximum transverse diameter is 14 mm. at the sixth cervical vertebra) and from the tenth to twelfth thoracic vertebrae. The lumbar swelling reaches a maximum transverse diameter of about 12 mm. at the twelfth thoracic vertebra, and then rapidly tapers to a point, forming the conus medullaris.

SPINAL NERVES

Thirty-one pairs of nerves are attached to the spinal medulla. Of these twelve are thoracic, five are lumbar, five are sacral, and one is coccygeal, and each of them leaves the vertebral canal below the vertebra to which it corresponds numerically. There are, however, eight cervical nerves, and these leave the vertebral canal above the corresponding vertebrae, with the exception of the eighth, which emerges between the seventh cervical and first thoracic vertebrae.

Spinal Nerve Roots [Figs. 19, 20]

Each spinal nerve is attached to the spinal medulla by a ventral and a dorsal root. The dorsal root is larger (except in the first cervical which frequently has no dorsal root) and has, in addition, an oval swelling, the spinal ganglion, where it joins the ventral root. The dorsal root is composed of afferent (sensory) nerve fibres, the ventral root of efferent (motor) nerve fibres. The two roots unite at

33

the ganglion to form the mixed spinal nerve, which contains both types of fibres.

Each of the two roots is made up of a number of separate rootlets which diverge as they approach the spinal medulla. The rootlets of the dorsal roots enter the dorsolateral aspect of the spinal medulla consecutively in a continuous straight line at the bottom of a slight furrow **(posterolateral sulcus).** The rootlets of the ventral roots emerge from the ventrolateral surface of the spinal medulla over an area of some breadth.

The portion of the spinal medulla to which any one pair of nerves is attached is called a **spinal segment.**

The **size** of the roots varies greatly, and is

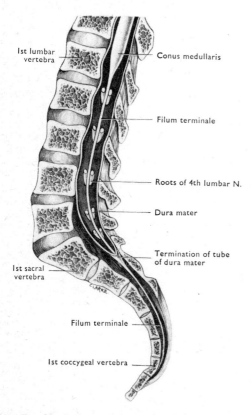

1st lumbar vertebra

Conus medullaris

Filum terminale

Roots of 4th lumbar N.

Dura mater

Termination of tube of dura mater

1st sacral vertebra

Filum terminale

1st coccygeal vertebra

F<small>IG</small>. 22   Sagittal section through the lower part of the vertebral canal.

34

directly related to the amount of tissue each supplies; thus the lower lumbar and upper sacral roots, which innervate the lower limb, are much the largest, and the lower sacral and coccygeal roots are the smallest. The thoracic roots are small and of uniform size, apart from the first, which innervates part of the upper limb. In the cervical region the lower roots are larger than the upper ones, and the dorsal root of the first cervical nerve may be absent.

The roots show great differences also in their **length,** and in the **direction** they follow in the vertebral canal. These differences are due to the spinal medulla being so much shorter than the vertebral canal—a relative shortening which occurs during development and causes the lower end of the spinal medulla to rise progressively higher in the vertebral canal, its relation to the foramen magnum remaining unaltered. Thus by birth the lower end of the spinal medulla is at the third lumbar vertebra, and in the adult between the first and second. This shortening is made good by the progressive elongation of the roots of the spinal nerves within the subarachnoid space, the junctions of the roots and the spinal ganglia remaining in the intervertebral foramina, except in the sacral and coccygeal nerves where the ganglia lie in the sacral canal and dural sac respectively.

The upper part of the spinal medulla remaining fixed, its roots are short (1·5–2 cm.) and horizontal, while the lower roots are progressively elongated (up to 27 cm.) and become increasingly oblique. The lumbar, sacral, and coccygeal nerves descend vertically as a leash of nerves in the subarachnoid space inferior to the termination of the spinal medulla, the **cauda equina.**

Lumbar Puncture. The importance of the high level of termination of the spinal medulla, and the presence only of a leash of roots in the subarachnoid space inferior to it is twofold. (1) Injuries to the vertebral column below the second lumbar vertebra can only damage spinal nerve roots and not the spinal medulla. (2) Samples of cerebrospinal fluid for diagnostic purposes can be obtained without injury to the spinal medulla, by introducing a hollow needle into the subarachnoid space between the laminae of the third and fourth lumbar vertebrae, an operation known as lumbar puncture.

Levels of Spinal Segments. The shortening of the spinal medulla also results in individual spinal segments being displaced from their corresponding vertebral levels, a fact of great clinical importance.

Spinal Segments	Vertebral Levels (Spines)
Cervical 1–8.	Foramen magnum— 6th Cervical.
Thoracic 1–6.	6th Cervical—4th Thoracic.
Thoracic 7–12.	4th Thoracic—9th Thoracic.
Lumbar and Sacral.	10th Thoracic—1st Lumbar.

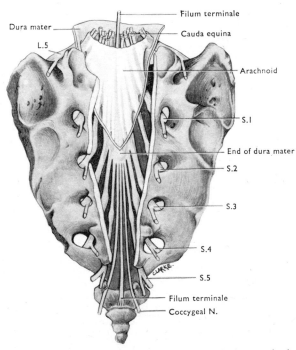

Filum terminale
Dura mater
L.5
Cauda equina
Arachnoid
S.1
End of dura mater
S.2
S.3
S.4
S.5
Filum terminale
Coccygeal N.

FIG. 23 Posterior view of the meninges and spinal nerves in the sacral canal.

Exit of Spinal Nerves

Most of the nerves emerge through the intervertebral foramina. Each of the two rami of the upper four sacral nerves passes out by a sacral foramen. The first cervical emerges above the posterior arch of the atlas, the second by passing above the vertebral arch of the axis. The fifth sacral and coccygeal nerves leave the sacral canal through its lower end [FIG. 23].

DISSECTION. Follow the nerve roots of one or two spinal nerves in each region into the corresponding intervertebral foramina by snipping away the articular processes with bone forceps. Note the position of the spinal ganglia, and study the dural sheaths of the roots. Note the union of the two roots, the spinal nerve, and its two rami. Attempt to find the recurrent meningeal branch.

Meningeal Branch. This fine recurrent twig is formed by the union of two fine filaments, one from the spinal nerve, the other from the sympathetic trunk. It runs back through the intervertebral foramen, and is sensory to the walls and contents of the vertebral canal, and supplies the blood vessels therein.

Spinal Ganglia. These ganglia consist of the cell bodies of nerve cells (neurons) which give rise to the sensory fibres in the peripheral nerves, and the nerve fibres of the dorsal roots. They lie in the intervertebral foramina except in the case of the sacral and coccygeal nerves (see above) and the first two cervical which are placed in the corresponding position above and below the atlas.

Spinal Nerves

The spinal nerve is formed by the union of the nerve roots and begins immediately distal to the ganglion. The nerve is exceedingly short and divides almost immediately into a ventral and a dorsal ramus.

35

DISSECTION. Divide the spinal nerves in the intervertebral foramina leaving as long a piece of each nerve attached to the dura as possible. Cut across the spinal medulla and its membranes at the upper limit of the dissection, and pulling on the dura, remove the whole specimen to a tray filled with water. Slit the dura mater along the median plane anteriorly, and display in turn the arachnoid mater and the pia mater with the ligamenta denticulata. Note the rootlets of the spinal part of the accessory nerve which ascends posterior to the ligamentum denticulatum in the upper cervical region [Figs. 24, 45].

Examine the exit of the roots of a spinal nerve through the dura from the inside. Note that the dorsal and ventral root each receive a separate dural sheath; examine these by passing a fine blunt probe into each foramen. It is usually possible to reach the distal part of the ganglion along the sheath of the dorsal root without piercing the dura.

ARTERIES OF THE SPINAL MEDULLA

The numerous, thin-walled arteries which supply the spinal medulla reach it along the roots of the spinal nerves, and arise from the vertebral artery, the posterior branches of the intercostal and lumbar arteries, and the lateral sacral arteries. They feed into three longitudinal vessels (one anterior and two posterior spinal arteries) on the surface of the spinal medulla.

The **anterior spinal artery** is formed superiorly by a branch from each intracranial vertebral artery, and runs along the mouth of the anterior median fissure dorsal to the linea splendens [p. 33], throughout the length of the spinal medulla. It receives three to ten tributaries over the ventral roots, the largest of these usually enters it from the left and often on the tenth thoracic ventral root, and supplies the lumbar swelling.

The anterior spinal artery sends branches: (1) into the anterior median fissure to supply most of the grey matter (nerve cells) in the interior of the spinal medulla, and the deeper parts of the surrounding white matter (nerve fibres); (2) branches which pass around the surface of the spinal medulla and may reach the line of entry of the dorsal roots. Here they join the **posterior spinal arteries**

which course longitudinally among the dorsal rootlets at their point of entry to the spinal medulla, and send branches over its posterior surface.

On the conus medullaris, each posterior spinal artery sweeps ventrally to join the caudal end of the anterior spinal artery, from which a slender branch continues on to the filum terminale. The posterior spinal arteries are fed by numerous small arteries on the dorsal roots, and are formed at their cranial ends by a branch of the vertebral artery or of its posterior inferior cerebellar branch. They are much smaller than the anterior spinal artery.

VEINS OF THE SPINAL MEDULLA

The veins, though small, numerous, and very tortuous, are larger than the arteries, and form a plexus with elongated meshes. Six more or less perfect longitudinal venous trunks may be seen: one in the median plane anteriorly; one in the median plane posteriorly; a pair behind the ventral roots; a pair behind the dorsal roots.

Superiorly they are continuous with the veins of the medulla oblongata, and they drain laterally along the nerve roots into the internal vertebral venous plexuses.

STRUCTURE OF THE SPINAL MEDULLA

The spinal medulla if cut across can be seen to consist of an internal core of **grey**

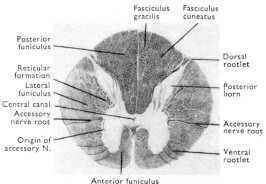

Fig. 24 Transverse section of the upper part of the cervical spinal medulla.

36

matter and an external layer of **white matter.**

It is partially divided into right and left halves by an anterior median fissure, and a posterior median septum.

The **posteromedian sulcus** is a mere groove on the surface marking the position of the **posteromedian septum** [FIG. 25] which is a thin sheet of **neuroglia,** the connective tissue peculiar to the central nervous system. The septum extends from the sulcus inwards to the centre, or even further in the upper part of the spinal medulla, but diminishes in depth in the lower part. The **anteromedian fissure** is a narrow cleft which extends into the substance of the spinal medulla, almost reaching the grey commissure [FIG. 25].

The **grey matter** (principally nerve cell bodies and neuroglia) is roughly H-shaped in cross section with the horizontal bar of the H formed by the **grey commissure** (crossing) traversed longitudinally by a narrow tunnel, the **central canal.** This canal is continuous superiorly with the central canal which traverses the lower half of the medulla oblongata and opens out into the fourth ventricle of the brain. Inferiorly it ends blindly in the filum terminale after a slight expansion in the conus medullaris, the terminal ventricle. It is filled with cerebrospinal fluid, but is often absent in the spinal medulla of aged individuals. The posterior median septum reaches the grey commissure, but the anterior median fissure is separated from it by nerve fibres crossing the midline, the **white commissure.**

The anterior and posterior limbs of the H-shaped grey matter form the anterior and posterior **horns** as seen in transverse section. The dorsal roots enter the posterior horns, the ventral roots arise in the ventral horns. Since the horns form continuous ridges of grey matter throughout the length of the spinal medulla, they are known as the **anterior** and **posterior grey columns.**

DISSECTION. If the spinal medulla is fairly firm, or if a well preserved specimen is available, make sections across it at different levels. Examine the cut surface with the naked eye and with a hand lens, and compare what you see with Figures 24 and 25.

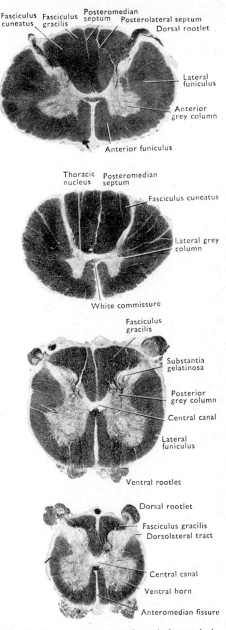

FIG. 25 Transverse sections through the cervical (A), thoracic (B), lumbar (C), and sacral (D) regions of the spinal medulla.

Spinal Medulla in Section

The amount of **grey matter** varies considerably at different levels, and at any level is proportional to the volume of tissue supplied by the spinal nerves arising at that level. Thus the horns are largest in the swellings and are mainly responsible for them, and smallest in the thoracic and upper cervical regions. In the thoracic region there is an additional spike-like extension of the lateral aspect of the grey matter, the **lateral grey column** or horn [FIG. 25]. It contains the nerve cells which give rise to the preganglionic fibres of the sympathetic system. These form the white rami communicantes of the thoracic and upper two lumbar nerves. A similar spike appears in the sacral region, and this gives rise to the pelvic parasympathetic nerves.

The **white matter** forms a thick coating around the grey matter, and is composed of longitudinally running nerve fibres, some of which ascend towards the brain while others descend. Fibres are added to the ascending pathways throughout their length, and descending fibres end in the grey matter at every level. Thus the number of fibres, and hence the volume of white matter, increases steadily from below upwards. Many of these groups of fibres are gathered together into special pathways known as **tracts** or fasciculi.

The white matter may be divided into posterior, lateral, and anterior **funiculi** on each side of the spinal medulla by the presence of the dorsal and ventral roots piercing it. In the upper half of the spinal medulla there is a **posterolateral septum** in each posterior funiculus, and this divides it into a slender, medial **fasciculus gracilis**, and a broader, lateral **fasciculus cuneatus**. The position of this septum is marked on the surface by the posterior intermediate sulcus.

THE DEEPER DISSECTION OF THE FACE

In the following dissection a number of structures will be displayed that are dissected more fully and described later; in order to avoid confusion the dissectors should refer to the appropriate illustrations as indicated.

DISSECTION. Detach the risorius and cut through the posterior half of the platysma along the lower border of the mandible. Reflect both towards the mouth, avoiding injury to vessels and nerves [Figs. 26, 27].

Find the branches of the great auricular nerve which ascend over the lower part of the parotid gland.

Clean the facial artery and vein at the antero-inferior angle of masseter, but do not trace them further at present.

Cut through the fascial covering of the parotid gland immediately in front of the auricle from the zygomatic arch to the angle of the mandible. Dissect the fascia carefully forwards to the margins of the gland, look for the nerves, vessels, and the duct of the gland which emerge at the borders. The duct appears at the anterior border about a finger's breadth below the zygomatic arch. It is of considerable size, is easily recognized [Fig. 60] and can be palpated in the living by rolling it against the anterior border of the clenched masseter.

Above the duct, find: (1) a small, detached part of the parotid gland, the accessory parotid; (2) the transverse facial artery and vein; (3) the zygomatic branches of the facial nerve. Below the duct, find the buccal and mandibular branches of the facial nerve [Fig. 27].

It is important to find the branches of the facial nerve issuing from the parotid gland and trace them forwards to their termination, as they form the only motor supply to the muscles of facial expression [p. 11]. The dissection is difficult because of the communications between the motor branches of the facial nerve and those of the sensory trigeminal nerve.

Follow the upper zygomatic branches first. When you reach the orbicularis oculi, reflect the lateral part of the muscle and find the zygomaticofacial nerve emerging from the zygomatic bone. As you reach the zygomaticus major, reflect it, the zygomaticus minor, and the levator labii superioris from their origins, and turning them downwards, clean the facial artery and vein and their branches. Find the deep facial vein which passes posteriorly from the facial vein to disappear into the fat of the cheek and pass deep to masseter. Trace the lower zygomatic branches forwards beneath the orbit, and find their communications with the infra-orbital nerve (sensory) which appears through the infra-orbital foramen. Clean the branches of this nerve.

Find the buccal branch of the facial nerve at the anterior border of the parotid, and trace it forwards through the fat of the cheek to the buccinator muscle. Find its communication with the buccal (sensory) branch of the trigeminal nerve, and follow that nerve posteriorly till it disappears deep to the ramus of the mandible.

Trace the mandibular branch of the facial nerve forwards from the lower border of the parotid gland to the depressor anguli oris. Divide that muscle and find the communication of the nerve with the mental nerve (sensory) which issues from the mental foramen. Clean the mental nerve.

At the upper border of the parotid gland, identify: (1) the superficial temporal artery and veins; (2) the auriculotemporal nerve lying behind the vessels, close to the auricle; (3) the temporal branches of the facial nerve anterior to the vessels. Clean them a short distance downwards.

At the lower border of the gland, find: (1) the anterior and posterior branches into which the lower end of the retromandibular vein divides [Fig. 11]; (2) the cervical branch of the facial nerve. Clean them as they emerge from the gland, but do not trace them further at present.

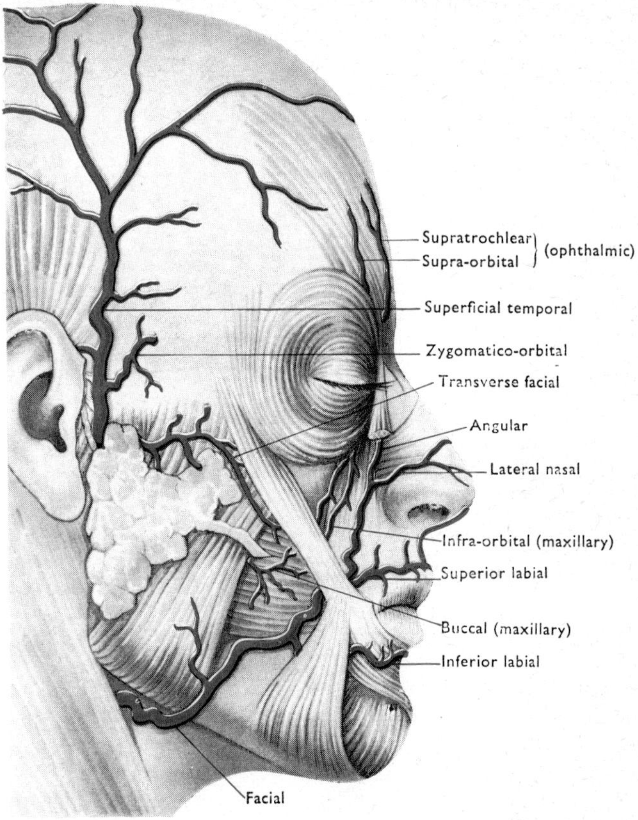
Supratrochlear
Supra-orbital
(ophthalmic)
Superficial temporal
Zygomatico-orbital
Transverse facial
Angular
Lateral nasal
Infra-orbital (maxillary)
Superior labial
Buccal (maxillary)
Inferior labial
Facial

FIG. 26 The arteries of the face.

ARTERIES OF THE FACE

The face has a very rich arterial supply: thus wounds of the face bleed freely and heal rapidly. The various arteries anastomose freely with each other, with the various small arteries which accompany branches of the trigeminal nerve into the face, and with the arteries of the opposite side, especially in the lips.

Transverse Facial Artery [FIG. 26]

This small vessel arises from the superficial temporal artery under cover of the parotid gland, and escapes near its upper end to run forwards over the masseter below the zygomatic arch.

Facial Artery [FIG. 26]

This is the main artery of the face, and it runs a sinuous course to accommodate to the mobility of the structures through which it passes. It arises from the external carotid artery, and after turning round the lower border of the mandible and piercing the deep cervical fascia, appears on the face at the antero-inferior border of masseter, where it can be palpated against the jaw. On the face it runs anterosuperiorly to a point 1·5 cm. from the angle of the mouth, and then ascends more vertically to end near the medial angle of the eye.

Branches. The larger branches pass to the chin, lips, and nose, but smaller branches run into the adjacent muscles. An important anastomosis is present at the medial angle of the eye between the facial vessels and those of the orbit. In this way venous blood may drain from the face into the orbit and skull, and arterial blood may flow from the facial artery (external carotid) to the internal carotid in the skull.

VEINS OF THE FACE

The veins anastomose freely in the face, and are drained by veins which accompany all of the arteries that supply it.

Facial Vein

This is the major route of venous drainage from the face. It is formed by the union of the supra-orbital and supratrochlear veins at the medial angle of the eye (angular vein). At first superficial to the artery, it runs postero-inferiorly in the same plane as the artery, but takes a straighter course and lies posterior to it. It joins the artery again at the antero-inferior angle of masseter, on the surface of the mandible. Here it pierces the deep fascia and descends into the neck, where it is joined by the anterior branch of the retromandibular vein. Thence it crosses the carotid arteries and enters the internal jugular vein.

Tributaries. In addition to those mentioned above, it receives tributaries which correspond with the branches of the facial artery. On the surface of buccinator it gives off the **deep facial vein,** which connects it with the pterygoid plexus of veins in the infratemporal fossa: an important route for the spread of infection.

NERVES OF THE FACE [p. 8]

Branches of two sensory nerves (trigeminal and great auricular) and one motor nerve (facial) are found on the face.

Branches of Trigeminal Nerve in Face [FIG. 27]

The trigeminal nerve is the main sensory nerve of the face. It gives rise to three divisions, each of which supplies cutaneous branches to one of three roughly concentric areas of the face.

Ophthalmic Nerve. This is the first division, and it supplies the skin of the superomedial

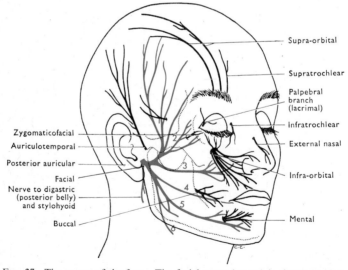

FIG. 27 The nerves of the face. The facial nerve (motor) is shown in blue, the branches of the trigeminal (sensory) in black. 1. Temporal branches of facial and zygomaticotemporal branch of trigeminal. 2 and 3. Zygomatic branches. 4. Buccal branch. 5. Marginal mandibular branch. 6. Cervical branch.

region, including the dorsum and root of the nose, the upper eyelid, and the forehead and scalp as far as the vertex. This is achieved through its three branches, lacrimal, frontal, and nasociliary, which pass through the orbit and give rise to five terminal branches on the face:

1. The **palpebral branch of the lacrimal,** which supplies the lateral part of the upper eyelid.

2 and 3. The **supra-orbital** and **supratrochlear** branches of the frontal [p. 8] nerve. They supply the forehead and scalp.

4. The **infratrochlear** branch of the nasociliary emerges from the orbit just above the medial palpebral ligament. It gives branches to the medial parts of the eyelids and the root of the nose.

5. The **external nasal** branch comes from the nasociliary nerve in the orbit, which sends its anterior ethmoidal branch through the cranial cavity, and nose, to emerge between the nasal bone and the upper nasal cartilage. It supplies the skin of the lower half of the dorsum of the nose.

Maxillary Nerve. This is the second division, and it supplies a zone of skin inferior and lateral to the eye by three branches:

1. The **infra-orbital nerve** [FIG. 29] emerges from the infra-orbital foramen under cover of the orbicularis oculi and levator labii superioris. It supplies the skin and mucous membrane of the upper lip and lower eyelid, the skin between them, and the side of the nose, through labial, palpebral, and nasal branches. These branches form a plexus with each other and with the zygomatic branches of the facial nerve. It should be appreciated that such plexuses are not the site of union of the various nerve fibres in the nerves, but merely that these fibres run together, and that there is an opportunity for sensory nerve fibres from the muscles of the face to enter the brain via the trigeminal nerve.

2. The **zygomaticofacial nerve** supplies the skin over the bony part of the cheek by passing from the orbit through the zygomatic bone to its facial surface [FIG. 27].

3. The **zygomaticotemporal nerve** [p. 8] also pierces the zygomatic bone, but appears on its temporal surface. It passes through the temporal fascia, and supplies the skin over the anterior part of the temple.

Mandibular Nerve. This is the third division and it supplies a zone of skin posterior and inferior to the previous area, also through three branches:

1. The **auriculotemporal nerve** emerges from the upper end of the parotid gland beside the auricle. It supplies the upper part of the auricle, the external acoustic meatus, and the skin of the side of the head [FIG. 27].

2. The **buccal nerve** passes antero-inferiorly from the infratemporal fossa, and running deep to masseter and the ramus of the mandible, appears in the cheek on the lowest part of buccinator. It supplies the skin over buccinator, and sends branches through it to the underlying mucous membrane. It is a purely sensory nerve.

3. The **mental nerve** appears through the mental foramen from the interior of the mandible. It divides into branches under cover of depressor anguli oris, and supplies the skin and mucous membrane of the lower lip, and the skin over the mandible from the symphysis to the anterior border of masseter.

Thus the trigeminal nerve supplies all the skin of the face with the exception of the area over the parotid gland and the angle of the mandible, which is supplied by the **great auricular nerve.** Inferiorly the trigeminal area abuts on the region supplied by the second cervical nerve **(transverse nerve of the neck)** along the inferior margin of the body of the mandible [FIG. 10].

Terminal Branches of Facial Nerve [FIG. 27]

The facial nerve is the motor nerve to the muscles of facial expression. It has five terminal branches, or groups of branches, all of which emerge from the parotid gland:

1. **Temporal** branches are described on page 8.

2. The **zygomatic** branches. The upper filaments run forwards across the zygomatic bone and supply orbicularis oculi. The lower filaments are larger, and run forwards on the

lower border of the zygomatic bone to supply the muscles of the nose, and those between the eye and the mouth.

3. The **buccal** branches run towards the angle of the mouth and supply the muscles of the soft part of the cheek.

4. The **marginal mandibular** branch runs forwards along the mandible, and usually curves down into the neck before running with the inferior labial branch of the facial artery to supply the muscles of the lower lip.

5. The **cervical branch** leaves the lower border of the parotid gland, runs forwards and downwards into the neck, to supply the platysma and communicate with the transverse nerve of the neck [p. 16].

DISSECTION. Clean the levator anguli oris and the buccinator. Remove the buccal fat from the buccinator, avoiding injury to the buccal nerve, and note the small buccal glands that lie in it. Remove the fascia covering buccinator, define its attachments to the maxilla and mandible, and trace its fibres towards the angle of the mouth.

STRUCTURES IN THE CHEEKS AND LIPS

Buccinator [Figs. 6, 111, 112]

This muscle lies next to the mucous membrane of the cheek. Its horizontal fibres arise from the outer surfaces of the maxilla and mandible opposite the sockets of the molar teeth. Between these two bony attachments it springs from the **pterygomandibular raphe.** The raphe is formed by the interlacing tendinous fibres of the buccinator and the superior constrictor muscle of the pharynx, where these muscles meet edge to edge. The superior constrictor will be seen later when the pharynx is dissected.

Anteriorly, the fibres of buccinator converge on the corner of the mouth, and blend with the orbicularis oris to form a large part of it. The upper and lower fibres pass directly into the corresponding lips, but the middle fibres decussate towards the angle of the mouth, so that the upper fibres enter the lower lip and vice versa. Some of the internal posterosuperior fibres pass almost vertically downwards from the maxilla to the mandible.

Nerve supply: the facial nerve. Action: the buccinator is used during mastication to press the cheek against the teeth and prevent food escaping into the vestibule of the mouth; it can also compress the blown out cheek.

Buccopharyngeal Fascia

This thin sheet of fascia clothes the external surface of buccinator, and continues backwards over the constrictor muscles of the pharynx. The **parotid duct** on its way to the vestibule of the mouth, pierces this fascia and the buccinator, and becomes continuous with the mucous membrane opposite the upper second molar tooth. The fascia and muscle are pierced also by the nerves and vessels of the mucous membrane.

Molar Glands and Buccal Lymph Nodes

Four to five small, molar, mucous salivary glands lie on the buccopharyngeal fascia around the parotid duct. Their ducts follow the parotid duct to the vestibule of the mouth. The buccal lymph nodes are one or two nodules found on the buccopharyngeal fascia.

Buccal Pad of Fat

This is an encapsulated mass of fat which lies on the buccopharyngeal fascia and is partly tucked between it and the masseter. It is pierced by the buccal nerve and the parotid duct, and thickens the cheek to help it resist the external pressure during sucking. This sucking pad is relatively much larger in the infant than the adult, and accounts for the fullness of the cheeks in children.

Levator Anguli Oris

This muscle arises from the canine fossa below the infra-orbital foramen, under cover of orbicularis oculi, levator labii superioris, and the zygomatic muscles. It runs to the angle of the mouth, blends with orbicularis oris, and sends some fibres into the lower lip.

DISSECTION. Evert the lips and remove the mucous membrane from their deep surfaces. This exposes a number of small labial glands, and the incisive muscles near the bases of the lips opposite the sockets of the incisor teeth. **Remove these from the lower lip and expose the mentalis.**

Mentalis

This small muscle arises from the outer walls of the canine sockets. Its slips converge to be inserted into the skin of the chin.

Labial and Buccal Glands

These are small, closely set, mucous salivary glands that lie in the submucosa of the lips and cheeks. They are palpable as small nodules when the tongue is pressed against them, and their ducts open into the vestibule of the mouth.

THE EYELIDS

The eyelids or palpebrae consist of the following layers from without inwards:
1. Skin and superficial fascia devoid of fat.
2. Orbicularis oculi [p. 12].
3. Tarsus and palpebral fascia. It is in this layer that the tendon of levator palpebrae superioris enters the upper eyelid. Immediately deep to it lie the tarsal glands.
4. Conjunctiva.

The skin of the eyelids is very thin, and its hairs (except the eyelashes) are so short that few of them appear above the surface. The superficial fascia is thin and loose. It allows the skin to move freely over the lid, and can become greatly swollen with fluid or blood after an injury.

DISSECTION. **Separate the palpebral part of orbicularis oculi from the remainder by a circular incision, and turn the palpebral part towards the palpebral fissure, avoiding injury to the palpebral fascia, vessels, and nerves. At the medial angle of the eye, this dissection will expose the medial palpebral ligament [p. 44]: elsewhere it uncovers the palpebral fascia and tarsi.**

Tarsi

The tarsi are two thin plates of condensed fibrous tissue which lie close to the free margins of the eyelids, and stiffen them.

The **inferior tarsus** is a narrow strip attached to the inferior orbital margin by the palpebral fascia.

The **superior tarsus** is much larger, and can be felt if the upper lid is pinched sideways between finger and thumb. Its deep surface is adherent to the palpebral conjunctiva, and the palpebral fascia is attached to its anterior surface some distance below its upper border, together with the greater part of the expanded tendon of **levator palpebrae superioris,** which is attached to the deep surface of the palpebral fascia [FIG. 28]. As a result, when the upper lid is everted to expose the conjunctival surface of the superior tarsus, it tends to remain in this position and is not immediately replaced by contraction of the levator. The lower edge of the tarsus is adherent to the skin of the margin of the lid.

The **tarsal glands** lie in furrows on the deep surfaces of the tarsi, and can be seen through the conjunctiva as closely placed, parallel, yellow streaks that run at right angles to the margin of the lid. Their ducts open on the margin behind the eyelashes.

The **ciliary glands** are arranged in several rows immediately behind the roots of the eyelashes, and their

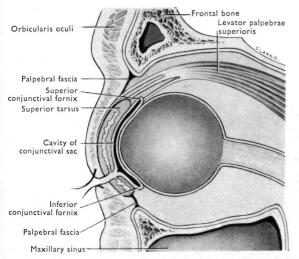

Orbicularis oculi

Frontal bone
Levator palpebrae superioris

Palpebral fascia
Superior conjunctival fornix
Superior tarsus

Cavity of conjunctival sac

Inferior conjunctival fornix

Palpebral fascia

Maxillary sinus

FIG. 28   Diagram of the structure of the eyelids as seen in section.

ducts open on the margin close to the lashes. They are too small to be seen by dissection, but when infected, they produce a red swelling of the margin of the lid known as a 'stye'.

The **palpebral fascia** is a thin fibrous membrane which connects the tarsi to the orbital margins, and forms an **orbital septum** with them. Medially it passes posterior to the lacrimal sac and is attached to the posterior margin of the groove which lodges the sac. In the lower lid it is attached to the inferior margin of the tarsus, but in the upper lid, it is attached to its anterior surface (see above). It is pierced by the nerves and vessels which pass from the orbit to the exterior.

Palpebral Ligaments

The **medial** palpebral ligament is a strong fibrous band that connects the two tarsi with the medial margin of the orbit. It lies under cover of the skin, anterior to the lacrimal sac, and gives origin to many of the fibres of orbicularis oculi.

The **lateral** palpebral ligament is a slender fibrous band which connects the two tarsi with a small tubercle on the lateral orbital margin. It lies posterior to the palpebral fascia and is separated from it by a little fat.

Levator Palpebrae Superioris

The tendon of this muscle expands into a wide, thin sheet which enters the upper eyelid from the orbit, and blends with the deep surface of the palpebral fascia. A few of the fibres of the tendon pass through orbicularis oculi to be inserted into the skin; others are attached to the front of the tarsus. Through its fascial sheath, the tendon is attached to the superior fornix of the conjunctiva, which is, therefore, raised with the eyelid [FIG. 28].

Vessels and Nerves of Eyelids

The **arteries** are derived from the ophthalmic, and pierce the palpebral fascia to enter the lids. They anastomose to form arches near the margins of the lids, between the tarsus and the orbicularis oculi.

The **veins** run medially and end in the supratrochlear and facial veins.

The **motor nerves** to the orbicularis oculi come from the temporal and upper zygomatic branches of the facial nerve. The **sensory nerves** to the upper lid are the palpebral branch of the lacrimal nerve and twigs from the supraorbital, supratrochlear, and infratrochlear nerves. The infra-orbital nerve supplies the lower lid.

THE LACRIMAL APPARATUS

Lacrimal fluid, produced by the lacrimal gland, passes through numerous ducts into the superolateral part of the conjunctival sac. Thence it flows to the medial angle of the eye, aided by the contraction of the orbicularis oculi, and enters the lacrimal canaliculi through the puncta [FIG. 3]. These canaliculi discharge into the lacrimal sac, which transmits the fluid into the nose through the nasolacrimal duct.

DISSECTION. Cut through the superolateral part of the

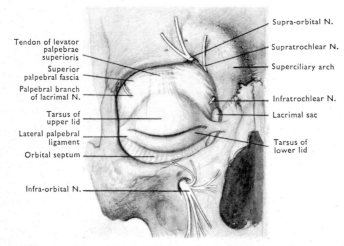

Tendon of levator palpebrae superioris
Superior palpebral fascia
Palpebral branch of lacrimal N.
Tarsus of upper lid
Lateral palpebral ligament
Orbital septum
Infra-orbital N.

Supra-orbital N.
Supratrochlear N.
Superciliary arch
Infratrochlear N.
Lacrimal sac
Tarsus of lower lid

FIG. 29 Dissection of the right eyelids. Orbicularis oculi has been completely removed.

palpebral fascia and expose the lacrimal gland. Raise the gland, and moving the points of a fine pair of forceps up and down in the loose tissue below the gland, find its ducts.

Find the lacrimal papillae at the medial ends of the eyelids, and attempt to pass a fine bristle along the lacrimal canaliculi through the puncta.

Clean the medial palpebral ligament and the lacrimal sac which lies posterior to it. Note the lacrimal part of the orbicularis oculi passing round the lateral side of the sac. Make an opening into the sac, and passing a probe into it, explore its extent, and then pass the probe downwards into the nose through the nasolacrimal duct.

Lacrimal Gland

This gland [FIGS. 30, 47, 48, 108] lies mainly in the orbit, but a part of it (the **palpebral process**) extends into the lateral part of the upper eyelid between the conjunctiva and the palpebral fascia. When the lid is everted it may be seen bulging the conjunctiva.

The **ducts** of the lacrimal gland (twelve or less) are short and slender, and open into the conjunctiva near the superior fornix.

Conjunctiva

This membrane is covered with moist, stratified, squamous epithelium, and it lines the deep surfaces of the eyelids and covers the exposed surface of the eyeball. Over the cornea it is known as the anterior epithelium of the cornea and is firmly attached to it. The fornices are produced where the thick, vascular, palpebral part is reflected from the roots of the eyelids on to the eyeball. Here it is thin and transparent and is loosely attached to the sclera. As a whole it is known as the conjunctival sac, which is closed when the eye is shut. The cavity is no more than a capillary interval which is moistened by lacrimal fluid. It opens to the exterior through the **palpebral**

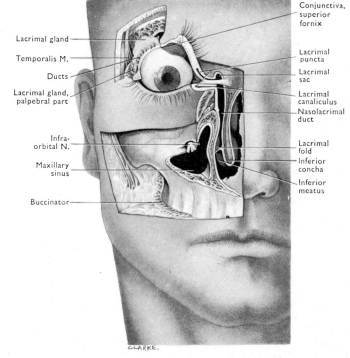

FIG. 30 Dissection of the lacrimal apparatus.

fissure and into the lacrimal sac through the canaliculi [FIG. 30].

Lacrimal Canaliculi

These two slender tubes are about 1 cm. in length. Each begins as a tiny hole (the **lacrimal punctum**) which is situated in the anterior wall of the closed conjunctival sac on the summit of a lacrimal papilla. Thence it runs medially in the margin of the eyelid, and opens into the lacrimal sac posterior to the medial palpebral ligament.

Lacrimal Sac

This sac lies posterior to the medial palpebral ligament, lodged in the lacrimal groove just posterior to the medial orbital margin. The sac is approximately 1 cm. long by 0·5 cm. wide. Its upper end is blind; its lower end is continuous with the nasolacrimal duct.

Nasolacrimal Duct [FIGS. 30, 123]

This tube is about 1·5 cm. long and 0·5 cm. wide. It begins at the anteromedial corner of the floor of the orbit, and passes downwards through the nasolacrimal canal, to end in the inferior meatus of the nasal cavity. The mucous membrane at the medial side of its opening is raised up as the **lacrimal fold**. This acts as a flap valve which prevents air and secretions being blown up the nasolacrimal duct when the nasal pressure is raised.

Lacrimal Fluid. This fluid flows downwards over the eyeball, and most of it evaporates in ordinary circumstances. It is also carried medially by the frequent involuntary contractions of orbicularis oculi which move the eyelids medially owing to the attachment to the medial palpebral ligament. Thus, in paralysis of the orbicularis oculi, the fluid is not spread over the permanently open eye and the cornea dries. Also the sagging lower lid forms a pond in which tears collect and spill over on to the face.

Excessive secretion by the gland, due to irritation of the conjunctiva or other causes, floods the conjunctiva and the fluid overflows as tears.

Accessory Lacrimal Glands. These are minute glands that lie near the fornices; they can be effective in moistening the conjunctiva if the lacrimal gland is removed.

DISSECTION. Strip the muscles and skin from the nose, and define the cartilages. Details of these are available in the larger textbooks.

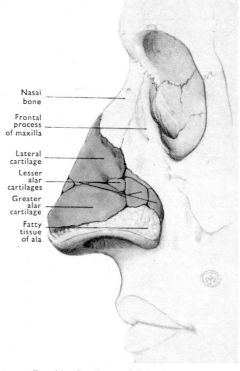

Nasal bone

Frontal process of maxilla

Lateral cartilage

Lesser alar cartilages

Greater alar cartilage

Fatty tissue of ala

FIG. 31   Cartilages of the external nose.

THE CRANIAL CAVITY

DISSECTION. Support the head on a block under the occiput. Make a sagittal cut through the epicranial aponeurosis from the root of the nose to the external occipital protuberance. Pull each half laterally with the scalp and detach it from the temporal lines. Strip the periosteum (pericranium) from the external surface of the vault of the skull, and carry this below the upper attachment of the temporalis muscle, detaching it from the skull. It is necessary to cut through the periosteum at the sutures of the skull for it is continuous through these with the periosteum on the inside of the skull (endocranium). In this way turn each half of the scalp down over the auricles together with the periosteum and the upper parts of both temporal muscles.

Sutural Ligaments

The pericranium is loosely attached to the surface of the bones of the skull cap, but is continuous through the sutures with the endocranium. This fibrous periosteum between the bones forms the sutural ligaments, and it holds the bones together and allows growth between them. As the skull consolidates from the third to fourth decade onwards, the adjacent bones unite by ossification of the sutural ligaments, a process which begins internally and is known as synostosis.

DISSECTION. To remove the skull cap or calvaria; mark a line with pencil on the skull by encircling it horizontally with a piece of string from a point 1 cm. above the orbital margin anteriorly, to a point 1 cm. above the external occipital protuberance posteriorly. Make a saw cut along this line, continuing only until the sawdust becomes red. This indicates that the marrow cavity (diploë) has been entered and the outer table of the skull divided. Introduce a blunt chisel into the saw cut, split the inner table along the line by a series of short, sharp strokes with a mallet. Introduce the thick part of the chisel into the cut, and using it as a lever prise off the skull cap from the underlying endocranium to which it is still adherent.

Endocranium

The brain, like the spinal medulla, is enclosed in three distinct membranes or meninges: the dura mater, the arachnoid mater and the pia mater. The cranial dura mater, unlike its spinal counterpart, is fused with the endocranium wherever it is directly in contact with it.

When the skull cap is detached, the outer surface of the endocranium is exposed. It is rough, owing to a multitude of fine fibrous and vascular processes by which it is connected with the bones. The torn blood vessels are most numerous close to the median line, where the superior sagittal sinus, one of the intracranial venous channels, runs. If a blunt instrument is run from before backwards, pressing on the sinus, a considerable quantity of blood will ooze out, showing that a number of small veins from the cranial bones have been ruptured. The endocranium, like the periosteum, is strongly

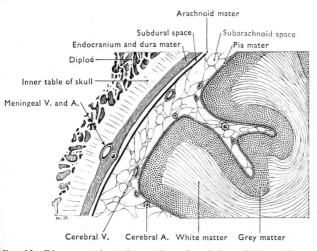

Arachnoid mater
Subdural space
Subarachnoid space
Endocranium and dura mater
Pia mater
Diploë
Inner table of skull
Meningeal V. and A.

Cerebral V.   Cerebral A.   White matter   Grey matter

FIG. 32   Diagrammatic section to show the relation of the meninges to the skull and brain. Note that the meningeal vessels are in the endocranium, while the cerebral vessels lie in the subarachnoid space. Cf. FIG. 4.

47

adherent to the sutural ligaments, and is more firmly attached to the base than to the vault of the cranium. The degree of adhesion varies with age and from individual to individual.

On the outer surface of the endocranium a number of vessels are seen ascending towards the vertex and branching. These are the branches of the **middle meningeal artery** with the corresponding veins on their external surfaces. These vessels groove the inner table of the skull, and so stand out in relief from the surface of the membrane. They supply the skull (particularly its diploë, which contains red bone marrow) as well as the endocranium and the dura fused to it. The branches do *not* cross the subdural space, and hence play *no* part in supplying the other layers of the meninges or the brain.

DISSECTION. Make a median sagittal incision through the endocranium and open the superior sagittal sinus as far forwards and backwards as the removal of the calvaria will allow.

Arachnoid Granulations [FIG. 34]

These are small, granular bodies, ranged along the sides of the superior sagittal sinus. They are formed by protrusions of the arachnoid mater, and they pass through apertures in the dura to enter the spaces between that membrane and the endocranium in which the venous sinuses of the dura mater and their

extensions lie. The granulations are normal enlargements of similar but microscopic processes of the arachnoid (**arachnoid villi**) which alone are present in children. In old age they may reach considerable proportions and even erode the inner table of the skull. They have been described in relation to most of the venous sinuses of the dura mater, and even in relation to the middle meningeal veins, but they are most plentiful in the superior sagittal sinus, particularly in the posterior parietal region. They are valvular structures which allow cerebrospinal fluid to pass into the venous system, but prevent the reflux of blood.

DURA MATER

Within the skull the dura mater is fused to the endocranium except: (1) where it passes between the major parts of the brain to form rigid folds or partitions which incompletely subdivide the cranial cavity, and help to support the brain within it [FIGS. 35, 36]; (2) where the venous sinuses of the dura mater separate the dura mater from the endocranium. These venous sinuses lie in the same plane as the internal vertebral venous plexuses, and some of them are continuous with these plexuses through the foramen magnum. The largest venous sinuses lie along the lines where the dural folds are attached to the endocranium and thus to the skull.

Structure of Venous Sinuses of Dura Mater. These are venous channels which are lined with endothelium and lie external to the dura mater. They transmit venous blood from the brain, meninges, and skull, mainly to the internal jugular vein. They also communicate with a number of other extracranial veins through **emissary veins** which pass through foramina in the skull. Most of these sinuses lie in shallow grooves on the internal surface of the cranial cavity, and are separated from the bone by endocranium, and from the subdural space and

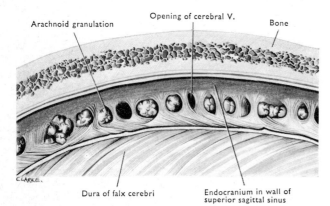

Arachnoid granulation   Opening of cerebral V.   Bone

CLARKE.

Dura of falx cerebri   Endocranium in wall of superior sagittal sinus

FIG. 33 Median section through the skull and superior sagittal sinus. Note arachnoid granulations protruding into the sinus.

48

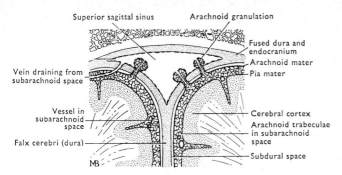

FIG. 34 Diagrammatic transverse section through the superior sagittal sinus and surrounding brain. Note the arrangement of the arachnoid granulations.

arachnoid mater by the dura mater; the endocranium and dura supporting their endothelial walls. Only two sinuses, the straight and the inferior sagittal, are enclosed entirely in dura by lying in the folds of that membrane which separate the major parts of the brain.

Internally the cranial dura mater has the same arrangement as the spinal dura mater; its surface is smooth and glistening, and is separated from the arachnoid by the capillary subdural space, except where the arachnoid villi and granulations are present, and where structures pierce it to enter or leave the brain.

DISSECTION. Tilt the head forwards, and make an incision through the dura mater and endocranium on each side of the superior sagittal sinus along its whole length. From the mid-point of each incision, make another cut downwards to the cut margin of the skull immediately above the auricle. It is best to raise the dura and endocranium as you make the incisions, so as to avoid cutting the underlying arachnoid, pia, and brain. Turn the flaps downwards over the cut margin of the skull to prevent its sharp edge from injuring the brain or your fingers during subsequent dissections.

Subdural Space

This capillary interval between the dura mater and the arachnoid contains a very small quantity of serous fluid which moistens their smooth apposed surfaces. It is in the nature of an extensive bursa which allows movement between the brain and pia-arachnoid on the one hand and the dura mater and skull on the other.

SUPERIOR CEREBRAL VEINS

These superficial vessels lie immediately external to the pia mater which covers the surface of the brain, and are entirely separate from the meningeal vessels. They can be seen through the thin arachnoid, and most of them lie in grooves on the cerebral surface. They run upwards towards the median plane, converging on the superior sagittal sinus which they enter by piercing the arachnoid and dura and crossing the subdural space between them. The anterior and posterior veins enter the sinus obliquely.

SUPERIOR SAGITTAL SINUS
[FIGS. 35, 36, 38]

This long sinus begins anteriorly at the crista galli, where it communicates with the veins of the frontal sinus, and sometimes with the veins of the nose, through the **foramen caecum.** The sinus runs posteriorly, grooving the cranial vault in the median plane, to become continuous with the right transverse sinus at the internal occipital protuberance [FIG. 46]. Arachnoid granulations bulge into the sinus, particularly towards its posterior part where its triangular lumen is of considerable size.

Lacunae Laterales. These are cleft-like, lateral extensions of the sinus between the dura mater and endocranium. The largest, 2–3 cm. in diameter, overlies the upper part of the motor area of the brain (q.v.); arachnoid villi and granulations perforate the dura to enter the lateral lacunae. Both lacunae and granulations increase in size with age, and may produce shallow depressions and clean cut pits, respectively, in the skull vault on either side of the groove for the sinus. The superior cerebral veins pass inferior to the lacunae to enter the sinus, but meningeal and diploic veins enter the lacunae.

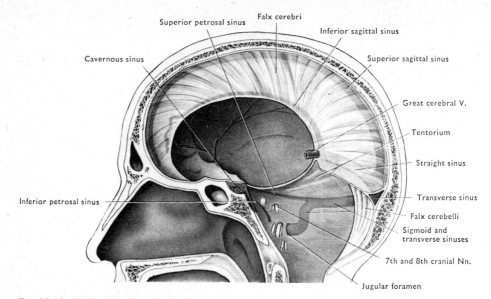

Superior petrosal sinus • Falx cerebri • Inferior sagittal sinus • Cavernous sinus • Superior sagittal sinus • Great cerebral V. • Tentorium • Straight sinus • Inferior petrosal sinus • Transverse sinus • Falx cerebelli • Sigmoid and transverse sinuses • 7th and 8th cranial Nn. • Jugular foramen

FIG. 35 Sagittal section through the skull to the left of the falx cerebri. The brain has been removed to show the folds of dura mater which incompletely partition the cranial cavity.

DISSECTION. To expose the falx cerebri, divide the superior cerebral veins on each side, and displace the upper parts of the cerebral hemispheres laterally.

FALX CEREBRI
[FIGS. 35, 36]

The falx cerebri is a sickle-shaped fold of the dura mater which descends between the two cerebral hemispheres. Anteriorly it is attached to the **crista galli,** is shallow and often cribriform, and may even resemble a lacework. As it passes posteriorly it increases in depth, and its convex, upper border is attached to the lips of the groove for the sagittal sinus on the vault of the skull. Posteriorly it is continuous, in the median plane, with the upper surface of another fold of dura mater (the tentorium cerebelli) which roofs over the posterior cranial fossa [FIGS. 36, 38]. Elsewhere the lower border is free and concave, and over-hangs a part of the brain (the corpus callosum) which connects the two halves of the cerebrum, but is not in contact with it except to a very slight extent posteriorly. Along its borders the two layers of the falx enclose blood sinuses: the superior sagittal sinus in its fixed margin; the inferior sagittal sinus in its free margin; the straight sinus in its attachment to the tentorium cerebelli.

REMOVAL OF THE BRAIN

The following dissection separates the major parts of the brain from each other, and should not be used if it is essential to retain the brain intact for future dissection; in which case the alternative dissection should be followed [p. 51].

DISSECTION. Draw one hemisphere gently away from the falx, and expose a mass of white matter (the corpus callosum) running between the hemispheres at a depth of approximately 5 cm. Make a sagittal cut with a scalpel through the corpus callosum. Start at its posterior end, and cut forwards in the median plane, between the anterior cerebral arteries which run posteriorly on the medial aspect of each hemisphere. Proceed carefully so as to divide no more than the corpus callosum, the posterior end of which is thicker than the remainder.

As the two parts of the corpus callosum are separated, a thin layer of pia mater will be exposed passing

50

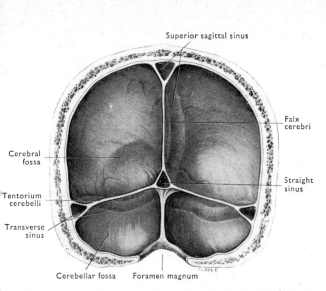

Superior sagittal sinus

Falx
cerebri

Cerebral
fossa

Straight
sinus

Tentorium
cerebelli

Transverse
sinus

Cerebellar fossa   Foramen magnum

Fig. 36   Coronal section through the skull at the level of the foramen
magnum.   The brain has been removed to show the fossae which lodge
the occipital lobes of the hemispheres and the cerebellum. The fossae are
separated by the falx cerebri and tentorium cerebelli, and the cerebellar
fossa is partly divided by the falx cerebelli.

anteriorly beneath the corpus callosum, while further
forwards is a thin, white, vertical sheet (septum pellucidum). This is composed of right and left parts,
and these can be separated by slight pressure from the
handle of a knife, provided the division of the corpus
callosum is strictly in the median plane.

When the two parts of the septum pellucidum are
separated, and the whole extent of the layer of pia
mater is exposed beneath it, two veins (internal cerebral)
may be seen lying in the pia mater, one on each side of
the median plane. Posteriorly, these internal cerebral
veins join to form the great cerebral vein which emerges
from beneath the posterior end of the corpus callosum,
and curving round it, enters the straight sinus [Fig. 35].
Divide the pia mater between the internal cerebral
veins, and thus open into a deep, slit-like cavity, the
third ventricle of the brain [Fig. 229].

Complete the division of the corpus callosum, and
note that its anterior extremity curves inferior to the
septum. Continue the median sagittal cut through the
anterior wall and floor of the third ventricle as far
posteriorly as the upper part of the midbrain [Fig. 213]
which can be seen under the posterior end of the corpus
callosum.

Lift the frontal lobe of one hemisphere gently from
the anterior cranial fossa, and expose the anterior part
of the falx attached to the crista galli. Lift the olfactory

bulb out of the narrow slit immediately lateral to the base of the
crista galli.

Raise the frontal lobe still further,
and note the temporal lobe slipping
out of the middle cranial fossa, and
the optic nerve and internal carotid
artery appearing near the midline
close to it. Divide the artery and
nerve, and note another nerve (oculomotor) smaller than the optic, passing horizontally forwards [Fig. 46].

Turn to the lateral side of the
hemisphere, elevate its posterior part
and identify the tentorium cerebelli
beneath it. Slip a knife medially and
upwards between the tentorium and
the hemisphere, and cut through one
half of the midbrain where it passes
through the median aperture of the
tentorium (tentorial notch) joining
this cut to the median sagittal cut
previously made.

Lift out the free hemisphere; examine the hemisphere which remains in situ [Figs. 37, 202] and
the exposed parts of the base of the
skull [Fig. 38].

Note the sharp posterior margin of the anterior
cranial fossa, which is formed by the lesser wing of the
sphenoid bone. It overlies the tip of the temporal lobe
which is inserted into the anterior extremity of the
middle cranial fossa. Medially, the lesser wing of the
sphenoid is continued into the anterior clinoid process,
which is immediately lateral to the internal carotid
artery and the optic nerve. Posteromedial to these lies
the infundibulum, a narrow funnel extending inferiorly
from the floor of the third ventricle to pierce the dura
mater (diaphragma sellae) and reach the hypophysis.

Identify the oculomotor nerve, and the free edge of the
tentorium passing forwards to be attached to the anterior clinoid process.

Gently elevate the intact hemisphere to expose the
optic nerve, the internal carotid artery and its anterior
cerebral branch. Free the arteries from the base of the
brain as far as possible, and then remove this hemisphere
in the same manner as the first, leaving the carotid
artery and its main branches in situ.

ALTERNATIVE DISSECTION. To remove the
brain in one piece, proceed as follows. Detach the falx
cerebri from the crista galli, and pull the falx posteriorly. Remove the block from under the head allowing it to drop backwards. The frontal lobes of the
brain usually fall away from the anterior cranial fossa;
if not, gently pull them away and separate each olfac-

51

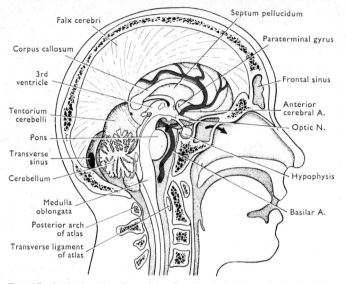

Labels on figure:
Falx cerebri
Corpus callosum
3rd ventricle
Tentorium cerebelli
Pons
Transverse sinus
Cerebellum
Medulla oblongata
Posterior arch of atlas
Transverse ligament of atlas
Septum pellucidum
Paraterminal gyrus
Frontal sinus
Anterior cerebral A.
Optic N.
Hypophysis
Basilar A.

FIG. 37 Sagittal section through head and neck slightly to the right of the median plane.

tory bulb from its fossa at the side of the crista galli. This process tears the fine olfactory nerves which pass from the nose through the cribriform plates of the ethmoid into the olfactory bulbs.

The large optic nerves then come into view and should be divided. This exposes the internal carotid arteries with the infundibulum passing vertically to the hypophysis between them. Divide both [Fig. 38].

Allow the brain to fall backwards as each structure is divided, but support it posteriorly so as to avoid damaging it on the skull.

Posterior to the infundibulum, identify the dorsum sellae, and the oculomotor nerves passing forwards, one on each side of it [Figs. 38, 39].

Lateral to each oculomotor nerve is the free edge of the tentorium cerebelli. Turn the margin of the tentorium laterally and divide a slender nerve, the trochlear, which lies just under its free margin [Fig. 46].

Turn the head forcibly round to one side, raise the posterior part of the upper hemisphere with the fingers, and note that it lies on the tentorium. Divide the tentorium along its attachment to the petrous temporal bone [Figs. 38, 39], taking care not to injure the cerebellum beneath it. Then turn the head in the opposite direction and repeat the procedure on the opposite side.

Let the brain fall well backwards so as to draw the brain stem away from the anterior wall of the posterior cranial fossa and bring the nerves into view.

Divide the oculomotor nerves, and allowing the brain to fall first to one side and then the other, identify and divide the trigeminal, abducent, facial, and vestibulocochlear nerves; the latter two entering the internal acoustic meatus. Then identify and cut the nerves passing to the jugular foramen [Fig. 46], but leave the accessory nerve on one side in the skull. Look for the hypoglossal nerve, which is deeper and more medial, and cut it also [Fig. 45].

Press the pons further posteriorly, and identify the vertebral arteries running superiorly to form the basilar artery on its anterior surface. Pass the knife into the vertebral canal in front of the medulla oblongata, cut firmly from side to side, and divide the spinal medulla and vertebral arteries. Withdraw the brain from the cranial cavity, dividing any roots of the accessory nerve which are still attached to the spinal medulla, and those of any spinal nerves included in the specimen.

Removal of the brain in this way, without complete division of the tentorium from the skull, ruptures the great cerebral vein where it enters the straight sinus at the junction of the free margins of the falx and tentorium.

STRUCTURES SEEN AFTER REMOVAL OF THE CEREBRUM
[FIGS. 38, 39]

With the assistance of a skull, identify the structures which have been exposed, and in particular note the boundaries of the anterior and middle cranial fossae, and the taut but resilient tentorium cerebelli.

In the **anterior cranial fossa** note:

1. The **crista galli** with the falx attached.

2. The **cribriform plate** of the ethmoid from which the olfactory bulb was removed, and through which the olfactory nerves pass into the bulb from the nasal mucosa which lies immediately inferior to the cribriform plate.

3. The floor formed by the irregular **orbital part of the frontal bone.** This separates the frontal lobe of the brain from the orbit, and

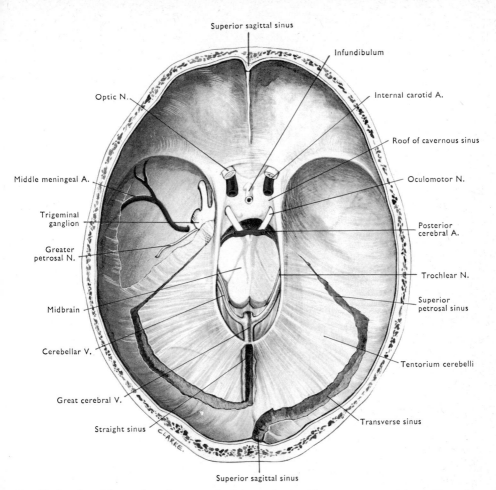

Superior sagittal sinus

Infundibulum

Optic N.

Internal carotid A.

Roof of cavernous sinus

Middle meningeal A.

Oculomotor N.

Trigeminal ganglion

Posterior cerebral A.

Greater petrosal N.

Trochlear N.

Superior petrosal sinus

Midbrain

Cerebellar V.

Tentorium cerebelli

Great cerebral V.

Straight sinus

Transverse sinus

Superior sagittal sinus

CLARKE

Fig. 38 Interior of the cranium after removal of the cerebrum. The transverse, straight, and superior petrosal sinuses have been opened, and the dura mater has been removed from the floor of the left middle cranial fossa.

its irregularities are due to the close fitting of the orbital surface of the frontal lobe to the bone.

4. The posterior margin of the **lesser wing of the sphenoid bone,** with the sphenoparietal venous sinus running medially along it outside the dura. The bony edge ends medially in the **anterior clinoid process,** to which the free margin of the tentorium is attached.

In the **middle cranial fossa** note:

1. The recess for the tip of the temporal lobe of the brain.

2. The middle meningeal vessels showing through the dura of the floor of the lateral part of the fossa.

3. The raised central area **(diaphragma sellae)** formed by the dura stretched between the four clinoid processes of the sphenoid bone. This dura is perforated by a number of structures:

53

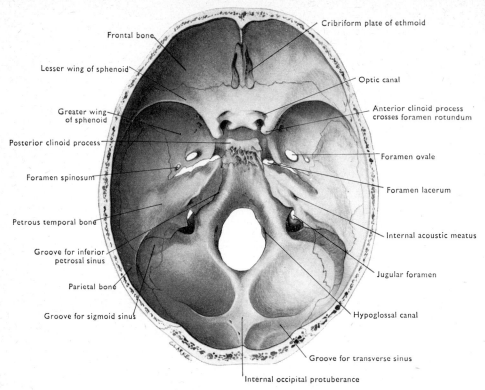

Cribriform plate of ethmoid

Frontal bone

Lesser wing of sphenoid

Greater wing of sphenoid

Posterior clinoid process

Foramen spinosum

Petrous temporal bone

Groove for inferior petrosal sinus

Parietal bone

Groove for sigmoid sinus

Optic canal

Anterior clinoid process crosses foramen rotundum

Foramen ovale

Foramen lacerum

Internal acoustic meatus

Jugular foramen

Hypoglossal canal

Groove for transverse sinus

Internal occipital protuberance

FIG. 39   Internal surface of the base of the skull.

(*a*) Centrally, by the **infundibulum** which is passing to the hypophysis beneath the central area.

(*b*) Laterally, the **oculomotor nerves,** which arise from the anterior surface of the mid-brain. Each nerve passes into the lateral wall of the corresponding **cavernous sinus,** which fills the lateral part of the central raised area, and lies inferior to the ridge formed by the free border of the tentorium passing to the anterior clinoid process. Between the cavernous sinuses (one on each side) anterior and posterior **intercavernous sinuses** pass in front of and behind the hypophysis, outside the dura mater.

(*c*) The **optic nerve** and **internal carotid artery** medial to the anterior clinoid process. Note also the branches of the internal carotid

artery; the anterior and middle cerebral arteries, the posterior communicating artery passing to the posterior cerebral, and the **ophthalmic artery** which runs anteriorly with the optic nerve [FIG. 50].

4. The **posterior cerebral artery** curves over the oculomotor nerve and the free border of the tentorium. Trace it to its origin from the median basilar artery, and note its small posterior communicating branch.

5. At the meeting point of the free edges of the falx and tentorium, note the **great cerebral vein** with tributaries entering it from the mid-brain and cerebellum [FIG. 38].

Tentorium Cerebelli

This wide, sloping fold of dura mater is attached to the margin of the posterior cranial fossa peripherally. At the attachment, the two layers of dura that form the fold diverge and enclose a venous sinus. Thus, between the internal occipital protuberance and the base of the petrous temporal bone, it encloses the **transverse sinus.** Anterior to this it is attached to the lips of a narrow groove along the superior border of the petrous temporal bone, and this lodges the **superior petrosal sinus** [FIG. 46].

At the apex of the petrous temporal bone the tentorium, greatly diminished in width, comes to lie in a vertical plane; the free margin, which is passing towards the anterior clinoid process, lying vertically above the margin attached to the petrous temporal bone. Anterior to this the two layers of the tentorium are separated by the cavernous sinus. The **medial layer** passes towards the posterior clinoid process and forms the diaphragma sellae and the roof of the cavernous sinus, which is pierced by the oculomotor nerve. The **lateral layer** forms the lateral wall of the cavernous sinus by sweeping inferolaterally from the free margin to become continuous with the dural floor of the middle cranial fossa.

The tentorium slopes upwards from its peripheral attachment to an apex situated at the point of meeting of its free border with that of the falx. Here the **great cerebral vein** pierces the dura mater and joins the inferior sagittal sinus to form the **straight sinus.**

The free margin of the tentorium extends almost horizontally backwards from the anterior clinoid processes to the apex of the tentorium. The **tentorial notch,** so formed, is converted into a foramen by the dorsum sellae and the dura covering the posterior surface of the cavernous sinus. This foramen connects the posterior cranial fossa with the supratentorial compartments of the cranial cavity, and it transmits the midbrain, the posterior cerebral arteries, and cerebrospinal fluid in the subarachnoid space.

Functions of Falx and Tentorium

These tough folds of dura mater play an important part in stabilizing the brain within the cranial cavity, and preventing the tendency of this semifluid structure to oscillate freely within it when the head is moved suddenly. It should be appreciated that when the brain does move within the cranial cavity, it carries the pia and arachnoid with it, and throws a considerable stress on the very thin-walled veins which pass across the subdural space to the venous sinuses which are held fast by the dura.

DISSECTION. Open the straight sinus by incising the falx cerebri along its line of union with the tentorium on the left side. Carry this incision forwards along the free edge of the falx and open the inferior sagittal sinus. Continue the incision laterally from the internal occipital protuberance to the base of the petrous temporal bone, in the fixed margin of the tentorium, opening the transverse sinus. Note the continuity of the transverse sinus with the sigmoid sinus at this point, and continue the incision along the fixed margin of the tentorium to the petrous temporal bone, thus opening the superior petrosal sinus [Fig. 46].

On the right side, follow the superior sagittal sinus into the transverse sinus and check for continuity of all the sinuses at the internal occipital protuberance.

VENOUS SINUSES [p. 67]

Inferior Sagittal Sinus

This narrow venous channel is enclosed in the posterior two-thirds of the free margin of the falx cerebri. It drains the falx and part of the medial surface of the hemisphere into the straight sinus.

Straight Sinus

Formed by the union of the great cerebral vein and the inferior sagittal sinus at the meeting point of the free edges of falx and tentorium, it runs postero-inferiorly in the line of union of the two folds. At the internal occipital protuberance it becomes continuous with one of the transverse sinuses, usually the left. It drains the posterior part of the cerebrum, part of the cerebellum, falx and tentorium, and may communicate with the superior sagittal sinus at the internal occipital protuberance. In this case the four sinuses (superior sagittal, straight, and two transverse) meet at this point in the **confluence of the sinuses,** which makes a wide, shallow impression on the bone.

Transverse Sinus

This is a paired sinus, and the widest of all the venous sinuses. Whichever transverse sinus receives the superior sagittal is larger than the other, but if the sinuses communicate they may be equal.

The transverse sinus runs horizontally from the internal occipital protuberance to the base of the petrous temporal bone. It lies in the fixed margin of the tentorium, and grooves the occipital, parietal, and temporal bones. In this position it lies below the occipital lobe of the cerebrum, and above the cerebellum.

Tributaries. It receives veins from the cerebrum (occipital lobe) and cerebellum, the occipital diploic vein, and the superior petrosal sinus. Anteriorly it is continuous with the sigmoid sinus.

Superior Petrosal Sinus

This narrow sinus drains the posterior end of the cavernous sinus to the junction of the transverse and sigmoid sinuses. It lies in the fixed margin of the tentorium on the petrous temporal bone.

The remaining venous sinuses are dealt with later.

PARANASAL SINUSES

These air-filled extensions of the nasal cavities pass into a number of skull bones. Each is lined by a ciliated columnar epithelium, which wafts the mucus on its surface towards the opening into the nose, and is adherent to the endosteum lining the bone in which it lies, to form a muco-endosteum. They replace the marrow cavities of the maxilla and ethmoid, and part of this tissue in the frontal, sphenoid, and temporal bones, and thereby greatly diminish the weight of the skull. Their apertures into the nose are all relatively narrow and easily obstructed, even by swelling of the vascular muco-endosteum.

Frontal Air Sinuses

When the calvaria was removed, one or other of these sinuses was probably opened. If not, chisel off part of the frontal bone close

to the median plane till one of the sinuses is opened. Explore the cavity with a probe and attempt to find its opening into the nose.

The frontal sinuses are paired cavities in the anterior part of the frontal bone, immediately above the root of the nose and the upper margins of the orbits. They lie between the outer and inner tables of the bone, and are separated from each other by a bony septum which is not median. They are not symmetrical in size or shape, and vary remarkably in extent. Normally about 2–3 cm. in height and width, they may be smaller, especially in women, or even absent. On the other hand, they may be much larger, and extend superiorly, laterally, and even posteriorly between the two tables of the roof of the orbit.

Like the other air sinuses they tend to become larger in old age owing to absorption of the diploë. The funnel-shaped passage from the frontal sinus to the nose (the infundibulum, Fig. 50) opens into the middle meatus of the nasal cavity [Fig. 122].

THE ANTERIOR CRANIAL FOSSA

DISSECTION. Carefully remove the dura mater from the cribriform plate, and clean the anterior ethmoidal nerve which runs anteriorly on its lateral margin.

The Anterior Ethmoidal Nerve. This is a terminal branch of the nasociliary nerve in the orbit. It enters the cranial cavity by passing with the **anterior ethmoidal artery** between the frontal and ethmoid bones, and appears at the lateral edge of the cribriform plate under the overhanging edge of the orbital part of the frontal bone. It runs anteriorly, and passes into the cavity of the nose through a small hole at the side of the crista galli. Its terminal branch is the external nasal nerve.

The **posterior ethmoidal artery** arises in the orbit. It is smaller than the anterior ethmoidal artery, and follows a more posterior course on to the cribriform plate.

The meningeal vessels of the anterior cranial fossa arise as twigs from the ethmoidal and middle meningeal arteries.

THE MIDDLE CRANIAL FOSSA

DISSECTION. Incise the diaphragma sellae radially, and dislodge the hypophysis from the hypophysial fossa. Chip away the floor of the fossa and open the sphenoidal air sinuses which lie below and in front of it. Explore them with a probe, and pass it through the small openings in their anterior walls into the postero-superior part of the nose. Make a median section of the hypophysis, and examine it with a hand lens.

HYPOPHYSIS (PITUITARY BODY OR GLAND)

This is an exceedingly important ductless gland with a wide range of functions, including the control of the other ductless glands and of body growth.

It is a flattened oval structure which lies in the hypophysial fossa under cover of the diaphragma sellae, and is connected to the hypothalamic part of the inferior surface of the brain by the infundibulum. The hypophysis has two lobes. (1) The **posterior lobe** is the small, expanded, inferior end of the infundibulum, and is developed from the brain. (2) The **anterior lobe.** This is much larger than the posterior lobe (which is lodged in a hollow on the back of it) and has three parts: the **anterior part,** which forms most of the anterior lobe, is separated from the posterior lobe by a narrow cleft and a thin sheet of glandular tissue applied to the posterior lobe; this is the **intermediate part.** The **tuberal part** is an upward, tongue-like projection of the anterior part, and it partly encircles the infundibulum and reaches the tuber cinereum of the brain [FIG. 230]. The anterior lobe is developed from the ectoderm of the roof of the primitive mouth, and has no direct nervous connexion with the brain. It loses its connexion with the roof of the nasal part of the pharynx early in development.

Blood Supply. This is by twigs from the internal carotid and anterior cerebral arteries, and the anterior lobe also receives venous blood from the hypothalamus via the hypothalamo-hypophysial portal system of veins. The veins of the hypophysis drain into the cavernous sinuses.

Position. It lies above and behind the sphenoidal air sinuses, below the optic chiasma, in front of the dorsum sellae, and has a cavernous sinus on each side of it. Several venous channels connect the two cavernous sinuses around the hypophysis.

Sphenoidal Air Sinuses [FIGS. 37, 44, 113]

These are an unequal pair of sinuses, separated by a bony septum which is never median. They occupy a variable amount of the body of the sphenoid, and may even extend beyond it into the bases of its wings and pterygoid processes, and even into the basi-occiput. Each opens by a small, round hole in the upper part of its anterior wall into the postero-superior part of the nasal cavity, the spheno-ethmoidal recess.

Position. Although better seen when the nose is dissected, the position of these sinuses can be ascertained from a skull split in the median plane.

Each sinus is related to the nasal cavity anteriorly, and to that cavity and nasal part of the pharynx inferiorly. Posteriorly a thick layer of bone separates it from the cranial

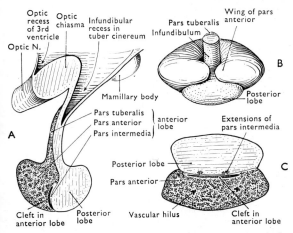

FIG. 40 Three diagrammatic views of the hypophysis. A. In median section. B. From above and behind. C. In horizontal section.

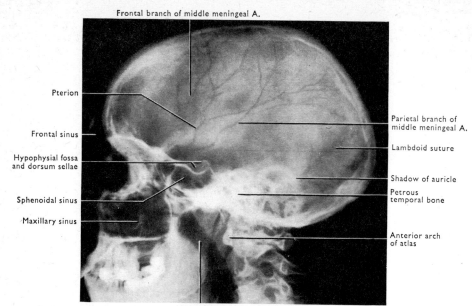

Frontal branch of middle meningeal A.

Pterion

Frontal sinus

Hypophysial fossa
and dorsum sellae

Sphenoidal sinus

Maxillary sinus

Parietal branch of
middle meningeal A.

Lambdoid suture

Shadow of auricle

Petrous
temporal bone

Anterior arch
of atlas

Air in pharynx

FIG. 41 Lateral radiograph of the skull. The region marked pterion indicates the position where the lesser wing of the sphenoid reaches the lateral wall of the cranium and the middle meningeal artery is enclosed in bone.

cavity, the basilar artery and the pons. Above lie the hypophysis and intercavernous sinuses, while the cavernous sinuses and their contents lie laterally.

DISSECTION. If the entire brain has not been removed, incise the dura mater on the posterior border of the lesser wing of the sphenoid and find the spheno-parietal sinus; trace it to the cavernous sinus.

Cut through the tentorium along the line of the straight and transverse sinuses, remove the falx, and turn each half of the tentorium anterolaterally on its attachment to the petrous temporal bone. Find the trochlear nerve [Fig. 45]; this arises from the dorsal surface of the midbrain, sweeps anteriorly round it, and pierces the inferior surface of the tentorium close to its free border, near the apex of the petrous temporal bone. Divide the nerve before it enters the dura.

Inferior to the trochlear nerve, find the large trigeminal nerve [Fig. 45] entering the dura mater. Pass a fine, blunt seeker along the line of the nerve, and demonstrate the dural sac (cavum trigeminale) which surrounds the nerve and the greater part of its ganglion beneath the dural floor of the middle cranial fossa.

Elevate the seeker so that it raises the dural floor of the middle cranial fossa and outlines the position of the nerve and ganglion.

Carefully remove the dura mater from the floor of the middle cranial fossa by cutting through on to the seeker in the cavum trigeminale, anterior to the superior petrosal sinus. Strip the dura forwards and laterally to uncover the trigeminal nerve and ganglion, and the three large nerves which issue from the convex, peripheral border of the ganglion. Trace the mandibular nerve inferolaterally to the foramen ovale (close to the entry of the middle meningeal artery). Follow the maxillary nerve to the foramen rotundum, and the ophthalmic nerve into the lateral wall of the cavernous sinus. Trace the three branches of the ophthalmic nerve forwards to the superior orbital fissure [Figs. 43, 48].

As you trace the ophthalmic nerve and its branches, you will encounter the trochlear, oculomotor and abducent nerves in the lateral wall of the cavernous sinus. Pick up the oculomotor and trochlear nerves as they enter the dura, pull gently on them, and thus identify them in the cavernous sinus. Preserve the margins of the holes through which the nerves enter the dura, in order to keep them in place, but remove the dura in

58

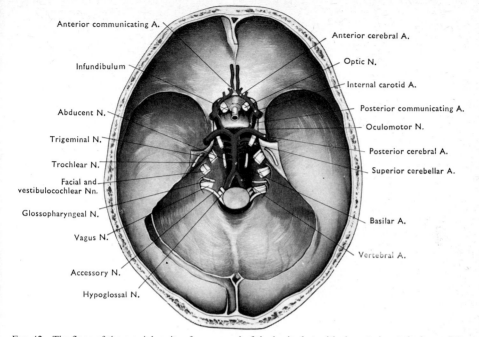

Anterior communicating A.
Infundibulum
Abducent N.
Trigeminal N.
Trochlear N.
Facial and vestibulocochlear Nn.
Glossopharyngeal N.
Vagus N.
Accessory N.
Hypoglossal N.

Anterior cerebral A.
Optic N.
Internal carotid A.
Posterior communicating A.
Oculomotor N.
Posterior cerebral A.
Superior cerebellar A.
Basilar A.
Vertebral A.

FIG. 42   The floor of the cranial cavity after removal of the brain, but with the arteries at the base of the brain *in situ.*

front of that to follow them to the superior orbital fissure. Remove the remains of the lateral wall of the cavernous sinus, and clean the internal carotid artery within it. Note that the abducent nerve lies in the sinus, lateral to the artery; trace the nerve forwards and backwards.

Carefully strip the rest of the dura from the anterior surface of the petrous temporal bone, and look for the petrosal nerves. These slender nerves emerge from slits in the temporal bone and run anteromedially. One disappears through the base of the skull; the other, larger and more medial, disappears under the trigeminal ganglion [Fig. 46]. Lift up the trigeminal ganglion; identify the motor root on its inferior surface, and trace it to the foramen ovale.

TRIGEMINAL NERVE

This is the fifth and largest of the cranial nerves. It is the principal sensory nerve of the head and is sensory to: (1) the skin of the face and anterior half of the head; (2) the mucous membrane of the nose, air sinuses, mouth, and anterior two-thirds of the tongue; (3) the

teeth and temporomandibular joint; (4) the contents of the orbit, except the retina; (5) part of the dura mater.

The **motor fibres** pass only into its mandibular division, and they supply the four muscles of mastication, and also mylohyoid, the anterior belly of digastric, tensor palati, and tensor tympani.

The **sensory fibres** arise in the large trigeminal ganglion, and the central processes of its cells converge to form the sensory root which enters the pons; their peripheral processes are distributed through the three divisions, the ophthalmic, maxillary, and mandibular nerves. The motor root arises in the pons and joins the mandibular nerve at the foramen ovale.

Trigeminal Ganglion

This semilunar, sensory ganglion lies in a shallow depression on the anterior surface of the petrous temporal bone near the apex, and

59

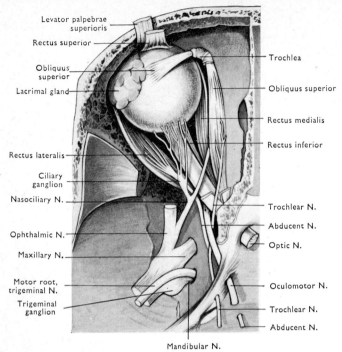

Levator palpebrae superioris
Rectus superior
Obliquus superior
Lacrimal gland
Rectus lateralis
Ciliary ganglion
Nasociliary N.
Ophthalmic N.
Maxillary N.
Motor root, trigeminal N.
Trigeminal ganglion

Trochlea
Obliquus superior
Rectus medialis
Rectus inferior
Trochlear N.
Abducent N.
Optic N.
Oculomotor N.
Trochlear N.
Abducent N.
Mandibular N.

Fig. 43   Dissection of the orbit and middle cranial fossa.   The trigeminal nerve and ganglion have been turned laterally to expose the motor root.

on the adjacent margin of the greater wing of the sphenoid. It lies in a pocket of dura mater (**cavum trigeminale**) tucked forwards from the posterior cranial fossa between the dural and endocranial layers of the floor of the middle cranial fossa. Posteriorly, the narrow neck of the cavum contains the motor and sensory roots (in a sleeve of pia, arachnoid, and sub-arachnoid space) which groove the upper margin of the petrous temporal bone close to the apex, and lie inferior to the superior pe-trosal sinus. The distal part of the root crosses the internal carotid artery in the carotid canal, and the superomedial part of the ganglion lies in the lateral wall of the cavernous sinus, lateral to the artery. Sympathetic filaments run to the ganglion from the plexus on the carotid artery. These supply the arteries in the ganglion and are distributed through its branches.

Sensory Root

The sensory root narrows as it passes from the con-cave aspect of the ganglion, through the neck of the cavum trigeminale, to enter the anterolateral surface of the pons.

Motor Root

This small root leaves the pons beside the sensory root, and passes under the ganglion to the foramen ovale.

Mandibular Nerve

This, the largest of the three divisions, arises from the inferolateral part of the ganglion, and giving a meningeal twig to the floor of the middle cranial fossa, immediately enters the fora-men ovale.

Maxillary Nerve

This nerve arises from the anterior surface of the ganglion close to the ophthalmic nerve. It runs forwards along the lower border of the cavernous sinus, between dura and endo-cranium, applied to the thin, bony wall of the sphenoidal sinus. It gives off a fine meningeal branch, and leaves the cranial cavity through the foramen rotundum [Fig. 39].

Ophthalmic Nerve

This is the smallest of the three divisions. It arises from the superomedial part of the ganglion, runs forwards in the lateral wall of the cavernous sinus, and dividing into **naso-ciliary, lacrimal,** and **frontal** branches, enters the orbit through the superior orbital fissure. Near its origin it gives off a small meningeal branch which curves back into the tentorium cerebelli, and it communicates with the oculo-motor, trochlear, and abducent nerves in the lateral wall of the cavernous sinus. These communications carry sensory fibres from the extrinsic ocular muscles to the trigeminal nerve. It receives sympathetic fibres from the plexus on the internal carotid artery.

OCULOMOTOR NERVE

The third cranial nerve supplies all but two of the muscles of the orbit, and two of the three muscles in the eyeball. It emerges through the front of the midbrain, passes anterolaterally between the posterior cerebral and superior cerebellar arteries, and pierces the triangular area of dura mater in the roof of the cavernous sinus. Outside the dura mater, it runs forwards in the lateral wall of the cavernous sinus (above the other nerves there) and splits into two branches (superior and inferior) which enter the orbit through the superior orbital fissure.

TROCHLEAR NERVE

This fourth cranial nerve is very slender and supplies only the superior oblique muscle of the eye. The nerve emerges from the dorsal surface of the lower midbrain, curves forwards round the side of it, and passes anteriorly between the posterior cerebral and superior cerebellar arteries. It pierces the tentorium through a small aperture hidden under the free margin near the point where that margin crosses the petrous temporal bone. The nerve runs forwards in the lateral wall of the cavernous sinus between the oculomotor and ophthalmic nerves, and passing anterosuperiorly across the lateral side of the oculomotor nerve, enters the orbit through the superior orbital fissure.

ABDUCENT NERVE

The sixth cranial nerve is also very slender, and supplies only the lateral rectus muscle of the eyeball. It emerges at the lower border of the pons, at once bends upwards between it and the clivus of the skull, to pierce the dura mater 1 cm. below the root of the dorsum sellae. Outside the dura, it runs superolaterally to reach the apex of the petrous temporal bone, and crossing the sphenopetrous suture, curves round the lateral side of the internal carotid artery to enter the cavernous sinus. Here it courses anteriorly on the lateral side of the horizontal part of the carotid artery, within the sinus, and leaving the sinus anteriorly, enters the orbit through the superior orbital fissure.

Communications. Apart from the communications with the ophthalmic nerve, all these nerves receive sympathetic fibres from the carotid plexus while in the wall of the cavernous sinus.

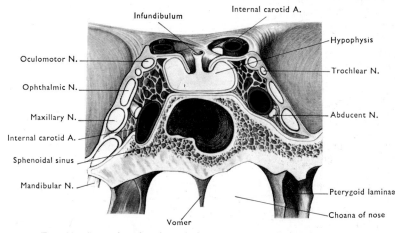

FIG. 44   Coronal section through the sella turcica and cavernous sinuses.

61

CAVERNOUS SINUS

The cavernous sinus is important because of its intimate relationships (see below), and because it may be involved in inflammatory processes which can spread to it from the face via the ophthalmic veins.

Position. It lies on the side of the body of the sphenoid, and extends from the medial end of the superior orbital fissure to the apex of the petrous temporal bone. Like the other venous sinuses, it lies between the dura mater and the endocranium and is lined with endothelium. Its cavity, however, consists of a large number of intercommunicating channels or 'caverns' from which the sinus derives its name, and structures which appear to pierce the sinus, in fact pass between its many channels.

Tributaries and Communications. Anteriorly, it receives the ophthalmic veins and the sphenoparietal sinus. Posteriorly, it is drained by the superior and inferior petrosal sinuses. Medially, a number of small intercavernous sinuses connect it with its fellow around the hypophysis. Superiorly, it receives the superficial middle cerebral vein and one or more small cerebral veins from the medial aspect of the temporal lobe. Inferiorly, it communicates with venous plexuses outside the skull by means of emissary veins which pass: (1) through the carotid canal to the pharyngeal plexus; (2) through the foramen ovale, and the sphenoidal emissary foramen (if present) to the pterygoid plexus. In this way the sinus forms a point of communication between the veins of the face, cheek, brain, and the internal jugular vein, and if infected may involve the structures within it or in its walls. It is sometimes involved in injuries to the base of the skull, and leakage from the carotid artery into it leads to a great increase in pressure in the veins entering it, with distension of the ophthalmic veins and protrusion of the eye. Its immediate relations are, therefore, of some importance.

Relations. The hypophysis and sphenoidal air sinus are its superior and inferior medial relations. The trigeminal ganglion, its maxillary and ophthalmic divisions, and the oculomotor and trochlear nerves are all in its

lateral wall. The internal carotid artery and the abducent nerve lie within its mesh, separated only by endothelium from the blood it contains.

INTRACRANIAL PART OF THE INTERNAL CAROTID ARTERY

The tortuous course of this vessel within the cranial cavity is clearly marked by a wide, shallow, sinuous groove on the side of the body of the sphenoid.

Course. It enters the cranial cavity through the carotid canal, crosses the foramen lacerum, and bends upwards to pierce the endocranium and enter the cavernous sinus. Almost immediately it bends forwards at a right angle, and runs along the side of the body of the sphenoid to the root of the lesser wing. Here it curves sharply upwards and backwards, and leaves the cavernous sinus by piercing the dura mater at the medial side of the anterior clinoid process, behind the optic canal. It passes through the arachnoid, and, bending backwards, runs for a short distance above the cavernous sinus [FIG. 50]. Finally, it turns upwards and divides into the anterior and middle cerebral arteries on the surface of the brain [FIG. 171]. Throughout its course it is surrounded by the internal carotid plexus of sympathetic nerves [FIG. 94].

Branches. (1) The ophthalmic artery leaves it as it pierces the roof of the cavernous sinus. (2) Small twigs to the hypophysis, trigeminal ganglion, and dura mater arise in the cavernous sinus. (3) The posterior communicating, anterior choroidal, and its two terminal branches arise at the base of the brain.

MENINGEAL VESSELS OF THE MIDDLE CRANIAL FOSSA

The meningeal vessels are embedded in the endocranium, but, being thicker than it, they stand out from its external surface, and groove the inner table of the skull. Despite their name, their branches are chiefly distributed to bone, and their intimate relation to the bones of the skull leads to a risk of their rupture in fractures. The veins are particularly liable to injury for they lie between the arteries and the bone.

Middle Meningeal Artery

This is a small but important artery, because its frontal branch is the commonest source of extradural haemorrhage, and it lies adjacent to the motor area of the brain, which may be compressed by such a collection of blood.

Course and Branches. It arises from the maxillary artery and enters the skull through the foramen spinosum. Thence it runs antero-laterally across the floor of the middle cranial fossa, and divides into a frontal and a parietal branch.

The **parietal branch** curves posteriorly and ascends gradually as it passes across the side wall of the cranial cavity towards the apex of the occipital bone (lambda).

The **frontal branch** is larger. It curves later-ally towards the lateral end of the lesser wing of the sphenoid, where it grooves the skull deeply, or even disappears into a short bony tunnel. It then runs obliquely upwards and backwards towards the mid point between the root of the nose and the occipital protuber-ance. In this part of its course, it runs on, or slightly behind the coronal suture, and it fre-quently sends a large branch posteriorly on the deep surface of the parietal bone.

Surface Anatomy. The student should check the position of the grooves for the middle meningeal artery on the inside of a skull, and mark their position on the external surface [FIG. 252].

The **middle meningeal vein** accompanies the artery through the foramen spinosum, and ends in the pterygoid plexus.

Small Meningeal Vessels of Middle Cranial Fossa

A small accessory meningeal is often found entering the cranial cavity via the foramen ovale, and supplying the trigeminal ganglion and the adjacent dura. It may arise from the maxillary or middle meningeal arteries. The ophthalmic and lacrimal arteries send small branches back through the superior orbital fissure to the middle cranial fossa. Occasion-ally the branch of the lacrimal is large and replaces the middle meningeal artery.

PETROSAL NERVES

The functions of the nerve fibres in the petrosal nerves are not entirely clear, but some are known to be concerned with the sense of taste in the palate, while others are secretory to the lacrimal, nasal, palatine, pharyngeal, and parotid glands.

The **greater** petrosal nerve arises from the facial nerve in the petrous temporal bone. It emerges through a slit in the anterior surface, and runs anteromedially in a slender groove to pass inferior to the trigeminal ganglion. Here it is joined by the deep petrosal nerve, to form the nerve of the pterygoid canal which runs to the **pterygopalatine ganglion.** It con-tains preganglionic parasympathetic fibres which synapse in the ganglion.

The **deep** petrosal nerve is a branch of the sympathetic plexus on the internal carotid artery. It consists of postganglionic sympa-thetic fibres which are distributed through the branches of the pterygopalatine ganglion without any synapse in the ganglion.

The **lesser** petrosal nerve is a slender nerve derived from fibres of the glossopharyngeal and facial nerves in the middle ear. It emerges through a tiny foramen lateral to that for the greater petrosal, and runs on the bony floor of the middle cranial fossa to leave the skull through or adjacent to the foramen ovale, and end in the **otic ganglion** on the medial side of the mandibular nerve. It contains pregan-glionic parasympathetic fibres which synapse in the otic ganglion.

THE POSTERIOR CRANIAL FOSSA

DISSECTION. If the entire brain has not been removed, detach the tentorium cerebelli from the petrous temporal bone and remove it. Examine the superior surface of the cerebellum, the superior cere-bellar artery, and the corresponding veins.

Split the cerebellum in the median plane, and carry the incision forwards until an aperture appears about the middle of the incision. This is the fourth ventricle of the brain which has an angular, posterior extension into the cerebellum. Now extend the incision superiorly

and inferiorly so as to divide the cerebellum completely, and open the full extent of the fourth ventricle, but do not cut into the midbrain.

Remove each half of the cerebellum in turn by cutting through its attachments to the brain stem with a coronal incision in the plane of the floor of the fourth ventricle.

The brain stem now lies free in the posterior cranial fossa, the various cranial nerves can be seen passing to their foramina, and the two vertebral arteries are visible running on to it from below.

With the help of Figures 39 and 46, and a dry skull, identify the cranial nerves arising from the lateral aspect of the brain stem: (1) the trigeminal nerve, already dissected; (2) the facial and vestibulocochlear nerves at the lower border of the pons (with the tiny nervus intermedius between them) passing to the internal acoustic meatus; (3) the glossopharyngeal, vagus, and accessory nerves which arise as a row of rootlets caudal to the previous two nerves. The spinal part of the accessory ascends beside the spinal medulla, posterior to the ligamentum denticulatum, to join the vagus, and pass out through the jugular foramen with it,

adjacent to the glossopharyngeal nerve, but in a separate dural sheath.

To expose the nerves arising from the ventral aspect of the brain stem, divide the oculomotor and trigeminal nerves, and draw the brain stem posteriorly. The abducent nerve comes into view as it emerges below the pons, and runs upwards anterior to it. Inferior to the abducent is the hypoglossal nerve. This arises as a row of rootlets which join together and pass out through the hypoglossal canal, often as two separate nerves.

Note the basilar artery lying on the front of the pons, and expose its continuity with the vertebral arteries on the medulla oblongata, by dividing the remaining cranial nerves (except the accessory) and drawing the brain stem further posteriorly. Separate the basilar and vertebral arteries and their main branches from the brain stem, and remove it by cutting through its junction with the spinal medulla. If the arteries were carefully removed from the base of the brain, the continuity between the vertebral and internal carotid systems will be visible.

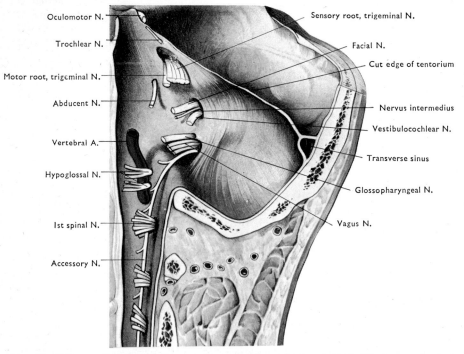

Fig. 45   Oblique section through the posterior cranial fossa seen from behind.   The brain and spinal medulla have been removed.

STRUCTURES SEEN AFTER REMOVAL OF THE BRAIN STEM

The upper end of the spinal medulla is attached to the margin of the foramen magnum by the first tooth of the ligamentum denticulatum, which has the vertebral artery anterior to it. In front of that, note the ventral rootlets of the **first cervical nerve,** and in the same sagittal plane at a higher level, the two parts of the **hypoglossal nerve** piercing the dura mater separately opposite the hypoglossal canal. The **accessory nerve** (spinal part) ascends through the foramen magnum, and turning laterally over the margin of the foramen magnum, joins the cranial part and the **vagus nerve.** Together they pierce the dura mater at the jugular foramen, and the glossopharyngeal nerve does likewise immediately above. Find the **facial nerve, nervus intermedius,** and **vestibulocochlear nerve** entering the internal acoustic meatus with the facial nerve above and the nervus intermedius between them.

The **vertebral artery** pierces the spinal dura mater near the skull, and ascends through the foramen magnum anterior to the first tooth of the ligamentum denticulatum. It gives a meningeal branch to the posterior cranial fossa before piercing the dura mater, and passes superomedially between the first cervical and hypoglossal nerves.

The **falx cerebelli** is a small fold of dura mater which fits into the posterior cerebellar notch, and contains the occipital venous sinus. It overlies the internal occipital crest.

DISSECTION. Slit up the falx cerebelli and look for the occipital sinus. Open the sigmoid sinus by passing a knife into it at the anterior end of the transverse sinus, and cutting along it to the base of the skull, and then forwards to the jugular foramen. Look for the mouth of the mastoid emissary vein about half way down the posterior wall of the sinus.

Remove the dura mater over the jugular foramen, but do not injure the nerves entering it. At the anterior end of the jugular foramen, find the end of the inferior petrosal sinus, and lay it open by cutting through the dura mater over the groove between the petrous temporal and the basi-occiput. In the medial wall of the petrosal sinus, find the mouths of the basilar sinuses, and trace them across to the opposite side.

Pull gently on the abducent nerve, and trace it to the apex of the petrous temporal bone by slitting the dura mater.

Make a transverse incision through the dura mater at the anterior margin of the foramen magnum. Strip it upwards and downwards. Then incise the endocranium and try to strip it in the same manner. Note that the dura separates from the endocranium at the lower margin of the foramen magnum.

Dura Mater of Base of Skull

The dura mater of the base is firmly attached not only at the suture lines but also between them. The endocranium is continuous, round the lips of each foramen, with the periosteum on the outside of the skull. At the foramen magnum, the cranial and spinal parts of the dura mater are continuous, and, at the foramina that transmit nerves, it gives sheaths to the nerves.

VENOUS SINUSES IN THE POSTERIOR CRANIAL FOSSA

Sigmoid Sinus

This S-shaped sinus begins in the attached margin of the tentorium, immediately behind the base of the petrous temporal bone, and is the continuation of the transverse sinus. It curves downwards, grooving the mastoid and petrous parts of the temporal bone opposite the back of the auricle. Here it is close to: (1) the mastoid air cells, laterally; (2) the mastoid antrum (a small cavity in the temporal bone which joins the mastoid air cells, in the mastoid process, to the middle ear) and the vertical part of the facial nerve, both anteriorly; (3) the cerebellum, medially.

Reaching the base of the skull, it curves forwards, and passes through the jugular foramen to become continuous with the internal jugular vein.

Tributaries and Connexions. The sigmoid sinus receives the **posterior temporal diploic vein.** It is connected with: (1) the occipital veins, through the mastoid emissary vein which traverses the mastoid foramen from the descending part of the sinus; (2) the suboccipital plexus, through the condylar emissary vein (when present) which passes posteriorly from its terminal part; (3) the

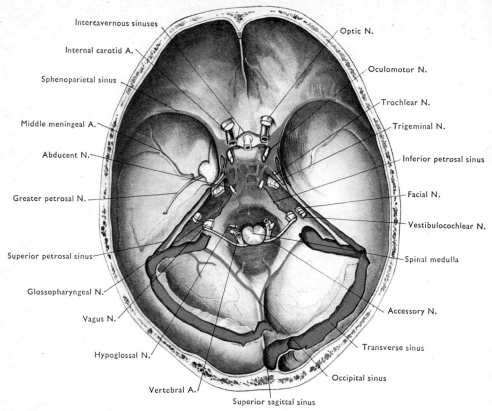

Intercavernous sinuses

Internal carotid A.

Sphenoparietal sinus

Middle meningeal A.

Abducent N.

Greater petrosal N.

Superior petrosal sinus

Glossopharyngeal N.

Vagus N.

Hypoglossal N.

Vertebral A.

Optic N.

Oculomotor N.

Trochlear N.

Trigeminal N.

Inferior petrosal sinus

Facial N.

Vestibulocochlear N.

Spinal medulla

Accessory N.

Transverse sinus

Occipital sinus

Superior sagittal sinus

FIG. 46   Dissection of the floor of the cranial cavity after removal of the brain.

beginning of the transverse sinus, through the occipital sinus [FIG. 46].

Occipital Sinus

When present, this long, narrow sinus arises at the beginning of the transverse sinus, descends in the falx cerebelli, and curves around the margin of the foramen magnum to end in the sigmoid sinus near its termination. It communicates through the foramen magnum with the internal vertebral venous plexus, and is usually single in the falx cerebelli.

Inferior Petrosal Sinus

It drains the posterior end of the cavernous sinus, runs in the groove between the basi-

occiput and the petrous temporal, and passes through the jugular foramen to join the internal jugular vein outside the skull.

Basilar Plexus of Sinuses

This network of sinuses on the clivus of the skull communicates with the inferior petrosal sinuses, and with the internal vertebral venous plexus through the foramen magnum.

DIPLOIC VEINS

These are wide venous spaces between the outer and inner tables of the flat bones of the skull. They are lined with endothelium, and communicate freely, but are difficult to display without special dissection.

66

VENOUS SINUSES

These are venous spaces formed either in the folds of dura (straight sinus and inferior sagittal sinus) or, more often, between the dura mater and the endocranium. They are lined by endothelium, and, for the most part, drain the venous blood from the brain and skull. Through the foramen magnum, they are continuous with the corresponding veins which surround the spinal dura mater (internal vertebral venous plexuses) and like them they have no valves; thus blood may flow in either direction along them according to the pressure gradients. Almost all of the blood which they transmit is drained into the internal jugular veins via the sigmoid and inferior petrosal sinuses; also there are subsidiary routes through the meningeal and diploic veins, and through the emissary veins passing to the exterior.

In addition to draining venous blood, they also drain cerebrospinal fluid directly from the **arachnoid villi** and **granulations.** The majority of these lie in relation to the superior sagittal sinus, and though there are other routes for the absorption of cerebrospinal fluid (especially along the sheaths of cranial and spinal nerves) blockage of the superior sagittal sinus materially affects the process, and is associated with a rapid rise in intracranial pressure.

The individual sinuses are described on pages 49, 55, 56, 62, and 65; the student should review their general arrangement, and be able to trace the potential routes of venous drainage through them with the help of FIGURES 35, 36, 46, and 50.

EMISSARY VEINS

These are veins which pass through foramina in the cranial wall and connect the venous sinuses of the dura mater with veins outside the skull. Like the venous sinuses, they have no valves, and the flow of blood may be in either direction along them. Thus extracranial infections involving the veins in the region of the emissary veins, may be transmitted to the venous sinuses along them. Not all emissary veins are invariably present; the parietal, the condylar, and the sphenoidal are frequently absent.

1. The **superior sagittal sinus** may be connected to the veins of the frontal air sinus through the **foramen caecum,** and to the occipital veins through the **parietal emissary foramen** in the top of the skull.

2. The **sigmoid sinus** is connected to the occipital or posterior auricular veins through the **mastoid emissary foramen,** behind the ear, and to the vertebral veins through the **condylar emissary foramen.**

3. The **cavernous sinus** has the greatest number of such communications: (*a*) through the **ophthalmic veins** to the face and infra-temporal region (pterygoid venous plexus); (*b*) through a plexus of veins along the internal carotid artery, to the **pharyngeal veins;** (*c*) through the foramen ovale to the **pterygoid plexus;** (*d*) occasionally through the **sphenoidal emissary foramen** to the pterygoid plexus.

Meningeal Veins. These are very thin-walled, and it is difficult to isolate them by dissection. They lie between the meningeal arteries and the bone, and end either in the venous sinuses, or in the veins outside the skull by passing through the foramina with the corresponding arteries.

THE ORBIT

DISSECTION. To remove the roof of the orbit, strip the periosteum from the floor of the anterior cranial fossa, except over the cribriform plate of the ethmoid. With a gentle tap from a mallet, crack the orbital roof with a chisel, and lever up the broken pieces of bone from the underlying orbital periosteum. Extend the opening with bone forceps, keeping outside the orbital periosteum, until all but the anterior margin of the orbital roof is removed. Occasionally the frontal air sinus extends into the roof of the orbit; in this case, two layers of bone and the contained part of the sinus must be removed.

The most medial part of the orbital plate of the frontal bone, which forms the roof of the orbit, also roofs in the

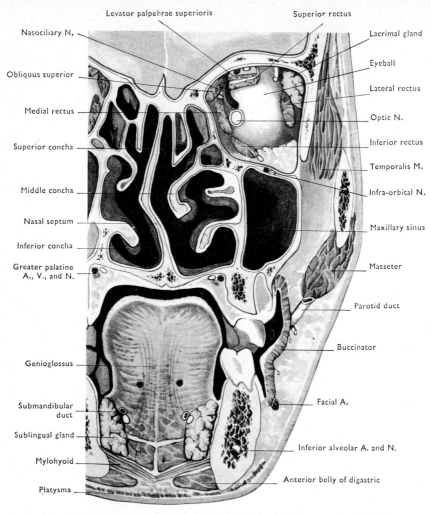

Levator palpebrae superioris

Superior rectus

Nasociliary N.

Lacrimal gland

Eyeball

Obliquus superior

Lateral rectus

Medial rectus

Optic N.

Inferior rectus

Superior concha

Temporalis M.

Middle concha

Infra-orbital N.

Nasal septum

Inferior concha

Maxillary sinus

Greater palatine A., V., and N.

Masseter

Parotid duct

Buccinator

Genioglossus

Submandibular duct

Facial A.

Sublingual gland

Mylohyoid

Inferior alveolar A. and N.

Platysma

Anterior belly of digastric

FIG. 47   Coronal section through the head at the level of the second molar teeth.

ethmoidal sinuses, and between the ethmoid and this bone lie the ethmoidal vessels and nerves. Chip away this part of the frontal bone, avoiding injury to the vessels and nerves, and expose the ethmoidal sinuses; open some of them.

Remove the remains of the lesser wing of the sphenoid, but leave the margin of the optic canal intact. The superior orbital fissure is now opened and the nerves which have been followed from the wall of the cavernous sinus can be traced into the orbit.

Ethmoidal Sinuses

These are small, thin-walled cavities or cells that occupy the whole of the ethmoidal labyrinth, between the orbit and the upper part of the cavity of the nose [FIGS. 50, 120]. They form three groups, of which the anterior and middle cells open into the middle meatus of the nose, while the posterior open into the superior meatus [FIG. 122]. Explore them with a blunt probe, and attempt to find an opening into the nose.

Orbital Periosteum

The orbital periosteum forms a funnel-shaped sheath which is loosely attached to the bony walls, and encloses all the contents of the orbit except the zygomatic nerve and the infra-orbital nerve and vessels. It is continuous with the endocranium through the optic canal and the superior orbital fissure, and with the periosteum of the face and forehead at the orbital margin.

DISSECTION. Divide the periosteum of the orbital roof transversely, close to the anterior margin of the orbit, and then anteroposteriorly along the middle line of the orbit.

Take care not to injure the nerves which pass through the superior orbital fissure, posteriorly. The trochlear nerve which lies immediately beneath the periosteum is most likely to be damaged. Find the trochlear nerve and trace it forwards and medially to the superior oblique muscle in the upper medial part of the orbit. In the midline of the orbit, the frontal nerve will be found lying on levator palpebrae superioris. Trace the nerve forwards to its division into supra-orbital and supratrochlear nerves; each runs with the corresponding artery. Follow the supratrochlear to the medial angle of the orbit, where it passes above the pulley (trochlea) of the superior oblique muscle.

Clean the superior oblique muscle, and follow its tendon through the pulley at the superomedial angle of the orbit, then posterolaterally to disappear beneath the levator palpebrae superioris and the superior rectus.

Clean levator palpebrae superioris. Raise it and identify the superior rectus muscle beneath, and the branch of the oculomotor nerve which pierces the latter to enter the levator.

Find the lacrimal nerve and artery which lie in the fat along the superolateral part of the orbit. Trace them to the lacrimal gland and define it.

THE STRUCTURES IN THE ORBIT

Frontal Nerve [FIG. 48]

This is the direct continuation of the ophthalmic nerve. It enters the orbit through the superior orbital fissure, and runs forwards, above all the muscles, on levator palpebrae superioris, to divide into supra-orbital and supratrochlear branches at a variable point.

Supratrochlear Nerve. This, the medial and smaller branch, runs towards the pulley of the superior oblique muscle, pierces the palpebral fascia above it, and leaves the orbit to run upwards into the forehead [p. 8]. In the orbit it communicates with the infratrochlear nerve.

Supra-orbital Nerve. This branch continues in the line of the parent stem, passes through the supra-orbital notch or foramen, and turns upwards into the forehead [p. 8]. Normally it divides into two in the scalp, but if this occurs in the orbit, the larger, lateral part occupies the supra-orbital notch.

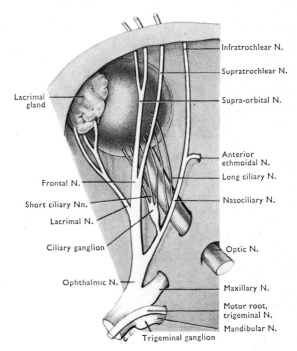

Infratrochlear N.

Supratrochlear N.

Supra-orbital N.

Lacrimal gland

Anterior ethmoidal N.

Long ciliary N.

Nasociliary N.

Frontal N.

Short ciliary Nn.

Lacrimal N.

Ciliary ganglion

Optic N.

Ophthalmic N.

Maxillary N.

Motor root, trigeminal N.

Mandibular N.

Trigeminal ganglion

FIG. 48   The left ophthalmic nerve. The trigeminal nerve and ganglion have been turned laterally.

69

Lacrimal Nerve

The smallest of the three branches of the ophthalmic, it passes through the lateral part of the superior orbital fissure [FIG. 54] and runs forwards above the lateral rectus muscle. At the anterior part of the orbit it receives a filament of postganglionic parasympathetic fibres from the zygomatic nerve, sends numerous twigs to the lacrimal gland, and one branch below it to the upper eyelid, the **palpebral branch.**

Trochlear Nerve

This fourth cranial nerve supplies only the superior oblique muscle. Having entered the orbit through the superior orbital fissure, it passes forwards and medially above the other structures, and enters the superior oblique. The remaining nerves are seen later.

Lacrimal Gland [FIGS. 30, 47, 108]

The lacrimal gland is a lobulated structure, about the size and shape of a bean. It

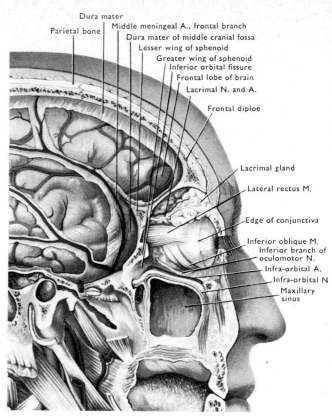

FIG. 49 Dissection of the orbit and maxillary sinus from the lateral side.

lies at the superolateral angle of the orbit, in the hollow on the medial side of the zygomatic process of the frontal bone. It is mostly hidden by the orbital margin, and is bound to it by short fibrous strands. The concave, medial surface rests on levator palpebrae superioris and the lateral rectus, which separate it from the eyeball. The **palpebral part** projects down into the upper lid between the palpebral fascia and the conjunctiva.

Nine to ten slender ducts open on the deep surface of the upper eyelid in the neighbourhood of the conjunctival fornix [FIG. 30].

The parasympathetic secretory nerve fibres arise in the pterygopalatine ganglion and reach the gland through the orbital branches of the ganglion, more especially through the branch from the zygomatic nerve.

Levator Palpebrae Superioris [FIG. 28]

It arises from the roof of the orbit immediately anterior to the optic canal, and passes forwards above rectus superior. Anteriorly, it widens into a broad, membranous expansion which is inserted into the skin of the eyelid, the superior tarsus, and the superior conjunctival fornix. In addition there is a layer of **involuntary** (smooth) **muscle** which arises from the aponeurosis and is attached to the superior tarsus. This smooth muscle is supplied by nerve fibres from the cervical sympathetic and its denervation leads to drooping of the eyelid (ptosis).

Nerve supply: oculomotor nerve, superior division, and cervical sympathetic via the carotid plexus. Action: it opens the eye by raising the upper eyelid and the superior conjunctival fornix.

DISSECTION. Divide the frontal nerve and the levator palpebrae superioris, and turn them out of the way. If possible, inflate the eyeball through a small cut in the white part (sclera).

Posterior to the eyeball, note a quantity of loose tissue. This is the fascial sheath of the eyeball. Pick up and cut out a small portion. Insert a blunt seeker between it and the eyeball, and gauge the extent of the sheath, defining the extensions it gives over the muscles at their attachments to the eyeball.

Rectus Superior

It arises from the upper margin of the optic canal, passes anterolaterally above the optic nerve, and is inserted into the sclera about 6 mm. posterior to the sclero-corneal junction.

Nerve supply: superior division of the oculomotor nerve. Action: the actions of the extrinsic ocular muscles are complicated by the fact that the axis of the orbit passes anterolaterally, and the rectus superior and inferior run in this direction. The visual axis is, however, anteroposterior, and so the superior and inferior recti are not simple elevators and depressors of the cornea respectively, except when the eye is turned laterally and the two axes correspond. In more medial positions of the cornea, they tend to rotate the cornea further medially, and this becomes more pronounced the further the cornea is turned medially [FIG. 56].

Obliquus Superior

It arises from the roof of the orbit immediately anteromedial to the optic canal, and passes anteriorly along the upper part of the medial orbital wall. Anteriorly, it ends in a slender tendon which enters the trochlea, and at once turns posterolaterally to pass between the superior rectus and the eyeball. Lateral to the superior rectus, the tendon flattens out and is inserted into the sclera midway between the entrance of the optic nerve and the cornea.

The **trochlea** is a small fibrocartilaginous ring attached by fibrous tissue to the trochlear fossa cn the frontal bone. It is lined with a synovial sheath which allows the tendon to slide freely in it. Nerve supply: the trochlear nerve. Action: it turns the cornea downwards when it is already turned medially; a position in which the inferior rectus is ineffective as a depressor of the cornea [p. 76].

DISSECTION. Divide and reflect the superior rectus. Clean out the fat beneath it and expose the optic nerve. Posteriorly, three structures cross the optic nerve; the nasociliary nerve, the ophthalmic artery, and the superior ophthalmic vein. Clean these and follow their branches. Two thread-like branches from the nasociliary nerve (long ciliary nerves) pass along the optic nerve to the eyeball. The short ciliary branches are much more numerous, and run forwards in the fat around the optic nerve. Select one of these and follow it posteriorly to a small swelling (the ciliary ganglion) which lies between the optic nerve and the lateral rectus. With care, the branches to the ciliary ganglion from the nasociliary and oculomotor (inferior division) nerves can be found, and even the sympathetic branch from the internal carotid plexus may appear.

Remove the fat lateral to the ganglion, and expose and clean the abducent nerve on the medial side of the lateral rectus muscle. Clean the optic nerve.

Optic Nerve

This nerve enters the orbit through the optic canal, and carries with it sheaths of dura mater, arachnoid mater, and pia mater which enclose extensions of the subdural and subarachnoid spaces as far as the eyeball. The nerve runs anterolaterally and slightly downwards, and pierces the sclera a short distance medial to the centre of its posterior surface. The nasociliary nerve, ophthalmic artery and vein cross above it, and the ciliary nerves and vessels surround it near the eyeball. The nerve is slightly longer than the distance it has to run, so that it does not restrict the movements of the eyeball. It is a sensory nerve, and the great majority of its fibres originate in the retina (the light sensitive layer of the eye), though there are efferent fibres passing from the brain to the retina in the nerve.

71

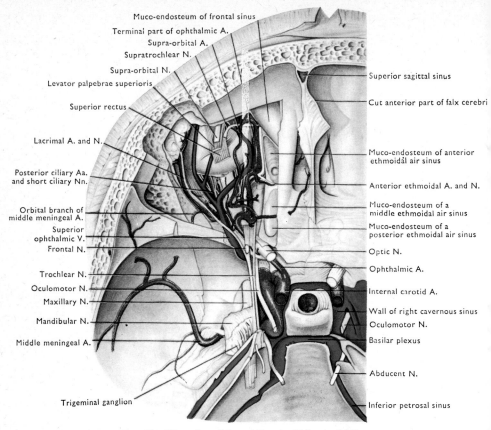

Muco-endosteum of frontal sinus
Terminal part of ophthalmic A.
Supra-orbital A.
Supratrochlear N.
Supra-orbital N.
Levator palpebrae superioris
Superior rectus
Lacrimal A. and N.
Posterior ciliary Aa. and short ciliary Nn.
Orbital branch of middle meningeal A.
Superior ophthalmic V.
Frontal N.
Trochlear N.
Oculomotor N.
Maxillary N.
Mandibular N.
Middle meningeal A.
Trigeminal ganglion

Superior sagittal sinus
Cut anterior part of falx cerebri
Muco-endosteum of anterior ethmoidal air sinus
Anterior ethmoidal A. and N.
Muco-endosteum of a middle ethmoidal air sinus
Muco-endosteum of a posterior ethmoidal air sinus
Optic N.
Ophthalmic A.
Internal carotid A.
Wall of right cavernous sinus
Oculomotor N.
Basilar plexus
Abducent N.
Inferior petrosal sinus

FIG. 50   Dissection of the orbit and middle cranial fossa.

Nasociliary Nerve

The nasociliary nerve arises from the ophthalmic nerve in the anterior part of the cavernous sinus. It passes through the superior orbital fissure and between the two heads of the lateral rectus muscle [FIG. 54]. It runs anteromedially above the optic nerve to the medial wall of the orbit. Here it continues forwards between the superior oblique and medial rectus muscles, and ends by dividing into infratrochlear and anterior ethmoidal nerves. It also gives off: (1) a branch to the ciliary ganglion; (2) the long ciliary nerves; (3) the posterior ethmoidal nerve.

The **communicating branch to the ciliary ganglion** runs along the lateral side of the optic nerve to reach the ganglion.

The two **long ciliary nerves** pass along the medial side of the optic nerve and pierce the sclera in this position. Their nerve fibres are sensory to the eyeball except the retina, but they also transmit some postganglionic sympathetic fibres, which enter the nasociliary nerve from the internal carotid plexus, and pass to supply the dilator of the pupil.

The **posterior ethmoidal nerve** arises at the medial wall of the orbit, passes through the posterior ethmoidal foramen, and supplies the mucous membrane of the ethmoid and sphenoid sinuses.

Infratrochlear Nerve. This is the smaller terminal branch, and it runs forwards to leave the orbit below the trochlea. It appears on the face above the medial angle of the eye, and supplies the skin of the eyelids and the upper half of the external nose.

Anterior Ethmoidal Nerve. This nerve leaves the orbit by the anterior ethmoidal foramen, which crosses above the ethmoidal sinuses [Fig. 50] and appears at the lateral margin of the cribriform plate of the ethmoid. Here it turns forwards under the dura mater, and descends into the nasal cavity through a slit-like aperture at the side of the crista galli. It gives **internal nasal branches** to the mucous membrane, and running down on the deep surface of the nasal bone, emerges between it and the upper nasal cartilage **(external nasal nerve)** to supply the skin of the lower half of the nose.

Ciliary Ganglion

This small collection of parasympathetic nerve cells, about the size of a large pin head, lies in fatty tissue between the optic nerve and the lateral rectus muscle.

Connexions. (1) The long, slender filament from the nasociliary nerve consists of **sensory** fibres to the eyeball, and postganglionic **sympathetic** fibres which enter the ophthalmic nerve from the internal carotid plexus and supply the dilator of the pupil and blood vessels in the outer coats of the eye. Both of these pass straight through the ganglion and on to the eyeball through the short ciliary nerves. (2) The oculomotor root is a short, stout branch from the nerve to the inferior oblique muscle. It enters the ganglion from below, and contains preganglionic **parasympathetic** fibres from the oculomotor nerve which synapse with the cells of the ganglion. The postganglionic fibres, which arise from these cells, pass with the short ciliary nerves to the eyeball, and innervate the sphincter of the pupil and the ciliary muscle. Changes in the tension of the ciliary muscle alter the focal length of the lens in the eye and allow focusing (accommodation) to occur.

The **short ciliary nerves,** about six in number, pass along the optic nerve and divide, so that twelve to twenty pierce the sclera around the entrance of the optic nerve.

Parasympathetic Ganglia

The four small ganglia associated with the branches of the trigeminal nerve (ciliary, pterygopalatine, otic, and submandibular) belong to the parasympathetic division of the autonomic nervous system. They receive preganglionic fibres either

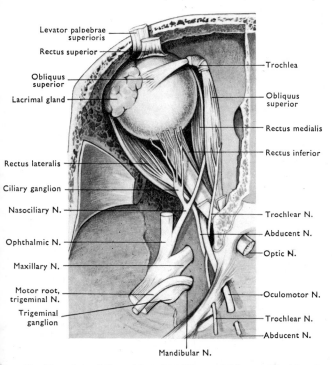

Levator palpebrae superioris
Rectus superior
Obliquus superior
Lacrimal gland
Rectus lateralis
Ciliary ganglion
Nasociliary N.
Ophthalmic N.
Maxillary N.
Motor root, trigeminal N.
Trigeminal ganglion
Trochlea
Obliquus superior
Rectus medialis
Rectus inferior
Trochlear N.
Abducent N.
Optic N.
Oculomotor N.
Trochlear N.
Abducent N.
Mandibular N.

FIG. 51 Dissection of the orbit and middle cranial fossa. The trigeminal nerve and ganglion have been turned laterally.

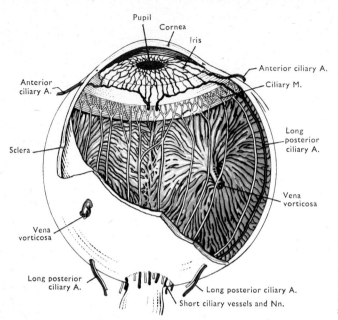

Pupil

Cornea

Iris

Anterior ciliary A.

Anterior ciliary A.

Ciliary M.

Long posterior ciliary A.

Sclera

Vena vorticosa

Vena vorticosa

Long posterior ciliary A.

Long posterior ciliary A.

Short ciliary vessels and Nn.

FIG. 52 Dissection of the eyeball to show the vascular coat and the arrangement of the ciliary nerves and vessels.

nerve. It lies below the optic nerve at first, but gradually pierces its arachnoid and dural sheaths, and winding round the lateral side of the nerve, crosses above it to reach the medial wall of the orbit. Thence the artery runs forwards below the superior oblique muscle, and ends by dividing into the **supratrochlear** and **dorsal nasal** arteries near the front of the orbit.

Branches. These are very numerous and difficult to display [FIG. 53]. The largest is the lacrimal; the most important is a small branch **(central artery of the retina)** which enters the optic nerve in the optic canal, and runs in it to the retina. It is the sole arterial supply to the retina, and its occlusion leads to blindness in the affected eye.

from the oculomotor, facial, or glossopharyngeal nerves, and the cells they contain give rise to postganglionic nerve fibres. These are distributed, mainly through the branches of the trigeminal nerve, to glands of the orbit, nose, nasal part of the pharynx, and mouth, and to the sphincter of the pupil and ciliary muscle of the eyeball. Fibres of the sympathetic system and the trigeminal nerve frequently run through these ganglia, but have no functional connexion with them. The parasympathetic ganglia lie closer to the structures they supply than the sympathetic ganglia, which are situated in the neck. The latter send postganglionic fibres to the same structures, often through plexuses on the arteries which supply them.

Ophthalmic Artery

This artery arises from the internal carotid artery as soon as it pierces the arachnoid mater [FIG. 50].

Course. It enters the orbit through the optic canal, inside the arachnoid sheath of the optic

Ophthalmic Veins

The **superior** ophthalmic vein begins in the anterior part of the orbit close to the artery, and communicates with the supra-orbital and supratrochlear branches of the facial vein. It runs with the ophthalmic artery in the orbit.

The **inferior** ophthalmic vein is smaller, and lies below the optic nerve. It communicates through the inferior orbital fissure with the pterygoid venous plexus. Both veins receive numerous tributaries in the orbit, and passing through the superior orbital fissure, open into the cavernous sinus either separately or by a common trunk.

Origins of the Muscles that Move the Eyeball

The four rectus muscles arise from a common tendinous ring which surrounds the orbital end of the optic canal, and encloses a part of the superior orbital fissure. The superior, inferior, and medial recti arise from the ring above, medial to, and below the optic canal respectively. The lateral rectus arises by two heads

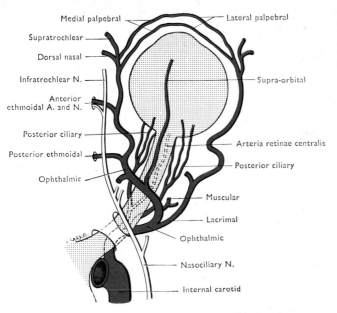

Medial palpebral — — Lateral palpebral
Supratrochlear —
Dorsal nasal —
Infratrochlear N. — — Supra-orbital
Anterior
ethmoidal A. and N.
Posterior ciliary —
Posterior ethmoidal — — Arteria retinae centralis
— Posterior ciliary
Ophthalmic —
— Muscular
— Lacrimal
Ophthalmic
— Nasociliary N.
— Internal carotid

FIG. 53   Diagram of the ophthalmic artery and its branches.

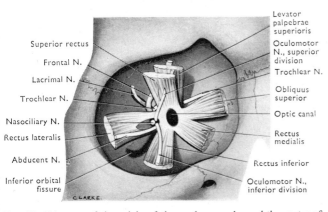

Levator
palpebrae
superioris
Superior rectus — Oculomotor
N., superior
Frontal N. — division
Lacrimal N. — Trochlear N.
Trochlear N. — Obliquus
superior
Nasociliary N. — Optic canal
Rectus lateralis — Rectus
medialis
Abducent N. —
Rectus inferior
Inferior orbital
fissure — Oculomotor N.,
inferior division

FIG. 54   Diagram of the origin of the ocular muscles and the routes of entry of nerves into the right orbit.

from the lateral part of the ring and the adjoining margins of the orbital fissure. The two divisions of the oculomotor nerve, the nasociliary nerve, the abducent nerve, and the ophthalmic veins enter or leave the orbit between the two heads of the muscle.

The superior oblique arises from the body of the sphenoid between the superior and medial recti. The inferior oblique is entirely separate from the others, and arises from the floor of the orbit far forward on the medial side.

DISSECTION. To display the attachments of the muscles of the eyeball, divide the optic nerve close to the canal and turn it forwards with the eyeball. Clean the origins, but do not damage the structures between the two heads of lateral rectus.

Replace the eyeball, and make an ncision through the inferior fornix of the conjunctiva. Raise the eyeball slightly and dissect away the fat and loose connective tissue to expose the inferior oblique muscle.

Clean the rectus muscles and trace the nerves into the inferior oblique, and inferior and medial recti from the inferior division of the oculomotor nerve.

Obliquus Inferior

It arises from a small area of the floor of the orbit just lateral to the opening of the nasolacrimal canal. It passes laterally and slightly backwards below the inferior rectus, and curving upwards [FIGS. 49, 55] ends in a flattened tendon which is inserted into the lateral side of the sclera under cover of the lateral rectus, close to the insertion of the superior oblique.

Nerve supply: the inferior division of the oculomotor nerve.

Action: it turns the cornea upwards when the cornea is rotated medially.

Insertions of the Muscles that Move the Eyeball

The recti are inserted into the sclera about 6 mm. behind the cornea. Both medial and

75

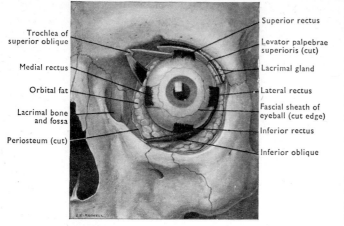

Trochlea of superior oblique

Medial rectus

Orbital fat

Lacrimal bone and fossa

Periosteum (cut)

Superior rectus

Levator palpebrae superioris (cut)

Lacrimal gland

Lateral rectus

Fascial sheath of eyeball (cut edge)

Inferior rectus

Inferior oblique

FIG. 55 Dissection of the left orbit to show the insertions of the muscles of the eyeball after removal of the fascial sheath.

lateral recti are inserted a little further forward than the superior and inferior recti. The oblique muscles are inserted much further back, their attachments to the sclera lying behind the equator of the eyeball, lateral to its sagittal meridian.

Actions of the Ocular Muscles

The **medial** and **lateral recti** have the simple function of rotating the eye around a vertical axis, thus turning the cornea medially and laterally. The **superior** and **inferior recti** produce simple elevation and depression of the cornea only when the eye is turned laterally so that the visual axis corresponds with that of these muscles [FIG. 56]. As the cornea is turned medially, they become progressively less effective in elevating and depressing the cornea, but tend to turn it further medially. At the same time the visual axis is moving progressively nearer to that of the **oblique muscles,** and they become increasingly effective in elevation and depression of the cornea as movement continues; their tendency to turn the cornea laterally helping to offset the medial movement produced by the superior and inferior recti.

The eye muscles may be used in any combination to produce intermediate movements, but it should be appreciated that very delicate control of eye movements is essential for normal vision. Thus failure to train both eyes exactly on to an object leads to double vision, because the images thrown on the two retinae

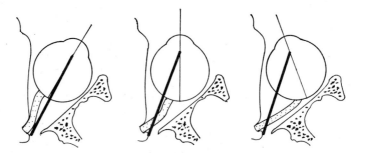

FIG. 56 ⁻ Three diagrams to show the changing relationship and actions of the superior and inferior rectus muscles (thick line) as the cornea is turned from lateral to medial. When the cornea is turned laterally the two muscles elevate and depress it respectively. As the cornea is turned further medially they become progressively less effective in this action, tending instead to turn the cornea further medially. It is in this position that the oblique muscles become effective elevators (inferior oblique) and depressors (superior oblique) of the cornea.

76

do not fall on exactly corresponding parts. To test this, hold up your finger about 30 cm. from your nose and look past it at a distant object. In this situation the finger appears double and out of focus. Now slowly change your direction of vision on to the finger; the two images move together and come into focus as a single object. This is due to convergence of the eyes throwing the image of the finger on to the corresponding parts of the two retinae, and the automatic focusing process which is linked to convergence (convergence-accommodation reflex) coming into play. Double vision is always found in paralysis of one or more of the ocular muscles, but only in those movements which the paralysed muscle or muscles produce.

Once again trace the nerves forwards from the cavernous sinus into the orbit, and note the relative positions which they take up in the fissure [FIG. 54].

Oculomotor Nerve

Both divisions of this nerve enter the orbit between the two heads of the lateral rectus muscle. The superior division passes to the rectus superior and, through it, to the levator palpebrae superioris. The inferior division is larger. It divides into three branches to supply the inferior and medial recti and the inferior oblique. The branches to the recti enter their internal surfaces. The branch to the inferior oblique runs forwards between the inferior and lateral rectus muscles, and gives the parasympathetic root to the ciliary ganglion.

Abducent Nerve

This nerve enters the orbit between the two heads of the lateral rectus, and continues forwards closely applied to the medial surface of that muscle. It supplies only the lateral rectus.

Fascial Sheath of the Eyeball

The connexions of this sheath cannot be satisfactorily demonstrated in an ordinary dissection, but some of the following points can be confirmed.

Relation of Sheath to Eyeball. It forms a membranous socket for the eyeball, but is deficient in front over the cornea. It is separated from the eyeball by some soft, semi-fluid areolar tissue which allows the eyeball to slide freely in the sheath. The free anterior margin of the sheath fuses with the ocular conjunctiva close to the margin of the cornea, while posteriorly, it is adherent to the dural sheath of the optic nerve. The sheath is loosely attached to the orbital fat.

Relation of Sheath to Extrinsic Ocular Muscles. Each of these muscles pierces the fascial sheath at the equator of the eyeball, and receives a covering sleeve from it which fades out posteriorly in continuity with the epimysium. Each of these sleeves is strengthened by a slip of fibrous tissue which passes to the bony wall of the orbit, and makes the sleeve act as a pulley which prevents the muscle compressing the eyeball when it contracts. The sheath of the superior oblique passes to the trochlea and fuses with it, while that of the inferior oblique reaches the floor of the orbit.

Relation of Sheath to Bony Orbit. The fascial sheath is connected to the orbital walls by: (1) The **suspensory ligament.** This is a hammock-shaped sling stretched across the anterior part of the orbit between the lacrimal and zygomatic bones. It is broadest beneath the eyeball where it is attached to the fascial sheath, and it helps to support the eyeball and steady the fascial sheath. (2) The **check ligaments.** These are strong bands which pass from the sheaths around the lateral and medial rectus muscles to be attached to the zygomatic and lacrimal bones close to the attachments of the suspensory ligament. These ligaments limit the amount of movement which the lateral and medial rectus muscles can produce. Similar checks are present on the superior and inferior rectus muscles, the former by an intimate connexion with the levator palpebrae superioris, the latter by attachment to the suspensory ligament.

DISSECTION. Separate the eyelids completely by incisions from the angles to the orbital margins, and pull them apart. Divide the conjunctiva immediately beyond the cornea by a circular incision which will also divide the fascial sheath. Turn the conjunctiva and fascial sheath outwards, thus exposing the openings for the passage of the tendons through the sheath.

There remain only the zygomatic and infra-orbital nerves to be dissected, but as these lie outside the orbital periosteum they are most conveniently dissected later with the maxillary sinus.

THE ANTERIOR TRIANGLE OF THE NECK

This is the large area on the front of the neck which is bounded by the midline, the mandible and the sternocleidomastoid muscle.

SURFACE ANATOMY

Pass the finger from the chin to the sternum along the median line, and identify, in sequence, the body of the **hyoid bone** immediately below the level of the mandible, the sharp protuberance of the anterior border of the **thyroid cartilage (laryngeal prominence)** which is notched superiorly, the rounded arch of the **cricoid cartilage,** and the rings of the **trachea,** which are partly masked by the isthmus of the thyroid gland [FIG. 111].

Grasp the U-shaped hyoid bone between finger and thumb, and trace its greater horns backwards. Note that their tips are very close to the sternocleidomastoid muscles, which may overlap them. From its notch, trace the superior border of the thyroid cartilage posteriorly, and note that it ends in a projection (the superior horn) immediately anterior to the sternocleidomastoid.

Press the fingers into the neck along a line from the mastoid process towards the tip of the shoulder, the deep bony resistance is due to the **transverse processes of the cervical vertebrae.** Only the first can be felt at all clearly immediately antero-inferior to the tip of the mastoid process. The fourth is on the level of the upper border of the thyroid cartilage, and the sixth at the level of the cricoid arch. These points are best felt on the living subject, especially the **isthmus of the thyroid gland** which forms a soft, cushion-like mass on the second to fourth tracheal rings.

DISSECTION. Incise the skin from chin to sternum in the midline, and reflect the flap of skin inferolaterally. Do not cut deeply, but remain superficial to the fibres of platysma in the superficial fascia of the postero-superior part.

Reflect the platysma upwards, keeping close to its deep surface and dividing the nerve bundles which enter it. Find the cervical branch of the facial nerve as it leaves the lower border of the parotid gland, and trace it antero-inferiorly. Find the branches of the transverse nerve of the neck as they cross the sternocleido-mastoid, and follow them to their termination anteriorly [Fig. 10].

Find the anterior jugular vein near the median line, and trace it inferiorly till it pierces the deep fascia about 2 cm. above the sternum. Clean the deep fascia of the triangle.

Make a transverse incision through the first layer of the deep fascia immediately above the sternum, and extend the incision upwards for 4 cm. along the anterior border of sternocleidomastoid. Reflect this flap of fascia upwards and uncover the suprasternal space between the first and second (deep) layers of fascia. Trace the anterior jugular vein and second layer of fascia laterally deep to sternocleidomastoid, and follow he fascia upwards till it fuses with the first layer (mid-way between the sternum and thyroid cartilage) and downwards to its attachment to the back of the sternum.

SUPERFICIAL FASCIA

In this region the superficial fascia contains a variable amount of fat, and is only loosely connected to the skin and deep fascia; the skin is, therefore, freely movable.

Platysma

This is a wide, thin sheet of muscle which lies in the superficial fascia superficial to the cutaneous branches of the cervical plexus and the external jugular vein. It extends from the lower face to the upper part of the chest, and it covers the superior part of the anterior triangle, and the antero-inferior part of the posterior triangle.

It arises from the fascia and skin over the upper part of pectoralis major and deltoid. The anterior fibres are either attached to the lower border of the anterior part of the mandible, or interdigitate with corresponding fibres of the opposite side immediately below the chin. The posterior fibres curve upwards across the mandible, are attached to the skin of the lower part of the face, and mingle with the muscles of the lips, helping to form risorius.

Nerve supply: the cervical branch of the facial nerve.

It is part of a much more extensive sheet of cutaneous muscle which is found in many animals, and part of which arises in the axilla.

Cervical Branch of Facial Nerve. It emerges at the lower border of the parotid gland, pierces the deep fascia, and sweeping forwards in the neck deep to platysma, supplies that muscle and sends a number of fine branches across the mandible to the muscles of the lower lip.

Anterior Jugular Vein [FIG. 57]

This is usually the smallest of the jugular veins, but it varies in width inversely with the external jugular vein. It begins below the chin by the union of small veins from the chin and lip, and descends in the superficial fascia, about 1 cm. from the median plane, draining the surrounding tissues. Approximately 2 cm. above the sternum, it pierces the first layer of the deep fascia and enters the suprasternal space. Here it runs laterally to join the external jugular vein, by passing deep to sternocleidomastoid. It is joined to its fellow by a transverse channel in the suprasternal space. This **jugular arch** is often of considerable size, and is an important anterior relation of the trachea and thyroid gland.

The anterior jugular vein is very variable; sometimes absent on one side or represented by a single median vein. It has no valves.

DISSECTION. Clean the surface of sternocleidomastoid, but retain the external jugular vein and the nerves on it. Remove the fat and lymph nodes from the posterior border of the muscle up to its cranial attachment, but avoid injury to the nerves that emerge at that border, especially the accessory. Push the parotid gland forwards and define the anterior border of the upper part of the muscle. Find the accessory nerve and the artery which accompanies it as they enter this part of the muscle. Once all the borders of the muscle are defined, lift up the anterior and posterior borders and clean beneath it, noting the vessels which enter it anteriorly.

STERNOCLEIDOMASTOID

This is an important landmark in the neck which is easily defined in a living subject. When it contracts and turns the face towards the opposite side, it stands out as a well defined ridge between the anterior and posterior triangles.

It arises inferiorly by two heads. (1) The **sternal head** (rounded, tapering, and tendinous) is attached to the upper part of the anterior surface of the manubrium sterni. Superiorly, it widens rapidly, crosses the medial part of the sternoclavicular joint, and a short distance above the clavicle, meets and overlaps the clavicular head, with which it fuses about half way up the neck. (2) The **clavicular head** (broad, thin, and fleshy) arises from the upper surface of the medial third of the clavicle. At first its fibres run more vertically than those of the sternal head, so that the two meet, fuse, and run posterosuperiorly to be inserted into the mastoid temporal bone and the superior nuchal line. The anterior part is thick and is attached to the anterior surface of the mastoid process; posteriorly, it becomes thin and aponeurotic and is attached to the lateral surface of the mastoid process, and the lateral half or more of the superior nuchal line.

Its deep part is pierced by the accessory nerve, and it receives its main blood supply from the occipital and superior thyroid arteries.

Nerve supply: the accessory nerve is motor, the ventral ramus of the second cervical nerve is sensory. Action: acting alone, it bends the head to its own side and rotates it so that the face is turned towards the opposite side. The two muscles acting together flex the neck, but if the neck is kept extended by the postvertebral muscles, the sternocleidomastoid muscles raise the sternum and thus assist in violent inspiration.

THE MEDIAN REGION OF THE FRONT OF THE NECK

This is a strip 2–3 cm. in width between the chin and the sternum.

Superficial Fascia

This layer contains the upper parts of the anterior jugular veins, the decussating fibres of platysma for 1–2 cm. below the chin, and a few small **submental lymph nodes** lie between it and the deep fascia. The lymph which drains to these nodes comes from the anterior part of the floor of the mouth, and they can usually be felt in the living person as little nodules when the thumb is pressed upwards behind the chin.

Deep Fascia [p. 134]

The **investing layer** is attached to the mandible, hyoid bone, and the sternum. Superiorly it splits to enclose the anterior belly of the digastric muscle, while inferiorly it divides to enclose the **suprasternal space.** This contains the jugular arch, the sternal head of sternocleidomastoid, the lowest parts of the anterior jugular veins, and an occasional lymph node. Inferior to the thyroid cartilage is the deeper layer of **pretracheal fascia.** This is attached to the thyroid and cricoid cartilages and envelops the thyroid gland. It descends over the front and sides of the trachea to blend with the back of the upper part of the pericardium, in the thorax.

DISSECTION. Remove the deep fascia from the anterior bellies of digastric and from the area between them, looking for the submental nodes on its surface. The exposed area of muscle is part of the two mylohyoid muscles which unite in the midline.

Below the hyoid, remove the same layer of fascia and expose the infrahyoid muscles, which lie on each side of the midline from the hyoid to the sternum. Remove the fascia between these muscles in the midline, and pulling them apart, expose the pretracheal fascia. Below the isthmus of the thyroid gland, clear away this fascia and identify the trachea with the inferior thyroid veins running on it. The small thyroidea ima artery may be seen ascending to the thyroid in this region.

At the upper border of the isthmus, look for a slender fibromuscular band (levator glandulae thyroideae) which connects the isthmus to the hyoid bone, and which, when present, usually lies to the left of the midline. Divide the pretracheal fascia along the upper border of the isthmus, clean the isthmus and the vessels on its surface, and note that it can be pulled downwards when the pretracheal fascia is divided above it. Detach the pretracheal fascia from the cricoid and thyroid cartilages, and note the cricothyroid ligament between them, with the anastomosis of the cricothyroid arteries on it. On each side of the ligament, clean the small cricothyroid muscle.

Between the thyroid cartilage and hyoid bone, clean the median thyrohyoid ligament with the anastomosis of the infrahyoid arteries on it. Note that the ligament ascends posterior to the body of the hyoid and is separated from it by the small hyoid bursa.

Suprahyoid Region

In the midline is the submental triangle which is outlined by the hyoid bone and the anterior bellies of the digastric muscles. The roof of the triangle is formed by the mylohyoid muscles, which separate it from the mouth and which are united by a median fibrous raphe extending from the symphysis menti to the hyoid bone. The submental lymph nodes lie superficial to the deep fascia which forms the floor of the triangle.

Infrahyoid Region

In the midline, between the infrahyoid muscles of the two sides, are a number of structures. From above downwards, these are:

1. The **median thyrohyoid ligament** which passes from the upper border of the thyroid cartilage, behind the body of the hyoid bone, to be attached to its upper border. It is separated from the hyoid bone by the hyoid bursa, which reduces friction between them during the movements of swallowing.

2. The **laryngeal prominence** is formed by the thyroid cartilage, and is notched on its superior margin.

3. The **cricothyroid ligament** attaches the thyroid cartilage to the arch of the cricoid. On each side of this ligament lies the **cricothyroid muscle,** which radiates postero-superiorly from the cricoid to the thyroid carti-

age. It is an important muscle of speech, and the only laryngeal muscle which appears on the external surface of the larynx.

4. The **isthmus of the thyroid gland** is separated from the cricoid cartilage by the first tracheal ring, and it lies on the second to fourth tracheal rings. It has a rich vascular anastomosis on its surface, and occasionally a small, pointed, **pyramidal lobe** projects from its superior margin, often on the left side. When present it may give rise to a slender slip

of muscle (**levator glandulae thyroideae**) or fibrous tissue which attaches it to the hyoid bone above. This is an embryological remnant of the tubular, epithelial downgrowth from the tongue (**thyroglossal duct**) which forms the greater part of the thyroid gland.

5. Below the isthmus of the thyroid gland, the **jugular arch** and the **inferior thyroid veins** lie anterior to the trachea. Occasionally the left brachiocephalic vein and the brachiocephalic artery are high enough to appear

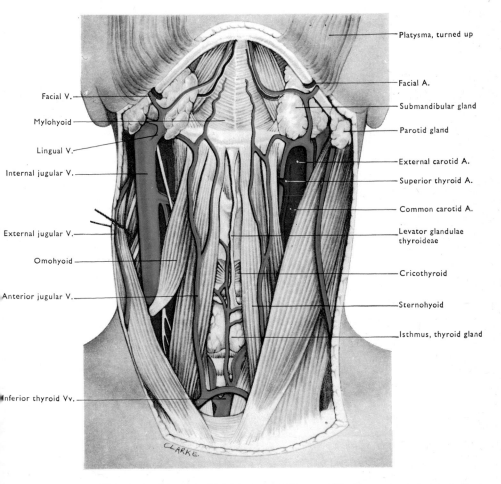

Facial V.

Mylohyoid

Lingual V.

Internal jugular V.

External jugular V.

Omohyoid

Anterior jugular V.

Inferior thyroid Vv.

Platysma, turned up

Facial A.

Submandibular gland

Parotid gland

External carotid A.

Superior thyroid A.

Common carotid A.

Levator glandulae thyroideae

Cricothyroid

Sternohyoid

Isthmus, thyroid gland

CLARKE.

FIG. 57   Dissection of the front of the neck. The right sternocleidomastoid has been retracted posteriorly.

81

in front of the trachea at the root of the neck.

THE SUBDIVISIONS OF THE ANTERIOR TRIANGLE

In addition to the submental triangle, the anterior triangle of the neck is divided into three subsidiary triangles [FIG. 58] by the digastric and omohyoid muscles crossing it.

DISSECTION. Identify the facial artery and vein at the lower border of the mandible. Cut the deep fascia from the mandible and turn it down on its attachment to the hyoid bone, thus partly exposing the submandibular gland. Identify both bellies of the digastric muscle at the lower border of the gland, and follow the facial vein postero-inferiorly across the gland and the posterior belly of digastric.

At the lower border of the mandible, find the submental branch of the facial artery, and trace it forwards, pushing aside the submandibular gland and removing the fat and submandibular lymph nodes. The artery runs with the mylohyoid nerve, the branches of which should be traced to the mylohyoid and the anterior belly of digastric.

Raise the lower border of the submandibular gland, and holding it away, identify the intermediate tendon of digastric and the fascial sling which loops over it from the hyoid. Find the stylohyoid muscle, a slender slip on the upper surface of the posterior belly of digastric, and note that it splits to embrace the intermediate tendon. Clean the stylohyoid and posterior belly of digastric as far as the angle of the mandible.

Find the posterior border of the mylohyoid muscle, and clean it to the point at which the hypoglossal nerve and one of the veins of the tongue disappear deep to it. The thin muscular sheet overlapped by the mylohyoid is the hyoglossus. Clean mylohyoid and hyoglossus [FIG.73].

DIGASTRIC TRIANGLE

This triangle is bounded by the digastric and stylohyoid muscles and the lower border of the mandible. The roof is formed by parts of the mylohyoid and hyoglossus, and the triangle forms part of the submandibular region. Note the position of its contents.

The inferior part of the **submandibular salivary gland** almost fills the triangle, and may overlap the digastric muscle. The **submandibular lymph nodes** lie on the surface of the gland, cniefly along the lower border of the mandible. They drain lymph from the side of the tongue, teeth, lips, and cheek, and transmit it to the deep cervical lymph nodes which lie deep to sternocleidomastoid.

The **facial vein** pierces the deep fascia at the lower border of the mandible, and crossing the submandibular gland, joins the anterior branch of the retromandibular vein, and ends in the internal jugular vein. The **facial artery** curves round the lower border of the mandible and gives off the submental artery before piercing the deep fascia. The **submental artery** passes forwards with the corresponding vein to run with the mylohyoid nerve.

The **mylohyoid nerve** lies on mylohyoid near the mandible; it supplies mylohyoid and the anterior belly of digastric. The **hypoglossal**

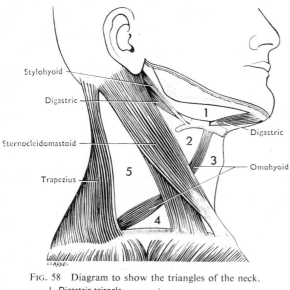

FIG. 58   Diagram to show the triangles of the neck.

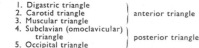

1. Digastric triangle
2. Carotid triangle   } anterior triangle
3. Muscular triangle
4. Subclavian (omoclavicular)
   triangle   } posterior triangle
5. Occipital triangle

nerve lies on a slightly deeper plane, on hyoglossus, and passes medial to mylohyoid. The **intermediate tendon** of digastric lies on hyoglossus immediately above the hyoid bone, and is held down to the bone by a loop of fascia which forms a pulley for it.

DISSECTION. Remove the remains of the deep fascia and the underlying fat from the area between the posterior belly of digastric and the superior belly of omohyoid; the carotid triangle [Fig. 58]. In so doing identify: the internal jugular vein, most laterally, with the common and internal carotid arteries medial to it, and the external carotid anteromedial to the internal carotid.

The lingual and facial veins enter the internal jugular in the upper part of the region, the superior thyroid in the lower part. Identify these veins and trace them till they leave the triangle.

Find the hypoglossal nerve at the lower border of the digastric as it appears between the internal carotid and internal jugular. Trace it forwards, and find its two branches in the triangle: (1) the superior root of the ansa cervicalis, given off where it appears; (2) the thyrohyoid branch, close to the point where it leaves the triangle. Note that the nerve curves round the lower border of the occipital artery as it enters the triangle.

Remove the superficial part of the carotid fascial sheath which surrounds the internal jugular vein, the vagus nerve, and the carotid arteries, but avoid injury to the superior root of the ansa cervicalis on the surface of the arteries and a similar nerve on the internal jugular vein. The latter is derived from the second and third cervical nerves, and forms a loop communication with the superior root of the ansa cervicalis on the artery, at a lower level.

Clean the external carotid artery and its branches.

The superior thyroid is the lowest branch in the triangle [Figs. 73, 92].

The lingual, facial, and occipital arteries arise in the upper part of the triangle, the occipital opposite the facial [Fig. 92].

Find the internal laryngeal nerve in the thyrohyoid interval. Trace it posterosuperiorly to the superior laryngeal branch of the vagus, deep to the carotid arteries. Find the slender external laryngeal nerve, which arises from the superior laryngeal nerve, and follow it downwards deep to the superior thyroid artery.

Clean the part of hyoglossus that lies in the triangle immediately above the hyoid bone. Note the hypoglossal nerve on its surface, and the lingual artery passing deep to it. The muscle on which the lingual artery lies is the middle constrictor muscle of the pharynx [Fig. 111] and this separates it from the mucous membrane lining the pharyngeal cavity. Elevate the posterior belly of the digastric, and clean the part of the middle constrictor near the hyoid bone [Fig. 111].

Clean the thyrohyoid muscle in the triangle; push the superior thyroid and carotid arteries posteriorly, and remove the fat in which the external laryngeal nerve lies. This exposes a part of the inferior constrictor muscle passing backwards from the side of the thyroid cartilage.

Separate the carotid arteries from the internal jugular vein and find the vagus nerve in the posterior part of the carotid sheath between them. Pull the carotid arteries anteromedially and find the sympathetic trunk posterior to the carotid sheath and these arteries.

CAROTID TRIANGLE

This triangle is bounded by the sternocleidomastoid, the posterior belly of digastric, and the superior belly of omohyoid, and it includes the neurovascular bundle, which lies mainly under cover of the corresponding part of sternocleidomastoid. The hyoglossus and thyrohyoid muscles form the anterior part of its floor, the middle and inferior constrictors form the posterior part.

The contents of the triangle will be dealt with in detail later, but their relative positions should be examined now.

Carotid Sheath

In the posterolateral part of the triangle this fascial sheath encloses the internal jugular vein, the carotid arteries, the vagus nerve, and the roots of the ansa cervicalis. The sympathetic trunk is embedded in the posteromedial part of its wall. Numerous lymph nodes cover the superficial surfaces of the sheath, and these transmit the lymph which they receive from adjacent regions and from nodes higher in the neck and head, to the nodes at the root of the neck.

Within the sheath, the internal jugular vein descends vertically to the level of the upper border of the thyroid cartilage with the internal carotid artery medial to it, and below that, with the common carotid in the same position; the common carotid dividing at that level into internal and external branches.

External Carotid Artery. It ascends along the side of the pharynx, anteromedial to the internal carotid, and gives off most of its branches in the carotid triangle:

1. The **superior thyroid artery**, arises low in the triangle, curves antero-inferiorly, and disappears deep to omohyoid. It gives infrahyoid, sternocleidomastoid, and superior laryngeal branches in the triangle. The last of these enters the larynx with the internal laryngeal nerve.

2. The **ascending pharyngeal artery** arises from the lowest part of the external carotid, and ascends between the internal carotid and the side of the pharynx.

3. The **lingual artery** arises behind the tip of the greater horn of the hyoid bone. It runs forwards on the middle constrictor, hooks above the tip of the greater horn, and disappears medial to hyoglossus.

4. The **facial artery** arises above the lingual, and leaves the triangle at once by ascending deep to the posterior belly of digastric.

5. The **occipital artery** runs posterosuperiorly along the lower border of the posterior belly of digastric to the upper angle of the triangle.

Veins

The **facial vein** crosses the posterior belly of the digastric, enters the carotid triangle, and uniting with the anterior branch of the retromandibular vein, takes a variable course. Usually it crosses the carotid arteries and ends in the internal jugular vein, but it may be joined by the lingual and superior thyroid veins. [FIG. 108]

The **lingual vein** is formed at the posterior border of hyoglossus by the union of veins that run with the lingual artery and the hypoglossal nerve. It crosses the carotid arteries and ends either in the facial or the internal jugular vein.

The **superior thyroid vein** takes a variable course to the internal jugular or facial vein.

Nerves

The **accessory nerve** runs postero-inferiorly across the upper angle of the triangle, either superficial or deep to the internal jugular vein.

The **hypoglossal nerve** (which supplies the muscles of the tongue) appears at the lower border of the posterior belly of digastric, curves forwards round the root of the occipital artery, crosses the carotid arteries and the bend of the lingual artery, and disappears into the digastric triangle deep to the posterior belly of digastric. In the triangle it gives off the **superior root** of the **ansa cervicalis** and the **thyrohyoid branch** ; the former runs down on the internal and common carotid arteries, the latter passes forwards to its muscle. Both are composed of fibres of the ventral ramus of the first cervical nerve, which join the hypoglossal close to the skull and run with it [FIG. 95].

Another slender nerve (the **inferior root of the ansa cervicalis**) arises from the ventral rami of the second and third cervical nerves behind the internal jugular vein. It curves forwards round the vein, usually on its lateral surface, and passing downwards out of the triangle on the vein, runs on to the common carotid artery. Here it joins the superior root from the hypoglossal nerve to form a loop called the ansa cervicalis.

Ansa Cervicalis. This slender nerve loop is formed by the union of the superior and inferior roots on the common carotid artery at the level of the lower part of the larynx. As indicated above, this complex consists of nerve fibres from the first three cervical ventral rami, some of which pass in the thyrohyoid nerve (C. 1) and possibly also to the suprahyoid muscle, geniohyoid, through the hypoglossal. The ansa cervicalis supplies the remaining **infrahyoid muscles** (sternohyoid, sternothyroid, and omohyoid). Thus the hypoglossal nerve and the first three cervical ventral rami form a secondary plexus responsible for the nerve supply to the ventral strip of muscles from the tongue to the sternum, including omohyoid. The phrenic nerve (C. 3, 4, 5) may be considered as continuing this complex into the thorax for the supply of the diaphragm.

MUSCULAR TRIANGLE

This is the space bounded by the sternocleidomastoid, the superior belly of omohyoid, and the median plane. It contains the infrahyoid muscles and a number of important

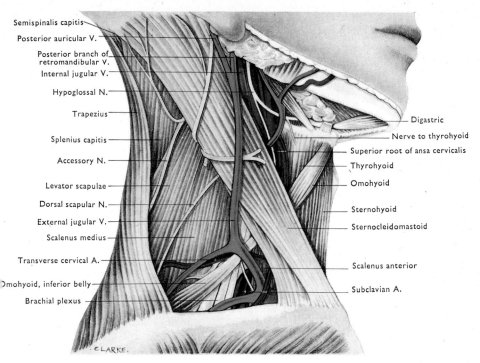

Semispinalis capitis
Posterior auricular V.
Posterior branch of retromandibular V.
Internal jugular V.
Hypoglossal N.
Trapezius
Splenius capitis
Accessory N.
Levator scapulae
Dorsal scapular N.
External jugular V.
Scalenus medius
Transverse cervical A.
Omohyoid, inferior belly
Brachial plexus

Digastric
Nerve to thyrohyoid
Superior root of ansa cervicalis
Thyrohyoid
Omohyoid
Sternohyoid
Sternocleidomastoid
Scalenus anterior
Subclavian A.

CLARKE.

FIG. 59   Lateral view of the triangles of the neck.

ructures in the midline which have been seen ready [p. 80].

DISSECTION. Draw the sternal head of sterno-eidomastoid aside and clean the part of the anterior gular vein deep to it. Expose also the intermediate ndon of omohyoid, and raise its superior belly exposing s nerve. Trace this nerve to the ansa cervicalis; define e ansa and find and trace its other branches.

Clean the infrahyoid muscles, retaining their nerves if ossible. Start with sternohyoid; define its attachments, e sternal one by passing the handle of a knife down tween it and the sternum. Then divide it low down, d expose the other muscles by reflecting it upwards the hyoid. Clean and define the attachments of the hers.

frahyoid Muscles

These ribbon-like muscles are sternohyoid, ernothyroid, thyrohyoid, and omohyoid. hey lie on the trachea, thyroid gland, larynx, d thyrohyoid membrane, and form two layers; the sternothyroid and thyrohyoid forming the deeper layer. The thin **fascia** which encloses them is attached to the second layer of cervical fascia by areolar tissue, and is thickened around the intermediate tendon of omohyoid to hold it down to the sternum and clavicle.

Nerve supply: the ventral rami of the first three cervical nerves through the thyrohyoid nerve and the ansa cervicalis. Action: they move the larynx and hyoid bone in speech and swallowing. They can: (1) depress the hyoid bone, or, when acting with the suprahyoid muscles, fix the hyoid to form a stable base for the tongue; (2) draw the larynx towards the hyoid (thyrohyoid) as in the first phase of swallowing; (3) depress the larynx, leaving the hyoid in position (sternothyroid) as in the second phase of swallowing.

Sternohyoid. It arises from the back of the

manubrium and the medial end of the clavicle, and is inserted into the lower border of the hyoid bone adjacent to the midline. Its upper part is covered only by skin and fasciae, but inferiorly, the anterior jugular vein and sterno-cleidomastoid lie in front of it.

Omohyoid. The intermediate tendon lies on the internal jugular vein under sternocleido-mastoid, at the level of the cricoid cartilage. It is held in place by a fascial sheet which con-nects it to the sternum and clavicle. The superior belly passes upwards from the tendon to the inferior surface of the body and greater horn of the hyoid immediately lateral to sternohyoid. It crosses the carotid sheath, and its upper part appears from under sternocleido-mastoid. Inferior belly, see page 19.

Sternothyroid. It is shorter and wider than the sternohyoid, and being deeper, it arises lower down from the back of the manubrium and first costal cartilage. It is inserted into the oblique line on the lateral surface of the thyroid cartilage [FIG. 125] superficial to the attachment of the pretracheal fascia and cricothyroid muscle. It lies anterior to the large vessels of the upper thorax and root of neck, and the thyroid gland.

Thyrohyoid. This is the upward continuation of sternothyroid, and passes from the oblique line on the thyroid cartilage to the lower border of the greater horn of the hyoid bone. It is concealed by omohyoid and sternohyoid, and covers the entry of the internal laryngeal nerve to the larynx.

If the dissection of the thorax has already begun, the dissectors of the head and neck should proceed to dissect the root of the neck [pp. 108–121] and return later to the following section on the deeper dissection of the parotid, infratemporal, and submandibular region. This latter dissection is necessary before the whole extent and branches of the vessels of the neck can be shown. If the dissection of the thorax has not begun, proceed to the study of the parotid region, but before doing so take care to protect the neck from drying so that its later dissection is not prejudiced.

THE PAROTID REGION

[FIGS. 26, 60–65]

This is the largest of the salivary glands, and it has a very irregular shape because it is wedged in among a number of structures. In its development it differs from the submandib-ular gland, in that it grows into the fascia of its region and becomes disseminated through it, enclosing structures which run through that fascia, rather than growing within a well-defined capsule. It lies in the fossa posterior to the ramus of the mandible, and extends from the external acoustic meatus above, to the upper part of the carotid triangle below. Medially, it extends to the styloid process (close to the side wall of the pharynx) and wraps round the neck of the mandible. Pos-teriorly, it overlaps sternocleidomastoid, and extends anteriorly over masseter for a variable distance; a portion of this facial part is often detached from the rest, the **accessory parotid gland.**

A part of the cervical fascia (in which it is embedded) deep to the gland is thickened to form the **stylomandibular ligament.** This passes from the styloid process to the posterior border of the ramus of the mandible, and separates the parotid from the submandibular gland.

Branches of the facial, great auricular, and auriculotemporal nerves pierce the substance of the parotid gland, and so may the external carotid, superficial temporal and transverse facial arteries, and the retromandibular vein. All of these have been seen already and their position should be reviewed [pp. 16, 39–40].

Parotid Duct

This is a thick-walled tube formed within the gland by the union of the ductules which drain its lobules. It appears at the anterior

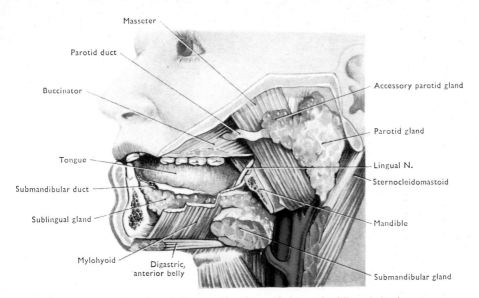

Masseter

Parotid duct

Buccinator

Accessory parotid gland

Parotid gland

Tongue

Lingual N.

Submandibular duct

Sternocleidomastoid

Sublingual gland

Mandible

Mylohyoid

Digastric,
anterior belly

Submandibular gland

FIG. 60   Dissection of the parotid, submandibular, and sublingual glands.

border of the gland on the surface of masseter a finger's breadth, or less, below the zygomatic arch. It runs anteriorly across the masseter, below the accessory parotid gland in company with the zygomatic branches of the facial nerve. At the anterior border of masseter (where it can be felt by rolling it against the muscle with the jaw clenched) it hooks medially over the anterior margin of the muscle, and pierces the buccal pad of fat, the buccopharyngeal fascia, and the buccinator muscle. It then runs obliquely forwards and opens into the vestibule of the mouth on a small papilla opposite the second upper molar tooth.

Structures within the Parotid Gland

1. The **external carotid artery** enters and leaves the gland on its deep surface. It gives off the posterior auricular artery immediately before entering the gland, and divides into its two terminal branches (maxillary and superficial temporal arteries) where it emerges behind the neck of the mandible. Deep to the gland, the superficial temporal gives off the transverse facial and middle temporal arteries.

2. The **retromandibular vein** receives the maxillary and transverse facial veins, and divides into anterior and posterior branches at the lower end of the gland.

3. The **facial nerve** enters the deep surface of the gland close to the stylomastoid foramen, and divides into five terminal branches in the gland. These radiate forwards, superficial to the artery and the vein, and branching repeatedly, appear at the borders of the gland as numerous smaller branches. Within the gland they receive communicating branches from the great auricular and auriculotemporal nerves.

4. The **parotid lymph nodes** are embedded in the gland, especially near its superficial surface. The superficial nodes drain the auricle, the anterior part of the scalp, and the upper part of the face; the deeper nodes receive lymph from the external acoustic meatus, middle ear, auditory tube, nose, palate, and deeper parts of the cheek. Both groups drain to the cervical lymph nodes.

DISSECTION. Clean the surface of the parotid gland, and follow its duct to the buccinator muscle.

87

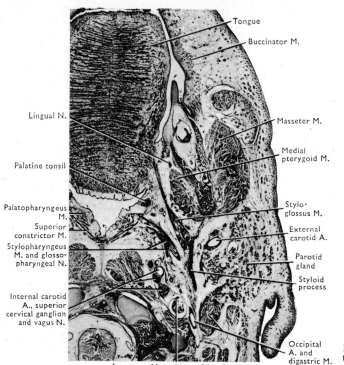

Tongue

Buccinator M.

Lingual N.

Masseter M.

Medial
pterygoid M.

Palatine tonsil

Palatopharyngeus
M.

Stylo-
glossus M.

Superior
constrictor M.

External
carotid A.

Stylopharyngeus
M. and glosso-
pharyngeal N.

Parotid
gland

Internal carotid
A., superior
cervical ganglion
and vagus N.

Styloid
process

Occipital
A. and
digastric M.

Accessory N. on internal jugular V.

FIG. 61 Horizontal section
through part of the head of a
seven-month human foetus.

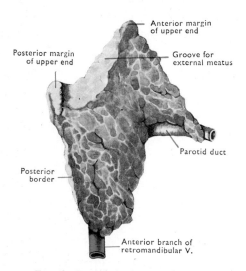

Anterior margin
of upper end

Posterior margin
of upper end

Groove for
external meatus

Parotid duct

Posterior
border

Anterior branch of
retromandibular V.

FIG. 62   Parotid gland, lateral surface.

Follow one of the branches of the facial nerve back
through the gland to the trunk of the nerve, and then
trace the others out through it, looking for the the communicating branches from the auriculotemporal nerve
which are relatively large. Trace the trunk of the facial
nerve to the stylomastoid foramen, and find its posterior
auricular branch and the branch to the posterior belly
of digastric and the stylohyoid which are given off deep
to the gland. Find and trace the posterior auricular
artery.

Clean the retromandibular vein and the external
carotid artery by removing more of the gland. Remove
the remainder of the gland piecemeal and expose the
structures which surround it, retaining, as far as possible, the structures which pass through it.

Shape and Position of the Parotid Gland

Compare FIGURES 62–64 with the space
from which the gland was removed and note
that its shape is determined by the surrounding structures [FIG. 65].

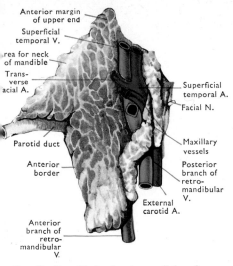

Labels for Fig. 63:
- Anterior margin of upper end
- Superficial temporal V.
- Area for neck of mandible
- Transverse facial A.
- Superficial temporal A.
- Facial N.
- Parotid duct
- Maxillary vessels
- Anterior border
- Posterior branch of retromandibular V.
- External carotid A.
- Anterior branch of retromandibular V.

FIG. 63   Parotid gland, anteromedial surface.

The upper end is grooved by the external acoustic meatus and is wedged between it and the back of the temporomandibular joint; the auriculotemporal nerve and the superficial temporal vessels pierce the gland through the latter part [FIG. 26].

The lower end lies between sternocleido-

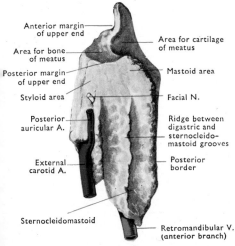

Labels for Fig. 64:
- Anterior margin of upper end
- Area for cartilage of meatus
- Area for bone of meatus
- Posterior margin of upper end
- Mastoid area
- Styloid area
- Facial N.
- Posterior auricular A.
- Ridge between digastric and sternocleido-mastoid grooves
- External carotid A.
- Posterior border
- Sternocleidomastoid
- Retromandibular V. (anterior branch)

FIG. 64   Parotid gland, posteromedial surface.

mastoid and the angle of the mandible, on the posterior belly of digastric. It is pierced by the cervical branch of the facial nerve and the two branches of the retromandibular vein, and is separated from the submandibular gland by the stylomandibular ligament.

The deep surface is very irregular. Anteriorly it is deeply concave where it fits over the posterior part of the mandible covered by the masseter and medial pterygoid muscles. Posteriorly it is grooved to fit the mastoid process and sternocleidomastoid muscle, the posterior belly of digastric, and the styloid process and stylohyoid muscle.

Vessels and Nerves

The vascular supply is from the adjoining vessels. Sensory nerve fibres reach it through the great auricular and auriculotemporal nerves, and postganglionic parasympathetic secretory fibres come from the otic ganglion through the auriculotemporal nerve. The preganglionic parasympathetic fibres reach the otic ganglion from the **glossopharyngeal nerve.** Sympathetic postganglionic fibres enter the gland from the plexus on the external carotid or middle meningeal arteries [FIG. 71].

FACIAL NERVE

This cranial nerve leaves the brain at the lower border of the pons [FIG. 163], passes with the vestibulocochlear (eighth cranial) nerve into the internal acoustic meatus, and emerges from the temporal bone at the stylomastoid foramen after a complicated course through that bone. The facial nerve then curves anteriorly round the lateral side of the styloid process and the internal jugular vein, and enters the posteromedial surface of the parotid gland. Before entering the gland, it gives off the posterior auricular nerve (to the occipital belly of occipitofrontalis and the auricular muscles), and a small branch which divides to supply the posterior belly of digastric and the stylohyoid muscle. In the gland it divides into its main branches [FIG. 27] and of these, the temporal and zygomatic can sometimes be felt as they cross the lateral border of the neck of the mandible.

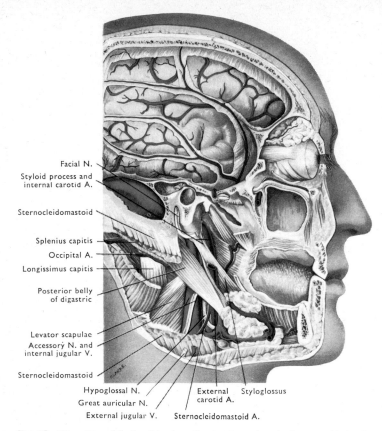

Facial N.

Styloid process and
internal carotid A.

Sternocleidomastoid

Splenius capitis

Occipital A.

Longissimus capitis

Posterior belly
of digastric

Levator scapulae

Accessory N. and
internal jugular V.

Sternocleidomastoid

Hypoglossal N.

Great auricular N.

External jugular V.

External
carotid A.

Styloglossus

Sternocleidomastoid A.

FIG. 65   Dissection of the head to show the structures deep to the parotid gland.

THE TEMPORAL AND INFRATEMPORAL REGIONS

Begin by revising the superficial part of the temporal region [pp. 5-8].

Temporal Fascia

This strong, glistening membrane is stretched over the temporal fossa and the temporalis muscle. Superiorly, it is attached to the upper temporal line. Inferiorly, it splits into two layers, of which the superficial is attached to the upper margin of the zygomatic arch, while the deep layer, separated from the superficial by a little fat, passes medial to the arch to become continuous with the fascia deep to masseter.

Masseter [FIGS. 6, 8]

This thick, quadrate muscle covers the lateral aspect of the ramus and coronoid process of the mandible, but leaves its head and neck uncovered and therefore palpable. It arises from the inferior margin and deep surface of the zygomatic arch, from the tubercle at its root posteriorly, to the junction with the zygomatic process of the maxilla

90

teriorly. It is inserted into the lateral surface of the ramus and coronoid process of the mandible; its deep fibres passing vertically, its superficial fibres running postero-inferiorly. Nerve supply: the mandibular nerve through a branch which enters its deep surface by passing through the mandibular notch immediately anterior to the capsule of the temporomandibular joint. Action: it raises the mandible, clenches the teeth, and its superficial fibres, running obliquely, help to protract the mandible.

DISSECTION. Turn the posterosuperior margin of the masseter forwards and find its artery and nerve.

Display the temporalis by removing the deep layer of temporal fascia, but preserve the temporal vessels and the zygomaticotemporal nerve. Divide the zygomatic arch anterior and posterior to the attachment of masseter, and turn it down with that muscle, dividing the neurovascular bundle (which enters the deep surface of the muscle immediately anterior to the temporo-mandibular joint) and any fibres of the temporalis that may join the masseter. Strip the masseter from the surface of the mandible as far as the angle, but leave it attached there. Clean temporalis.

Temporalis

This is a fan-shaped muscle which arises from the floor of the temporal fossa [FIG. 8] and from the temporal fascia. It converges on the coronoid process of the mandible, the anterior fibres descending vertically, the posterior fibres running almost horizontally forwards, and the intermediate fibres passing with varying degrees of obliquity. A tendon is formed on its superficial surface, and this is inserted into the summit and anterior margin of the coronoid process and the anterior margin of the ramus. The deeper, muscular fibres are attached to the medial side of the coronoid process and, becoming tendinous, reach down to the junction of the anterior border of the ramus with the body of mandible behind the third molar tooth. Some of the superficial fibres may join masseter and pass with it to the mandible [FIG. 67].

Nerve supply: deep temporal branches of the mandibular nerve. Action: the temporalis raises the mandible and its horizontal,

posterior fibres retract the mandible after protraction.

DISSECTION. Separate the coronoid process from the mandible by an oblique cut from the mandibular notch to the point where the anterior margin of the ramus meets the body of the mandible. Be particularly careful at the lower end of the cut, for here the buccal nerve and artery lie either on the deep surface of, or embedded in, the lowest, tendinous fibres of temporalis, and running parallel to the fibres are easily overlooked.

Turn the coronoid process and the attached temporalis upwards, and separate the muscle fibres from the lower part of the temporal fossa by blunt dissection to expose the deep temporal vessels and nerves which ascend between the muscle and the bone. The middle temporal artery [p. 9] will be exposed passing upwards on the squamous part of the temporal bone. Follow the zygomaticotemporal nerve, if it is still intact, to the small foramen through which it emerges from the temporal surface of the zygomatic bone.

The deeper structures in the infratemporal fossa may be exposed from the lateral side (1) by removal of part of the mandible, or (2) by dissection from the medial aspect at a later phase. A combination of the two methods gives the best view of this complicated region. Make one horizontal cut through the neck of the mandible, and another immediately above the mandibular foramen. The position of the latter cut can be found by sliding the handle of a knife between the ramus of the mandible and the subjacent soft parts, and pressing it inferiorly till it is arrested by the inferior alveolar nerve and vessels entering the foramen. Cut half way through the bone with a saw along the lower border of the knife handle, and complete the division with bone forceps, avoiding injury to the underlying structures. Remove the pieces of bone and clean the underlying muscles, vessels, and nerves. Remove the parts of the pterygoid plexus of veins which obscure your view.

THE SUPERFICIAL CONTENTS OF THE INFRATEMPORAL FOSSA

[FIG. 68]

When the fatty tissue is cleared away, the pterygoid muscles are exposed, as are the maxillary vessels and the branches of the mandibular nerve related to them.

DISSECTION. Follow the maxillary artery antero-superiorly till it disappears medially. Carefully remove the fat from the region just superior to this and expose the maxillary nerve passing towards the inferior orbital

91

fissure to become the infra-orbital nerve [Fig. 72]. Find its two branches given off in this region: (1) the zygomatic nerve passing through the inferior orbital fissure, and (2) the posterior superior alveolar nerve, which divides into branches that descend and disappear into small holes in the posterior surface of the maxilla.

Lateral Pterygoid Muscle [FIGS. 67, 68]

This muscle arises by two heads. The smaller, **upper head** springs from the infratemporal ridge and infratemporal surface of the greater wing of the sphenoid. The **lower head** arises from the lateral surface of the lateral pterygoid plate. The muscle narrows as it passes posteriorly, and is inserted into the front of the neck of the mandible and the articular disc through the capsule of the temporomandibular joint.

Nerve supply: the mandibular nerve. Action: acting together the two muscles protrude the mandible and depress the chin, drawing the head of the mandible and the disc forwards on to the articular tubercle. When one muscle acts alone, the head of the mandible on that side is drawn forwards, the mandible pivots around the opposite joint, and the chin is slewed towards the opposite side.

Medial Pterygoid Muscle

This muscle also has two heads of origin, and they embrace the lower head of the lateral pterygoid. The **superficial head** is a small slip arising from the maxillary tuberosity. The

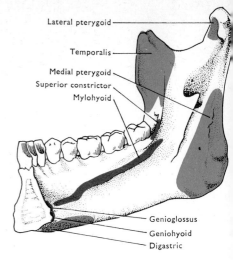

FIG. 67   Muscle attachments to the medial surface of the mandible.   Origins, red; insertions, blue.

deep head forms nearly the whole muscle, an arises deep to the lateral pterygoid from th medial surface of the lateral pterygoid plate The two heads unite inferior to the anteric part of the lateral pterygoid, and passing down wards, with a posterolateral inclination, ar inserted into a rough area between the mand bular foramen and the angle of the mandible Its fibres are nearly parallel to the anteric fibres of masseter.

Nerve supply: the mandibular nerve Action: it raises the mandible, assis protrusion, and slews the chin to th opposite side, but, unlike the later pterygoid, does not open the mouth The two muscles acting alternately pro duce a grinding movement similar t the action of the superficial fibres c masseter.

Maxillary Artery [FIG. 68]

This artery arises posterior to th neck of the mandible as the larger ter minal branch of the external carotid a tery. The first part runs horizontall forwards between the neck of the man dible and the sphenomandibular liga

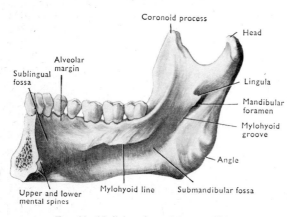

FIG. 66   Medial surface of the mandible.

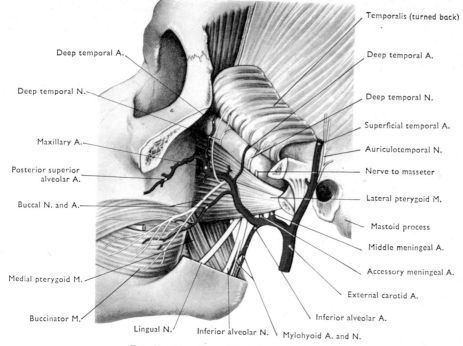

Deep temporal A.

Deep temporal N.

Maxillary A.

Posterior superior
alveolar A.

Buccal N. and A.

Medial pterygoid M.

Buccinator M.

Lingual N.

Inferior alveolar N.

Temporalis (turned back)

Deep temporal A.

Deep temporal N.

Superficial temporal A.

Auriculotemporal N.

Nerve to masseter

Lateral pterygoid M.

Mastoid process

Middle meningeal A.

Accessory meningeal A.

External carotid A.

Inferior alveolar A.

Mylohyoid A. and N.

Fig. 68   Dissection of the infratemporal fossa.

ment, on the lower border of the lateral ptery-goid muscle. The second part runs antero-superiorly, superficial to the lower head of the lateral pterygoid muscle and deep to the in-sertion of temporalis. The third part turns medially, between the two heads of the lateral pterygoid, and ends in the pterygopalatine fossa in a number of branches which are distri-buted over the surfaces of the maxilla. The second part of the artery may lie between the two pterygoid muscles, and bend laterally be-tween the heads of the lateral pterygoid muscle before entering the pterygopalatine fossa.

During its course the artery gives **branches** to the external acoustic meatus and the middle ear, the muscles of the region, the skull bones and dura mater (especially by the middle meningeal [p. 63]), and branches which ac-company the nerves of the infratemporal and pterygopalatine fossae.

The **inferior alveolar artery** descends with the inferior alveolar nerve, and entering the mandibular foramen, courses through the mandibular canal to supply the teeth, gums and mandible, and the skin over the chin and lip through the **mental artery**. It also gives a branch with the mylohyoid nerve, and the corresponding veins drain into the pterygoid venous plexus.

Pterygoid Plexus and Maxillary Vein

The numerous veins of the infratemporal fossa are difficult to dissect, since they form a dense pterygoid plexus around the lateral pterygoid muscle. The veins which correspond to the branches of the maxillary artery open into this network, which is drained posteriorly by one or two short, wide maxillary veins. These pass to the parotid gland, and drain into the retromandibular vein posterior to the neck of the mandible.

Communications of Pterygoid Venous Plexus.

This plexus has widespread communications with all the surrounding veins, but particularly with: (1) the **cavernous sinus** by an emissary vein which traverses the foramen ovale or the sphenoidal emissary foramen; (2) the **inferior ophthalmic vein** through the inferior orbital fissure; (3) the **facial vein,** through the deep facial vein which passes posteriorly on the buccinator muscle, deep to masseter and the ramus of the mandible, to join the plexus.

TEMPOROMANDIBULAR JOINT

This synovial joint is formed by the articulation of the head of the mandible with the mandibular fossa and the articular tubercle of the temporal bone. These two bones are separated by an articular disc which completely divides the joint cavity into upper and lower parts.

The **fibrous capsule** is attached to the margins of the articular area on the temporal bone and around the neck of the mandible. Laterally it is thickened to form the **lateral ligament.** This is a triangular band attached by its base to the zygomatic process of the temporal bone and the tubercle at its root, and by its apex to the lateral side of the neck of the mandible.

The **articular disc** is an oval plate of dense fibrous tissue which is fused with the fibrous capsule around its periphery, and, through this, is more firmly bound to the mandible than to the temporal bone. The upper surface of the disc is concavo-convex to fit the articular tubercle and the mandibular fossa; its inferior surface limits the smaller of the two cavities of the joint, and is concave to fit the head of mandible.

Remove the lateral ligament and expose the disc and the two separate synovial cavities.

The fibrous capsule and its thickened part, the lateral ligament, are the only proper ligaments of the joint. The sphenomandibular and stylomandibular [p. 86] ligaments also connect the mandible to the skull, but add little if anything to the strength of the joint, which is maintained principally by the muscles of mastication. As with any joint maintained mainly by muscles, the temporomandibular joint is relatively readily dislocated.

The **sphenomandibular ligament** is a long, membranous ribbon that passes from the spine of the sphenoid, superficial to the medial pterygoid muscle, to reach the lingula and lower margin of the mandibular foramen. At the latter point it is pierced by the mylohyoid vessels and nerve. The ligament is of considerable developmental interest, as it is the remnant of part of the first branchial arch cartilage, the superior part of which gives rise to the malleus (one of the middle ear ossicles) while the inferior part is fused to the medial aspect of the mandible which develops on its lateral side.

Movements [FIG. 70]

When the mandible is depressed to open the mouth, the articular disc and the head of the mandible move forwards on the upper articular surface until the head of the mandible lies inferior to the articular tubercle. At the same time the head of the mandible rotates on the lower surface of the disc in the inferior part of the joint. The latter movement alone is capable of permitting simple chewing movements over a small range, but if the mouth is opened wide the former element is added also. This can be confirmed by placing the forefinger in front of the head of the mandible and pressing posteromedially; then carry out the two types of movement and note the forward displacement of the head of the mandible

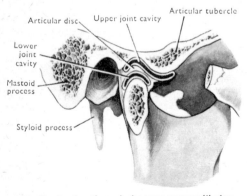

Articular disc Upper joint cavity Articular tubercle

Lower joint cavity

Mastoid process

Styloid process

FIG. 69   Section through the temporomandibular joint.

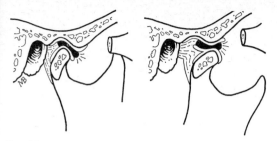

FIG. 70 Two diagrams to show the changing relationship between the head of the mandible and the temporal bone when the mouth is opened (right illustration). Note that the head of the mandible, together with the articular disc (black), slides forwards on to the articular tubercle, while the head of the mandible rotates on the disc.

when the mouth is opened wide. The axis of the two movements is different, the first movement is around an axis through the head of the mandible, while in the second movement the axis passes approximately through the mandibular foramen. Thus the vessels and nerves entering the mandible are not unduly stretched when the mouth is opened wide.

In **protraction** and **retraction** the head of the mandible slides, with the articular disc, forwards and backwards on the temporal articular surface, both sides moving in unison. When these movements of the joints alternate on the two sides, a grinding movement is produced.

The muscles which are active in these movements are: (1) depressors of the chin—the lateral pterygoid, and the suprahyoid and infrahyiod muscles acting with the digastric; (2) elevators—temporalis, masseter, and medial pterygoid; (3) protractors—lateral pterygoid, and less effectively medial pterygoid and the superficial fibres of masseter; (4) retractor—the posterior fibres of temporalis; (5) side to side movements are produced by the muscles of opposite sides acting alternately.

DISSECTION. Separate the two heads of the lateral pterygoid muscle, avoiding injury to the buccal nerve between them. Carefully remove the upper head by detaching it from the capsule of the temporomandibular joint and removing it piecemeal from the infratemporal fossa. In the latter position take care not to damage the deep temporal nerves which lie between it and the skull. Separate the lower head of the lateral pterygoid from the lateral pterygoid lamina, and strip it posteriorly from the underlying structures, leaving the buccal nerve intact. Disarticulate the head of the mandible from the articular disc and remove it with the lower head of the lateral pterygoid, taking care not to injure the auriculotemporal nerve which curves round the medial and posterior surfaces of the joint capsule. Clean the exposed structures.

Trace the middle meningeal artery to the foramen spinosum, and note the two roots of the auriculotemporal nerve which surround the artery close to the skull. Identify the origin of this nerve from the mandibular nerve and trace it posteriorly. Clean the branches of the mandibular nerve [Fig. 71] and identify the chorda tympani nerve entering the posterior surface of the lingual nerve; trace it towards the spine of the sphenoid.

THE DEEPER CONTENTS OF THE INFRATEMPORAL FOSSA

MIDDLE MENINGEAL ARTERY

This branch arises from the maxillary artery at the lower border of the lateral pterygoid muscle, and ascending between the roots of the auriculotemporal nerve, enters the skull through the foramen spinosum. It is posterolateral to the mandibular nerve, and lies on the lateral surface of the tensor palati muscle, which separates if from the auditory tube. Its intracranial course is described on page 63.

The **accessory meningeal** and **anterior tympanic arteries** arise either from the middle meningeal artery or from the maxillary. The accessory meningeal artery runs anterosuperiorly through the foramen ovale with the mandibular nerve; the anterior tympanic passes posterosuperiorly to enter the middle ear through the petrotympanic fissure, close to the chorda tympani [FIG. 93].

MANDIBULAR NERVE

The mandibular branch of the trigeminal nerve arises from the trigeminal ganglion in the cranium, and enters the infratemporal fossa through the foramen ovale. In the foramen ovale it is joined by the motor root of the trigeminal nerve, and emerges from the skull as a mixed nerve.

Immediately below the skull it gives off its meningeal branch and the nerve to the medial pterygoid, and lies between the lateral pterygoid muscle and the tensor palati which separates it from the auditory tube. It divides almost immediately into anterior (predominantly motor) and posterior (predominantly sensory) divisions.

The anterior division branches into the deep temporal nerves, the nerves to masseter and lateral pterygoid, and the buccal nerve, its only pure sensory branch.

The posterior division gives off the auriculotemporal nerve, and divides into the lingual and inferior alveolar nerves. Its only motor fibres are in the mylohyoid branch of the inferior alveolar nerve.

Branches of Trunk

The **meningeal branch** enters the skull with the middle meningeal artery. It supplies the dura mater and skull and sends a filament to the middle ear.

Nerve to Medial Pterygoid. This nerve passes forwards to enter the deep surface of the muscle, and, at its origin, lies close to the otic ganglion.

Anterior Division

Buccal Nerve. This is the largest branch of the anterior division. It passes between the two heads of the lateral pterygoid, and running antero-inferiorly, immediately deep to the anterior margin of the ramus of the mandible in contact with or through the lowest fibres of insertion of temporalis, reaches the surface of the buccinator muscle. Here it forms a plexus with the buccal branches of the facial nerve (which supply the motor fibres to the buccinator muscle) and supplies the skin and mucous membrane on the lateral and medial surfaces of buccinator.

Nerve to Lateral Pterygoid. It arises in common with the buccal nerve, and enters the muscle as that nerve passes between its heads.

Deep Temporal Nerves. These two nerves, anterior and posterior, pass into the temporal fossa between the skull and the lateral pterygoid, and grooving the bone, enter the deep surface of the temporalis. The anterior deep temporal nerve may be replaced by a branch of the buccal nerve which ascends lateral to the upper head of the lateral pterygoid [FIG. 68].

Nerve to Masseter. It arises with the posterior deep temporal nerve, runs laterally between the skull and the lateral pterygoid muscle (immediately anterior to the capsule of the temporomandibular joint) and enters the deep surface of masseter by passing through the mandibular notch. It gives one or two twigs to the temporomandibular joint.

Posterior Division

Auriculotemporal Nerve [FIGS. 71, 117]. It is formed by two sensory roots from the posterior division of the mandibular nerve. Each root receives a bundle of postganglionic parasympathetic fibres from the cells of the otic ganglion. These transmit secretory impulses to the parotid gland from the cells of the otic ganglion, which are activated by impulses reaching the ganglion from the glossopharyngeal nerve. The roots surround the middle meningeal artery, unite posterior to it, and run backwards, lateral to the spine of the sphenoid, to hook round the posterior surface of the neck of the mandible. Here the nerve turns superiorly in contact with the parotid gland, and crossing the root of the zygomatic process of the temporal bone with the superficial temporal artery, breaks up into its terminal branches on the temple [FIG. 27].

Branches. (1) A few slender filaments to the posterior part of the capsule of the temporomandibular joint. (2) One or two thick branches which enter and supply the parotid gland, and mingle with the branches of the facial nerve in its substance. (3) Cutaneous branches to the auricle and the temple.

Inferior Alveolar Nerve. This is the largest branch of the posterior division. It runs vertically downwards with the inferior alveolar artery, on the lateral surfaces of the sphenomandibular ligament and the medial pterygoid muscle, and together they enter the mandibular

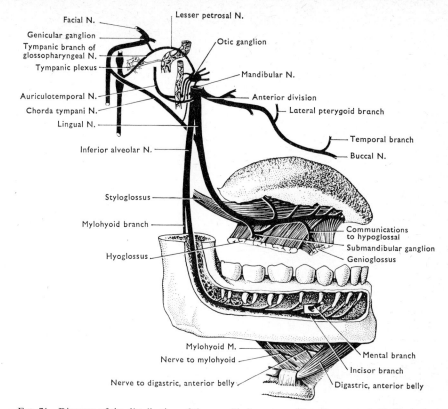

Labels on figure:
Facial N.
Genicular ganglion
Tympanic branch of glossopharyngeal N.
Tympanic plexus
Auriculotemporal N.
Chorda tympani N.
Lingual N.
Inferior alveolar N.
Styloglossus
Mylohyoid branch
Hyoglossus
Lesser petrosal N.
Otic ganglion
Mandibular N.
Anterior division
Lateral pterygoid branch
Temporal branch
Buccal N.
Communications to hypoglossal
Submandibular ganglion
Genioglossus
Mylohyoid M.
Nerve to mylohyoid
Nerve to digastric, anterior belly
Mental branch
Incisor branch
Digastric, anterior belly

Fig. 71 Diagram of the distribution of the mandibular nerve. Note the sympathetic filaments to the otic ganglion and the tympanic plexus from the plexuses on the middle meningeal and internal carotid arteries.

foramen [Fig. 66]. They course through the canal in the body of the mandible giving branches to the lower teeth and gums, and each sends a **mental branch** out through the mental foramen to supply the skin of the chin and the mucous membrane and skin of the lower lip.

The inferior alveolar nerve contains the only **motor fibres** in the posterior division and these leave it near the mandibular foramen to form the **mylohyoid nerve** [Figs. 68, 73].

The **mylohyoid nerve** pierces the spheno-mandibular ligament and runs antero-inferiorly in a groove on the medial aspect of the mandible, to enter the digastric triangle on the inferior surface of the mylohyoid muscle. In the digastric triangle it is joined by the sub-mental artery, and breaks into a number of branches to supply the mylohyoid muscle and the anterior belly of digastric [Fig. 73].

Lingual Nerve. The trigeminal fibres in this nerve are entirely sensory and are distributed to the mucous membrane of the anterior two-thirds of the tongue and the adjacent part of the floor of the mouth. It descends anterior to the inferior alveolar nerve on a slightly deeper plane. Emerging from beneath the lateral pterygoid muscle, it runs antero-inferiorly between the mandible and the medial pterygoid muscle. Just inferior to the last molar tooth, and above the posterior fibres of the mylohyoid muscle, it comes to lie between

97

the mandible and the mucous membrane covering it [FIGS. 67, 74]. Its further course will be followed later.

It gives no branches in the infratemporal fossa, but is joined by the chorda tympani branch of the facial nerve deep to the lateral pterygoid muscle, and it is sometimes joined to the inferior alveolar nerve by a communicating twig.

Chorda Tympani [FIG. 71]

This slender branch of the facial nerve contains preganglionic parasympathetic fibres destined to supply the submandibular and sublingual glands through the submandibular ganglion, and sensory fibres from the taste buds on the anterior two-thirds of the tongue. It arises from the facial nerve posterior to the middle ear cavity, runs anteriorly across the lateral wall of that cavity (tympanic membrane) and escapes from it through the petrotympanic fissure. Thence it runs antero-inferiorly, grooves the medial side of the spine of the sphenoid, and joins the posterior surface of the lingual nerve at an acute angle.

DISSECTION. Lift the mandibular nerve laterally and attempt to find the otic ganglion medial to it. If it cannot be found with ease, do not dissect further as it will be seen from the medial side later.

Clean as much as possible of the tensor palati medial to the middle meningeal artery and the mandibular nerve without damage to the nerve; the remainder of tensor palati will be seen from the medial side.

Otic Ganglion

This is a minute collection of parasympathetic nerve cells which lies between the mandibular nerve and the tensor palati, immediately below the foramen ovale. It is on the origin of the nerve to the medial pterygoid muscle [FIG. 71].

A number of different nerve fibres pass to the otic ganglion, but only the preganglionic parasympathetic fibres, which reach it from the glossopharyngeal nerve via the lesser petrosal nerve, synapse with the cells of the ganglion. The remainder traverse the ganglion but have no functional relation to it. The postganglionic fibres, which arise from the cells of the ganglion, pass as secretory fibres to the parotid gland through the auriculo-temporal nerve. The fibres which traverse the ganglion are: (1) Motor fibres to the tensor palati and tensor tympani muscles from the nerve to the medial pterygoid muscle. (2) Sympathetic fibres from the plexus on the middle meningeal artery, for distribution through the branches of the ganglion. (3) Sensory fibres of the trigeminal and glosso-pharyngeal nerves which are distributed through the branches of the ganglion.

Tensor Palati [FIGS. 111, 112, 117, 151]

This is a thin, flat, triangular muscle which separates the nasal part of the pharynx and the auditory tube from the infratemporal fossa. It will be seen more clearly later, but it is advisable to identify its position on a skull at this phase so that the relation to the pharynx of the structures just dissected can be appreciated. The muscle arises from the scaphoid fossa at the root of the medial pterygoid lamina, and from the posteromedial margin of the greater wing of the sphenoid as far posteriorly as the spine of the sphenoid [FIG. 93]. Here it lies between the groove for the auditory tube medially, and the foramina ovale and spinosum laterally, and forms the lateral wall of the uppermost part of the pharynx. It runs antero-inferiorly, and converges on a slender tendon which hooks round the base of the pterygoid hamulus, on the inferior margin of the medial pterygoid lamina. The tendon slides on a bursa on the hamulus, and spreads medially into the soft palate to form the palatal aponeurosis with the muscle of the opposite side.

Nerve supply: the mandibular nerve, the fibres traversing the otic ganglion.

The maxillary nerve will be fully dissected at a later stage, but its course and some of its branches should be studied now.

DISSECTION. Expose the contents of the orbit and push them upwards and medially, or remove them if they are too unyielding. Find the zygomatic nerve near the angle between the floor and lateral wall of the orbit, and trace it forwards till it enters the bone.

Remove the periosteum from the orbital floor, and identify the infra-orbital groove with the infra-orbital vessels and nerve lying in it.

MAXILLARY NERVE

The maxillary nerve is the second of the three divisions of the trigeminal nerve. It arises from the trigeminal ganglion [p. 60], and passes forwards in the dura mater, to the **foramen rotundum.** It lies on the side of the body of the sphenoid, at the lower border of the cavernous sinus. Passing through the foramen rotundum, it enters the upper part of the **pterygopalatine fossa,** and curves laterally through the pterygomaxillary fissure to the infratemporal fossa. It turns sharply forwards and enters the infra-orbital groove as the **infra-orbital nerve** [FIGS. 72, 123].

Confirm this course by passing a bristle through the foramen rotundum in a dried skull.

Branches. (1) A **meningeal** branch arises near the origin of the nerve. (2) Two **ganglionic** branches pass inferiorly in the pterygopalatine fossa to join the pterygopalatine ganglion. (3) The **posterior superior alveolar nerve** arises in the infratemporal fossa, and divides into two branches which descend over the posterior surface of the maxilla. They supply filaments to the gum and to the mucous membrane of the cheek, and then enter canals in the bone with the alveolar branches of the maxillary artery. In the canals they run forwards above the tooth sockets and form a plexus with the superior alveolar branches of the infra-orbital nerve. They give dental branches to the molar teeth. (4) The **zygomatic nerve** arises close to the foramen rotundum and enters the orbit through the inferior orbital fissure. It gives a delicate filament to the lacrimal nerve, pierces the periosteum, and divides into **zygomaticotemporal** and **zygomaticofacial** branches. These pass forwards in the periosteum of the lateral wall of the orbit, and pierce the zygomatic bone to reach the skin of the temple and face [pp. 8, 41]. (5) The **infra-orbital nerve** is the continuation of the maxillary nerve in the infra-orbital groove and canal. It is

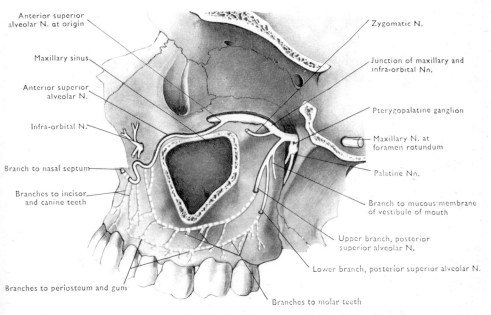

Anterior superior alveolar N. at origin

Maxillary sinus

Anterior superior alveolar N.

Infra-orbital N.

Branch to nasal septum

Branches to incisor and canine teeth

Branches to periosteum and gum

Zygomatic N.

Junction of maxillary and infra-orbital Nn.

Pterygopalatine ganglion

Maxillary N. at foramen rotundum

Palatine Nn.

Branch to mucous membrane of vestibule of mouth

Upper branch, posterior superior alveolar N.

Lower branch, posterior superior alveolar N.

Branches to molar teeth

FIG. 72   Diagram of the maxillary nerve. Cf. FIG. 123.

accompanied by the corresponding vessels, and emerges through the infra-orbital foramen on to the face, deep to the orbicularis oculi. It divides into sensory branches to the upper lip, nose, and lower eyelid.

About the middle of the floor of the orbit the infra-orbital nerve gives off the **anterior superior alveolar nerve** which descends through the anterior wall of the maxilla, and joining the plexus formed by the posterior dental nerves, supplies branches to the upper first molar and to the premolar, canine, and incisor teeth. It also supplies the adjacent gum, and sends branches to the maxillary sinus and to the mucous membrane of the antero-inferior part of the nose.

A **middle superior alveolar nerve** has been described, but it is seldom found as a separate branch of the infra-orbital nerve.

STRUCTURES WITHIN THE MANDIBULAR CANAL

The canal is traversed by the inferior alveolar vessels and nerve, which give dental branches to the roots of the lower teeth, and gingival branches to the adjacent gum.

The mental nerve and artery arise from the inferior alveolar nerve and artery in the canal, and emerge through the mental foramen.

THE SUBMANDIBULAR REGION

The submandibular region lies between the body of the mandible and the hyoid bone. The superficial part includes the submental and digastric triangles which have been dissected already. Its deeper parts, now to be dissected, include the root of the tongue and the floor of the mouth.

DISSECTION. To expose this region, extend the neck and flex it to the opposite side. Divide the facial artery and vein at the lower border of the mandible, and detach the anterior belly of the digastric from the mandible. Divide the mandible in the median plane with a saw, taking care not to extend the cut any deeper than is necessary just to divide the bone. Turn the mandible upwards and fix it with hooks.

Complete the cleaning of the posterior belly of digastric and the stylohyoid.

Digastric Muscle [Figs. 59, 67, 92]

The **anterior belly** of the digastric springs from the lower border of the mandible, close to the symphysis. The **posterior belly** arises from the floor of the mastoid notch on the medial side of the mastoid process. The two bellies are united by an intermediate tendon, which passes through a short, strong loop of fibrous tissue binding it down to the upper border of the hyoid bone. This fibrous pulley is attached at the junction of the body with the greater horn of the hyoid bone, and allows the tendon to slide backwards and forwards through it, in a synovial sheath.

Nerve supply: the posterior belly by the facial nerve, the anterior belly by the mylohyoid nerve. Action: if the hyoid bone is fixed, it helps to depress the mandible. The chief action of both bellies, acting together, is to raise the hyoid in the action of swallowing; an action which cannot be carried out when the mouth is open because the muscle is already shortened. Acting with the infrahyoid muscles, it fixes the hyoid bone, thus forming a stable platform on which the tongue can move.

The **anterior belly** is covered by deep fascia, and is overlapped by the submandibular gland; its deep surface is in contact with the mylohyoid muscle.

The **posterior belly** begins deep to the mastoid process. It passes antero-inferiorly, deep to the lower part of the parotid gland and the angle of the mandible. It is crossed by the facial vein, and overlapped by the submandibular gland, and runs obliquely across the neurovascular bundle of the neck, in contact with the internal jugular vein, both carotid arteries, and the accessory and hypoglossal nerves. The occipital artery runs postero-

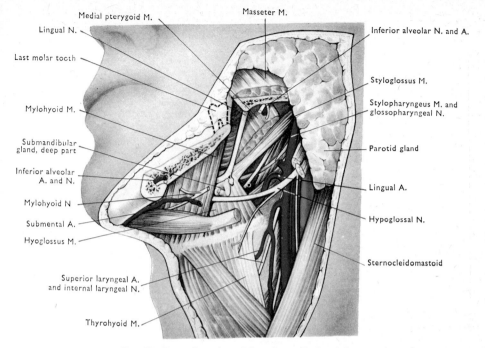

Labels (clockwise from top):
Medial pterygoid M.
Masseter M.
Lingual N.
Inferior alveolar N. and A.
Last molar tooth
Styloglossus M.
Mylohyoid M.
Stylopharyngeus M. and glossopharyngeal N.
Submandibular gland, deep part
Parotid gland
Inferior alveolar A. and N.
Lingual A.
Mylohyoid N
Hypoglossal N.
Submental A.
Hyoglossus M.
Sternocleidomastoid
Superior laryngeal A. and internal laryngeal N.
Thyrohyoid M.

FIG. 73   Deep dissection of the submandibular region.

superiorly along its deep surface, to reach and groove the temporal bone just medial to the origin of the posterior belly from the mastoid notch [FIG. 93].

Stylohyoid Muscle

This small slip of muscle arises from the styloid process, and descends along the upper border of the posterior belly of the digastric. Inferiorly, it divides to surround the intermediate tendon of the digastric, and is inserted into the hyoid bone at the junction of the body and greater horn. Nerve supply: the facial nerve. Action: it helps to pull the hyoid upwards and backwards during swallowing.

DISSECTION. Turn the submandibular gland posteriorly, and complete the cleaning of the mylohyoid muscle. Note the deep part of the gland which hooks round the free posterior border of the mylohyoid muscle, and runs forwards on its superior surface. Dissect out the facial artery from the deep surface of the gland, and trace its branches in this region. Identify

the mylohyoid nerve on the mylohyoid muscle.

Turn the submandibular gland anteriorly and identify the hypoglossal nerve lying on the hyoglossus muscle immediately superior to the greater horn of the hyoid bone. At a slightly higher level, the lingual nerve crosses the same muscle, and has the submandibular ganglion suspended from its lower margin. Identify this ganglion and the submandibular duct, which passes forwards from the deep part of the gland.

Submandibular Gland

This salivary gland is about half the size of the parotid gland [p. 86]. Its superficial part is wedged between the body of the mandible and the mylohyoid muscle, and reaches superiorly to the mylohyoid line on the medial surface of the mandible. Posterior to the free margin of the mylohyoid, the mucous membrane of the mouth lies superior to it, while inferiorly it is limited by the bellies of the digastric. It extends posteriorly to the angle of the mandible, where it is separated from the

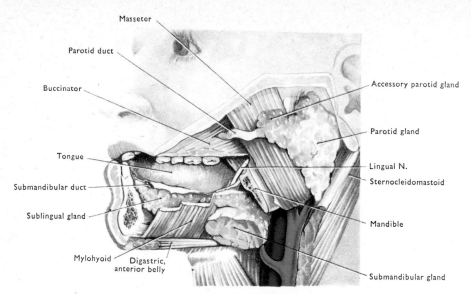

Labels on figure:
Masseter
Parotid duct
Buccinator
Tongue
Submandibular duct
Sublingual gland
Mylohyoid
Digastric, anterior belly
Accessory parotid gland
Parotid gland
Lingual N.
Sternocleidomastoid
Mandible
Submandibular gland

FIG. 74   Dissection of the parotid, submandibular, and sublingual glands.

parotid gland by the stylomandibular ligament, and anteriorly it reaches the level of the
mental foramen. The gland is loosely attached
to a capsule of deep cervical fascia which
ascends from the hyoid bone and splits to
enclose the gland.   The superficial layer is
attached to the inferior border of the mandible; the deep layer separates the gland from
the mylohyoid and hyoglossus muscles, and is
attached to the mylohyoid line [FIG. 66].

Surfaces. The **inferolateral** surface is covered
with: (1) superficial fascia containing platysma
and the cervical branch of the facial nerve;
(2) deep fascia; (3) deep to this the facial vein
and a few **submandibular lymph nodes,** most of
which lie in the groove between the submandibular gland and the mandible.   The **facial
artery** grooves the posterior surface of the
gland, then loops antero-inferiorly between it
and the medial pterygoid muscle to appear at
the inferior margin of the mandible.

The **lateral** surface is related, posteriorly, to
the medial pterygoid muscle and the facial
artery, and anteriorly, to the mandible.

The **medial** surface extends from the bellies
of the digastric muscle to the mylohyoid line,

and is applied to the mylohyoid and hyoglossus muscles. On the latter, it lies on the
hypoglossal and lingual nerves and the submandibular ganglion, while further posteriorly
it lies in contact with the pharynx and is
indented by the facial artery.

The duct arises from the medial surface, and
passes anteriorly in the angle between the side
of the tongue and mylohyoid. The **deep part
of the gland** is a thin, flat process which
extends anteriorly on the lateral side of the
duct [FIGS. 75, 118] superior to mylohyoid.

Nerves and Vessels. The nerve supply is
derived from the parasympathetic nerve cells
in the submandibular ganglion, and from the
sympathetic plexus on the facial artery. The
preganglionic parasympathetic fibres, which
synapse in the ganglion, come from the chorda
tympani via the lingual nerve, and the latter
sends sensory fibres to the gland. The arterial
supply comes from several small branches of
the facial and submental arteries.

Facial Artery [FIGS. 26, 75, 92]

This artery arises from the external carotid
immediately superior to the tip of the greater

102

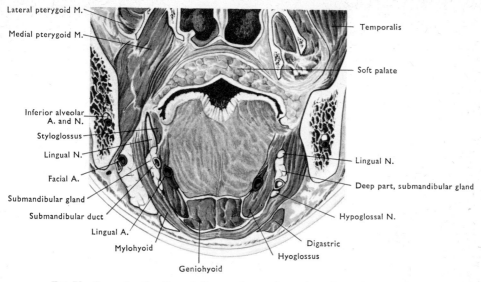

Labels on figure:

Lateral pterygoid M.
Medial pterygoid M.
Temporalis
Soft palate
Inferior alveolar A. and N.
Styloglossus
Lingual N.
Facial A.
Submandibular gland
Submandibular duct
Lingual A.
Mylohyoid
Geniohyoid
Lingual N.
Deep part, submandibular gland
Hypoglossal N.
Digastric
Hyoglossus

Fig. 75   Coronal section through the mouth posterior to the molar teeth. Cf. Fig. 79.

horn of the hyoid bone, in the carotid triangle. It passes vertically upwards on the middle and superior constrictor muscles of the pharynx, passing close to the palatine tonsil, and lying under cover of the digastric and stylohyoid muscles and the angle of the mandible. Turning forwards, it indents the posterior surface of the submandibular gland and reaching its lateral surface, hooks round the lower border of the mandible to appear on the face and pierce the deep fascia at the antero-inferior angle of the masseter.

Branches in the Neck. (1) **Ascending palatine** (q.v.). (2) The **tonsillar artery** ascends superficial to the styloglossus, and pierces the superior constrictor to reach the palatine tonsil. (3) Small **glandular** branches pass to the submandibular gland. (4) The **submental artery** leaves the facial as it escapes from the groove in the submandibular gland, runs forwards between the gland and the mandible, and then turns round the upper border of the gland to reach the inferior surface of the mylohyoid muscle. It supplies the submandibular and sublingual glands and the adjacent muscles and skin.

DISSECTION. Displace the submandibular gland and the submental vessels posteriorly; cut the mylohyoid nerve and turn the anterior belly of the digastric downwards. Clean the mylohyoid muscle and examine its attachments.

Mylohyoid Muscle [Figs. 67, 74, 78]

The mylohyoid muscle is a thin sheet that arises from the whole length of the mylohyoid line on the mandible. The fibres of both muscles pass downwards, medially, and forwards to meet in a median fibrous raphe which extends from the symphysis of the mandible to the body of the hyoid bone, into which a few of the most posterior muscle fibres are inserted. The two muscles form a supporting sling [Fig. 79] under the tongue, and separate it from the submandibular region. Posteriorly each muscle has a free border around which the superficial and deep parts of the submandibular gland become continuous; the deep part and the duct thus lie above mylohyoid in the floor of the mouth.

Nerve supply: the mylohyoid nerve. Action: it raises the hyoid bone and tongue in swallowing, and forms the muscular floor of the mouth.

DISSECTION. On one side cut the mylohyoid muscle a little below its origin and turn it downwards and forwards. Identify and take care not to injure the mucous membrane of the mouth. The superior surface of mylohyoid will be exposed on the opposite side by dissection from the medial side.

With the help of Figure 76, identify the hyoglossus, geniohyoid, and genioglossus muscles, and clean the structures on their lateral surfaces. Trace the styloglossus backwards to the styloid process, taking care of the branches of the facial artery which ascend beside it. Postero-inferior to the styloglossus, identify the stylopharyngeus, and find the glossopharyngeal nerve curving around its posterior border and passing forwards deep to the hyoglossus. Find and trace the stylohyoid ligament from the tip of the styloid process downwards towards the lesser horn of the hyoid bone. Define the upper edge of the middle constrictor of the pharynx, which passes superficial to stylopharyngeus and the lower border of the superior constrictor muscle [Fig. 111].

Hyoglossus [Figs. 76, 78]

The hyoglossus is a quadrate, flat muscle which arises from the whole length of the greater horn of the hyoid bone and also from its body. Its fibres pass superiorly and are inserted into the posterior half of the side of the tongue, medial to and interdigitating with the fibres of styloglossus.

Nerve supply: the hypoglossal nerve. Action: it depresses the side of the tongue and enlarges the cavity of the mouth in sucking.

Styloglossus [Figs. 76, 111]

This is an elongated fleshy slip which arises from the tip of the styloid process and the adjacent part of the stylohyoid ligament. It passes antero-inferiorly and is inserted into the whole length of the side of the tongue, intermingling with the fibres of hyoglossus.

Nerve supply: hypoglossal nerve. Action: it pulls the tongue posterosuperiorly during swallowing.

Geniohyoid

It is a short muscle which arises from the lower mental spine, and runs postero-inferiorly on the superior surface of mylohyoid, side by side with its fellow, to the body of the hyoid bone.

Nerve supply: the first cervical nerve through the hypoglossal nerve [p. 84]. Action: it pulls the hyoid bone anterosuperiorly.

Hyoid Bone [Fig. 77]

This is a U-shaped structure, deficient posteriorly, which lies between the root of the

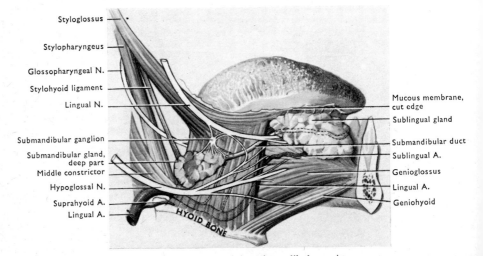

FIG. 76   Dissection of the submandibular region.

Styloglossus
Stylopharyngeus
Glossopharyngeal N.
Stylohyoid ligament
Lingual N.
Submandibular ganglion
Submandibular gland, deep part
Middle constrictor
Hypoglossal N.
Suprahyoid A.
Lingual A.
HYOID BONE
Mucous membrane, cut edge
Sublingual gland
Submandibular duct
Sublingual A.
Genioglossus
Lingual A.
Geniohyoid

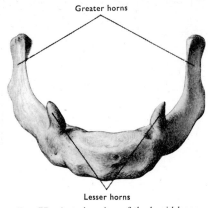

Greater horns

Lesser horns

FIG. 77   Anterior view of the hyoid bone.

ongue and the thyroid cartilage. It forms a movable base for the tongue, and is held in position by a large number of muscles which connect it to the mandible (mylohyoid, geniohyoid, and anterior belly of digastric); to the skull (stylohyoid and posterior belly of digastric); to the thyroid cartilage (thyrohyoid); to the sternum (sternohyoid); and to the scapula (omohyoid). It can be raised by the contraction of both bellies of the digastric; pulled forwards and upwards by the geniohyoid; moved posterosuperiorly by the stylohyoid; depressed by the infrahyoid muscles [p. 85], and held fixed by the contraction of these opposing muscles so that the tongue may be moved on it. The hyoid is also attached to the skull by the stylohyoid ligament (q.v.), to the thyroid cartilage by the thyro-

hyoid membrane, and is in continuity with the pharyngeal wall through the attachment of the middle constrictor muscle of the pharynx to it [FIG. 111].

Submandibular Duct [FIGS. 76, 79, 118]

It emerges from the medial surface of the submandibular gland and passes anterosuperiorly in the angle between the mylohyoid and the side of the tongue. It opens on the floor of the mouth, beneath the anterior part of the tongue, on the summit of the sublingual papilla, an elevation at the anterior end of the sublingual fold [FIG. 109]. Examine these structures in the floor of the living mouth.

At first the duct lies on the hyoglossus, between the lingual nerve above the hypoglossal nerve below, and separated from the mylohyoid muscle by the deep part of the gland. Next it passes on to the genioglossus, and has the sublingual gland between it and mylohyoid. Here the lingual nerve hooks round the inferior surface of the duct, and runs upwards into the tongue medial to the duct.

The wall of the duct is much thinner than that of the parotid gland, and is therefore not so easily palpated. Make an opening into it, and pass a fine probe along it into the mouth.

Sublingual Gland

This gland lies in the floor of the mouth between the mandible and the genioglossus muscle. It raises the mucous membrane covering its superior surface to form the sublingual fold [FIGS. 79, 109], and it rests on the anterior part of the mylohyoid muscle. It is the smallest of the large salivary glands (3 cm. long) and touches its fellow in the median plane above the origin of the genioglossus. The lingual nerve and submandibular duct lie medial to it.

Ducts. Numerous small ducts (eight to twenty) open into the mouth on the summit of the sublingual fold. It is predominantly a

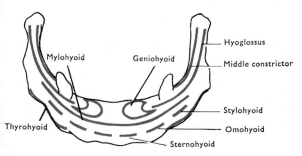

Mylohyoid   Geniohyoid   Hyoglossus

Middle constrictor

Thyrohyoid   Stylohyoid

Omohyoid

Sternohyoid

FIG. 78   Anterior view of the hyoid bone to show muscle attachments.

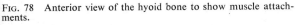

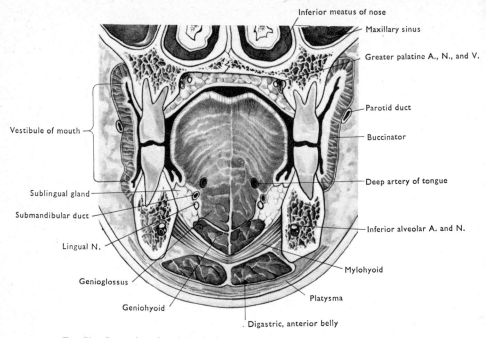

Labels on figure:
- Inferior meatus of nose
- Maxillary sinus
- Greater palatine A., N., and V.
- Parotid duct
- Buccinator
- Vestibule of mouth
- Deep artery of tongue
- Sublingual gland
- Submandibular duct
- Inferior alveolar A. and N.
- Lingual N.
- Mylohyoid
- Genioglossus
- Platysma
- Geniohyoid
- Digastric, anterior belly

FIG. 79   Coronal section through the mouth at the level of the second molar teeth.

mucous gland, in contrast to the serous parotid and the mixed submandibular glands.

Vessels and Nerves. The arterial supply is from the sublingual branch of the lingual artery, and its nerves are branches of the lingual nerve. The latter contain postganglionic parasympathetic fibres from the cells of the submandibular ganglion, as well as postganglionic sympathetic fibres [FIG. 118].

Lingual Nerve

The lingual nerve descends between the ramus of the mandible and the medial pterygoid muscle. It then inclines forwards and enters the mouth by passing inferior to the lower border of the superior constrictor muscle of the pharynx at its attachment to the posterior end of the mylohyoid line [FIG 118.]. It continues antero-inferiorly between the mucous membrane of the mouth and the body of the mandible, postero-inferior to the last molar tooth [FIG. 74]. In this position it is liable to

be injured by the clumsy extraction of the adjacent tooth, and is accessible to local anaesthetics. In its further course, the nerve lies close to the side of the tongue, crosses the styloglossus and the upper part of hyoglossus, and hooks round the submandibular duct.

Branches:	
Twigs of Communication.	(1) Two or more to the submandibular ganglion. (2) One or two which descend along the anterior border of the hyoglossus muscle to unite with the hypoglossal nerve.
Branches of Distribution.	(1) Slender filaments to the mucous membrane of the mouth and gums. (2) A few twigs to the sublingual gland. (3) Branches to the tongue.

The **lingual branches** pierce the substance of the tongue, and then incline superiorly to supply the mucous membrane over its anterior two-thirds.

Submandibular Ganglion [FIGS. 76, 118]. This small ganglion lies on the upper part of the hyoglossus muscle, between the lingual nerve and the submandibular duct. It is about 2 mm. in diameter, and is suspended from the lingual nerve by two short branches. The **posterior** of these may be made up of a number of filaments, and carries preganglionic **parasympathetic nerve fibres** to synapse on the cells of the ganglion.

These fibres reach the lingual nerve from the facial nerve through its chorda tympani branch. They may be accompanied by some sensory nerve fibres which traverse the ganglion and are distributed through its branches. The **anterior branch** carries axons of the ganglion cells (postganglionic fibres) to the lingual nerve for distribution to the sublingual gland and to the glands in the anterior two-thirds of the tongue. From the inferior border of the ganglion, several minute branches carry postganglionic fibres to the submandibular gland and duct, and to the mucous membrane of the mouth.

The **sympathetic fibres,** which also supply the glands, reach this territory from the plexus of postganglionic fibres on the facial and lingual arteries.

Hypoglossal Nerve

This nerve has already been traced to the posterior margin of the mylohyoid muscle [p. 83]. It can now be followed anteriorly across the hyoglossus muscle, with a lingual vein, between the hyoid bone and the submandibular duct. Anterior to hyoglossus, it passes on to and pierces the genioglossus muscle, breaking up into branches to the muscles of the tongue.

Branches. Through numerous purely muscular branches it supplies: (1) styloglossus; (2) hyoglossus; (3) genioglossus; (4) geniohyoid; (5) the intrinsic muscles of the tongue.

It communicates freely with the lingual nerve on the lateral surface of hyoglossus and in the substance of the tongue, and these communications transmit sensory nerve fibres from the muscles, which convey afferent information to the brain stem via the trigeminal nerve. For the distribution of nerve fibres from the first cervical nerve with the hypoglossal nerve, see page 84.

DISSECTION. Detach the hyoglossus carefully from the hyoid bone, and turn it upwards without dividing the structures on its lateral surface.

STRUCTURES EXPOSED BY THE REFLEXION OF HYOGLOSSUS

These are: (1) the lingual artery and its dorsal branches; (2) the lingual veins; (3) the posterior part of genioglossus, and the origin of the middle constrictor muscle of the pharynx; (4) the attachment of the stylohyoid ligament.

Genioglossus [FIGS. 138, 140]

This is a flat triangular muscle which is in contact with its fellow in the median plane. It arises from the upper mental spine, and its fleshy bundles fan out in a vertical plane into the tongue, and are inserted throughout its length, the most inferior fibres reaching the hyoid bone.

Nerve supply: hypoglossal nerve. Action: the two muscles, acting together, protrude the tongue. If one muscle only is active or the other is paralysed, the tip of the tongue deviates towards the inactive side. The middle and anterior fibres depress the central part of the tongue, and if the tongue is in the mouth, they increase the volume of that cavity as in sucking.

Lingual Artery [FIG. 76]

It springs from the front of the external carotid artery opposite the tip of the greater horn of the hyoid bone, and hooking over the top of it, runs anteriorly above the hyoid bone under cover of hyoglossus. It turns superiorly along the anterior border of hyoglossus, and ends by becoming the deep artery of the tongue.

Initially it lies deep to skin, fasciae, and the hypoglossal nerve (which crosses the bend of the artery) and gives off the **suprahyoid branch,** which runs along the superior border of the hyoid bone, superficial to hyoglossus.

Deep to hyoglossus, it gives off two or more **dorsal lingual branches,** which run postero-superiorly to supply the muscular substance of the tongue, and end in the mucous membrane of its pharyngeal surface and in the palatine tonsil.

At the anterior border of hyoglossus it is crossed by the branches of the hypoglossal nerve, by the submandibular duct, and by the lingual nerve. Here it gives off the **sublingual artery,** which runs anterosuperiorly to supply the sublingual gland and the neighbouring muscles.

It is continued as the **deep artery of the tongue,** which enters the tongue about its middle and runs forwards to the tip, separated only by the deep vein from the mucous membrane of the lower surface of the tongue near the frenulum linguae. It is a tortuous vessel to allow for the elongation of the tongue when protruded, and it sends numerous branches into the substance of the tongue.

Veins of the Tongue

The arrangement of these veins is variable. Two venae comitantes run with the lingual artery, and these are joined by the dorsal lingual veins. A vena comitans runs with the hypoglossal nerve. The **deep vein** is the principal vein. It begins at the tip and runs posteriorly near the median plane. It lies immediately deep to the mucous membrane on the inferior surface of the tongue and can be seen through it in life. It descends along the anterior margin of hyoglossus, and crosses the superficial surface of that muscle below the hypoglossal nerve. All the veins unite at the posterior border of hyoglossus to form the **lingual vein.** This either joins the facial vein, or, crossing the external and internal carotid arteries, joins the internal jugular vein.

Stylohyoid Ligament [FIGS. 76, 112]

This is a fibrous cord which passes from the tip of the styloid process to the lesser horn of the hyoid bone. It may be stout or slender, and it is not uncommon to find it partly cartilaginous or ossified. Occasionally it may contain muscle fibres.

It is of embryological interest for it represents the remnant of part of the cartilage of the second pharyngeal arch of the embryo, the remainder of which forms the styloid process and the lesser horn and upper part of the body of the hyoid bone. It may also form the stapes, one of the three ear ossicles, and it corresponds to the sphenomandibular ligament [p. 94] in the first pharyngeal arch.

THE DEEP DISSECTION OF THE NECK

Most of the structures in this dissection lie under cover of the sternocleidomastoid, and therefore were not seen in the dissections of the anterior or posterior triangles of the neck. Some of the structures are hidden by the infrahyoid muscles and others by the parotid gland and adjacent structures. The dissection should be carried out, so far as possible, without dividing the attachments of the sternocleidomastoid.

DISSECTION. Identify the sternohyoid, sternothyroid, and superior belly of the omohyoid. Displace the sternocleidomastoid and the omohyoid laterally, divide the sternothyroid near its inferior end and turn it upwards to its attachment to the thyroid cartilage, preserving its nerve supply. Clean the fat from the front of the trachea, but preserve the inferior thyroid veins. The upper ends of the two lobes of the thymus may lie in the fat, and though difficult to differentiate from it, they are darker in colour, firmer, and ensheathed in fascia.

Remove the fascia from the thyroid gland, and clean the vessels that enter and leave it. Lift the lower part of the gland and clean the trachea, oesophagus, and the recurrent laryngeal nerve which lies in the groove between them. On the left side, look for the thoracic duct on the left border of the oesophagus, and clean it. Trace the external branch of the superior laryngeal nerve to the cricothyroid muscle; clean the superficial part of this muscle and the lower part of the inferior constrictor muscle which arises from a fibrous arch crossing the cricothyroid muscle [Fig. 111].

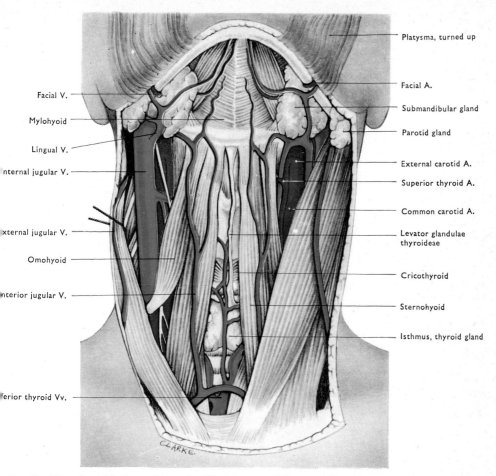

Facial V.

Mylohyoid

Lingual V.

Internal jugular V.

External jugular V.

Omohyoid

Anterior jugular V.

Inferior thyroid Vv.

Platysma, turned up

Facial A.

Submandibular gland

Parotid gland

External carotid A.

Superior thyroid A.

Common carotid A.

Levator glandulae
thyroideae

Cricothyroid

Sternohyoid

Isthmus, thyroid gland

CLARKE.

FIG. 80   Dissection of the front of the neck. The right sternocleidomastoid has been retracted posteriorly.

THYMUS

The thymus is an important lymphoid structure in the child, but in the adult it consists chiefly of fat and fibrous tissue. Its lobes are two slender, elongated, yellowish bodies that lie side by side anterior to the pericardium and great vessels of the upper part of the thorax. Their superior parts may extend into the neck anterior to the trachea, a feature which results from the fact that they develop as lateral outgrowths of the pharynx in the neck, and descend into the thorax.

THYROID GLAND

This highly vascular ductless gland clasps the upper part of the trachea, and extends from the fifth or sixth tracheal ring inferiorly, to the side of the thyroid cartilage superiorly. It is enclosed in a **sheath** of pretracheal fascia, which is attached to the arch of the cricoid cartilage and the oblique line of the thyroid cartilage superiorly; the gland moves therefore with the larynx in all its movements. Internal to the sheath it is enclosed in its own fibrous capsule, and between these, lie the

109

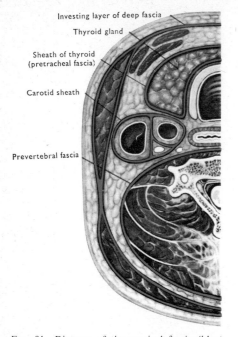

Investing layer of deep fascia

Thyroid gland

Sheath of thyroid
(pretracheal fascia)

Carotid sheath

Prevertebral fascia

FIG. 81 Diagram of the cervical fascia (blue) in transverse section at the level of the thyroid isthmus.

arteries and veins of the gland; the latter forming a network from which the various thyroid veins arise. The gland varies greatly in size, and is always relatively larger in women and children than in men. It consists of a pair of lobes joined across the median plane by a narrow isthmus.

Lobes

Each lobe is conical in shape, and has a convex superficial surface which is covered by the sternohyoid, sternothyroid, and omohyoid muscles, and is overlapped by the anterior border of sternocleidomastoid [FIG. 84]. The medial surface is moulded inferiorly on the trachea and oesophagus with the recurrent laryngeal nerve between them; while superiorly it is fitted to the cricoid and thyroid cartilages, with the cricothyroid and inferior constrictor muscles and the external branch of the superior laryngeal nerve intervening.

The posterior surface varies in width; it is applied to the prevertebral muscle (longus colli) and overlaps the medial part of the carotid sheath. The **parathyroid glands** are embedded in this surface.

Isthmus

This is a band of variable width which lies on the second to fourth tracheal rings, under cover of the skin and fasciae in the median line of the neck. It is nearer the lower than the upper ends of the lobes which it connects.

The **pyramidal lobe** is an elongated, slender process which frequently springs from the upper border of the isthmus on one or other side of the median plane (more usually the left). It extends superiorly towards the hyoid bone, and may be attached to it by a narrow slip of muscle, the **levator glandulae thyroideae,** or a fibrous strand. This strand is the remnant of the **thyroglossal duct,** from which the greater part of the thyroid gland is developed. It originates as an epithelial downgrowth from the region of the foramen caecum in the tongue, and passing inferiorly, anterior to the body of the hyoid, hooks up posterior to it and descends in the midline of the neck to expand into the thyroid gland. The suprahyoid part of this structure only rarely persists as a rudiment.

Blood Supply

Arteries. This is a very vascular gland. At the apex of each lobe the superior thyroid artery divides into two or three branches. The inferior thyroid artery sends its branches to the basal part and deep surface of the lobe. An occasional small artery (**thyroidea ima**) may arise from the brachiocephalic trunk, or the left common carotid artery, or the aortic arch. It ascends to the isthmus over the anterior surface of the trachea. The various arteries anastomose freely on the surface of the lobe (especially posteriorly); but there is little anastomosis across the median plane except for a branch of the superior thyroid artery which runs along the upper border of the isthmus, and joins with the same artery of the opposite side.

110

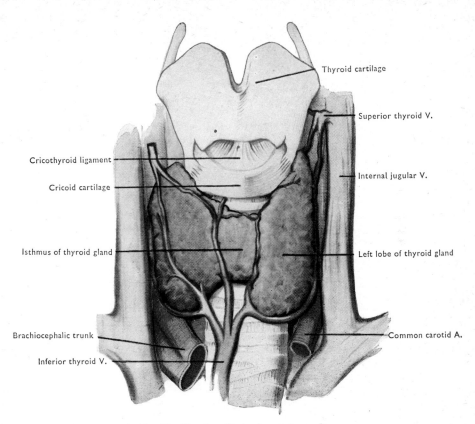

FIG. 82 The thyroid gland, anterior surface.

Labels (clockwise from top):
Thyroid cartilage
Superior thyroid V.
Internal jugular V.
Left lobe of thyroid gland
Common carotid A.
Inferior thyroid V.
Brachiocephalic trunk
Isthmus of thyroid gland
Cricoid cartilage
Cricothyroid ligament

Veins. Three pairs of veins drain the venous network on the superficial surface of the gland, but the main tributaries emerge from its substance through its deep surface.

The **superior thyroid vein** arises near the upper end of the lobe, and either crosses the common carotid to join the internal jugular vein, or ascends with the superior thyroid artery to the facial vein. It drains the territory supplied by the superior thyroid artery. The **middle thyroid vein** is very short. It arises near the lower end of the lobe, and crossing the common carotid, enters the internal jugular vein. The **inferior thyroid veins** arise from the network on the isthmus or from its inferior continuation. They descend side by side into the thorax on the anterior surface of the trachea, and inclining to the right, each ends in the corresponding brachiocephalic vein close to the junction of these veins. Occasionally they form a single stem [FIG. 82] which ends in one or other of the brachiocephalic veins. They receive tributaries from the larynx, trachea, and oesophagus.

Nerve Supply

It is supplied by branches from the cervical ganglia of the sympathetic trunk and from the cardiac and laryngeal branches of the vagus.

DISSECTION. Divide the isthmus. Cut the vessels of one lobe and remove it. Examine the posterior surface of this lobe, and note a longitudinal anastomotic

111

vessel between the superior and inferior thyroid arteries towards the medial side. Look for the yellowish brown parathyroid glands immediately lateral to that anastomotic vessel.

Structure and Function

Examine the cut surface of the gland with a hand lens. It is composed of a large number of closed vesicles which are held together by a stroma of delicate, highly vascular fibrous tissue. Each vesicle is filled with a semi-liquid colloid substance, coagulated by preservatives, in which the active principle of the gland is stored in normal circumstances. The vesicles vary greatly in size (normally up to 1 mm. in diameter) and many are visible to the unaided eye. The active principle of the gland contains iodine, is known as thyroxin, and is a powerful stimulant of the metabolism of the body. Accumulation of colloid occurs in the inactive gland, but it disappears during excessive activity of the organ (hyperthyroidism); the cuboidal cells lining the vesicles release the active principle into the surrounding capillaries.

Lymph Vessels

The lymph vessels drain mostly to nodes on the surface of the gland, on the front and sides

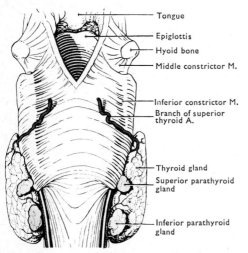

FIG. 83 Posterior surface of the thyroid gland to show the parathyroid glands.

Tongue
Epiglottis
Hyoid bone
Middle constrictor M.
Inferior constrictor M.
Branch of superior thyroid A.
Thyroid gland
Superior parathyroid gland
Inferior parathyroid gland

of the trachea, and on the carotid sheath (deep cervical nodes). Occasionally some pass from the apex of the lobe to a retropharyngeal node; others may descend into the thorax with the inferior thyroid veins and end in a mediastinal node. Yet others may pass to the thoracic duct, or even directly into the internal jugular vein without passing through a lymph node.

PARATHYROID GLANDS

These are two pairs of small (approximately $6 \times 3 \times 2$ mm.) yellowish brown ductless glands, which are embedded in the posterior surface of the capsule of the thyroid gland; one pair in each lobe. Their secretion has an importance quite out of proportion to their small size, for it is effective in stimulating the mobilization of calcium from the bones to maintain the normal blood calcium level. Thus overactivity of these glands leads to demineralization of the bones, while underactivity is associated with a low blood calcium which, if severe, can lead to a condition known as tetany in which there are extensive muscle spasms.

The **superior** parathyroid is the more constant in position, and is therefore more readily found. It lies about the middle of the posterior surface of the lobe, while the **inferior** parathyroid is close to the inferior surface of the lobe, and may even lie some distance below it. The reason for this variability is that the inferior parathyroid develops with the thymus, and usually leaves it to become attached to the thyroid as the thymus descends into the thorax; occasionally it may pass into the thorax with the thymus. The best guide to the parathyroids is the small individual twig which the inferior thyroid artery gives to each.

The parathyroid glands consist of clumps of small cells divided into columns by sinusoidal capillaries.

DISSECTION. Complete the cleaning of the trachea and oesophagus, and examine their relations.

TRACHEA AND OESOPHAGUS

Both these structures begin at the level of the cricoid cartilage, anterior to the sixth cervical vertebra, and descend into the thorax.

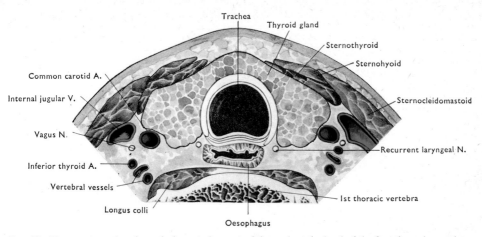

FIG. 84   Transverse section through the anterior part of the neck at the level of the first thoracic vertebra.

Trachea or Windpipe

This is a wide tube (approximately 12 cm. in length) kept constantly patent by the curved cartilaginous bars embedded in its walls. Posteriorly, the bars are deficient where it lies against the oesophagus, and here the wall is flat and composed of smooth muscle and connective tissue. Superiorly, the trachea is continuous with the larynx, and lies in the median plane of the neck. Anterior relations, see page 80. Laterally are the common carotid arteries and the lobes of the thyroid gland, and on the right side the brachiocephalic trunk is related to its lower part. The recurrent laryngeal nerves ascend, one on each side, in the angle between the oesophagus and the trachea in the neck.

Oesophagus or Gullet

This is a thick, distensible, muscular tube (approximately 25 cm. long) which extends from the pharynx to the stomach [FIGS. 81, 83, 84, 88, 97] and is surrounded by loose connective tissue. In the neck it lies between the trachea and the anterior longitudinal ligament on the vertebrae, and overlaps the longus colli muscles. On the right, it is in contact with the cervical pleura at the root of the neck, and the thyroid gland at a higher level. On the left, the subclavian artery and thoracic

duct separate it from the pleura, but superiorly its relations are the same as on the right side. As it descends it inclines to the left [FIG. 84]; thus it is more closely related to the thyroid gland on that side, and is more readily accessible to the surgeon.

DISSECTION. Remove the carotid sheath, fat, and lymph nodes from the common carotid artery and the internal jugular vein, and find the vagus nerve between them. Clean the vagus and find the right recurrent laryngeal nerve arising from it as it crosses the subclavian artery; follow it around that artery to the groove between the trachea and oesophagus. On the left side, find the thoracic duct, first behind the common carotid artery and internal jugular vein and then curving inferiorly anterior to the subclavian artery.

On both sides, clean the cervical part of the brachiocephalic vein and its tributaries. On the right side, clean the small part of the brachiocephalic trunk which lies in the neck.

Identify the phrenic nerve and trace it inferiorly till it enters the thorax.

Displace the internal jugular vein medially, and clean the part of the subclavian artery thus exposed, and the cervical pleura above and below it. Avoid injury to the thoracic duct (left side) and the vertebral veins. Trace the internal thoracic artery inferiorly from the subclavian. Identify the thyrocervical trunk arising from the anterior surface of the subclavian artery, and clean its suprascapular, transverse cervical, and inferior thyroid branches.

113

Pull scalenus anterior laterally and find the costo-cervical trunk which arises from the subclavian artery close to the medial margin of the muscle. Follow the trunk over the cervical pleura to the neck of the first rib.

Separate the internal jugular vein and the common carotid artery, and, avoiding injury to the vertebral veins and the thoracic duct, clean the vertebral artery posterior to them. Trace the vertebral artery superiorly from the subclavian. It passes anterior to the transverse process of the seventh cervical vertebra and disappears into the transverse process of the sixth. Clean out the fatty tissue posterior to the vertebral artery, and expose the ventral rami of the seventh and eighth cervical nerves, respectively above and below the seventh transverse process.

Displace the common carotid artery laterally, and find the sympathetic trunk posterior to it. Trace the trunk superiorly and inferiorly, and find the cervico-thoracic ganglion between the seventh transverse process and the neck of the first rib (posterior to the vertebral artery). Find also the tiny middle cervical ganglion on the inferior thyroid artery close to the sixth transverse process. Note the grey rami communicantes passing from the ganglia to the ventral rami of the spinal nerves.

BRACHIOCEPHALIC TRUNK

This great artery arises from the arch of the aorta in the thorax, passes superiorly and to the right, and divides into the right subclavian and common carotid arteries behind the upper margin of the right sternoclavicular joint. The part posterior to the joint is separated from it by the sternohyoid and sternothyroid muscles, and lies between the trachea and the right brachiocephalic vein. It is separated from the pleura posteriorly by some fat, in which the right vagus descends obliquely to the trachea.

SUBCLAVIAN ARTERY

This is the artery of the upper limb, but it supplies a considerable part of the neck and the brain through its branches.

On the left it arises from the arch of the aorta and ascends on the parietal pleura to enter the neck posterior to the sternoclavicular joint. On the right it arises from the brachio-cephalic trunk posterior to the sternoclavicular joint. On each side it arches laterally across the anterior surface of the cervical pleura and the first rib, and behind the scalenus anterior. At the outer border of the first rib it becomes the axillary artery.

For descriptive purposes the artery is divided into three parts, the second of which lies posterior to scalenus anterior. The short, third part has been described already [p. 19].

First Part

On the right, this part extends supero-laterally to a point 1 cm. above the level of the clavicle at the medial edge of scalenus anterior. It lies deeply, and is covered anteriorly by sternocleidomastoid, sternohyoid, and sterno-thyroid, and by the internal jugular and vertebral veins at the medial border of scalenus anterior. Running across it anteriorly are the vagus (which sends the recurrent laryngeal nerve hooking round it), a loop from the sympathetic trunk (**ansa subclavia**), and, occasionally, the cardiac branches of the vagus and sympathetic passing to the thorax.

It arches over the anterior surface of the cervical pleura, but is separated from it by the suprapleural membrane [p. 120]. If the lung has already been removed, investigate the position of the artery from the thoracic side.

The first part of the left subclavian ascends vertically from the aortic arch to the sterno-clavicular joint. Thereafter the course and relations are the same as on the right side, except that, posterior to the sternoclavicular joint, the nerves lie parallel to the artery which is crossed by the left brachiocephalic vein, and the phrenic nerve and the thoracic duct descend anterior to it close to scalenus anterior [FIG. 85]. Also, the left recurrent laryngeal nerve hooks round the aorta and so is medial to the artery.

Second Part

This is the summit of the arch of the artery, and rises 1·5–2·5 cm. above the level of the clavicle. Anteriorly, it is covered by the scalenus anterior and, on the right side, the phrenic nerve is anterior to the muscle. Posteriorly and inferiorly, the artery is in contact with the suprapleural membrane which separates it from the pleura.

The subclavian vein is described on page 19, but it should be noted that the external jugular vein is its only tributary; the veins which

114

accompany the branches of the subclavian artery do not end in the subclavian vein, though blood from the transverse cervical and suprascapular veins reaches it through the external jugular vein.

Branches of the Subclavian Artery

From the first part:
(1) Vertebral
(2) Thyrocervical
{ Inferior thyroid
Transverse cervical
Suprascapular
(3) Internal thoracic

From the second part:
Costocervical
{ Highest intercostal
Deep cervical

A branch of considerable size may arise from the third part of the subclavian artery. Usually this replaces the deep branch of the transverse cervical artery and is called the **descending scapular artery**, while the branch from the thyrocervical trunk forms only the superficial branch of the transverse cervical artery; it is then called the **superficial cervical artery.**

Vertebral Artery [FIGS. 86, 100]

This is the first branch of the subclavian. It arises opposite the upper part of the sterno-clavicular joint, and ascends into the angle between the longus colli and scalenus anterior muscles, passing into the foramen transversarium of the sixth cervical vertebra. It is deeply placed posterior to the common carotid artery and its own vein, and runs anterior to the ventral rami of the seventh and eighth cervical nerves with the seventh transverse process between them. The sympathetic trunk lies along its medial side, and the cervicothoracic ganglion, which is partly behind it, sends branches to form a plexus on the artery. It is crossed anteriorly by the thoracic duct on the left, and by the inferior thyroid artery immediately below the sixth vertebra on both sides.

The **vertebral vein** issues from the foramen transversarium of the sixth cervical vertebra. It descends posterior to the internal jugular

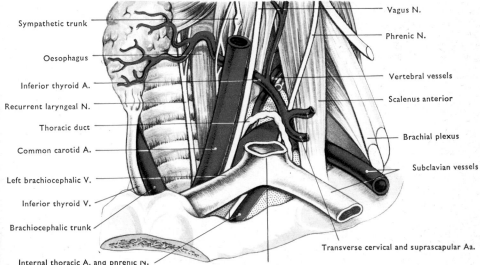

Sympathetic trunk	Vagus N.
Oesophagus	Phrenic N.
Inferior thyroid A.	Vertebral vessels
Recurrent laryngeal N.	Scalenus anterior
Thoracic duct	
Common carotid A.	Brachial plexus
Left brachiocephalic V.	Subclavian vessels
Inferior thyroid V.	
Brachiocephalic trunk	
	Transverse cervical and suprascapular Aa.
Internal thoracic A. and phrenic N.	
	internal jugular V.

FIG. 85   Deep dissection of the root of the neck on the left side. The clavicle, sternocleidomastoid, and infrahyoid muscles have been removed, and the thyroid gland is displaced anteriorly. Pleura, blue stipple.

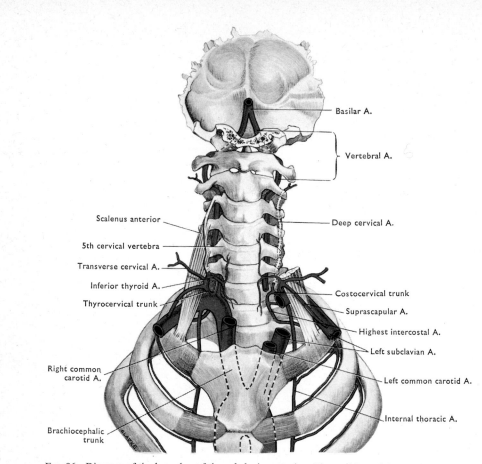

Basilar A.

Vertebral A.

Scalenus anterior

Deep cervical A.

5th cervical vertebra

Transverse cervical A.

Inferior thyroid A.

Costocervical trunk

Thyrocervical trunk

Suprascapular A.

Highest intercostal A.

Left subclavian A.

Right common
carotid A.

Left common carotid A.

Internal thoracic A.

Brachiocephalic
trunk

FIG. 86   Diagram of the branches of the subclavian arteries. The position of the left deep cervical
artery is shown though it is completely hidden from view as it lies deep among the muscles of the
back of the neck.

vein, and opens into the brachiocephalic vein
close to its formation.

Thyrocervical Trunk [Figs. 85, 86]

This short, wide vessel springs from the
anterior surface of the subclavian close to
the medial margin of scalenus anterior, and
posterior to the internal jugular vein, between
phrenic and vagus nerves. It branches immediately into (1) suprascapular and (2)
transverse cervical arteries, which are described on page 19, and (3) the **inferior thyroid**

artery which ascends for a short distance along
the medial border of scalenus anterior, posterior to the internal jugular vein. At the
level of the cricoid cartilage, it turns medially,
and crossing the vertebral artery, passes
posterior to the vagus, sympathetic trunk, and
common carotid artery to reach the middle
of the posterior surface of the thyroid gland.
It next descends to the lower pole of the
gland, and gives off tracheal, oesophageal,
and glandular branches. The main glandular
branch ascends over the posterior surface of

116

e lobe of the gland. No vein accompanies
ie artery.

The **ascending cervical artery** is a small
ranch which ascends anterior to the trans-
erse processes. It gives branches to the pre-
rtebral muscles, and spinal branches to the
rtebral canal along the spinal nerves.

The **inferior laryngeal artery** is a small
ranch which accompanies the recurrent
ryngeal nerve to the larynx.

Small irregular twigs supply the trachea,
esophagus, pharynx, and adjacent muscles.

The main glandular branch supplies the
arathyroid glands on its way to anastomose
ith the superior thyroid artery.

ternal Thoracic Artery [FIG. 88]

This long artery arises from the inferior
rface of the subclavian near the medial
order of scalenus anterior. It passes infero-
edially and enters the thorax posterior to the
rst costal cartilage after a short cervical
ourse. In the neck it lies on the pleura behind
ie medial part of the clavicle. The left artery
posterior to the junction of the subclavian
id brachiocephalic veins, while the right
rtery is posterior to the internal jugular and
rachiocephalic veins, which lie in a straight
ne. The phrenic nerve passes obliquely
ross the artery, usually anterior to it.

The **internal thoracic vein** joins the brachio-
ephalic vein at the superior aperture of the
iorax.

ostocervical Trunk [FIG. 86]

It arises from the posterior surface of the
ibclavian artery opposite the thyrocervical
unk. It arches posteriorly over the pleura
id divides into two branches at the neck of
ie first rib.

1. The **deep cervical artery** passes posteriorly
etween the transverse process of the seventh
ervical vertebra and the neck of the first rib
. 25]. The corresponding **deep cervical vein**
, a large vessel which joins the vertebral
ein.

2. The **highest intercostal artery** descends
nterior to the neck of the first rib, between
the first thoracic nerve and the cervicothoracic
ganglion of the sympathetic trunk. It gives the
posterior intercostal arteries to the first and
second intercostal spaces. If the lung has been
removed, examine these from the interior of
the thorax.

BRACHIOCEPHALIC VEINS

The brachiocephalic veins collect the blood
from the head and neck, the upper limbs, the
walls of the thorax, and even from the anterior
wall of the abdomen (internal thoracic veins).
They lie in the neck and in the thorax, and they
end by joining to form the superior vena cava
opposite the lower border of the right first
costal cartilage behind the margin of the
sternum. They have no valves. Each brachiocephalic vein begins by the union of the internal jugular vein with the subclavian vein,
between the cervical pleura and the medial
part of the clavicle [FIG. 88].

The **right vein** descends, with a slight medial
inclination, to enter the thorax behind the
first costal cartilage. It lies on the cervical
pleura, with the phrenic nerve and the internal
thoracic artery between it and the pleura. It
is lateral to the brachiocephalic trunk, with
the vagus behind and between them, while
anterior to it are the sternohyoid and sternothyroid muscles, the clavicle, and the costo-
clavicular ligament.

The **left brachiocephalic vein** crosses the
median plane posterior to the upper part of
the manubrium to join the right vein, and is
therefore much longer than it. In the neck, the
left vein is at first posterior to the clavicle, and
then to the sternoclavicular joint with the
sternohyoid and sternothyroid muscles. In
the first position it lies anterior to the pleura
and internal thoracic artery, and, in the second,
is anterior to the phrenic and vagus nerves
with the ascending part of the left subclavian
and common carotid arteries [FIG. 87].

Tributaries in the Neck

Both brachiocephalic veins receive the vertebral and highest intercostal veins, and one
or two lymph trunks. In addition the left vein
receives the thoracic duct.

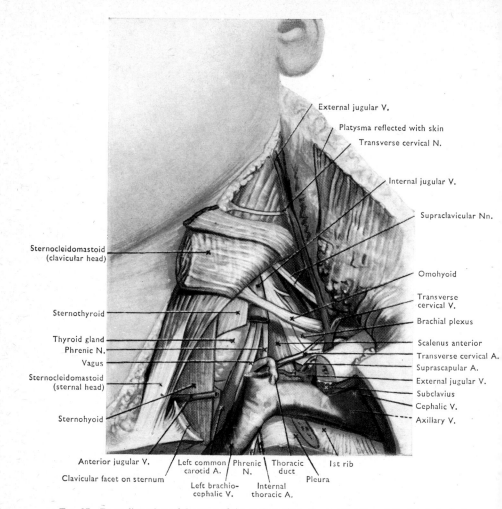

External jugular V.

Platysma reflected with skin

Transverse cervical N.

Internal jugular V.

Supraclavicular Nn.

Sternocleidomastoid (clavicular head)

Omohyoid

Transverse cervical V.

Brachial plexus

Sternothyroid

Thyroid gland
Phrenic N.
Vagus

Scalenus anterior

Transverse cervical A.

Suprascapular A.

Sternocleidomastoid (sternal head)

External jugular V.

Subclavius

Cephalic V.

Sternohyoid

Axillary V.

Anterior jugular V.

Clavicular facet on sternum

Left common carotid A.

Left brachio-cephalic V.

Phrenic N.

Internal thoracic A.

Thoracic duct

Pleura

1st rib

Fig. 87   Deep dissection of the root of the neck to show the termination of the thoracic duct.

THORACIC DUCT

This is the vessel through which lymph from both sides of the body below the diaphragm (except the upper part of the right lobe of the liver and the upper right quarter of the abdomen) and from the left half of the body above the diaphragm may be drained into the venous system. More usually one or more of the three lymph trunks which drain the upper part of each half of the body enters the veins separately. The lymph in the thoracic duct has a milky appearance owing to the fat containing lymph (chyle) which enters it from the small intestine.

The thoracic duct is a slender, thin-walled vessel which is frequently mistaken for a vein. It ascends from the thorax along the left margin of the oesophagus, and, at the level of the seventh cervical vertebra, arches laterally between the carotid sheath and the cervical

118

leura. It then turns inferiorly, and passing
nterior to the subclavian artery, ends by
pening into the brachiocephalic vein in the
ngle between the internal jugular and sub-
lavian veins [FIGS. 87, 88]. Its opening is
uarded by a valve, but the proximal part is
ften filled with blood in the cadaver.

There are three other **terminal lymph trunks**
a the root of the neck on each side. (1) The
ubclavian trunk drains the upper limb; (2)
ne **jugular** trunk drains half of the head and
eck; (3) the **bronchomediastinal** trunk drains
ne lung, half the mediastinum, and, through
ne internal thoracic tributary, part of the an-
erior wall of the thorax and abdomen. None
f these trunks is visible in an ordinary dissec-
on, and their mode of termination is extreme-
y variable, but a common arrangement is:

1. On the **left side,** the jugular trunk ends
a the thoracic duct with the other two trunks.
But the subclavian trunk often ends in the
ubclavian vein, and the bronchomediastinal
runk usually ends in the brachiocephalic vein.

2. On the **right side,** the three trunks commonly end in the internal jugular, subclavian,
and brachiocephalic veins respectively. But
the subclavian and jugular trunks frequently
unite to form the **right lymph duct,** and this
enters the venous system at a point corresponding to that of the thoracic duct on the left side.
It is uncommon for the right bronchomediastinal trunk to join the right lymph duct.

CERVICAL PLEURA
[FIGS. 85, 88]

The pleural sac on each side, with the apex
of the lung, bulges upwards into the root of
the neck for a variable distance. Its height
varies from 2·5–5·0 cm. above the sternal end
of the first rib, though posteriorly it usually
reaches to the level of the neck of the first
rib, the variability anteriorly depending on the
the degree of obliquity of the superior aperture
of the thorax. The cervical pleura forms the
dome of each pleural cavity, and is strengthened by a membrane which arises from the

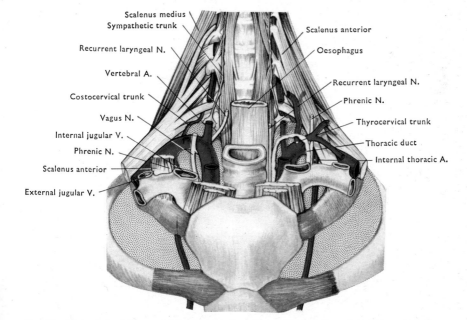

Scalenus medius
Sympathetic trunk
Recurrent laryngeal N.
Vertebral A.
Costocervical trunk
Vagus N.
Internal jugular V.
Phrenic N.
Scalenus anterior
External jugular V.

Scalenus anterior
Oesophagus
Recurrent laryngeal N.
Phrenic N.
Thyrocervical trunk
Thoracic duct
Internal thoracic A.

FIG. 88 Dissection of the root of the neck to show the structures adjacent to the cervical pleura
(blue stipple).

transverse process of the seventh cervical vertebra, and spreads over the pleura like a fan to be attached to the inner margin of the first rib, the **suprapleural membrane.** It may contain muscle fibres, the **scalenus minimus.**

Posterior to the cervical pleura lie the first two ribs and intercostal spaces, and the sympathetic trunk; while anterior to it are the great vessels of the upper limb and head and neck. Superiorly, the space occupied by the cervical pleura disappears as the carotid sheath comes to lie on the prevertebral muscles and sympathetic trunk.

Medial to the cervical pleura are the oesophagus and vertebral bodies, with the thoracic duct and recurrent laryngeal nerve on the left, and the trachea further anteriorly. Laterally, is the scalenus anterior with the subclavian artery and the lower trunk of the brachial plexus behind it. Because the subclavian artery lies on the anterior surface of the cervical pleura, its ascending (vertebral and inferior thyroid) and descending (internal thoracic) branches run over that surface, while the costo-cervical trunk and its highest intercostal branch arch over the apex of the pleura from the anterior to the posterior surface.

COMMON CAROTID ARTERY

The right common carotid arises from the brachiocephalic trunk behind the sterno-

clavicular joint. The left artery arises from the arch of the aorta, and ascends to enter th neck posterior to the left sternoclavicular join

From the sternoclavicular joint each arter ascends, with a slight posterolateral inclina tion, to the upper border of the thyroid car tilage (opposite the disc between the thir and fourth cervical vertebrae) where it divide into the internal and external carotid arterie These are its only branches.

It is enclosed in the **carotid sheath** [FIG. 90] a fascial condensation which also surround the internal jugular vein, the vagus nerve, an the ansa cervicalis. The vein overlaps the arter anterolaterally, and the vagus is postero intermediate in position.

Posterior Relations. The artery ascends o the cervical transverse processes, but is sepa rated from them by the prevertebral muscle the prevertebral fascia, and the sympatheti trunk. In addition the vertebral artery inter venes between the carotid artery and th seventh transverse process, and the inferio thyroid artery separates it from the sixt transverse process. The recurrent laryngea nerve passes posterior to the right artery jus above its origin, and the thoracic duct turn laterally between the left artery and the verte bral artery.

Anterior Relations. In its lower part it i covered by the sternocleidomastoid, sterno

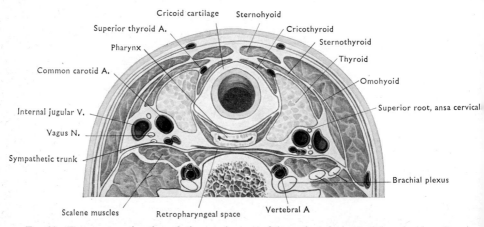

FIG. 89   Transverse section through the anterior part of the neck at the level of the cricoid cartilage.

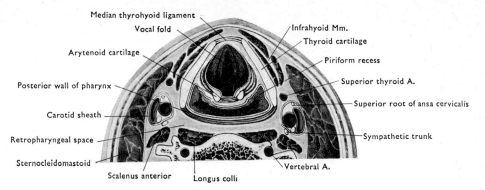

Fig. 90 Transverse section through the anterior part of the neck at the level of the upper part of the thyroid cartilage.

hyoid, sternothyroid, and omohyoid muscles, and is overlapped by the thyroid gland and ansa cervicalis posterior to these muscles. At the root of the neck the left artery lies posterior to the sternoclavicular joint, with the sternothyroid and sternohyoid muscles and the brachiocephalic vein between. In the carotid triangle, it is covered by deep fascia and is overlapped by the anterior border of sternocleidomastoid.

Medial Relations. Inferiorly, it is related to the oesophagus and trachea, with the recurrent laryngeal nerve between them. Superiorly, it is related to the larynx and pharynx. The lobe of the thyroid gland is either medial to the artery, or overlaps it anteriorly [Figs. 81, 89].

Carotid Sinus and Carotid Body

The carotid sinus is a slight dilatation of the upper part of the common carotid and the adjacent part of the internal carotid artery. The wall of this dilatation is more elastic than the rest of the arteries, and is heavily innervated. It is a pressure receptor, and distension of the wall stimulates the nerve endings and leads to a reflex slowing of the heart and a fall in blood pressure.

The carotid body is a small gland-like structure placed on the deep surface of the carotid bifurcation; it may be seen by twisting the arteries round and cleaning between them.

It consists of clusters of epithelial-like cells arranged around capillaries. Both sinus and body are innervated principally by the glossopharyngeal nerve through its branch, the **carotid sinus nerve,** but they are also supplied by the vagus and the sympathetic. The carotid body responds either to decreased oxygen tension or increased carbon dioxide tension in the blood. It gives rise to afferent discharge in the sensory nerve fibres, and these induce the appropriate reflex changes in respiration.

THE VESSELS AND NERVES IN THE UPPER PART OF THE NECK

DISSECTION. The external carotid artery and its branches have been partly or wholly dissected already. Identify its branches again, and complete the cleaning of any not yet fully traced. Lift up the sternocleidomastoid and follow the occipital artery deep to it. Push the posterior belly of the digastric out of the way, and clean the part of the external carotid artery which it conceals.

EXTERNAL CAROTID ARTERY

This terminal branch of the common carotid artery is so named because it supplies structures external to the skull.

It extends posterosuperiorly from the level of the upper border of the thyroid cartilage to a point between the neck of the mandible and the lobule of the auricle. Here it divides into

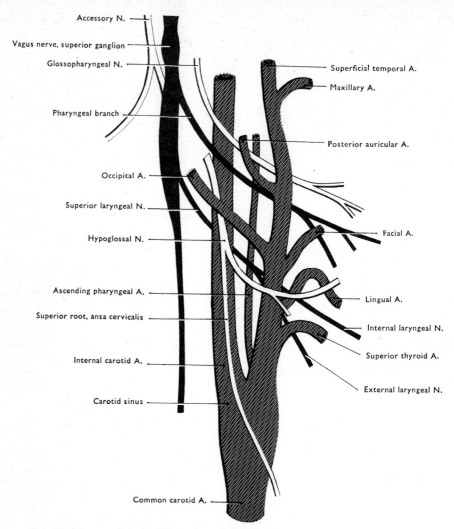

Accessory N.

Vagus nerve, superior ganglion

Glossopharyngeal N.

Pharyngeal branch

Occipital A.

Superior laryngeal N.

Hypoglossal N.

Ascending pharyngeal A.

Superior root, ansa cervicalis

Internal carotid A.

Carotid sinus

Common carotid A.

Superficial temporal A.

Maxillary A.

Posterior auricular A.

Facial A.

Lingual A.

Internal laryngeal N.

Superior thyroid A.

External laryngeal N.

FIG. 91 Diagram of the carotid arteries and the nerves associated with them in the neck.

the superficial temporal and maxillary arteries. At first it is superficially placed, anteromedial to the internal carotid artery. It then passes deep to the posterior belly of digastric and the stylohyoid muscle, superior to which it enters a deep groove in the parotid, and ends between the gland and the neck of the mandible [FIG. 92].

Superficial Relations. In the carotid triangle it is crossed by branches of the transverse nerve of the neck and the cervical branch of the facial nerve in the superficial fascia, and by the facial and lingual veins and the hypoglossal nerve beneath the deep fascia. Superior to the triangle it is overlapped by the angle of the mandible, and crossed by the posterior belly of digastric and the stylohyoid. In the parotid gland, it is deep to the retromandibular vein, and both vessels are deep to the branches of the facial nerve.

Deep Relations. In the carotid triangle, it lies on the lateral aspect of the pharynx with the branches of the superior laryngeal nerve intervening. The deep relations superior to this will be seen later.

The **external carotid plexus** is a net of sympathetic nerve fibres around the external carotid artery. These fibres are derived from the superior cervical ganglion of the sympathetic trunk, and they are distributed along all the branches of the artery.

Branches of External Carotid Artery [see also pp. 9, 39, 92, 102, 107]

Superior Thyroid Artery. This artery arises from the anterior surface of the external carotid close to its origin. It runs antero-inferiorly, deep to the infrahyoid muscles, and breaks into three terminal branches at the apex of the lobe of the thyroid gland. In addition it gives a number of small muscular branches and:

The **infrahyoid artery** is a small branch which runs along the lower border of the hyoid bone.

The **superior laryngeal artery** is a larger vessel [FIGS. 73, 92] which enters the pharynx by piercing the thyrohyoid membrane with the internal branch of the superior laryngeal nerve, and descends to the larynx.

The **sternocleidomastoid branch** is a small vessel which runs postero-inferiorly across the carotid sheath.

The **cricothyroid branch** arises deep to the sternothyroid muscle, runs anteriorly across the cricothyroid muscle, and anastomoses with its fellow on the cricothyroid membrane.

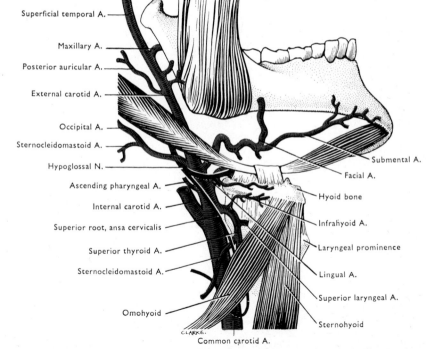

FIG. 92 Diagram of the external carotid artery and its branches. The mandible has been tilted upwards.

123

Occipital Artery. This artery arises from the posterior surface of the external carotid artery opposite the origin of the facial branch. It runs along the lower border of the posterior belly of digastric, under cover of sternocleidomastoid, to reach and groove the base of the skull medial to the origin of the posterior belly of digastric. Its further course is described on pages 9 and 25. In its course to the base of the skull, it crosses the internal carotid artery, the hypoglossal nerve which hooks anteriorly around its origin, the internal jugular vein, and the accessory nerve.

Branches. Several muscular twigs, one of which runs with the accessory nerve to sternocleidomastoid. A meningeal branch which accompanies the internal jugular vein through the jugular foramen.

Posterior Auricular Artery. This small branch arises from the posterior surface of the external carotid at the superior border of the posterior belly of digastric. It runs along this muscle, and passing superficial to the mastoid process, accompanies the posterior auricular nerve [p. 8]. It supplies the adjacent muscles and the parotid gland, and sends a stylomastoid branch superiorly into the stylomastoid foramen [FIG. 93] to supply the facial nerve and structures within the temporal bone.

DISSECTION. Divide the posterior belly of the digastric close to its origin. Turn it antero-inferiorly, and clean the stylopharyngeus, avoiding damage to the glossopharyngeal nerve which forms a spiral round it. If necessary to obtain proper exposure, cut the occipital and posterior auricular arteries.

At the posterior part of the thyrohyoid interval, clean the margins of the middle and inferior constrictor muscles, and expose the lowest part of stylopharyngeus through the aperture between them [Fig. 111].

STYLOPHARYNGEUS

The longest of the three styloid muscles, stylopharyngeus arises from the medial surface of the styloid process close to its root, and runs antero-inferiorly, between the external and internal carotid arteries, to the lateral wall of the pharynx. It then passes obliquely through the pharyngeal wall between the

superior and middle constrictor muscles [FIG. 111], and deep to the latter, blends with the anterior fibres of palatopharyngeus, with which some of its fibres are inserted into the posterior margin of the lamina of the thyroid cartilage, the remainder passing mainly into the lateral aspect of the epiglottis.

Nerve supply: the glossopharyngeal nerve. Action: it helps to lift the larynx during swallowing and phonation.

THE VESSELS AND NERVES AT THE BASE OF THE SKULL

The following dissection is designed to expose the superior parts of the internal carotid artery and the internal jugular vein, together with the last four cranial nerves, which are all close together in a dense mass of connective tissue in the angle between the anterior surface of the vertebral column and the base of the skull. Before beginning the dissection, identify the carotid canal, jugular foramen, and hypoglossal canal on the base of a dried skull [FIG. 93], and compare the openings of these foramina on its internal [FIG. 39] and external surfaces. The carotid canal, which transmits the internal carotid artery with a plexus of sympathetic nerves and small veins, lies furthest anteriorly. Immediately posterior to it is the jugular foramen which transmits the sigmoid sinus, the inferior petrosal sinus, and the glossopharyngeal, vagus, and accessory nerves between the two veins. The hypoglossal canal transmits the hypoglossal nerve, and lies posteromedial to the jugular foramen. As it emerges, the hypoglossal nerve joins the other nerves, and forms a spiral round the vagus, adhering to it [FIG. 94]. Thus all the nerves lie in a tight bundle between the artery and vein close to the skull, but they separate inferiorly. The accessory runs postero-inferiorly, either superficial or deep to the internal jugular vein. The glossopharyngeal passes antero-inferiorly, lateral to the internal carotid. The hypoglossal leaves the vagus at a lower level and curves anteriorly superficial to both internal and external carotid arteries. The vagus

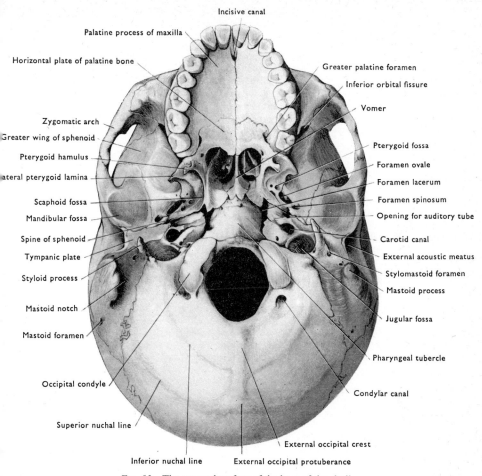

Incisive canal

Palatine process of maxilla

Horizontal plate of palatine bone

Greater palatine foramen

Inferior orbital fissure

Vomer

Zygomatic arch

Greater wing of sphenoid

Pterygoid hamulus

Lateral pterygoid lamina

Scaphoid fossa

Mandibular fossa

Spine of sphenoid

Tympanic plate

Styloid process

Mastoid notch

Mastoid foramen

Pterygoid fossa

Foramen ovale

Foramen lacerum

Foramen spinosum

Opening for auditory tube

Carotid canal

External acoustic meatus

Stylomastoid foramen

Mastoid process

Jugular fossa

Occipital condyle

Pharyngeal tubercle

Condylar canal

Superior nuchal line

Inferior nuchal line

External occipital crest

External occipital protuberance

FIG. 93   The external surface of the base of the skull.

descends vertically between the artery and vein in the carotid sheath.

DISSECTION. The dissectors of the two sides should co-operate in the following dissection as certain features are best shown on one or other side.

The dissection removes the right half of the skull, mandible, cervical viscera, and neurovascular bundle from the vertebral column. It facilitates the dissection of the deep structures of the upper part of the neck by allowing a posterior approach, and dissection of the nose, pharynx, larynx, and ear from the medial side.

On the right side only, free the greater occipital nerve from the scalp and turn it inferiorly. Divide the descending branch of the occipital artery and any muscular branches and veins which might prevent it being removed with the skull. If not already divided, free the great auricular, lesser occipital, and transverse nerve of the neck at their distal ends, and turn them towards their origins. In the suboccipital triangle, separate the superior oblique and rectus capitis posterior major and minor from their bony attachments and remove them, thus exposing the posterior atlanto-occipital membrane. Divide this membrane close to the skull but avoid damage to the vertebral arteries on the posterior arch

125

of the atlas. Detach the longissimus capitis from the skull without damaging the occipital artery which may lie on either side of the muscle.

Cut across the sternocleidomastoid 2–3 cm. above the clavicle, and turn it superiorly. Clean its deep surface to the skull and identify the accessory nerve entering it. Cut the nerve in the posterior triangle so that its superior part remains with the sternocleidomastoid, and divide any communications which the nerve may have with the cervical plexus.

Pass a finger behind the carotid sheath and pharynx, and separate them from the anterior surface of the vertebral column and sympathetic trunk as far superiorly as the superior cervical ganglion. Clean away all remnants of the parotid gland, and expose the lateral surface of the atlanto-occipital joint by dividing rectus capitis lateralis [Fig. 99] but avoid injury to the neurovascular bundle anterior to it and to the ventral ramus of the first cervical nerve on its medial side.

Saw through the mandible in the midline, and continue this cut with a knife, splitting the tongue and epiglottis in the median plane to the hyoid bone. Divide the hyoid in the midline, and extend the incision inferiorly through the larynx, pharynx, and trachea to the inferior border of the isthmus of the thyroid gland. Cut transversely through the right half of the trachea, oesophagus, and neurovascular bundle (sparing the sympathetic trunk, the phrenic nerve, and scalenus anterior) and separate them from the posterior structures, dividing the inferior thyroid artery.

Make a sagittal saw cut through the skull slightly to the right of the midline (so as to leave the nasal septum with the left half) and continue the cut to the foramen magnum without damage to the atlas. Within the skull, detach the membrana tectoria [Fig. 106] from the anterior margin of the foramen magnum and turn it inferiorly, thus exposing the alar ligaments and the longitudinal fibres of the cruciate ligament [Fig. 107]. Divide the right alar ligament, and flexing the right half of the head on the vertebral column, lever the right occipital condyle out of its articulation, and divide any remaining parts of the capsule together with rectus capitis anterior, longus capitis [Fig. 99] and, if necessary, part of the anterior atlanto-occipital membrane [Fig. 106].

Complete the division of the soft palate and the posterior pharyngeal wall with a knife. Lift the right half of the skull and attached structures off the left half and vertebral column, dividing the branches of the superior cervical ganglion which pass to join the cranial nerves and internal carotid artery, thus leaving the sympathetic trunk and ganglia on the vertebral column. Identify and divide the communication between the first cervical nerve and the hypoglossal nerve.

The upper part of the cervical neurovascular bundle can now be dissected from the posterior aspect on th right half.

On both sides, find the internal laryngeal branch o the superior laryngeal nerve, and trace it superiorly t its parent nerve and follow that nerve to the vagus Find the pharyngeal branch of the vagus (which arise from the vagus above the superior laryngeal nerve) an trace it inferomedially between the carotid arteries t the pharynx.

Trace the glossopharyngeal, vagus, accessory, an hypoglossal nerves superiorly. Separate the nerves fron each other and identify the connexions between then and the superior cervical ganglion and first cervica nerve on the left side.

Clean the internal carotid artery, and, on the left side displace it anteriorly to expose the superior cervica ganglion. This ganglion is a spindle-shaped body abou 2·5 cm. long. Identify the branches of the ganglio which pass posterior to the internal jugular vein to th upper four cervical nerves, and also its branches to th adjacent cranial nerves and the internal carotid artery

Define the margins of the longus capitis muscle, prevertebral muscle on which the artery and sympa thetic trunk lie.

Separate the carotid arteries and find the ascendin pharyngeal artery arising from the medial side of th external carotid artery near its origin. Follow th ascending pharyngeal artery superiorly on the side c the pharynx to the base of the skull, and clean th superior part of the ascending palatine artery.

Ascending Pharyngeal Artery

This is the first and smallest branch of th external carotid artery, and it ascends on th pharynx medial to the carotid arteries.

Its branches are: (1) **pharyngeal,** to pharynx auditory tube, tonsil and palate; (2) **muscular** to the prevertebral muscles; (3) **inferio tympanic,** a branch which passes with th tympanic branch of the glossopharyngea nerve to the middle ear; (4) **meningeal,** number of branches which pass through th foramen lacerum, jugular foramen, and hypo glossal canal.

INTERNAL CAROTID ARTERY

The internal carotid artery arises from th common carotid artery at the level of th upper border of the thyroid cartilage. I ascends almost vertically to the base of th skull, and enters the carotid canal, throug which it reaches the cranial cavity.

126

The **cervical part** lies on the longus capitis and the sympathetic trunk. The vagus lies posterolateral to it throughout this part, while the glossopharyngeal, accessory, and hypoglossal nerves bear a similar relation to it at the base of the skull. The artery lies between the internal jugular vein and the constrictors of the pharynx [Fig. 108].

Inferiorly it is overlapped by the sternocleidomastoid and is crossed by the lingual and facial veins, by the hypoglossal nerve and the occipital artery, and has the superior root of the ansa cervicalis anterior to it. As it ascends, it passes deep to the posterior belly of digastric, stylohyoid, stylopharyngeus and the styloid process (which separate it from the parotid gland). It then passes anterior to the internal jugular vein and enters the carotid canal.

Inferiorly, the external carotid artery lies anteromedial to the internal carotid, but superiorly it lies on the lateral side of the internal carotid, and is separated from it by: (1) The styloid process, the stylopharyngeus muscle and the glossopharyngeal nerve. (2) The pharyngeal branch of the vagus. (3) A portion of the parotid gland.

GLOSSOPHARYNGEAL NERVE

The ninth cranial nerve is a mixed nerve. Its motor fibres supply the stylopharyngeus; its parasympathetic fibres reach the parotid gland by a circuitous route; its sensory fibres arise in the cells of two small ganglia which lie in the jugular foramen on the trunk of the nerve, and their central branches end in the medulla oblongata.

Course. The nerve arises from the side of the upper medulla oblongata, passes through the anterior part of the jugular foramen in its own sheath of dura mater, between the sigmoid and inferior petrosal sinuses. Below the skull, it descends between the internal jugular vein and the internal carotid artery; curves round the lateral surface of stylopharyngeus, passing with it between the internal and external carotid arteries. It then runs anteriorly into the pharynx between the superior and middle constrictors, and passing deep to hyoglossus,

breaks up into its terminal branches. These supply sensory nerve fibres (including taste) to the posterior third of the tongue, the palatine tonsil, the soft palate, and the anterior surface of the epiglottis.

Branches. The **tympanic nerve** is a very slender branch which enters a minute canal on the ridge of bone between the jugular foramen and the carotid canal, and ascends to the middle ear, breaking up into the tympanic plexus on its medial wall. This plexus is joined by two minute caroticotympanic nerves from the sympathetic plexus around the internal carotid artery [Fig. 152]. The tympanic plexus supplies the mucous membrane of the middle ear, auditory tube, mastoid antrum, and mastoid air cells [Fig. 147], and it sends a root to the lesser petrosal nerve [p. 63] through which preganglionic parasympathetic fibres pass to the otic ganglion. These carry impulses which are eventually distributed to the parotid gland.

The **nerve to stylopharyngeus** is a small branch which supplies the muscle, and passes through it to the pharyngeal mucous membrane.

The **pharyngeal branches** are: (1) One or two twigs which pass to the pharyngeal mucous membrane through the superior constrictor. (2) A larger branch which arises more proximally and accompanies the pharyngeal branch of the vagus to the pharyngeal plexus. One of its branches joins a branch of the vagus and forms the **carotid sinus nerve** [p. 121] which supplies the carotid sinus and the carotid body.

VAGUS NERVE

The tenth cranial nerve is a mixed nerve which supplies structures from the inside of the skull to the abdomen. Its motor fibres to striated muscle pass to the pharynx, larynx and oesophagus. Its parasympathetic fibres are distributed to the heart, the respiratory system, a great part of the digestive system and its associated glands, and to the kidney. Its sensory fibres supply the dura mater, the skin of the external acoustic meatus, and the areas supplied by its efferent fibres. These

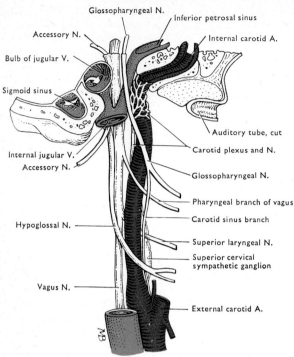

Glossopharyngeal N.

Inferior petrosal sinus

Accessory N.

Internal carotid A.

Bulb of jugular V.

Sigmoid sinus

Auditory tube, cut

Internal jugular V.

Carotid plexus and N.

Accessory N.

Glossopharyngeal N.

Pharyngeal branch of vagus

Carotid sinus branch

Hypoglossal N.

Superior laryngeal N.

Superior cervical
sympathetic ganglion

Vagus N.

External carotid A.

FIG. 94 Diagram of structures in and below the right jugular foramen.

sensory fibres arise in two ganglia situated on the trunk of the nerve.

Course

The vagus arises by a row of rootlets attached to the side of the medulla oblongata [FIG. 163]. It leaves the skull through the middle compartment of the jugular foramen in the same dural sheath as the accessory nerve, and descends vertically through the neck between and behind the internal jugular vein and, at first, the internal carotid artery, and subsequently the common carotid artery. All three structures are enclosed in the carotid sheath.

At the root of the neck, both vagi cross the anterior surface of the subclavian artery. The right vagus then descends posterior to the brachiocephalic vessels to reach the right side of the trachea in the thorax. The left vagus descends to the arch of the aorta between the subclavian and common carotid arteries, passing posterior to the left brachiocephalic vein.

Branches [FIGS. 91, 94]

It has numerous communications with the other nerves in the jugular foramen, and is joined by the cranial part of the accessory nerve which is distributed through the branches to the pharynx and larynx.

Meningeal Branch. This minute twig arises in the jugular foramen, and passes to the dura mater of the posterior cranial fossa.

Auricular Branch. This slender branch arises in the jugular foramen, and enters a tiny, horizontal canal in the lateral wall of the jugular fossa. This conducts it to the tympanomastoid fissure. It supplies the skin on the posterior aspect of the external acoustic meatus, and piercing the cartilage of the meatus supplies the cutaneous lining of its lower half and of the lower half of the tympanic membrane.

Pharyngeal Branch. It arises immediately below the skull, and runs antero-inferiorly between the carotid arteries, to reach the pharyngeal wall and form a large part of the **pharyngeal plexus.** The nerve may be double. The pharyngeal plexus is a mesh of fine nerve fibres in the fascia covering the middle constrictor muscle, and it is formed by branches of the vagus, glossopharyngeal, and superior cervical sympathetic ganglion. It supplies the muscles and mucous membrane of the pharynx and it communicates with the hypoglossal nerve.

Superior Laryngeal Nerve. This nerve is larger than the pharyngeal branch, and arises inferior to it. It runs antero-inferiorly, deep to both carotid arteries, and divides into:

1. The **internal branch** descends on the

128

lateral wall of the pharynx, meets the superior laryngeal artery, and together they pass deep to the thyrohyoid muscle and pierce the thyrohyoid membrane. They descend between the membrane and the mucous lining of the pharynx, to supply the mucous membrane of the larynx down to the vocal folds.

2. The **external branch** is very slender, and descends on the side of the pharynx deep to the carotid and superior thyroid arteries. It passes deep to the sternothyroid muscle and the thyroid gland, enters and supplies the cricothyroid muscle [FIG. 134] the only laryngeal muscle not supplied by the recurrent laryngeal nerve, and it sends branches to the inferior constrictor muscle [FIG. 111].

Cardiac Branches. Two slender cardiac branches arise from each vagus at variable points in the neck; one in the upper part, the other in the lower. They descend with the vagus to the root of the neck, and enter the thorax with the vagus on the left side, but pass posterior to the subclavian artery on the right. They are distributed to the cardiac plexuses.

Recurrent Laryngeal Nerve. The right nerve arises as the vagus crosses the first part of the subclavian artery: the left as the vagus crosses the arch of the aorta in the thorax. Each nerve hooks round the corresponding artery, and passes to the groove between the oesophagus and trachea; ascends in the groove deep to the lobe of the thyroid gland (either anterior or posterior to the branches of the inferior thyroid artery), and enters the larynx by passing deep to the inferior border of the inferior constrictor muscle. Within the larynx, it communicates with the internal laryngeal branch of the superior laryngeal nerve, and supplies all the intrinsic muscles except cricothyroid, and the mucous membrane below the level of the vocal fold. It also gives off cardiac branches near its origin; twigs to the trachea, oesophagus, and the inferior constrictor muscle.

ACCESSORY NERVE

The eleventh cranial nerve is mainly motor, and has two sets of roots: (1) The cranial roots emerge from the side of the medulla oblongata as a vertical row in series with those of the vagus, and in line with the dorsal rootlets of the cervical nerves. (2) The spinal rootlets arise from the upper five cervical segments of the spinal medulla, between the ligamentum denticulatum and the dorsal roots of the cervical nerves, the upper rootlets lying further posteriorly than the lower rootlets [FIG. 24]. The spinal rootlets unite and ascend through the foramen magnum, to be joined by the cranial rootlets within the skull [FIG. 163].

Course and Termination

The trunk of the nerve leaves the skull through the jugular foramen in the same dural sheath as the vagus. As the nerve leaves the foramen its cranial and spinal parts separate; the cranial part passing with the vagus to enter its pharyngeal and laryngeal branches.

The spinal part descends with the internal jugular vein, inclines posteriorly, either anterior or posterior to the vein, and crosses the tip of the transverse process of the atlas and the upper part of the carotid triangle. It then sinks into and supplies the sternocleidomastoid, and emerging from the middle of its posterior border, runs postero-inferiorly in the fascial roof of the posterior triangle, and disappears deep to trapezius, supplying it. The communicating branches which it receives from the ventral rami of the second to fourth cervical nerves are sensory to the sternocleidomastoid and trapezius.

HYPOGLOSSAL NERVE

This is a purely motor nerve which supplies styloglossus, hyoglossus, genioglossus, and the intrinsic muscles of the tongue. Some of its branches supply the geniohyoid and infrahyoid muscles, but these are composed of nerve fibres from the first cervical nerve which join the hypoglossal nerve as it leaves the skull, and run with it [FIG. 95].

Origin and Course

The hypoglossal nerve arises as a row of rootlets which emerge from the anterior surface of the medulla oblongata, and unite to form two roots which pierce the dura mater separately. They leave the skull through the hypoglossal canal, and, uniting at its external orifice, form the single nerve which inclines laterally to become adherent to the vagus and make a half spiral twist round it. The hypoglossal nerve then descends between the internal jugular vein and the internal carotid artery, and passing deep to the posterior belly of digastric, curves anteriorly round the root of the occipital artery to enter the anterior triangle of the neck [pp. 84, 107].

Branches

(1) A **meningeal branch** (composed of recurrent nerve fibres from the first cervical nerve) arises in the hypoglossal canal, and enters the cranial cavity through it. It supplies the dura mater around the foramen magnum. (2) A descending branch, the **superior root of the ansa cervicalis** (C. 1, p. 84). (3) The nerves to **thyrohyoid** and **geniohyoid** (C. 1, p. 84). (4) Branches to all the **intrinsic muscles of the tongue,** and to its extrinsic muscles except palatoglossus.

DISSECTION. Identify the cervicothoracic ganglion of the sympathetic trunk, and expose it completely by displacing the vertebral artery laterally. Clean the branches that arise in this ganglion, and also the branches of the other cervical sympathetic ganglia, demonstrating the grey rami communicantes to the cervical nerves on the right side.

SYMPATHETIC TRUNK

In the neck, this trunk runs almost vertically, lying posterior to the common and internal carotid arteries, on the longus colli and longus capitis muscles, opposite the roots of the transverse processes. Inferiorly it lies close to the medial side of the vertebral artery, and is crossed by the thoracic duct (on the left) and by the inferior thyroid artery. Usually this artery passes posterior to the trunk, but may pierce it.

Superiorly, the trunk ends in the superior cervical ganglion, but it is continued into the skull on the internal carotid artery as the **internal carotid nerve** [FIG. 94]. Inferiorly, it

enters the thorax across the neck of the first rib.

Ganglia and Rami Communicantes

All three cervical ganglia (superior, middle, and cervicothoracic) send grey rami communicantes to the ventral rami of the cervical nerves, but they receive no white rami from them. The grey rami may pass between the prevertebral muscles to reach the cervical nerves, or they may pierce these muscles or the scalenus anterior. Through the grey rami, the communications with the cranial nerves, and the branches passing to the major arteries, postganglionic sympathetic fibres are distributed to the head, neck, and upper limb.

Superior Cervical Ganglion. This is the largest ganglion of the trunk. It is about 2·5 cm. long, and lies between the internal carotid artery and the longus capitis, opposite the second and third cervical vertebrae.

Branches. (1) Communicating branches to the ninth, tenth, and twelfth cranial nerves. (2) **Grey rami communicantes** pass to the upper four cervical nerves. (3) The **internal carotid nerve** passes to the internal carotid artery and forms the internal carotid plexus around it. (4) **Laryngopharyngeal** branches pass medially to the pharyngeal plexus. (5) The **external carotid nerves** form a plexus around the external carotid artery and its branches. (6) The **superior cervical cardiac branch** is a slender nerve which descends with the common carotid artery to end in the superficial cardiac plexus on the left. On the right, it also runs with the common carotid artery, crosses anterior or posterior to the subclavian artery at the root of the neck, and runs posterior to the brachiocephalic artery to reach the deep cardiac plexus on the tracheal bifurcation.

Middle Cervical Ganglion. This small ganglion lies on the inferior thyroid artery at the level of the cricoid cartilage.

Branches. (1) **Grey rami communicantes** pass to the fifth and sixth cervical nerves. (2) **Thyroid branches** form a plexus on the inferior thyroid artery, and communicate with the recurrent and external laryngeal nerves. (3) The **middle cervical cardiac branch** is a slender nerve to the deep cardiac plexus. On the left, it runs between the subclavian and common carotid arteries to the trachea; on the right, it accompanies the superior cervical cardiac nerve. (4) The **ansa subclavia** is a slender branch which loops round the subclavian artery to join the cervicothoracic ganglion. It supplies the subclavian artery and sends nerve fibres to the phrenic nerve.

Cervicothoracic Ganglion. This ganglion may consist of one or two parts. When single, it represents the fused inferior cervical and first, or first and second thoracic ganglia. When there is a separate **inferior cervical ganglion** it is small and lies behind the common carotid and vertebral arteries, anterior to the eighth cervical nerve. When the ganglia are fused, the compound mass lies across the neck of the first rib, receives a white ramus communicans from the first thoracic ventral ramus, and sends a grey ramus to it and sometimes to the second thoracic ventral ramus also. When separate, the inferior cervical ganglion has the following **branches**, which also arise from the fused cervicothoracic ganglion.

(1) **Grey rami communicantes** pass to the seventh and eighth cervical ventral rami. (2) Fine filaments pass from the ansa subclavia to form the **subclavian plexus** on the subclavian artery. (3) Larger filaments form the **vertebral plexus** on the vertebral artery. (4) An **inferior cervical cardiac branch** passes with the middle cervical cardiac nerve to the deep cardiac plexus.

INTERNAL JUGULAR VEIN

This is usually the largest vein in the neck. It begins at the jugular foramen as the continuation of the sigmoid sinus [FIG. 94] and descends vertically through the neck applied to the lateral side of the internal and common carotid arteries, enclosed with them and the vagus in the carotid sheath [FIG. 90]. It ends posterior to the medial part of the clavicle by joining the subclavian vein to form the brachiocephalic vein. In the lower part of the neck, both veins deviate to the right. The left vein therefore overlaps the common carotid considerably, while the right vein recedes from it.

The upper end of the vein is dilated in the jugular fossa to form the **superior bulb,** the walls of which adhere to the fossa. Near the termination of the vein is a smaller dilatation, the **inferior bulb,** in association with which is a valve of two or three cusps.

The right internal jugular vein is usually larger than the left, since the superior sagittal sinus normally turns to the right, and therefore the greater flow of blood from the cranial cavity is to this vein. This can be confirmed by a comparison of the sizes of the grooves for the transverse and sigmoid sinuses on the two sides of the dried skull. On the base of a dried skull, note the position of the jugular foramen and its relation to the carotid and hypoglossal canals, the occipital condyle, the styloid process, the stylomastoid foramen, and the external acoustic meatus [FIG. 93]. This gives a clear picture of the relative positions of the structures at the base of the skull.

Superiorly, the vein lies posterolateral to the internal carotid artery with the last four cranial nerves intervening. As it descends the vein rapidly becomes lateral to the artery, and continues in this position throughout the neck, enclosed in the carotid sheath with the vagus and with the internal carotid first and later with the common carotid artery.

Superficially, it is separated from the parotid gland by the styloid process and its muscles, and by the posterior belly of digastric with the occipital artery. Immediately inferior to this it passes deep to the sternocleidomastoid, and is associated with numerous deep cervical lymph nodes and the inferior root of the ansa cervicalis. Caudal to this it is crossed by the inferior belly of omohyoid, by the anterior jugular vein, and by the sternohyoid and sternothyroid muscles.

Posteriorly, it lies on the prevertebral muscles and cervical plexus, and on the scalenus anterior with the phrenic nerve posterolateral to the vein. It crosses the thyrocervical trunk, the subclavian artery, the cervical pleura, and, on the left side, the thoracic duct.

Tributaries. (1) The **inferior petrosal sinus** joins it at, or immediately inferior to, the jugular foramen. (2) It drains the **pharyngeal**

plexus by two or more veins which join its upper part. (3) In the carotid triangle it receives the **facial, lingual,** and **superior thyroid veins.** (4) At the root of the neck it drains the **middle thyroid vein,** and may receive the **jugular lymph trunk** [p. 119].

DISSECTION. Clean the prevertebral muscles and the cervical plexus on the right side. Find the part of rectus capitis lateralis attached to the superior surface of the transverse process of the atlas. Find the ventral ramus of the first cervical nerve at the medial side of the muscle, and trace its communication with the second cervical ventral ramus. Clean the ventral rami of the cervical nerves and their branches, noting the communications between the first five. Define the attachments of the scalene muscles, and trace the lower cervical and first thoracic nerves as far medially as possible, detaching the scalenus anterior if necessary.

CERVICAL PLEXUS
[Fig. 95]

This plexus is formed by communications between the ventral rami of the upper four cervical nerves, which emerge superior to the corresponding vertebrae. It lies posterior to the internal jugular vein and the prevertebral fascia, between the level of the root of the auricle and the superior border of the thyroid cartilage.

The ventral ramus of the first cervical nerve appears between the rectus capitis lateralis and the rectus capitis anterior. It descends over the anterior surface of the transverse process of the atlas, and joining the second, passes inferolaterally to meet the third on the anterior surface of scalenus medius. A communicating loop joins the third to the fourth, and a slender branch from the fourth passes to the fifth, thus joining the cervical and brachial plexuses.

Branches

(1) **Communicating.** (a) Grey rami communicantes from the superior cervical sym-

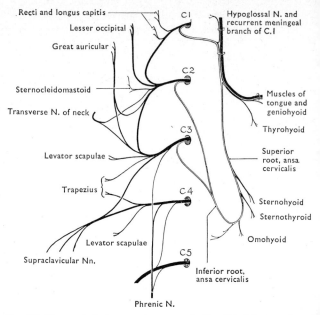

FIG. 95 The cervical plexus and ansa cervicalis. C.1-C.5, ventral rami of the upper five cervical nerves. Note that the nerves to the geniohyoid and thyrohyoid muscles and the superior root of the ansa are derived from the first cervical ventral ramus although they appear to arise from the hypoglossal nerve.

pathetic ganglion. (b) A branch from the first cervical ventral ramus to the hypoglossal nerve. This supplies geniohyoid and thyrohyoid, and forms the superior root of the ansa cervicalis. (c) Branches from the second, third, and fourth to the accessory nerve. (2) The **cutaneous** branches are described on page 16. (3) **Muscular** branches pass to the diaphragm (phrenic), the infrahyoid (ansa cervicalis, C. 1–3, p. 84), the prevertebral, scalene, intertransverse, and levator scapulae [p. 18] muscles, and sensory branches to sternocleidomastoid (C. 2), and trapezius [p.18].

Phrenic Nerve. It arises chiefly from the fourth cervical ventral ramus, and from the third and fifth to a lesser extent.

It begins at the lateral border of the scalenus anterior, opposite the upper border of the thyroid cartilage, and posterolateral to the internal jugular vein. On both sides the nerve retains this relation to the vein, and descends with it obliquely across scalenus anterior, reaching the medial border of the muscle at a higher level on the left than on the right. Thus it crosses the first part of the subclavian artery on the left, but on the right it lies on scalenus anterior in front of the second part of the artery.

On both sides the nerve passes posterior to the subclavian vein where it joins the brachiocephalic, and crosses the internal thoracic artery. The right nerve descends into the thorax posterolateral to the right brachiocephalic vein and the superior vena cava. On the left, the brachiocephalic vein passes to the right, and the nerve descends into the thorax between the common carotid artery and the pleura.

The root from the fifth cervical ventral ramus usually joins the phrenic nerve on the surface of scalenus anterior, but it may either descend into the thorax before joining it, or may reach the phrenic through a communication from the nerve to subclavius.

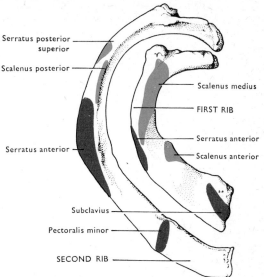

FIG. 96   Muscle attachments to the first two ribs, excluding the intercostals. Origins, red; insertions, blue.

SCALENE MUSCLES
[FIG. 99]

These muscles form the thick fleshy mass that extends from the cervical transverse processes to the first two ribs.

Nerve supply: twigs from the ventral rami of the lower five or six cervical nerves. Actions: they elevate the first two ribs in forced inspiration, and produce lateral flexion of the cervical vertebrae when acting unilaterally.

Scalenus Anterior [FIGS 85–88]

It arises from the anterior tubercles of the transverse processes of the third to sixth cervical vertebrae, and tapering as it descends, is inserted into the scalene tubercle on the first rib between the grooves for the subclavian artery and vein [FIG. 96].

It is separated from the scalenus medius posteriorly by the roots of the brachial plexus and the subclavian artery. Anteriorly, it is crossed obliquely by the internal jugular vein

and the phrenic nerve, and its lowest part is separated from the clavicle by the subclavian vein.

It is crossed by the inferior belly of omohyoid, and by the transverse cervical and suprascapular arteries which pass between the muscle and the internal jugular vein, but lie anterior to the phrenic nerve. Medially is the thyrocervical trunk [FIG. 86] and posterior to that, the suprapleural membrane [p. 120] and the pleura.

Scalenus Medius

This is a larger and more powerful muscle than scalenus anterior. It arises from the posterior tubercles of the transverse processes of all the cervical vertebrae, and is inserted into a rough, oval area on the superior surface of the first rib between its tubercle and the groove for the subclavian artery [FIG. 96].

Position. It lies in the floor of the posterior triangle of the neck, immediately posterior to the emerging ventral rami of the cervical and first thoracic nerves and the third part of the subclavian artery. It lies anterior to the levator

133

scapulae, and is only separated from it by the dorsal scapular nerve and the deep branch of the transverse cervical artery. It is pierced by the dorsal scapular nerve and by the upper two roots of the long thoracic nerve, and the lower part of its anteromedial surface is in contact with the cervical pleura.

Scalenus Posterior

This small muscle is only partially separated from the posterior surface of scalenus medius. It arises from the fourth to sixth cervical transverse processes with scalenus medius, and is inserted into the external surface of the second rib [FIG. 96].

CERVICAL FASCIA

In the dissection of the neck, the layers of fascia are often difficult to identify as they are

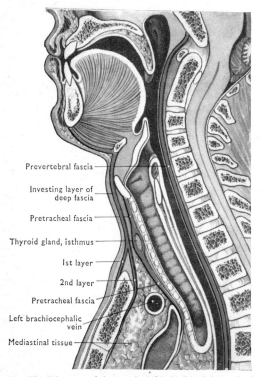

Prevertebral fascia

Investing layer of deep fascia

Pretracheal fascia

Thyroid gland, isthmus

1st layer

2nd layer

Pretracheal fascia

Left brachiocephalic vein

Mediastinal tissue

FIG. 97   Diagram of the cervical fascia (blue) in sagittal section.

134

laminar condensations of the general areolar tissue, and are produced by the stresses of the structures moving within it. These laminae ensheathe muscles and other moving structures, and are joined to them and to each other by loose areolar tissue. This allows movement between the sheaths and within them. They also form planes which tend to direct the spread of infection in the neck.

Investing Fascia. This deep fascia encircles the neck and surrounds the sternocleidomastoid and trapezius muscles, forming the roof of the posterior triangle between them. *Superiorly*, it is attached to the body and greater horn of the hyoid bone, and above this it splits to enclose the submandibular gland, the two layers passing to be attached to the inferior border and mylohyoid line of the mandible respectively. Posterior to the submandibular gland, the layers form the stylomandibular ligament [p. 86] and the rest of the fascia of the parotid gland. *Inferiorly*, it splits to surround the suprasternal space [FIG. 97 and p. 80] and is attached to the sternum, clavicle, and to the acromion and spine of the scapula. In contact with its deep layer is the fascia of the infrahyoid muscles, and this encloses the inferior belly and intermediate tendon of omohyoid, and binds it down to the clavicle.

Pretracheal Fascia. This fascia covers the front and sides of the trachea, splits to enclose the thyroid gland, and is attached to the oblique line on the thyroid cartilage [FIG. 125] and to the arch of the cricoid cartilage anteriorly. These attachments lead to the thyroid gland rising and falling with the larynx, *e.g.*, in swallowing. Inferiorly, it surrounds the inferior thyroid veins, and ends by fusing with the posterior surface of the pericardium.

Carotid Sheath. This is a tubular condensation around the common and internal carotid arteries, the internal jugular vein, the vagus nerve, and the ansa cervicalis. It extends from the base of the skull to the root of the neck, and is wedged between the investing, pretracheal, and prevertebral fasciae.

Prevertebral Fascia. This layer passes an-

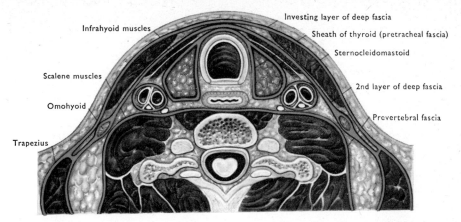

Labels on figure:
Infrahyoid muscles
Investing layer of deep fascia
Sheath of thyroid (pretracheal fascia)
Sternocleidomastoid
Scalene muscles
2nd layer of deep fascia
Omohyoid
Prevertebral fascia
Trapezius

FIG. 98   Diagram of the cervical fascia (blue) in transverse section of lower part of neck.

terior to the prevertebral muscles and separates them from the loose areolar tissue in which the distensible oesophagus lies. It extends from the base of the skull to the third thoracic vertebra where it fuses with the anterior longitudinal ligament inferior to the termination of longus colli. *Laterally*, it is continuous with the fascia which covers the scalene muscles, levator scapulae, and splenius capitis (the fascia of the floor of the posterior triangle) and surrounds the deep muscles of the back of the neck. *Inferiorly*, it covers scalenus anterior to the first rib, and is carried laterally as a sleeve around the subclavian and axillary arteries and the brachial plexus **(fascia of the cervico-axillary canal)**. Medial to scalenus anterior, it is continuous with the suprapleural membrane which passes from the seventh cervical transverse process to the inner border of the first rib. Occasionally a fleshy slip (scalenus minimus) arises with it and forms radiating tendinous fibres on the superficial surface of the suprapleural membrane. Anteromedially it fades into the loose areolar tissue between the pleura and the brachiocephalic vein.

Buccopharyngeal Fascia.   This is a delicate, distensible layer which clothes the constrictor muscles of the pharynx and buccinator, and extends from the base of the skull to the wall of the oesophagus. Together with a similar layer (**pharyngobasilar fascia,** p. 147) on the internal surface of these muscles, it closes the gaps in the muscular wall of the pharynx [FIG. 111].

LYMPH NODES AND LYMPH VESSELS OF THE HEAD AND NECK

Some of the lymph nodes may already have been encountered, especially those along the carotid sheath and in the root of the neck, but neither the nodes, nor the lymph vessels which drain into them, can be demonstrated satisfactorily except with special injection techniques. The following brief account is intended to give an introduction to the main features of this system in the head and neck.

The lymph nodes of the head and neck are very numerous, and fall into two sets. One set consists of relatively **superficial groups** which are situated around the junction of the head with the neck, and drain all the superficial structures of the head and some deep parts. They are assisted in the drainage of the deeper structures by nodes situated posterior to the pharynx. Most of the efferent vessels from these groups pass to the second set. These consist of a **deep, vertical chain** composed of numerous nodes arranged along the internal jugular vein from the digastric to the root of the neck. There are also subsidiary superficial groups on the external and anterior jugular

135

veins, and these drain to the deep, vertical chain of nodes, which may receive direct lymph vessels from the tongue and the structures in the neck. A further group, in the posterior triangle, lies along the anterior border of trapezius.

Superficial Lymph Nodes

Occipital Lymph Nodes. These are a few small nodes that lie on the upper end of trapezius and on the fascia at the apex of the posterior triangle. They drain the occipital part of the scalp and the superior part of the back of the neck. Their efferent vessels pass to the deep nodes under cover of the sterno-cleidomastoid muscle.

Mastoid Lymph Nodes. These nodes lie on the superior end of the sternocleidomastoid posterior to the auricle. They drain the posterior half of the side of the head and the posterior surface of the auricle. Their efferent vessels either pass through, or sweep round the anterior border of the sternocleidomastoid, to enter the deep nodes.

Parotid Lymph Nodes. These are several small nodes which are scattered throughout the parotid gland from its lateral to its medial surface. They drain a great part of the head, including the anterior part of the scalp, the upper half of the face, the upper molar teeth and gums, the temporal and infratemporal regions, the auricle, the external acoustic meatus, the middle ear and auditory tube, and the lacrimal and parotid glands. The deep members of this group drain the deeper structures, the superficial nodes drain the more superficial tissues. The final efferent vessels arise from the nodes between the inferior end of the parotid gland and the sternocleido-mastoid. Some of them end in the nodes on the external jugular vein, the others pass to the deep nodes.

Submandibular Lymph Nodes. These nodes lie along the length of the submandibular salivary gland, in the groove between the mandible and the gland. They receive lymph from the lower part of the front and side of the face (including the lower lip and chin) from the submandibular and sublingual salivary glands, from the floor of the mouth, the side of the tongue, most of the teeth and gums, part of the palate and the anterior part of the walls of the nasal cavity. Their efferents pass to deep nodes medial to sternocleidomastoid. In addition there are a few inconstant facial nodes that lie beside the facial vein. One of these is relatively constant, the mandibular node, and it lies on the mandible immediately anterior to masseter. It drains lymph from the cheek and lateral parts of the lips, and thus may be involved in infections and cancer of the lips.

Submental Lymph Nodes. Three or four small submental nodes lie between the anterior bellies of digastric on the fascia covering the inferior surface of mylohyoid. They drain lymph from a wedge-shaped zone which includes the incisor teeth and gums, and the anterior part of the floor of the mouth. Their efferents pass to the nodes deep to sterno-cleidomastoid. Though small they are palpable even in healthy individuals.

Retropharyngeal Lymph Nodes. A few nodes lie in the fascia on the posterior wall of the upper pharynx, in a plane just anterior to the mastoid process. They drain lymph from the oral and nasal parts of the pharynx, the palate, nose, and air sinuses, the auditory tube and the middle ear. Their efferents pass to the lymph nodes deep to the upper part of sterno-cleidomastoid. In their turn, these nodes drain to nodes on the anterior border of trapezius through nodes lying with the accessory nerve.

Cervical Lymph Nodes

Superficial Cervical Nodes. (1) Three or four nodes extend inferiorly from the parotid group along the external jugular vein. They drain the adjoining skin and the parotid nodes and send lymph vessels around the anterior border of sternocleidomastoid to the deep nodes in the carotid triangle. A few vessels may also run with the external jugular vein to a deep node at the root of the neck. (2) A few small nodes on the anterior jugular vein receive lymph from the skin and muscles of the anterior part of the neck, and transmit it to the deep nodes, especially along the anterior jugular vein.

Anterior Cervical Lymph Nodes. Several small lymph nodes lie on the front and sides of the trachea, especially along the recurrent laryngeal nerve, where they form chains that are continuous with the tracheobronchial nodes in the thorax. One or two lie in the posterior surface of the thyroid gland and often one is associated with the isthmus. They drain lymph from the larynx, trachea, and thyroid gland, to the deep cervical nodes.

Deep Cervical Lymph Nodes. These are numerous and large, and they form a broad strip of nodes which extends from the digastric to the root of the neck. They lie in relation to the carotid sheath, and are mostly under cover of the sternocleidomastoid. Two of them, the jugulodigastric and the jugulo-omohyoid, are of special importance in the lymph drainage of the tongue (q.v.) and are named from their relation to the digastric and omohyoid muscles. There are several of these nodes in the posterior triangle: (1) three or four nodes extend along the accessory nerve from the point where it crosses the internal jugular vein into the posterior triangle. Lymph from the retropharyngeal nodes drains through this group. (2) Another chain extends along the transverse cervical artery across the upper part of the brachial plexus.

The deep cervical lymph nodes are linked by afferent and efferent vessels, and they receive the efferent vessels of all the other groups. Thus all the lymph of the head and neck passes through them, and is finally united in the jugular lymph trunk at the root of the neck. This trunk normally ends in the thoracic duct on the left, and in the internal jugular vein on the right [p. 119].

THE PREVERTEBRAL REGION

The prevertebral muscles have already been exposed on the right side, and can now be cleaned. Longus capitis and rectus capitis anterior and lateralis have been divided on the right, but their attachments to the base of the skull can be checked by reference to it on the detached right half, and the muscles can be seen on the left side by displacing the pharynx anteriorly.

PREVERTEBRAL MUSCLES

These muscles are covered anteriorly by the prevertebral fascia. They are supplied by the ventral rami of the cervical nerves, and they flex the neck and the head on the neck.

Longus Colli. This is the longest and most medial of the three muscles. It extends from the anterior tubercle of the atlas to the lower part of the body of the third thoracic vertebra. Between these points it is attached to all the vertebral bodies and to the third to sixth cervical transverse processes [FIG. 99].

Longus Capitis. This muscle lies antero-lateral to longus colli and overlaps rectus capitis anterior. It arises from the anterior tubercles of the third to sixth cervical transverse processes, medial to the scalenus anterior, and is inserted into the base of the skull in front of rectus capitis anterior [FIG. 15].

Rectus Capitis Anterior. This is a short, wide muscle that arises from the anterior surface of the lateral mass of the atlas and is inserted into the base of the skull immediately anterior to the occipital condyle.

Rectus Capitis Lateralis. This short muscle runs vertically between the superior surface of the transverse process of the atlas and the jugular process of the occipital bone. It lies immediately posterior to the jugular foramen, and is separated from the rectus capitis anterior by the ventral ramus of the first cervical nerve which supplies both muscles. The two rectus muscles act with the small muscles of the suboccipital triangle to stabilize the skull on the vertebral column.

DISSECTION. Re-examine the attachments of the scalene muscles on both sides of the neck. Then remove scalenus anterior and longus capitis from their origins, and expose the small intertransverse muscles. The anterior intertransverse muscles run between the anterior tubercles of adjacent transverse processes, the posterior between the posterior tubercles. They are separated by the ventral rami of the cervical nerves, and the dorsal rami pass posteriorly medial to the posterior

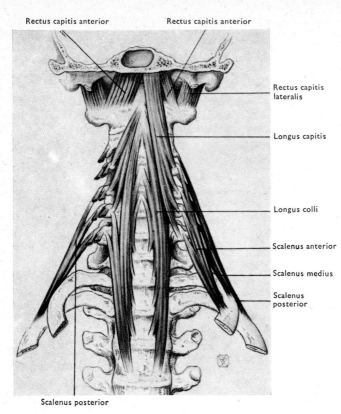

Rectus capitis anterior Rectus capitis anterior

Rectus capitis lateralis

Longus capitis

Longus colli

Scalenus anterior

Scalenus medius

Scalenus posterior

Scalenus posterior

FIG. 99 The prevertebral muscles of the neck.

intertransverse muscles. **The rectus capitis anterior and lateralis are enlarged intertransverse muscles.**

The vertebral artery may now be exposed in the intertransverse spaces by removal of the intertransverse muscles, but it can be more fully exposed by snipping off the anterior tubercles and costal processes [Fig. 101] of the third to sixth cervical vertebrae.

VERTEBRAL ARTERY

The vertebral artery is a very important vessel which joins its fellow of the opposite side to form the basilar artery. Through the branches of these vessels blood is supplied to the hindbrain, the midbrain, the posterior part of the cerebrum, and the superior part of the spinal medulla.

First Part. It begins in the root of the neck as a branch of the first part of the subclavian artery, and passes to the transverse process of the sixth cervical vertebra [p. 115; FIG. 88].

Second Part. The artery ascends vertically through the foramina transversaria, accompanied by the vertebral veins and a plexus of sympathetic nerve fibres which is derived from the cervicothoracic ganglion of the sympathetic trunk, and which accompanies all the branches of the artery. Between the transverse processes, it lies medial to the intertransverse muscles and anterior to the ventral rami of the cervical nerves. In the axis it turns laterally under the superior articular facet in the foramen transversarium, and bending upwards, enters the foramen transversarium of the atlas, which is placed further laterally than the others [FIGS. 86, 100].

Third Part [FIGS. 100, 104]. The artery emerges on the superior surface of the atlas between rectus capitis lateralis and the superior articular process of the atlas. Here it lies with the ventral ramus of the first cervical nerve, and curving with it horizontally around the lateral and posterior aspects of the superior articular process, grooves the process and the root of the posterior arch of the atlas. On the posterior arch, it lies superior to the dorsal ramus of the first cervical nerve, in the depths of the suboccipital triangle [FIG. 17] and leaves the triangle by passing anterior to the posterior atlanto-occipital membrane.

Fourth Part [p. 65, FIGS. 100, 169, 170]. The artery turns superiorly, and piercing the dura and arachnoid mater, enters the cranial cavity through the foramen magnum, anterior to the uppermost tooth of the ligamentum

138

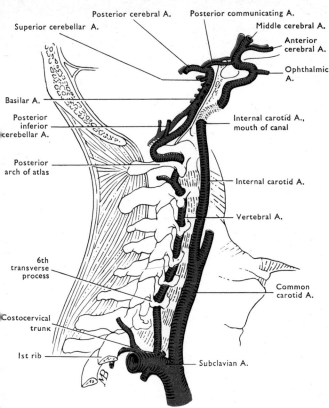

Fig. 100 The course and communications of the internal carotid and vertebral arteries.

and a series of branches to the central nervous system (see below).

VERTEBRAL VEIN

A plexus of veins is formed around the beginning of the third part of the vertebral artery by the union of veins from the internal vertebral venous plexus and the suboccipital triangle. This plexus runs with the second part of the artery through the foramina transversaria. It anastomoses with the internal vertebral venous plexus, and it ends inferiorly as one or two vertebral veins. They accompany the artery out of the foramen in the sixth cervical transverse process, and passing anterior to the subclavian artery, end by entering the posterior surface of the brachiocephalic vein near its origin. One of the two veins may pass through the foramen transversarium in the seventh cervical vertebra.

denticulatum. It then runs anterosuperiorly over the anterior surface of the medulla oblongata, between the rootlets of the first cervical and hypoglossal nerves, to meet and join the opposite vertebral artery at the inferior border of the pons, and form the basilar artery.

Branches

No branch of importance is given off from the first part. Spinal [p. 36] and muscular branches arise from the second part. The branches of the third part anastomose with branches of the occipital and deep cervical arteries, and supply adjacent muscles. The fourth part gives off a meningeal branch,

DISSECTION. Remove the muscles completely in order to examine the vertebral joints and their ligaments. Define and clean the ligaments. Clean the column of laminae and spines that was laid aside when the vertebral canal was opened, and expose the ligaments which connect its parts. Remove the remaining cervical laminae and spines below the axis by cutting through the laminae medial to the articular processes.

THE JOINTS OF THE NECK

The joints between the second to fifth cervical vertebrae are similar to those in the other parts of the vertebral column, and allow flexion and extension together with lateral flexion, but little or no rotation. The joints

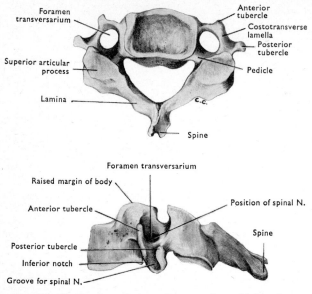

Foramen
transversarium

Superior articular
process

Lamina

Spine

c.c.

Anterior
tubercle

Costotransverse
lamella

Posterior
tubercle

Pedicle

Foramen transversarium

Raised margin of body

Anterior tubercle

Position of spinal N.

Spine

Posterior tubercle

Inferior notch

Groove for spinal N.

Fig. 101   The fourth cervical vertebra, superior and left surfaces.

between the first and second cervical vertebrae are designed to allow rotation, while those between the first cervical vertebra (atlas) and the skull are so arranged that they permit nodding movements of the skull on the vertebral column.

TYPICAL CERVICAL JOINTS

These are the joints between the lower six cervical vertebrae. The **bodies** of these vertebrae are firmly bound to each other by a flexible fibrous disc (**anulus fibrosus**) of moderate thickness. This contains a central gelatinous structure (**nucleus pulposus**) and allows a moderate degree of movement. The intervertebral discs are strengthened anteriorly and posteriorly by the anterior and posterior longitudinal ligaments, which are attached principally to the discs and the adjacent parts of the bodies. The discs are the major factor in producing the cervical curvature, and they do not cover the entire surfaces of the vertebral bodies, but are replaced laterally by small **synovial joints** situated where the margins of the inferior vertebra overlap the vertebral body above [FIG. 102].

The **vertebral arches** are united by the synovial joints between the articular processes and by a number of ligaments. The cervical articular processes lie in an oblique coronal

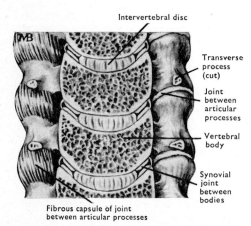

Intervertebral disc

Transverse
process
(cut)

Joint
between
articular
processes

Vertebral
body

Synovial
joint
between
bodies

Fibrous capsule of joint
between articular processes

Fig. 102   Coronal section through the joints between the bodies of the cervical vertebrae.

Pedicle
divided

Ligamentum
flavum

Lamina of
vertebra

Transverse
process

Ligamentum flavum

Fig. 103   Ligamenta flava seen from the front after removal of the bodies of the vertebrae by saw cuts through the pedicles.   Lumbar region.

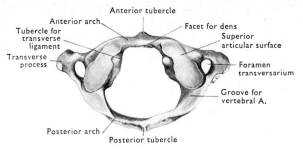

FIG. 104   The superior surface of the atlas.

stout transverse process projecting laterally from it. The atlas is held, like a washer, between the axis and the occipital bone because these two bones are firmly attached to each other by strong ligaments, but the articular surfaces which the atlas has with the skull and with the axis are of different configuration, those with the skull allowing for flexion and extension, while those with the axis permit rotation.

plane, which passes anterosuperiorly, and the processes on the two sides are parallel to each other, thus effectively preventing rotation between the lower six cervical vertebrae. The capsules of these joints are lax, and permit a considerable range of movement.

Ligaments of Vertebral Arches

Ligamenta Flava [FIG. 103]. These are flat bands of yellow elastic tissue which pass between the adjacent laminae. They are powerful ligaments of considerable width in the cervical region because of the width of the vertebral canal. They help to maintain the vertebral column in position, but are capable of being stretched on flexion, and of helping to restore it to its original position afterwards.

Interspinous Ligaments. These are weak in the cervical region. They pass between adjacent spines, and are directly continuous with the **supraspinous ligaments** and the **ligamentum nuchae** [p. 25].

JOINTS OF ATLAS, AXIS, AND OCCIPITAL BONE

The atlas consists of a ring of bone with a lateral mass on each side. The lateral masses articulate superiorly with the occipital condyles and inferiorly with the superior articular facets of the axis. Each has a long

Ligaments of Joints of Atlas

Anterior Longitudinal Ligament. This ligament tapers superiorly to be attached to the anterior tubercle of the atlas. Above this it continues as a narrow band to the base of the skull, and strengthens the median part of the thin **anterior atlanto-occipital membrane.** This passes from the superior margin of the anterior arch of the atlas to the base of the skull anterior to the foramen magnum [FIG. 106].

Ligamentum Flavum. Between the atlas and the axis this is a delicate structure, and the corresponding ligament between the posterior arch of the atlas and the occipital bone **(posterior atlanto-occipital membrane)** is also thin. The latter passes from the part of the posterior arch of the atlas between the grooves

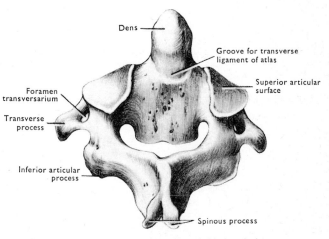

FIG. 105   The axis vertebra from behind and above.

141

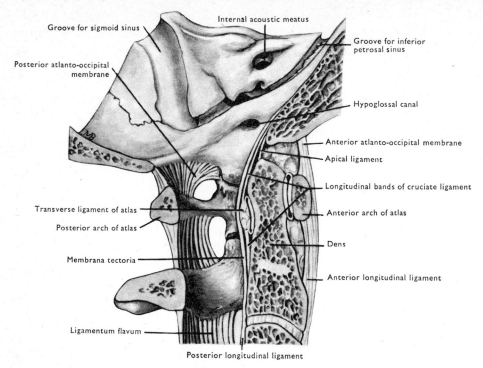

Groove for sigmoid sinus

Internal acoustic meatus

Groove for inferior petrosal sinus

Posterior atlanto-occipital membrane

Hypoglossal canal

Anterior atlanto-occipital membrane

Apical ligament

Longitudinal bands of cruciate ligament

Transverse ligament of atlas

Anterior arch of atlas

Posterior arch of atlas

Dens

Membrana tectoria

Anterior longitudinal ligament

Ligamentum flavum

Posterior longitudinal ligament

FIG. 106   Median section through the foramen magnum and first two cervical vertebrae.   The brain, spinal medulla, and meninges have been removed.

for the vertebral arteries to the margin of the foramen magnum posterior to the atlanto-occipital joints. Each of its lateral margins arches over the corresponding third part of the vertebral artery and the first cervical nerve, to reach the posterior surface of the lateral mass of the atlas. These margins may be ossified.

DISSECTION. To expose the other ligaments, remove the laminae of the axis and the posterior arch of the atlas with bone forceps. Remove the tube of spinal dura mater and any remains of the spinal medulla, and expose the membrana tectoria.

Membrana Tectoria. This broad ligamentous sheet is the superior continuation of the posterior longitudinal ligament. It passes from the posterior surface of the body of the axis to the cranial surface of the occipital bone [FIGS. 106, 107]. It holds the axis to the skull,

142

and covers the posterior surface of the dens and its ligaments and the anterior margin of the foramen magnum.

DISSECTION. Remove the membrana tectoria and expose and clean the cruciate and accessory atlanto-axial ligaments.

The **accessory atlanto-axial ligaments** [FIG. 107] pass from the posterior surface of the body of the axis to the corresponding lateral mass of the atlas. These strong ligaments help to limit the rotation of the atlas on the axis.

Cruciate Ligament. This ligament is formed by the transverse ligament of the atlas (which passes between the tubercles on the medial aspects of the lateral masses of the atlas) and the superior and inferior longitudinal bands which pass from the transverse ligament to the cranial surface of the occipital bone and

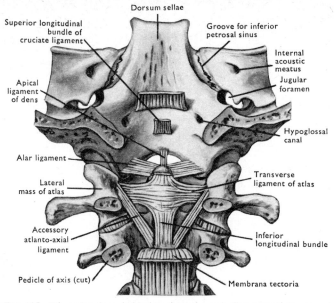

Superior longitudinal
bundle of
cruciate ligament

Dorsum sellae

Groove for inferior
petrosal sinus

Internal
acoustic
meatus

Jugular
foramen

Apical
ligament
of dens

Hypoglossal
canal

Alar ligament

Transverse
ligament of atlas

Lateral
mass of atlas

Accessory
atlanto-axial
ligament

Inferior
longitudinal bundle

Pedicle of axis (cut)

Membrana tectoria

FIG. 107 Dissection from behind to show the main ligaments that connect the occipital bone, the atlas, and the axis.

the body of the axis respectively. The **transverse ligament of the atlas** curves round the posterior surface of the dens of the axis, but is separated from it by a synovial joint. The ligament holds the anterior arch of the atlas firmly against the anterior surface of the dens, and these two bones are also separated by a synovial joint. Thus the atlas is held firmly to the dens and is capable of rotating round it, but cannot be displaced anteroposteriorly on the axis.

DISSECTION. If the division of the skull has been kept to the right of the midline, the apical ligament of the dens [Fig. 106] should still be visible on the left side. It lies anterior to the superior band of the cruciate ligament and may be exposed by removing this.

Identify the divided right alar ligament and clean out the left alar ligament which passes from the side of the apex of the dens to the medial aspect of the occipital condyle.

Apical Ligament of the Dens. The posterior part is a rounded cord-like ligament which stretches from the apex of the dens to the

cranial surface of the occipital bone immediately above the margin of the foramen magnum. It develops around a part of the notochord. The anterior part is a flat, weak band which joins the posterior part superiorly, but is attached to the dens immediately superior to its articular facet for the anterior arch of the atlas. Neither of these parts plays a significant role in strengthening the joints.

Alar Ligaments [FIG. 107]. These very powerful ligaments arise from the sloping sides of the summit of the dens. They pass laterally and slightly upwards to the medial sides of the occipital condyles. They hold the skull to the axis and they tighten when the atlas, carrying the skull, rotates around the dens. They are thus the main factor in limiting rotation at the atlanto-axial joints. The alar ligaments are attached to the skull on the axis of the nodding movements which the skull makes on the atlas, and so do not hinder these movements.

Atlanto-occipital Joint

The kidney-shaped occipital condyles lie on the anterolateral aspects of the foramen magnum, and are shaped as two segments of an obtuse, inverted cone. They fit into the superior articular facets of the atlas which are also kidney-shaped, and the joints allow flexion and extension and slight side to side rocking of the head, but no rotation. The stability of these joints does not depend on the loose articular capsule, but rather on the alar ligaments, the membrana tectoria, and the longitudinal bands of the cruciate ligament, all of which bind the skull to the axis.

143

The Atlanto-axial Joints

These joints are formed between the large, nearly circular, slightly curved facets on the adjacent surfaces of the atlas and axis. These facets slope downwards and outwards and form segments of a flat cone which permits the atlas to rotate round the dens of the axis. These joints are stabilized partly by the articulation of the anterior arch of the atlas and its transverse ligament with the dens, and partly by the ligaments which bind the axis and the skull together so that the atlas is held firmly between them.

In the atlanto-occipital and atlanto-axial joints there are no articular facets corresponding to the articular facets of the other cervical vertebrae, but the articular surfaces of these two joints correspond in position to the small synovial joints at the lateral edges of the vertebral bodies. Thus the emerging spinal nerves (first and second cervical) pass posterior to the joint capsules and not anterior to them as in the case of the articular facets between the vertebral arches of the remaining cervical vertebrae.

THE MOUTH AND THE PHARYNX

THE MOUTH

The mouth is the first division of the digestive tube, and is separable into two parts; a smaller, external part, the vestibule, which separates the lips and cheeks from the teeth and gums, and a larger part, the mouth proper, which is limited anteriorly and laterally by the teeth.

Vestibule of Mouth

The vestibule is a cleft into which the ducts of the parotid glands and the mucous glands of the lips and cheeks open. Superiorly and inferiorly, it is bounded by the reflexion of the mucous membrane from the lips and cheeks on to the maxillae and mandible. Posteriorly, it communicates, on each side, with the cavity of the mouth proper through the interval between the last molar tooth and ramus of the mandible. In paralysis of the facial muscles, the lips and cheeks fall away from the teeth and gums, and food is apt to lodge in the vestibule.

Lips

The superficial structures in the lips have been examined already [p. 42]. Each lip is a flexible structure which consists of a sheet of muscle covered externally by skin and internally by mucous membrane and submucosa. The mucous membrane is continuous with the skin at the margins of the lips, and here the stratified squamous epithelium changes from a non-keratinizing to a keratinizing type. At its reflexion on to the jaws, the mucous membrane forms a median, raised fold, the **frenulum** of the lip. The chief bulk of the lips is the muscular layer which is formed by orbicularis oris and the various facial muscles which converge on it [p. 13].

The submucous layer consists of areolar tissue which binds the mucous membrane to the muscular layer. It contains numerous mucous labial glands with ducts which pierce the mucous membrane and open into the vestibule. In each lip there is an arterial arch formed by the labial branches of the facial artery [FIG. 26].

The **lymph vessels** of the lower lip pass to the submandibular nodes; those of the upper lip pass to the submandibular and superficial parotid nodes.

Cheeks

The cheeks are directly continuous with the lips and have the same general structure. **Buccinator** forms the muscle layer, and it follows the line of the teeth, passing deep to masseter posteriorly, to become continuous with the superior constrictor muscle of the pharynx at the pterygomandibular raphe [FIG. 111]. It lies between the **buccopharyngeal fascia** externally and the **pharyngobasilar fascia** internally. There is a considerable quantity of subcutaneous fat in the cheek, particularly in infants where the buccal pad of fat is especially well formed in its deepest parts, and assists the

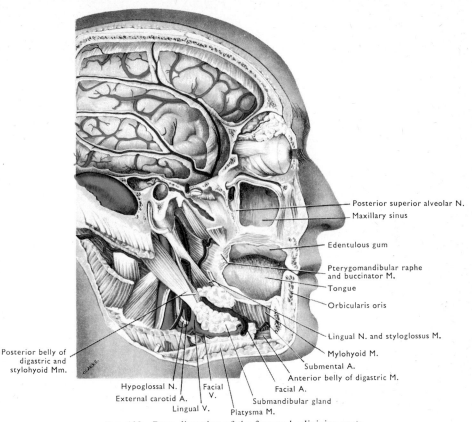

Posterior superior alveolar N.

Maxillary sinus

Edentulous gum

Pterygomandibular raphe
and buccinator M.

Tongue

Orbicularis oris

Lingual N. and styloglossus M.

Mylohyoid M.

Submental A.

Anterior belly of digastric M.

Posterior belly of
digastric and
stylohyoid Mm.

Hypoglossal N.

External carotid A.

Lingual V.

Facial
V.

Platysma M.

Facial A.

Submandibular gland

FIG. 108   Deep dissection of the face and adjoining parts.

ucking process. Numerous buccal glands lie
n the submucosa, and four to five larger
mucous, **molar glands** lie external to the
buccinator around the entry of the parotid
duct. The parotid duct pierces the buccal pad
of fat, buccinator and its coverings of fascia,
and enters the vestibule of the mouth opposite
the second upper molar tooth.

Gums and Teeth

The gums are composed of dense fibrous
tissue covered with a smooth, vascular mucous
membrane. They are attached to the alveolar
margins of the jaws and the necks of the teeth;
the fibrous tissue is continuous with the peri-
odontal membrane which attaches the teeth to

their sockets, and the epithelium is adherent
to the tooth surfaces.

In the adult there are 16 teeth in each jaw,
and these consist, on each side from the
median plane, of 2 incisors, 1 canine, 2 premolars, and 3 molars.

CAVITY PROPER OF MOUTH

This cavity is bounded anteriorly and laterally by the gums and teeth; posteriorly, it
communicates with the pharynx through the
isthmus of the fauces.

Floor of the Mouth

This is formed by the mucous membrane
which connects the tongue to the mandible.

145

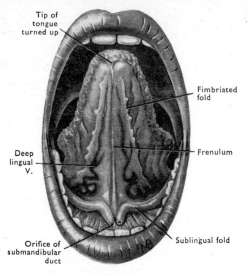

Tip of
tongue
turned up

Fimbriated
fold

Deep
lingual
V.

Frenulum

Orifice of
submandibular
duct

Sublingual fold

FIG. 109   The inferior surface of the tongue.

Laterally, the mucous membrane is reflected
directly from the side of the tongue on to the
mandible. Anteriorly it stretches across the
floor of the mouth from one half of the mandible to the other, beneath the free anterior
part of the tongue, and forms a
median fold which connects the
inferior surface of the tongue to
the floor of the mouth, the **frenulum of the tongue.** On both sides
of the frenulum, the sublingual
gland bulges upwards to form the
sublingual fold which ends anteriorly in the **sublingual papilla.**
On the apex of the papilla is the
opening of the submandibular
duct, while the sublingual ducts
form a series of minute apertures
on the summit of the sublingual
fold [p. 105].

Roof of Mouth

This is formed by the vaulted
hard and soft palate [FIGS. 110,
113]. The **soft palate** is attached
to the posterior border of the hard

palate, and has a free posterior margin from
the middle of which the **uvula** hangs down and
rests on the dorsum of the tongue. A poorly
marked median raphe runs forwards from
the uvula, and ends anteriorly, below the incisive fossa, in a slight elevation, the **incisive
papilla.** On each side of the raphe, the mucous
membrane of the anterior part of the hard
palate is thrown into three to four hard transverse ridges, the **transverse palatine folds,** but
posteriorly it is comparatively smooth. By
careful palpation with a finger or the tongue,
the pterygoid hamulus [FIG. 93] may be felt
immediately posterior to the lingual surface of
the third upper molar tooth.

Isthmus of Fauces

The term fauces is often used to indicate the
region between the mouth and the pharynx,
but it may be defined more precisely as that
part of the pharynx which contains the two
palatine tonsils between the palatoglossal and
palatopharyngeal arches.

The isthmus of the fauces is bounded by the
palatoglossal arches and is therefore the communication between the mouth proper and the
pharynx [FIG. 110]. The isthmus is best seen

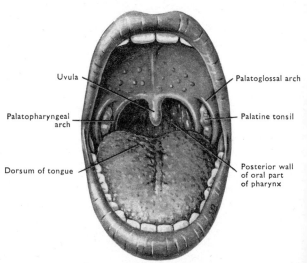

Uvula

Palatoglossal arch

Palatopharyngeal
arch

Palatine tonsil

Dorsum of tongue

Posterior wall
of oral part
of pharynx

FIG. 110   The fauces and its isthmus seen through the widely open
mouth.

146

the living body, and should be examined ith the mouth wide open and the tongue pressed. Its boundaries are the soft palate, e dorsum of the tongue, and the palato-ossal arches.

Palatoglossal Arch. This is a fold of mucous embrane which covers the palatoglossus uscle. It descends antero-inferiorly from the ferior surface of the soft palate to the pos-rior part of the side of the tongue. The alatopharyngeal arch and the palatine tonsil .n be seen also, but they are described with › .e pharynx to which they belong.

THE PHARYNX

The pharynx is a wide muscular tube, about 2 cm. long, which is lined throughout with ucous membrane, and extends from the ase of the skull to the level of the body of .e sixth cervical vertebra [FIG. 113] where it continuous with the oesophagus. It lies osterior to the nasal cavities and septum .asal part), the mouth (oral part) and the rynx **(laryngeal part),** and it conducts air to .d from the larynx and food to the oesopha-.s from the mouth; the oral part is common › both functions.

It is widest at the base of the skull, posterior › the orifices of the auditory tubes. Thence, narrows to the level of the hyoid bone, but idens again opposite the superior part of .e larynx and then rapidly narrows to the esophagus.

Above the opening of the larynx the walls re not in contact, and thus allow the passage f air via the mouth or nasal cavities to the .rynx. If the posterior part of the tongue is .ised and the soft palate drawn down on to it palatoglossus muscle) the oral cavity can be .ut off from the pharynx. If the soft palate is .ised and drawn posteriorly, the nasal part f the pharynx may be isolated from the oral .rt. Below the opening of the larynx, the nterior and posterior walls lie in contact.

osition

Posteriorly, the pharynx is separated from .e prevertebral fascia by some loose areolar tissue, and this allows free movement between them during deglutition. Lateral to the pharynx are the great vessels and nerves of the neck, and the styloid process and its muscles. The pharyngeal plexus ramifies over it, and supplies it with motor and sensory twigs. Anteriorly, it opens into the nasal cavities, mouth, and larynx, and its muscles are attached to structures which lie in proximity to those apertures.

PHARYNGEAL WALL

The wall of the pharynx consists of five layers. These are: (1) mucous membrane; (2) submucosa; (3) pharyngobasilar fascia; (4) pharyngeal muscles; (5) buccopharyngeal fascia.

The **buccopharyngeal fascia** covers the external surfaces of buccinator and the pharyngeal muscles. The **pharyngobasilar fascia** lines the internal surfaces of the pharyngeal muscles, attaches the pharynx to the base of the skull, to the auditory tubes and to the lateral margins of the choanae. It also fills the gap in the pharyngeal wall above the free superior margin of the superior constrictor muscle [FIG. 111].

The muscles of the pharynx consist of the three constrictors, the stylopharyngeus and palatopharyngeus muscles.

DISSECTION. On the right side, remove the buccopharyngeal fascia from the external surfaces of the pharyngeal muscles, moving the knife in the direction of their fibres [Fig. 111]. Note the plexuses of nerves and veins, and remove them.

On the left side, examine the interior of the pharynx [p. 150] and strip off its mucous membrane to expose the pharyngeal muscles from the medial side [Fig. 112].

Pharyngeal Veins

These veins lie on the posterior wall and borders of the pharynx, and form the **pharyngeal plexus of veins** which receives blood from the pharynx, soft palate, and prevertebral region. Two or more veins drain from it to the internal jugular vein, and it communicates with the pterygoid and cavernous sinuses.

Inferior Constrictor

This muscle arises from th[e] side of the cricoid cartilag[e] and the oblique line on th[e] thyroid cartilage. Its fibre[s] sweep posteriorly and med[i]ally to the median raphe; th[e] lowest fibres are horizonta[l] but those above this ascen[d] with increasing obliquity, th[e] highest fibres almost reachin[g] the base of the skull externa[l] to the other two constrictor[s]. Inferiorly, it overlaps th[e] beginning of the oesophagu[s] and the recurrent larynge[al] nerve and inferior larynge[al] artery ascending to the larynx.

Middle Constrictor

This fan - shaped musc[le] arises from the greater an[d] lesser horns of the hyoi[d] bone and from the lowe[r] part of the stylohyoid liga[ment. From this curved or[i]gin, the fibres fan out int[o] the pharyngeal wall, th[e] middle fibres running hor[i]zontally. The inferior pa[rt] passes deep to the inferic[r] constrictor posteriorly, b[ut] is separated from it lateral[ly] by an interval through whic[h] the internal branch of th[e] superior laryngeal nerve an[d] the superior laryngeal arter[y] pass to pierce the thyrohyoid membrane an[d] enter the pharynx [FIG. 111].

DISSECTION. On the right side, the superi[or] constrictor may be brought fully into view by detachin[g] the medial pterygoid muscle from its origin and turnin[g] it downwards.

Superior Constrictor

This muscle is in the wall of the nasal an[d] oral parts of the pharynx. It has a continuou[s] origin from: (1) the lower third of th[e]

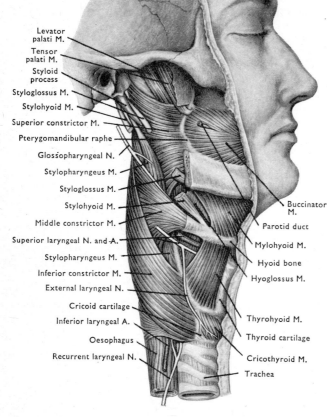

Levator palati M.
Tensor palati M.
Styloid process
Styloglossus M.
Stylohyoid M.
Superior constrictor M.
Pterygomandibular raphe
Glossopharyngeal N.
Stylopharyngeus M.
Styloglossus M.
Stylohyoid M.
Middle constrictor M.
Superior laryngeal N. and A.
Stylopharyngeus M.
Inferior constrictor M.
External laryngeal N.
Cricoid cartilage
Inferior laryngeal A.
Oesophagus
Recurrent laryngeal N.

Buccinator M.
Parotid duct
Mylohyoid M.
Hyoid bone
Hyoglossus M.
Thyrohyoid M.
Thyroid cartilage
Cricothyroid M.
Trachea

FIG. 111   Lateral view of the constrictors of the pharynx and associated muscles.

CONSTRICTOR MUSCLES

These three muscles form curved sheets which lie in the posterior wall and sides of the pharynx, and overlap each other from below upwards [FIG. 111]. They are inserted into a median fibrous **raphe** which descends in the posterior pharyngeal wall from the **pharyngeal tubercle** on the base of the skull [FIG. 93]. Nerve supply: the pharyngeal plexus of nerves, with an additional supply to the inferior constrictor from the external and recurrent laryngeal nerves. Actions: page 157.

148

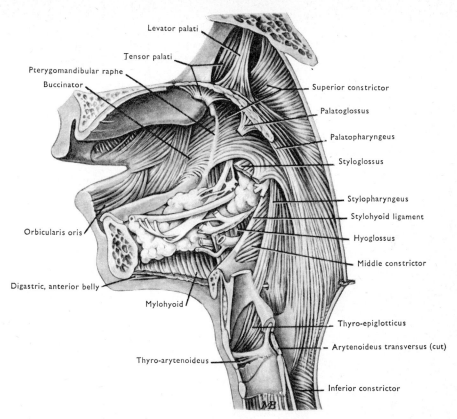

FIG. 112 Dissection of the constrictors of the pharynx and the associated structures which lie adjacent to the mucous membrane lining the mouth, pharynx, and larynx, from the medial side. The tongue has been removed to expose the structures which lie between it and the mylohyoid muscle. See also FIG. 118.

posterior margin of the medial pterygoid lamina and the pterygoid hamulus; (2) the pterygomandibular raphe; (3) the posterior end of the mylohyoid line on the mandible; (4) the mucous membrane of the mouth and side of the tongue. The fibres curve posteriorly around the pharynx to the median raphe, and some of the highest reach the pharyngeal tubercle.

The **lower part** of the superior constrictor lies medial to the middle constrictor, and the stylopharyngeus enters the pharynx through the interval between them (accompanied by the glossopharyngeal nerve [FIG. 111]) and

passes to its insertion on the posterior border of the lamina of the thyroid cartilage and the side of the epiglottis [FIG. 112].

The **upper border** of the superior constrictor is free and crescentic. It extends from the medial pterygoid lamina to the pharyngeal tubercle, and leaves a semilunar gap between it and the skull. This gap is filled by pharyngo-basilar fascia, which has the tensor and levator muscles of the palate immediately lateral to it, and the auditory tube passing through it between these muscles [FIG. 123]. The auditory tube and the levator muscle of the palate enter the pharynx above the superior margin

149

of the superior constrictor together with the ascending palatine artery.

The **pterygomandibular raphe** [FIGS. 111, 112] is a tendinous line stretching from the pterygoid hamulus to the posterior end of the mylohoid line on the mandible. It is formed by the interlacing tendinous fibres of the superior constrictor and buccinator muscles. These tendinous fibres run horizontally, and hence are capable of being separated when the raphe is stretched on opening the mouth.

INTERIOR OF THE PHARYNX

The pharynx is lined throughout with mucous membrane, and the submucosa contains numerous mucous pharyngeal glands and nodules of lymphoid tissue. Aggregations of these lymphatic follicles form the pharyngeal, tubal, and palatine tonsils.

The cavity of the pharynx is divided into nasal, oral, and laryngeal parts.

Nasal Part of Pharynx [FIGS. 113, 119]

It lies superior to the soft palate, and is continuous, inferiorly, with the oral part through the narrow pharyngeal isthmus, which lies posterior to the palate and is limited laterally by the palatopharyngeal arch. This arch is visible internally as a ridge of mucous membrane covering the palatopharyngeus muscle. It begins at the posterolateral margin of the soft palate, and sweeps postero-inferiorly to fade out on the lateral wall of the pharynx; its superior margin passes almost horizontally backwards around the pharyngeal isthmus.

Anteriorly, it communicates with the nasal cavities through the oval choanae (each approximately 2·5 cm. high by 1·5 cm. wide) which slope antero-inferiorly from the base of the skull to the posterior edge of the hard palate, and are separated by the nasal septum. Through the choanae can be seen the posterior ends of the middle and inferior nasal conchae.

The **roof** and **posterior wall** form a continuous curved surface of mucous membrane which covers the inferior surface of the sphenoid, the basilar part of the occipital bone, and the superior part of the longus capitis muscle. As the roof becomes continuous with the posterior wall, the mucous membrane is wrinkled

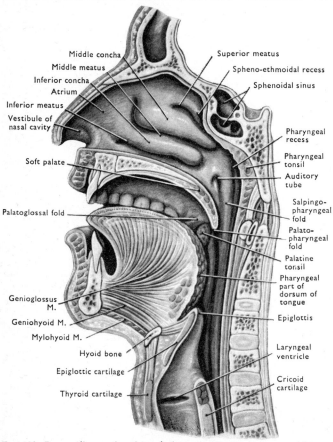

Middle concha
Middle meatus
Inferior concha
Atrium
Inferior meatus
Vestibule of nasal cavity
Soft palate
Palatoglossal fold
Genioglossus M.
Geniohyoid M.
Mylohyoid M.
Hyoid bone
Epiglottic cartilage
Thyroid cartilage

Superior meatus
Spheno-ethmoidal recess
Sphenoidal sinus
Pharyngeal recess
Pharyngeal tonsil
Auditory tube
Salpingo-pharyngeal fold
Palato-pharyngeal fold
Palatine tonsil
Pharyngeal part of dorsum of tongue
Epiglottis
Laryngeal ventricle
Cricoid cartilage

FIG. 113 Paramedian section through the nose, mouth, pharynx, and larynx.

nd protrudes into the cavity of the pharynx due to the presence of the **pharyngeal onsil** in the submucosa. This lymphoid tissue s often enlarged in children (adenoids) and nay be of sufficient size to block the nasal part of the pharynx. A minute, median pit pharyngeal bursa) may be found in its surace.

On each **lateral wall** is the **pharyngeal orifice of the auditory tube,** which lies at the level of he inferior concha of the nose. The tube leads o the middle ear, and its pharyngeal opening s bounded superiorly and posteriorly by a irm, rounded **tubal ridge** around which lies he tubal tonsil. From the ridge, the narrow **alpingopharyngeal fold** of mucous membrane escends and fades out on the lateral wall of he pharynx towards the pharyngeal isthmus. Vithin the fold lies the salpingopharyngeus nuscle. Posterior to the tubal ridge, the pharyngeal wall extends laterally to form the leep **pharyngeal recess.**

Note that the posterior wall and roof of the nasal part of the pharynx can be explored by a finger introduced through the mouth and pharyngeal isthmus.

When the nasal part of the pharynx is illuminated by light reflected from a mirror introduced through the mouth, a view may be obtained in the mirror of the choanae, the orifices of the auditory tubes, and the side walls and roof of the nasal part of the pharynx.

Structure. The **mucous membrane** lining the pharynx contains a considerable amount of elastic tissue and a number of glands, mainly mucous in type. The mucous membrane lining the nasal part of the pharynx is of the ciliated columnar type characteristic of the respiratory passages, while that of the oral and laryngeal parts is a stratified squamous epithelium of the non-keratinizing type, similar to that in the mouth.

The pharyngeal and tubal tonsils are collections of **lymphoid tissue** which lie in the

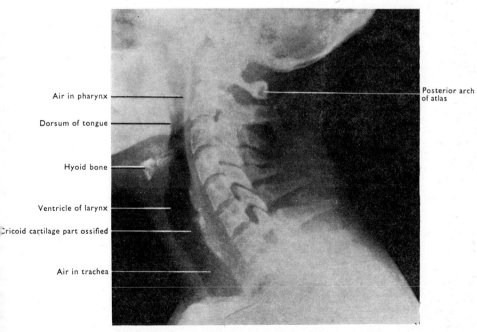

Air in pharynx

Dorsum of tongue

Hyoid bone

Ventricle of larynx

Cricoid cartilage part ossified

Air in trachea

Posterior arch of atlas

Fig. 114   Lateral radiograph of the neck.

mucous membrane, and are very closely associated with the epithelial lining, which tends to pass into the lymphoid tissue in the form of narrow clefts or pits (crypts). The lymphoid tissue is similar to that in a lymph node, but differs from it in having no afferent vessels, but only efferent vessels, and many of the lymphocytes which are produced in the germinal centres migrate through the covering epithelium into the crypts, and so into the lumen of the pharynx. Similar collections are found in the palatine and lingual tonsils in the oral part of the pharynx, the latter consisting of small scattered collections which give the pharyngeal part of the tongue its nodular appearance. Thus there is virtually a complete subepithelial ring of lymphoid tissue which surrounds the pharynx between the pharyngeal tonsil and the pharyngeal part of the tongue. This collection of lymphoid tissue, like that in the small and large intestines, appears to be concerned with protection against ingested and inspired bacteria etc., and is no doubt involved in the production of antibodies to such invading organisms. All this lymphoid tissue is normally much larger in children than in adults.

Oral Part of Pharynx

This part lies posterior to the palatoglossal arch.

Immediately posterior to the tongue is the epiglottis, a leaf-shaped, perforated plate of elastic cartilage covered by mucous membrane. The upper part of the epiglottis stands up prominently posterior to the tongue. Pull the epiglottis backwards and expose the **median glosso-epiglottic fold,** a median ridge of mucous membrane between the front of the epiglottis and the back of the tongue, with a depression on each side of it, the **epiglottic vallecula.** The **lateral glosso-epiglottic fold** is a ridge of mucous membrane that forms the lateral boundary of the vallecula, and extends from the margin of the epiglottis to the side wall of the pharynx at its junction with the tongue [Fig. 116].

The lateral wall of the oral part is the interval between the palatoglossal and palatopharyngeal arches, and it contains the palatine tonsil.

Palatine Tonsils. These masses of lymphoid tissue lie in the mucous membrane of the lateral wall of the pharynx opposite the angle of the mandible, above the back of the tongue, below the soft palate, and between the palatoglossal and palatopharyngeal arches. In children they are larger than the fossae between the arches, and extend superiorly into the soft palate, forwards external to the palatoglossal arch, and bulge into the pharynx [Fig. 113].

The medial surface is covered by mucous membrane which dips deeply into the substance of the tonsil to form about twelve narrow tonsillar **crypts.** Superiorly the tonsil

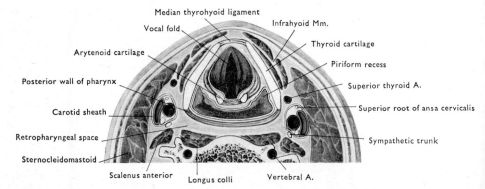

FIG. 115 Transverse section through the anterior part of the neck at the level of the upper part of the thyroid cartilage.

s bounded by a mucosal fold,
under which lies the supraton-
sillar fossa.

The lateral surface is covered
by a thin fibrous capsule which
is attached to the pharyngobasilar fascia by loose areolar
tissue, and to the sheath of the
palatoglossus muscle by a fibrous band which helps to hold
the tonsil in position. Lateral
to these structures lies the
superior constrictor muscle,
and this separates the tonsil
from the arch of the facial
artery.

**Vessels and nerves of the
Tonsil.** The chief **artery** is the
tonsillar branch of the facial
artery, which enters the inferior
part of its lateral surface. Two
veins pierce the superior constrictor near the artery, and
either end in the pharyngeal
venous plexus or unite to form
a single vessel which ends in
the facial vein. One or more
inconstant veins descend from the soft
palate, lateral to the tonsillar capsule, and
pierce the superior constrictor. They may
be a source of troublesome bleeding at tonsill-
ectomy, especially when they unite to form a
single larger vein. The **lymph vessels** pierce
the superior constrictor and pass laterally and
downwards to the nearest nodes, particularly
to those on the carotid sheath at the angle
of the mandible, and to the posterior submandibular and jugulodigastric nodes. Nerve
supply: the glossopharyngeal and lesser
palatine nerves.

Laryngeal Part of Pharynx

This part lies posterior to the larynx, and
decreases rapidly in width from above downwards.

The **posterior** and **lateral walls** are formed
by the middle and inferior constrictor muscles,
with the palatopharyngeus and stylopharyn-

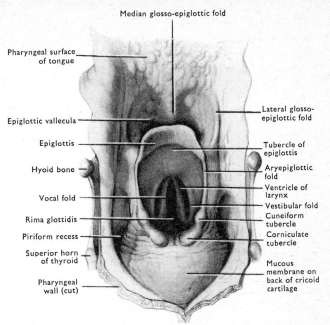

FIG. 116   Anterior wall of the laryngeal part of the pharynx seen from
above.

geus muscles internally, lined with smooth
mucous membrane.

The **anterior wall** is composed of: (1) the
inlet of the larynx with (2) a piriform recess on
each side of it, and (3) the mucous membrane
on the posterior surfaces of the arytenoid and
cricoid cartilages inferior to the inlet [FIG.
116]. Between this mucous membrane and
the cricoid cartilage is the attachment of the
longitudinal oesophageal muscle fibres to the
cricoid [FIG. 135].

Inlet of the Larynx. This is a large, oblique
opening bounded anterosuperiorly by the
epiglottis, on each side by the aryepiglottic
fold of mucous membrane, and postero-
inferiorly by the interarytenoid fold of mucous
membrane.

Each **aryepiglottic fold** is a narrow, deep
fold that extends postero-inferiorly from the
margin of the epiglottis to the arytenoid
cartilage. It contains the aryepiglottic muscle,
and, near its inferior end, two small pieces of

cartilage which form the cuneiform and corniculate tubercles in its free edge [FIG. 116].

The **arytenoid cartilages** are a pair of three-sided cartilages placed side by side on the superior border of the lamina of the cricoid cartilage [FIG. 126]. The interarytenoid fold of mucous membrane, passing between them, forms the inferior boundary of the inlet and encloses the muscles which pass between the posterior surfaces of the arytenoid cartilages [FIG. 135].

Piriform Recess. This is a fairly deep gutter which separates the lateral wall of the laryngeal inlet (the aryepiglottic fold) from the posterior part of the lamina of the thyroid cartilage and the thyrohyoid membrane. It is lined with mucous membrane and ends as a blind pocket inferiorly. In this pocket foreign bodies may lodge, and, if sharp, may pierce the mucous membrane.

The oesophageal orifice is the narrowest part of the pharynx, and lies opposite the inferior border of the cricoid cartilage.

Soft Palate

The soft palate is a flexible, muscular flap which extends postero-inferiorly from the posterior edge of the hard palate into the pharyngeal cavity. It may be raised and drawn posteriorly to meet the posterior pharyngeal wall. It thus cuts off the nasal part of the pharynx from the remainder to allow such actions as blowing out air through the mouth under pressure without any escaping through the nasal cavities. It may also be swung inferiorly against the posterior part of the tongue, and so cut off the mouth from the pharynx, allowing the cheeks to be distended with air while respiration is carried on through the nose. When it is tensed, it assists the tongue in directing food and fluids towards the laryngeal part of the pharynx in deglutition, and, by shutting off the pharyngeal isthmus, prevents regurgitation into the nose.

The soft palate is attached to the posterior edge of the hard palate and to the side walls of the pharynx, and has the uvula hanging down from the middle of its free posterior border. On each side the posterior border is

continuous with the palatopharyngeal arch.

Structure. The soft palate is made up of fold of mucous membrane which enclos parts of five pairs of muscles, of which on the uvular muscles are intrinsic. Each of t remaining pairs of muscles forms a slin the two muscles meeting in the midline of th palate where they are partly attached to th palatal aponeurosis—an intermediate fibro sheet formed from the tendons of the tens palati muscles. The convex superior surfac of the soft palate is continuous with the flo of the nasal cavities, and is covered by th same pseudostratified columnar ciliated ep thelium, except posteriorly where it is of stratified squamous type. The **mucous men brane** of the oral surface is much thicker, an contains a considerable layer of tightly packe mucous glands. It is covered by the or type of stratified squamous epithelium, an contains some taste buds, especially in chi dren.

Tensor Palati. This muscle arises from th scaphoid fossa at the base of the medi pterygoid lamina, from the spine of th sphenoid, and from the lateral side of th auditory tube between. It passes almos vertically downwards, anterior to the auditor tube, and tapering to a rounded tendon, hook round the lateral side of the pterygoid hamulu [FIG. 111]. It then spreads out horizontall into the soft palate to meet the opposite tendo in the midline and form the **palatal apo neurosis** [FIG. 151]. This aponeurosis is attache anteriorly to the palatine crests on the inferio surface of the hard palate, and is thick an rigid anteriorly, but rapidly thins posteriorl so that it cannot be identified in the posterio third of the soft palate. The uvular muscles li on the superior surface of the aponeurosis, an run side by side in the midline from the nasa spine of the palatine bones to the mucou membrane of the uvula. Action: tensor palat makes the anterior part of the soft palate rigid The **musculus uvulae** shortens and tenses th uvula, helping to prevent the soft palate fron being everted into the nasal part of the pharyn when it is in contact with the posterior pharyn geal wall, *e.g.*, in coughing.

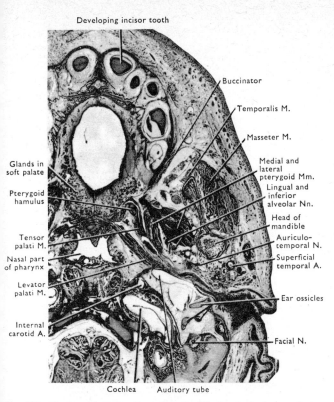

Developing incisor tooth

Buccinator

Temporalis M.

Masseter M.

Medial and lateral pterygoid Mm.

Lingual and inferior alveolar Nn.

Head of mandible

Auriculo-temporal N.

Superficial temporal A.

Ear ossicles

Facial N.

Glands in soft palate

Pterygoid hamulus

Tensor palati M.

Nasal part of pharynx

Levator palati M.

Internal carotid A.

Cochlea   Auditory tube

FIG. 117   Horizontal section through part of the head of a human foetus of seven months at the level of the soft palate.

Levator Palati. This muscle arises from the medial side of the auditory tube and the adjacent part of the petrous temporal bone. It descends inside the free upper border of the superior constrictor muscle, and passing posterior to the auditory tube, curves medially to join the opposite muscle and be partially attached to the superior surface of the palatal aponeurosis. Action: the two muscles raise the palate symmetrically [FIG. 112].

Palatoglossus. This is a small counterpart of the levator palati on the inferior surface of the palate. It is attached to the inferior surface of the palatal aponeurosis and meets the opposite muscle in the midline. Thence it converges on the palatoglossal arch, and runs through it to mingle with the muscles of the posterolateral part of the tongue. Action: the two muscles, acting together, draw the soft palate inferiorly on to the posterior part of the dorsum of the tongue.

Palatopharyngeus. The origin of this muscle from the superior surface of the palate is split by the levator palati into a lateral part (which arises from the posterior margin of the hard palate) and a medial part which is attached to the opposite muscle and to the palatal aponeurosis on the superior surface of the palate. Most of the muscle converges on the palatopharyngeal arch and runs inferiorly in it, on the internal surfaces of the constrictor muscles. Superiorly, it is joined by the salpingopharyngeus, and inferiorly by the stylopharyngeus at the interval between the middle and superior constrictors. It is inserted into the posterior border of the lamina of the thyroid cartilage and fans out into the posterior pharyngeal wall. A few of its fibres, which arise from the hard palate, pass horizontally backwards with the fibres of the superior constrictor and so surround the pharyngeal isthmus.

Action: the main mass of the muscle depresses the palate on to the posterior part of the dorsum of the tongue, and prevents the soft palate from being forced into the nasal part of the pharynx when blowing through the mouth against resistance. The horizontal fibres, with those of the superior constrictor, narrow the pharyngeal isthmus and raise a ridge in its wall against which the soft palate is elevated by the levator palati to separate the oral and nasal parts of the pharynx.

Salpingopharyngeus. This slender muscle arises by one or two slips from the inferior

155

border of the cartilage of the auditory tube at its pharyngeal end. It descends in the salpingopharyngeal fold to join palatopharyngeus.

Vessels and Nerves of Soft Palate. The ascending palatine branch of the facial artery is the principal supply. It ascends on the lateral pharyngeal wall to the superior border of the superior constrictor, and hooking over this, descends with the levator to the palate. This main arterial supply is supplemented by the lesser palatine branches of the greater palatine artery.

The **lesser palatine nerves** supply the mucous membrane. The tensor palati is supplied by the **mandibular nerve** through the otic ganglion; all the other muscles are supplied from the vago-accessory complex by fibres that reach the **pharyngeal plexus** through the pharyngeal branch of the vagus.

DISSECTION. The dissection of the soft palate is difficult, but with careful removal of the mucous membrane and gentle blunt dissection, the main muscles can be shown satisfactorily. Begin by removing the mucous membrane from both surfaces, from the palatoglossal and palatopharyngeal arches, and from the salpingopharyngeal fold, to expose the muscles within them. [Fig. 113].

To display the levator and tensor palati, remove the mucous membrane, the submucosa, and pharyngobasilar fascia from the lateral wall of the pharynx anterior and posterior to the opening of the auditory tube. Identify the levator posterior to the auditory tube, and follow it into the palate. The ascending palatine artery may be seen descending beside the levator to the palate. Trace the tensor inferiorly to the pterygoid hamulus and follow its tendon into the palatal aponeurosis [Fig. 112].

On the left side, identify the superior constrictor lateral to the levator palati. Clean its superior border and remove the mucous membrane from the parts of its medial surface which are not covered by the palatal muscles. Dissect out the tonsil and uncover the anterior part of the superior constrictor muscle. This part is difficult to define as some of its fibres sweep inferiorly into the tongue, and it is often partly covered by thin sheets of muscle fibres passing inferiorly from the palate lateral to the tonsil. Anterior to palatoglossus, strip the thick glandular mucous membrane from the inferior surface of the most anterior part of the soft palate, and uncover the pterygoid hamulus with the tendon of tensor palati hooking round it to form the palatal aponeurosis. Identify the pterygomandibular raphe passing from the

hamulus to the mandible, and follow the superior constrictor anteriorly to the raphe.

Note the styloglossus entering the posterolateral aspect of the tongue by passing inferior to the superior constrictor close to the medial side of the mandible. Pull the muscle medially and identify the posterior border of mylohyoid attached to the mandible inferior to the pterygomandibular raphe. In the angle between the mylohyoid, superior constrictor, and the styloglossus, note part of the submandibular gland and the lingual nerve passing anteriorly between the first two muscles.

Anterior to the pterygomandibular raphe, strip the mucous membrane from the internal surface of the buccinator and identify its attachments, and the opening of the parotid duct [Fig. 112].

Identify the greater horn of the hyoid bone, and clean the mucous membrane from the medial surface of the middle constrictor, leaving the palatopharyngeus in position on its medial aspect. Follow the latter muscle to the posterior border of the lamina of the thyroid cartilage. Anterior to palatopharyngeus, identify the stylopharyngeus entering the pharynx between the middle and superior constrictor muscles to spread anteroposteriorly in such a manner that its posterior fibres are inserted with those of the palatopharyngeus, while the anterior fibres pass to the lateral aspect of the epiglottis. The intermediate fibres form a thin layer medial to the superior part of the thyrohyoid membrane, and the internal laryngeal nerve may be found entering the pharynx through that membrane below the fibres of the muscle [Fig. 118]. Find the glossopharyngeal nerve anterior to the stylopharyngeus where it enters the pharynx, and trace the nerve to the tongue.

Pull the half tongue medially and remove the mucous membrane from the sulcus between it and the mandible. Identify the attachment of the mylohyoid to the mandible, and clean the structures on its superior surface, including the submandibular duct and gland, the sublingual gland, and the lingua and hypoglossal nerves. Trace these structures anteriorly, and clean the superior surface of the mylohyoid muscle to its attachments; the inferior part is best displayed by raising geniohyoid and cleaning beneath it [Fig. 113].

Finally clean the mucous membrane from the medial surface of the inferior constrictor, the upper part of the oesophagus, and the piriform recess. In the latter identify the medial surface of the thyroid cartilage and the thyrohyoid membrane with the superior laryngeal vessels and the internal branch of the superior laryngeal nerve piercing it.

Swallowing

Now that the walls of the pharynx have been seen from the medial aspect, it is possible

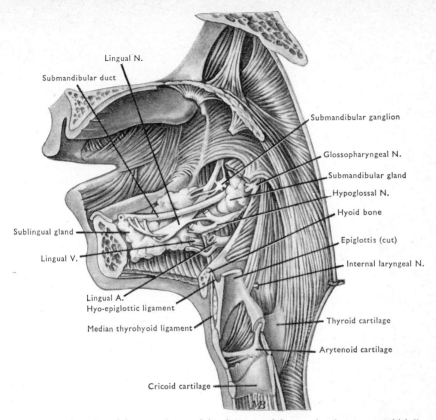

Lingual N.

Submandibular duct

Submandibular ganglion

Glossopharyngeal N.

Submandibular gland

Hypoglossal N.

Hyoid bone

Sublingual gland

Lingual V.

Epiglottis (cut)

Internal laryngeal N.

Lingual A.
Hyo-epiglottic ligament

Median thyrohyoid ligament

Thyroid cartilage

Arytenoid cartilage

Cricoid cartilage

FIG. 118   Dissection of the constrictors of the pharynx and the associated structures which lie adjacent to the mucous membrane lining the mouth, pharynx, and larynx, from the medial side.   The tongue has been removed to expose the structures which lie between it and the mylohyoid muscle.   See also FIG. 112.

visualize the mechanism of swallowing.

In the first phase, the tip of the tongue is raised against the hard palate anterior to the bolus of food or fluid, and this is squeezed posteriorly by pressing progressively more posterior parts of the tongue against the palate (intrinsic muscles of the tongue, mylohyoid and styloglossus).   As this movement passes backwards, the elevation of the posterior part of the tongue against the tensed anterior part of the soft palate (tensor palati) is achieved by raising the hyoid bone (digastric, stylohyoid, and geniohyoid).   Geniohyoid also carries the hyoid bone anteriorly, and this increases the

anteroposterior diameter of the oral part of the pharynx to receive the bolus, the middle and inferior constrictor muscles being relaxed. At this stage the superior constrictor muscle and horizontal fibres of palatopharyngeus contract to draw the upper part of the posterior pharyngeal wall against the raised posterior part of the soft palate (levator palati).   This effectively shuts off the nasal part of the pharynx from the oral part and prevents passage of food into the nasal part of the pharynx.

The second phase is very rapid.   There is a considerable elevation of the larynx and the inferior part of the pharynx which is attached

157

to it (thyrohyoid and stylopharyngeus muscles). When the larynx is raised, the thyroid cartilage is brought close to the hyoid bone and the arytenoid cartilages are approximated to the epiglottis (thyrohyoid). Contraction of the aryepiglottic muscles [FIG. 135] produces a sphincteric action on the pharyngeal orifice of the larynx and draws the tip of the epiglottis down into firmer contact with the arytenoid cartilages. This action is no doubt assisted by the elevation of the base of the epiglottis with the thyroid cartilage, and by the contraction of the fibres of stylopharyngeus which are inserted into the base of the epiglottis while the pharyngeal surface of the tongue bulges posteriorly pushing the tip of the epiglottis in this direction. These actions effectively close the pharyngeal aperture of the larynx. The bolus slips over the the lingual surface of the epiglottis, which now faces superiorly, and is caught by the middle constrictor to be carried inferiorly by a wave of contraction in this muscle and the inferior constrictor, aided by the downward displacement of the larynx and pharynx (infrahyoid muscles) which follows almost immediately.

AUDITORY TUBE

This tube connects the nasal part of the pharynx to the middle ear cavity, and beyond that to the mastoid air cells through the mastoid antrum. It is approximately 3·5 cm. long. The posterolateral 1·5 cm. has a bony wall where it lies between the tympanic and petrous parts of the temporal bone and opens into the middle ear cavity. The anteromedial part has a wall composed mainly of cartilage. It lies in the groove between the petrous part of the temporal bone and the posterior border of the greater wing of the sphenoid; identify the groove and the bony part of the tube on a dried skull.

Ascertain the direction of the cartilaginous part of the tube by passing a probe into its pharyngeal orifice. At first it runs superiorly and then posterolaterally, and passes for a considerable part of its extent between the tensor and the levator palati muscles [FIG 149, 151].

Note that the levator palati forms a round prominence inferior to the opening of th auditory tube. Remove the mucous membra from the mouth of the tube, and note that t superior and medial walls are formed by folded plate of cartilage; the inferolateral pa of the tube being completed by dense fibro tissue joining the edges of the cartilagino plate. The tubal ridge is formed by the base the cartilage plate. The lining of the tube respiratory, pseudostratified ciliated column epithelium, which is continuous with the sar epithelium in the pharynx and with simp cubical epithelium in the middle ear. In t tube it contains some goblet cells, and there a mixed mucous and serous glands in the su mucosa of the cartilaginous part near t pharynx. The lumen is narrowest (isthmu where the cartilaginous and bony parts me but it gradually increases in diameter from t isthmus to the pharyngeal orifice, which is t widest part of the tube.

The function of this tube is to equalize t pressure in the middle ear with the atmospher pressure, and so allow free movement of t tympanic membrane which separates t external acoustic meatus from the middle e cavity. It also forms a route through whi infections may pass from the nasal part of t pharynx to the middle ear, and is read blocked even by mild infections, because t walls of its cartilaginous part lie in appositio When the auditory tube is blocked, the residu air in the middle ear is liable to be absorb into the blood vessels of that cavity, th causing the pressure within it to fall. This i pedes the free movement of the tympar membrane and interferes with hearing.

DISSECTION. If a clear view of the otic gangl [p. 98] has not already been achieved, free the openi of the auditory tube from the medial pterygoid lami and turn it posteriorly, separating the cartilagine part from the base of the skull and tensor palati, a exposing a small slip of muscle arising from the petr temporal bone superomedial to the tube and passi posterolaterally with it—the tensor tympani. Deta the tensor palati from the base of the skull and turn inferiorly. **Remove the layer of fascia which is exposed and uncover the mandibular nerve with the otic ganglion on its anteromedial aspect. Immediately posterior to the mandibular nerve lies the middle meningeal artery at the foramen spinosum. Identify the branches of the mandibular nerve as far as possible from this aspect, and note how close is its relation to the pharyngeal wall. Confirm this on the base of a macerated skull.**

CAROTID CANAL

The carotid canal lies in the petrous part of the temporal bone. It contains the internal carotid artery, the internal carotid plexus of sympathetic nerve fibres, and a plexus of veins. Its position and course can best be seen by inspecting a macerated skull.

Internal Carotid Artery

The part of the internal carotid artery in the canal is approximately 2 cm. long. At first it ascends vertically; then bending anteromedially, it runs horizontally to the apex of the petrous temporal bone and enters the foramen lacerum through its posterior wall. The artery turns upwards in the foramen lacerum, pierces

the endocranium, and enters the middle cranial fossa [p. 62]. In the carotid canal, it lies inferomedial to the middle ear and inferior to the cochlea, the greater petrosal nerve, and the trigeminal ganglion [FIG. 151].

Internal Carotid Nerve and Plexus [FIG. 152]

The internal carotid nerve is a large branch which ascends from the superior cervical ganglion, and enters the carotid canal. It divides to form the internal carotid plexus around the internal carotid artery, and secondary plexuses extend from it around the branches of the artery.

Branches. The plexus consists predominantly of postganglionic sympathetic fibres which are distributed to the cerebral vessels, to the middle ear (caroticotympanic nerves) to the nose, palate, air sinuses and pharynx through the branches of the pterygopalatine ganglion (to which it sends the deep petrosal nerve), and to the contents of the orbit through branches which it gives to the 3rd, 4th, 6th, and ophthalmic branch of the 5th cranial nerves, and on the ophthalmic artery.

THE CAVITY OF THE NOSE

SEPTUM OF NOSE

The septum of the nose divides the nasal cavity into two narrow cavities. It is seldom placed accurately in the median plane, but bulges to one or other side (more frequently to the right). Immediately above the nostril, the septum is slightly concave where it forms the medial wall of the vestibule of the nose, the skin of which carries a number of stiff hairs or vibrissae. The remainder of the septum is covered with mucous membrane the epithelium of which is pseudostratified columnar ciliated epithelium. It is tightly adherent to the underlying periosteum and perichondrium (mucoperiosteum and mucoperichondrium). The lower, larger area is known as the **respiratory region**, while the upper third is called the **olfactory region** because its epithelium contains the olfactory nerve cells. The respiratory mucous membrane is thick, spongy, and

highly vascular. It contains numerous mucous glands and is capable of swelling to a considerable thickness when the vascular spaces in it are filled with blood. It also contains many arteriovenous anastomoses which facilitate the flow of blood through it and warm the air passing over it. The olfactory mucous membrane is more delicate, and is yellowish in the fresh state.

Structure. Strip the mucous membrane off the septum, and expose: (1) the vomer; (2) the perpendicular plate of the ethmoid; (3) the septal cartilage; (4) small parts of the maxillary, palatine, nasal, and sphenoid bones. The relative positions of these parts are shown in FIGURE 119.

Note that the anterior angle of the septal cartilage is blunt and rounded, and does not reach the point of the nose which is formed by the greater alar cartilages.

159

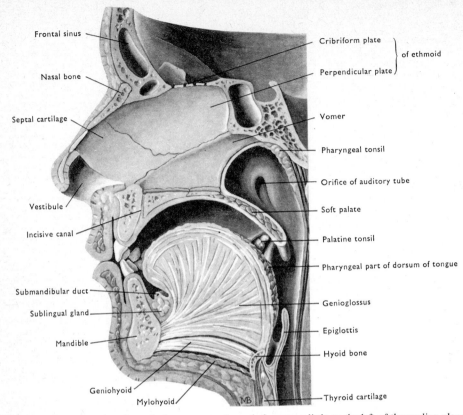

Frontal sinus

Nasal bone

Septal cartilage

Cribriform plate
Perpendicular plate
} of ethmoid

Vomer

Pharyngeal tonsil

Orifice of auditory tube

Vestibule

Soft palate

Incisive canal

Palatine tonsil

Pharyngeal part of dorsum of tongue

Submandibular duct

Sublingual gland

Genioglossus

Mandible

Epiglottis

Hyoid bone

Geniohyoid

Mylohyoid

Thyroid cartilage

Fig. 119   Sagittal section through the nose, mouth, and pharynx, a little to the left of the median plane.

DISSECTION. Remove the septum piecemeal from the mucous membrane on its opposite surface, taking care not to damage the structures in that mucous membrane.

Nerves of Septum. (nerves of smell, see p. 164). The **nasopalatine nerve** is a long, slender nerve that is easily identified on the deep surface of the mucous membrane of the septum. It springs from the pterygopalatine ganglion, and enters the nasal cavity through the sphenopalatine foramen with the spheno-palatine branch of the maxillary artery. It runs medially across the roof of the nasal cavity, and then antero-inferiorly, to the floor of the nose, in a groove on the surface of the vomer. It then runs through the incisive canal

and median incisive foramen to supply the mucous membrane in the anterior part of the hard palate.

The medial **posterosuperior nasal branches** of the pterygopalatine ganglion, together with twigs from the nerve of the pterygoid canal, supply the posterosuperior parts of the septum, but are too small to be dissected easily.

The medial nasal branches of the **anterior ethmoidal nerve** run on the anterosuperior part of the nasal septum as far as the vestibule.

Arteries of Septum. These are: (1) The sphenopalatine artery, a branch of the maxillary artery; (2) ethmoidal branches of the ophthalmic artery; (3) branches of the superior labial arteries [FIG. 26].

160

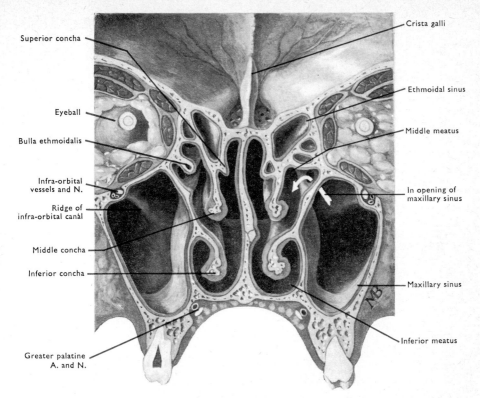

Labels on figure:
- Superior concha
- Eyeball
- Bulla ethmoidalis
- Infra-orbital vessels and N.
- Ridge of infra-orbital canal
- Middle concha
- Inferior concha
- Greater palatine A. and N.
- Crista galli
- Ethmoidal sinus
- Middle meatus
- In opening of maxillary sinus
- Maxillary sinus
- Inferior meatus

Fig. 120 Coronal section through the nasal cavities, paranasal sinuses, and orbits, seen from behind.

DISSECTION. Disengage the nerves from the mucous membrane of the septum, so that they may later be followed to their origins. Then remove the mucous membrane and open the nasal cavity.

CAVITY OF THE NOSE

Each cavity is approximately 5 cm. in height, and 5–7 cm. in length. It is narrow transversely, measuring approximately 1·5 cm. at the floor, and only 1–2 mm. at the roof. The width is further reduced by the conchae, which project into the cavity from the lateral wall.

The anterior apertures or nostrils are a pair of oval orifices which open on the inferior surface of the external nose. The posterior apertures or **choanae** open into the nasal part of the pharynx and face postero-inferiorly.

Roof

The roof, 7–8 cm. long, is curved. The middle part is formed by the cribriform plate of the ethmoid, and is nearly horizontal. The sloping anterior and posterior parts are formed respectively by: (1) the nasal part of the frontal bone, the nasal bone, and by the junction of lateral and septal cartilages; (2) the anterior and inferior surfaces of the body of the sphenoid and the bones in contact with these surfaces.

Floor

The floor is about 5 cm. long and 1–1·5 cm. in width. It is formed by the palatine process of the maxilla and the horizontal process of the palatine bone. It is concave transversely, and slightly higher anteriorly than posteriorly.

161

Lateral Wall

The lateral wall is very uneven owing to the projection of the three conchae. The different bones that form the lateral wall of the nose should be studied in a median section of a macerated skull, and the dissector should constantly refer to such a preparation during the dissection. Lateral to the lateral wall are the air sinuses. The air-filled spaces in the bones communicate with the nasal cavity. The ethmoidal sinuses lie between the upper part of the nasal cavity and the orbit, while inferior to these is the maxillary sinus which lies inferior to the orbit [FIGS. 47, 120].

The lateral wall of the nose is divisible into three areas:

1. The **vestibule** of the nose [FIGS. 119, 121] is the part immediately above the nostril. It is lined with skin from which stout hairs or vibrissae grow, and its shape can be changed by contraction of the nasal muscles. The anterior vibrissae are directed posteriorly, the

posterior are directed anteriorly, thus forming a fine filter of hairs.

2. The **atrium** of the middle meatus [FIG. 121] is above and slightly posterior to the vestibule, and immediately anterior to the middle meatus. Its lateral wall is concave, except close to the nasal bone where a feeble elevation, the **agger nasi,** represents an additional concha which is present in some mammals.

3. **Nasal conchae** and **meatuses** [FIGS. 121, 122].

The conchae are three bony plates which project from the lateral wall of the nose and curve inferiorly. The meatuses are the spaces inferior to conchae. The upper two conchae are processes of the ethmoid, the inferior concha is an independent bone, and all are covered with thick, highly vascular mucous membrane.

The **superior concha** lies in the postero-superior part of the cavity, and is very short

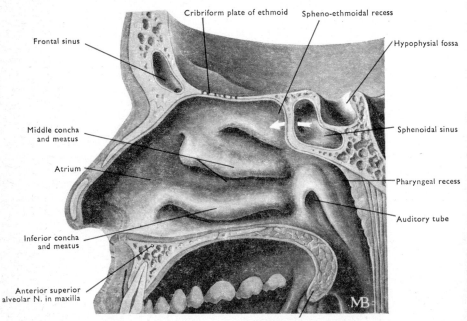

Frontal sinus

Cribriform plate of ethmoid   Spheno-ethmoidal recess

Hypophysial fossa

Middle concha and meatus

Atrium

Sphenoidal sinus

Pharyngeal recess

Auditory tube

Inferior concha and meatus

Anterior superior alveolar N. in maxilla

MB

Uvula turned forwards

FIG. 121   Sagittal section through the nose and palate to show the lateral wall of the nose.

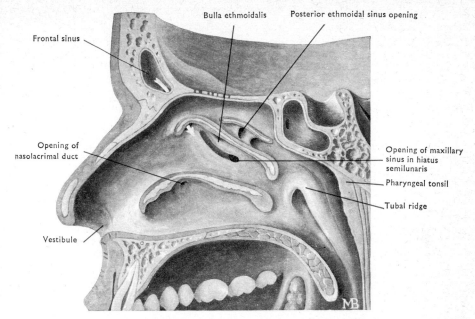

Frontal sinus

Bulla ethmoidalis

Posterior ethmoidal sinus opening

Opening of
nasolacrimal duct

Opening of maxillary
sinus in hiatus
semilunaris

Pharyngeal tonsil

Tubal ridge

Vestibule

MB

Fig. 122   Sagittal section through the nose and palate. The conchae have been cut away to expose the
meatuses and the openings into them. The opening of the infundibulum is unusual.

Its free border begins a little inferior to the
middle of the cribriform plate, and passes
postero-inferiorly to end immediately anterior
to the lower part of the body of the sphenoid.
The space posterosuperior to it is known as
the **spheno-ethmoidal recess**, and the sphenoidal
sinus opens into its posterior part [Fig. 121].

The **middle concha** is much larger and
extends from the atrium to the level of the
choanae.

The **inferior concha** is slightly longer than
the middle concha, and lies about midway
between the middle concha and the floor of the
nose.

The **superior meatus** is a narrow fissure between the superior and middle conchae. The
posterior ethmoidal sinuses open into its
anterosuperior part by one or more orifices.
These can be exposed by forcing the margin of
the superior concha upwards.

The **middle meatus** is a much longer and
wider passage than the superior meatus. To
expose it, tilt the middle concha forcibly up-

wards. The anterosuperior part of the middle
meatus leads into a funnel-shaped opening,
the **infundibulum**, through which it communicates with the frontal sinus [Fig. 122].

On the lateral wall of the middle meatus is
a deep, curved groove which begins at, or
slightly behind, the infundibulum and runs
postero-inferiorly. This is the **hiatus semilunaris** [Fig. 122] and the anterior ethmoidal
and maxillary sinuses open into it. The upper
margin of the hiatus semilunaris is formed by
a prominent bulge, the **bulla ethmoidalis**, on
which is the opening of the middle ethmoidal
sinuses.

The **opening of the maxillary sinus** [Fig. 120]
lies in the posterior part of the hiatus semilunaris, and enters the upper medial wall of the
sinus. Occasionally there is a second opening
and this leads into the middle meatus superior
to the middle of the attachment of the inferior
concha. It should be noted that the relative
positions of the openings of the maxillary and
frontal sinuses favours the flow of material

163

from the latter to the former, and the consequent spread of infection from the frontal to the maxillary sinus.

The **inferior meatus** is the horizontal passage between the inferior concha and the floor of the nose. The nasolacrimal duct opens into the anterior part of the inferior meatus close to the attached border of the inferior concha.

DISSECTION. Remove the anterior part of the inferior concha with scissors, and expose the opening of the nasolacrimal duct. Pass a probe upwards along the duct to confirm its continuity with the lacrimal sac. Separate the medial margin of the aperture from the overlying bone, and, passing a probe between the duct and the bone, break away the thin plate of bone which separates the duct from the nose, and expose the length of the duct and the sac at its superior end by continuing the bony removal to the level of the eye [Fig. 123].

Orifice of Nasolacrimal Duct. It may be wide, patent, and circular, or the mucous membrane may extend over the opening as a lacrimal fold, thus reducing its size and acting as a flap valve. In a few cases the orifice is so small that it is difficult to find.

Mucosa of Lateral Wall of Nasal Cavity. Apart from the vestibule, which is covered with skin, the lateral wall is covered with mucous membrane which is tightly adherent to the underlying periosteum and forms a **mucoperiosteum** — a lining which is found throughout the remainder of the nasal cavity. This mucoperiosteum is continuous: (1) through the nasolacrimal duct, with the ocular conjunctiva; (2) through the various apertures, with the lining of the air sinuses in the frontal, ethmoid, maxilla, and sphenoid; (3) through the posterior apertures with the mucous membrane of the nasal part of the pharynx.

The mucoperiosteum on the lateral wall is divisible into the upper, yellowish **olfactory region** in the general area of the superior concha, and the remainder which comprises the **respiratory region.** These regions cannot be differentiated by the naked eye because of the absence of any sharp line of demarcation between them. In the respiratory region, the mucoperiosteum is thick and spongy, especially on the free margins and posterior extremities of the middle and inferior conchae. These spongy, bulging regions are due to the presence of rich venous plexuses in the mucoperiosteum, and these may even have the character of cavernous tissue, more particularly on the inferior concha. Here the mucoperiosteum may be so swollen by distended venous channels that it extends medially to the septum, and reduces the cross sectional area of the nasal cavity to such an extent that the air passing through it comes into close association with the warm, moist surface. This effectively warms and moistens the inspired air which also deposits dust particles on the mucus covering its ciliated surface, whence they are wafted towards the anterior aperture of the nose. Numerous mucous glands are present over the surface of the mucoperiosteum, and their ducts are visible to the unaided eye.

Nerves and Vessels on Lateral Wall of Nasal Cavity. The nerves of common sensation all arise as branches of the maxillary nerve, except for the **anterior ethmoidal,** which is a branch of the nasociliary nerve in the orbit and reaches the anterosuperior part of the nasal cavity through the anterior ethmoidal foramen and cribriform plate of the ethmoid. The nerve fibres from the maxillary nerve reach the nose through branches of the pterygopalatine ganglion, the anterior superior alveolar nerve, and the greater palatine nerve. In addition to sensory fibres, they also convey postganglionic parasympathetic nerve fibres from the pterygopalatine ganglion, and these supply the glands in the mucoperiosteum.

The **olfactory nerves** are formed as the processes of the olfactory cells in the epithelium of the olfactory area. These fine, non-myelinated nerve fibres run in shallow grooves and small canals in the bone deep to the mucous membrane, but they are so soft that it is impossible to identify them by dissection. They form twelve to twenty olfactory nerves which pass through the cribriform plate of the ethmoid, and, piercing the meninges, enter the inferior surface of the olfactory bulb.

DISSECTION. Trace the nasopalatine nerve from the nasal septum across the roof of the nasal cavity to the sphenopalatine foramen in the lateral wall. Careful dissection in this region may display one or more of the nasal branches of the pterygopalatine ganglion, and will also display the sphenopalatine artery running with the nasopalatine nerve.

The **nasal branches of the pterygopalatine ganglion** are minute twigs which are accompanied by filaments from the nerve of the pterygoid canal. They pass through the sphenopalatine foramen, and supply the mucous membrane on the posterior part of the septum, the superior and middle conchae, the ethmoidal air sinuses, and the lateral wall of the nasal part of the pharynx [FIG. 123].

DISSECTION. Carefully reflect the mucous membrane on the medial pterygoid lamina anteriorly and attempt to find the nasal branches of the greater palatine nerve, which pierce the perpendicular plate of the palatine bone.

Two **nasal branches of the greater palatine nerve** pierce the perpendicular plate of the palatine bone, and supply the mucous membrane on the posterior parts of the conchae and meatuses.

The **anterior ethmoidal nerve** [FIG. 123] descends in a groove on the deep surface of the nasal bone and supplies the anterosuperior parts of the septum and lateral wall.

The **sphenopalatine branch of the maxillary artery** is the main supply to the mucoperiosteum. It enters through the sphenopalatine foramen and is distributed with the various nerves. The anterior and posterior **ethmoidal arteries** supplement this supply in the anterosuperior part.

PTERYGOPALATINE GANGLION,
MAXILLARY ARTERY, AND
MAXILLARY NERVE

The pterygopalatine ganglion lies in the pterygopalatine fossa, lateral to the sphenopalatine foramen and the perpendicular plate of the palatine bone.

DISSECTION. The mucoperiosteum has already been stripped from the perpendicular plate of the

palatine bone, and the greater palatine nerve can be seen shining through this very thin plate of bone, as it descends on the lateral side of the bone to reach the palate, with the descending palatine branch of the maxillary artery.

Break through the perpendicular plate of the palatine bone and expose part of the greater palatine nerve; then open up the whole length of the canal by levering off the remainder of the lamina lying medial to the nerve. Superiorly, the greater palatine nerve joins the pterygopalatine ganglion at the level of the sphenopalatine foramen, through which the nasopalatine nerve passes to the ganglion. Inferiorly, where the canal reaches the hard palate, cut out a narrow, transverse strip of the hard palate to open into the palatine foramen, through which the greater palatine nerve reaches the hard palate. Remove the fibrous sheath covering the greater palatine nerve and expose the lesser palatine nerves which run with it in the upper part of their course, but leave inferiorly to pass through separate bony canals. As far as possible open these canals, and follow the lesser palatine nerves to their termination in the soft palate. One of the lesser palatine nerves is more lateral in position, and hence difficult to follow from the medial side: it may be absent.

Turn to the inferior surface of the palate, and follow the greater palatine nerve and artery in the hard palate.

Greater Palatine Nerve

This is the largest branch of the pterygopalatine ganglion. It descends vertically through the greater palatine canal and foramen with the descending palatine branch of the maxillary artery, and enters the inferior surface of the hard palate at its posterolateral corner. It runs forwards in a groove on the inferior surface of the bony palate close to its lateral margin, and, reaching the incisive fossa, communicates there with the terminal branches of the nasopalatine nerve. It supplies the gum and the mucous membrane of the hard palate, including the numerous palatine mucous glands which indent the inferior surface of the bone.

Branches. (1) It sends two **nasal** branches through the perpendicular plate of the palatine bone to the mucous membrane of the nose (above). (2) The **lesser palatine nerves** descend through the lesser palatine canals. The more medial of these emerges immediately posterior to the palatine crest, and enters the soft palate to supply its mucous membrane and glands. The more lateral nerve, when present, supplies the mucous membrane of the soft palate near the palatine tonsil.

DISSECTION. Remove the three nasal conchae, and, beginning just posterior to the infundibulum, strip away the thin medial walls of the ethmoidal air cells, noting their continuity with the nasal mucous membrane through the apertures already described. Remove the mucous membrane lining these sinuses and the dividing walls between them, and thus expose the medial surface of the orbital lamina of the ethmoid.

Break away the medial wall of the maxillary sinus from the nasolacrimal duct anteriorly to the greater palatine canal posteriorly, and examine the interior of the sinus [p. 72]. Remove the orbital process of the palatine bone and as much of the posterior part of the roof of the maxillary sinus as may be necessary to expose the maxillary nerve in the pterygopalatine fossa [pp. 99–100]. This also exposes the anterior surface of the pterygopalatine ganglion and the terminal part of the maxillary artery. Chip away the sphenoid bone medial to the ganglion, taking care to preserve the pharyngeal branch of the ganglion and the nerve of the pterygoid canal, which enters the posterior surface of the ganglion.

Follow the infra-orbital nerve [p. 99] anteriorly by chipping away the floor of the infra-orbital groove and canal. Find the anterior superior alveolar branch of the nerve, and trace this through its sinuous, bony canal [Fig. 123], below the opening of the nasolacrimal duct, into the anterior part of the floor of the nose superior to the incisor teeth. Lift the latter nerve gently out of its canal, and note its branches to the upper teeth, gums, and mucous membrane of the maxillary sinus. Where necessary, remove the branches of the maxillary artery in order to get a clear view of the nerves.

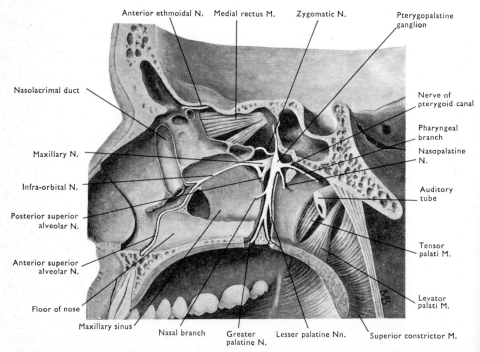

FIG. 123 The same specimen as FIG. 122. The mucous membrane and a large part of the bone of the lateral wall of the nose has been removed to expose the maxillary sinus and break through the ethmoidal sinuses into the orbit (cf. FIG. 120). The mucous membrane has also been stripped from the pharynx and lateral wall of the mouth, and the maxillary, infra-orbital, anterior superior alveolar, and palatine nerves exposed by removal of the bony wall of their canals. The pterygopalatine fossa and ganglion are also exposed.

Pterygopalatine Ganglion

This ganglion is a small, triangular body which lies in the superior part of the pterygopalatine fossa opposite the sphenopalatine foramen. It is surrounded by the terminal branches of the maxillary artery.

Roots. It is suspended from the inferior aspect of the maxillary nerve by two stout ganglionic branches. The sensory fibres of the trigeminal nerve in these branches pass directly through the ganglion into its branches. The sympathetic and parasympathetic roots enter the ganglion via the **nerve of the pterygoid canal,** which is formed by the union of the greater petrosal branch of the facial nerve (parasympathetic preganglionic fibres) and the deep petrosal branch of the internal carotid sympathetic plexus [FIG. 152]. Only the preganglionic parasympathetic fibres relay on the cells of the pterygopalatine ganglion, which give rise to secretory fibres that pass into all the branches of the ganglion, and run with the sensory fibres from the maxillary nerve. They supply glands in the nose, palate, pharynx, and the lacrimal gland.

Branches. (1) Palatine [p. 165]. (2) The **orbital branches** are two to three filaments which enter the orbit through the inferior orbital fissure to supply the orbital periosteum (sensory) and the lacrimal gland (secretory). (3) The **nasopalatine** and **nasal nerves** pass through the sphenopalatine foramen to the mucous membrane of the nose [p. 160]. (4) The **pharyngeal branch** passes posteriorly through the palato-vaginal canal to the mucous membrane of the sphenoidal air sinus and the roof of the pharynx.

Termination of Maxillary Artery

The third part of the maxillary artery enters the pterygopalatine fossa through the pterygomaxillary fissure. It breaks up into branches which accompany all the nerves in the fossa (infra-orbital, greater palatine, nasopalatine, pharyngeal, and nerve of the pterygoid canal) and receive the same names.

Maxillary Sinus [FIGS. 120, 123]

This is the largest of the paranasal air sinuses. It occupies the whole of the body of the maxilla, and has the shape of an irregular three-sided pyramid. The **apex** extends into the zygomatic process of the maxilla, and the **base** is the lower part of the lateral wall of the nose. The sides are the orbital, anterior, and infratemporal surfaces of the maxilla. Where the base and anterior surfaces meet, it lies superior to the molar and premolar teeth. The lowest part of this sinus is opposite the second premolar and first molar teeth, and is approximately 1 cm. below the level of the floor of the nose.

Nasal Opening. The sinus opens into the middle meatus of the nasal cavity through an aperture in the superior part of its base, a feature which makes it impossible for fluid in the sinus to escape until the sinus is nearly filled when the head is in the erect position.

The infra-orbital groove and canal run forwards in the bone of the roof of the sinus, and, as the canal bends inferiorly towards the infraorbital foramen, it produces a marked ridge in the angle between the orbital and anterior surfaces of the sinus. The posterior superior alveolar nerve and vessels run in the lower part of the infratemporal and anterior walls of the sinus; the anterior superior alveolar nerve and vessels are in the orbital and anterior surfaces. The **mucous membrane** of the sinus is supplied by branches of these nerves and by the branches of the greater palatine nerve which supply the lateral wall of the nose. It is covered with ciliated columnar epithelium, and the cilia waft the mucus on its surface towards the opening into the nose. In some situations, the bone which separates the nerves from the mucous membrane of the sinus may be absent, and this, combined with the fact that the alveolar nerves supply the teeth and the mucous lining of the sinus, may be responsible for the sensation of toothache which frequently accompanies inflammation in the sinus.

THE LARYNX

STRUCTURE AND POSITION

The larynx is the upper, expanded part of the windpipe which extends from the trachea (at the level of the sixth cervical vertebra) to the pharynx, and is specially modified for the production of the voice.

It lies anterior to and parallel with the laryngeal part of the pharynx, and opens into its anterior wall by a long, almost vertical orifice which stretches from the back of the tongue downwards to the level of the middle of the thyroid cartilage [FIG. 113]. The margin of this orifice (composed of the epiglottis, the aryepiglottic folds, and the arytenoid cartilages, all covered by mucous membrane, FIGURE 116) projects into the anterior part of the pharynx, which thus extends anteriorly on each side of it, to form deep gutters between the aryepiglottic folds and the laminae of the thyroid cartilage, the **piriform recesses.**

The walls of the larynx are supported by the cricoid, thyroid, epiglottic, and arytenoid cartilages [FIG. 126], and the rigidity of the lower part of each aryepiglottic fold is increased by two small nodules, the corniculate and cuneiform cartilages [FIG. 116].

Cricoid Cartilage

Inferiorly, the larynx is surrounded by the cricoid cartilage which is shaped like a signet ring and has a narrow bar or arch of hyaline cartilage anteriorly [FIG. 124]. It deepens laterally [FIG. 129], and posteriorly [FIG. 126] forms a vertical lamina which extends superiorly between the free posterior margins of the la-

minae of the thyroid cartilage. The superior surface of the lamina of the cricoid cartilage is surmounted by the two arytenoid cartilages, one on each side [FIG. 126] and it is here that the mucous membrane of the posterior wall of the larynx becomes continuous with that of the anterior wall of the pharynx by curving over the arytenoid cartilages. From this point the mucous membrane of the anterior wall of the pharynx may be followed inferiorly on the posterior surfaces of the arytenoid cartilages and the lamina of the cricoid cartilage and the muscles covering them. Thence it passes on to the muscle of the anterior wall of the oesophagus which is attached to the posterior surface of the lamina of the cricoid.

The arch of the cricoid cartilage is attached anteriorly to the inferior margin of the thyroid

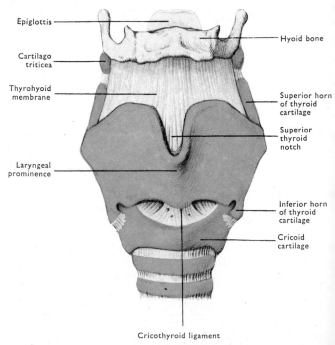

Epiglottis

Cartilago triticea

Thyrohyoid membrane

Laryngeal prominence

Hyoid bone

Superior horn of thyroid cartilage

Superior thyroid notch

Inferior horn of thyroid cartilage

Cricoid cartilage

Cricothyroid ligament

FIG. 124   Anterior aspect of the cartilages (blue) and ligaments of the larynx

168

artilage by the cricothyroid ligament. laterally the gap between these two cartilages filled by the cricothyroid muscle [FIG. 134] nd by the inferior horn of the thyroid cartilage hich descends across the gap to articulate ⸱ith the lateral surface of the cricoid cartilage ostero-inferiorly. The inferior margin of the ricoid cartilage is attached to the first acheal ring by the cricotracheal ligament.

DISSECTION. Turn the sternothyroid muscle pwards and define its attachment to the thyroid ⸱rtilage. Identify the arch of the inferior constrictor ⸱ossing the cricothyroid muscle, and expose the latter ⸱uscle by a horizontal cut through the inferior con- ⸱rictor superficial to it. Reflect the parts of the inferior ⸱nstrictor and identify their attachment to the ⸱yroid and cricoid cartilages. Clean the inferior horn ⸱f the thyroid cartilage to its articulation with the ⸱ricoid cartilage. Clean the cricothyroid ligament to ⸱ lateral margin at the anterior border of the crico- ⸱yroid muscle.

hyroid Cartilage

This is the largest of the laryngeal cartilages, nd it consists of two roughly quadrilateral laminae of hyaline cartilage. These fuse anteriorly in their inferior two-thirds, but are separated superiorly by the deep **thyroid notch** [FIG. 124] where they extend furthest anteriorly to form the **laryngeal prominence.** The angle at which these laminae meet anteriorly varies (90°–120°) and is smallest in the male, thus making the cartilage more prominent anteriorly, and deeper antero-posteriorly in the male than the female.

The thyroid cartilage is deficient posteriorly, the laminae ending in thick, rounded, vertical posterior margins which lie far apart and are separated from the laryngeal orifice by the piriform recesses of the pharynx. Each posterior margin extends superiorly and inferiorly to form the slender **horns** (cornua) of the thyroid cartilage [FIG. 125]. The superior horns are attached to the tips of the corresponding greater horns of the hyoid bone by the thyrohyoid ligaments.

Thyrohyoid Membrane and Ligaments. The **thyrohyoid ligaments** each contain a small cartilaginous nodule **(cartilago triticea)** and are the thickened posterior margins of the thyrohyoid membrane. This membrane connects the sinuous superior margin of the thyroid cartilage to the upper margin of the hyoid bone on its internal surface. It passes superiorly within the concavity of the hyoid bone, and it is partly lined by the mucous membrane of the piriform recesses, and pierced by the internal branch of the superior laryngeal nerve and the superior laryngeal vessels on their way to the larynx, Anteriorly, the membrane is thickened to form the **median thyrohyoid ligament,** and this is separated from the posterior surface of the body of the hyoid bone by a **bursa** which lessens the friction between them when the upper border of the thyroid cartilage is drawn superiorly behind the hyoid bone, as in swallowing.

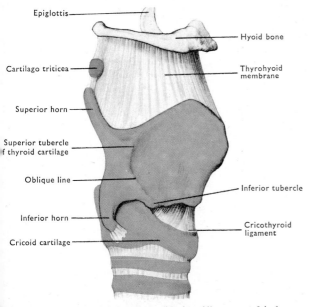

Epiglottis
Hyoid bone
Cartilago triticea
Thyrohyoid membrane
Superior horn
Superior tubercle f thyroid cartilage
Oblique line
Inferior tubercle
Inferior horn
Cricothyroid ligament
Cricoid cartilage

ɪɢ. 125 Profile view of the cartilages (blue) and ligaments of the larynx.

DISSECTION. Divide the thyrohyoid muscle and expose the thyrohyoid membrane and the vessels and nerve which pierce it. Clean and identify the parts of this membrane, and follow it superiorly inside the arch of the hyoid bone.

Cricothyroid Joint. The inferior horns of the thyroid cartilage each articulate with the postero-inferior part of the lateral surface of the cricoid cartilage by a synovial joint [FIG. 125], and these two joints allow the cricoid cartilage to rotate round a horizontal axis passing through both of them. This movement tilts the superior margin of the lamina of the cricoid cartilage and the attached arytenoid cartilages so that they move towards or away from the anterior part of the thyroid cartilage. This movement slackens or tightens the elastic **vocal ligaments** [FIG. 129] which pass between the arytenoid cartilages and the thyroid cartilage.

Each lateral surface of the thyroid cartilage is relatively flat, but where it thickens to form the posterior margin there is a raised **oblique line** which extends from the **superior tubercle** (just in front of the root of the superior horn) to the **inferior tubercle** (immediately posterior to the middle of the horizontal inferior border, FIGURE 125). To this oblique line are attached the inferior constrictor of the pharynx, the pretracheal fascia (sheath of the thyroid gland) and the thyrohyoid and sternothyroid muscles.

Epiglottis

The rigidity of the epiglottis is provided by a thin, leaf-like lamina of elastic fibro-cartilage. It forms the upper part of the anterior wall and the superior margin of the laryngeal orifice. It lies posterior to the base of the tongue, the body of the hyoid

bone, and the median thyrohyoid ligament and is covered over the whole of its posterior surface and the upper part of its anterior surface with mucous membrane. Numerous glands lie in the pits and perforations in the cartilage. The rigidity of the cartilage is increased because of its curved shape; it is convex anteriorly in the superior part, and posteriorly in the lower part where it bulges into the larynx to form the **epiglottic tubercle**.

Ligaments. The epiglottis has numerous attachments. Inferiorly it tapers to a point and is attached to the posterior surface of the thyroid cartilage in the midline by the strong **thyro-epiglottic ligament.** Anteriorly, it is attached (1) to the tongue by the **median and lateral glosso-epiglottic folds** of mucous membrane [FIGS. 116, 137] and (2) below these to the upper surface of the body of the hyoid bone by the loose, fibro-elastic, **hyo-epiglottic ligament.** The latter is separated from the

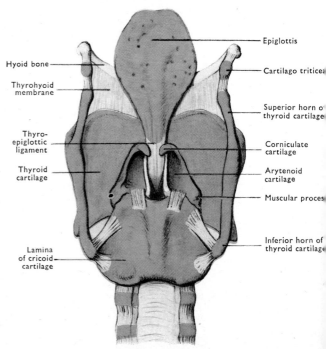

Hyoid bone

Thyrohyoid membrane

Thyro-epiglottic ligament

Thyroid cartilage

Lamina of cricoid cartilage

Epiglottis

Cartilago triticea

Superior horn of thyroid cartilage

Corniculate cartilage

Arytenoid cartilage

Muscular process

Inferior horn of thyroid cartilage

FIG. 126   Posterior aspect of the cartilages (blue) and ligaments of the larynx.

hyro-epiglottic and median thyrohyoid ligaments by a pad of soft fat which is displaced
vhen the thyroid cartilage is drawn up inside
he curve of the hyoid bone in swallowing.
Laterally the margins of the epiglottis are
continuous with the aryepiglottic folds.

DISSECTION. On the sectioned surface of the
arynx, identify the epiglottis, the thyro-epiglottic and
yo-epiglottic ligaments. Note their relation to the
hyroid cartilage, the hyoid bone, and the thyrohyoid
igament [Fig. 118].

Arytenoid Cartilages

These cartilages are a pair of three-sided
pyramids [Fig. 126] that rest on the superior
border of the lamina of the cricoid cartilage,
each forming a synovial joint with it [Figs.
126, 129]. The **apex** of each cartilage passes
superiorly, and curving posteromedially, sup-
ports the corniculate cartilage. The base
articulates with the cricoid, and
extends laterally to form the
muscular process (to which the
crico-arytenoid muscles are attached) and anteriorly to form
the **vocal process** (to which the
vocal ligament is attached).
The transverse arytenoid
muscle is attached to the posterior surface of each arytenoid
cartilage [Fig. 135] while the
anterolateral surfaces have the
thyro-arytenoid and vocalis
muscles attached to them
[Figs. 127, 136].

Crico-arytenoid Joints. These
synovial joints allow the arytenoid cartilages to glide transversely on the lamina of the
cricoid cartilage, so that they
are able to move closer together
or further apart. Rotation of
each arytenoid cartilage around
its vertical axis swings the vocal
process laterally and medially,
thus separating or approxima-
ting the vocal ligaments. The
arytenoid cartilages are pre-

vented from slipping anteriorly by the strong
posterior capsule of the joint [Fig. 126],
and thus they are carried posteriorly with the
lamina of the cricoid cartilage when it is tilted
backwards.

Structure of Laryngeal Cartilages. The
thyroid, cricoid, and basal parts of the
arytenoid cartilages are composed of hyaline
cartilage, and tend to ossify even in early adult
life; in old age they may be completely trans-
formed into bone. The apex and vocal process
of the arytenoid cartilage and the other
cartilages are formed of elastic fibrocartilage
and do not ossify.

INTERIOR OF LARYNX

The cavity of the larynx is nearly divided
into superior and inferior parts by two anteroposterior **vocal folds** of mucous membrane, one
of which projects from each lateral wall [Fig.

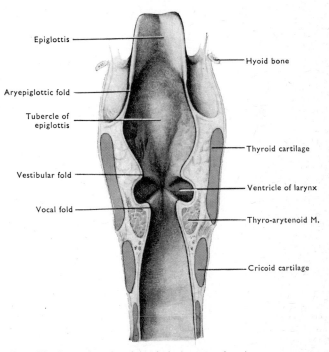

Epiglottis

Hyoid bone

Aryepiglottic fold

Tubercle of
epiglottis

Thyroid cartilage

Vestibular fold

Ventricle of larynx

Vocal fold

Thyro-arytenoid M.

Cricoid cartilage

Fig. 127   Coronal section through the larynx to show its compartments.
Cartilage blue.

127]. Above each of these is a subsidiary **vestibular fold** which is separated from the corresponding vocal fold by a narrow, horizontal groove (the **ventricle of the larynx**) and together the two pairs of folds narrow the middle part of the laryngeal cavity.

Vestibule of Larynx

The superior part, or vestibule of the larynx, extends from the pharyngeal opening of the larynx to the vestibular folds. It has a long **anterior wall** which consists of the mucous membrane covering the epiglottis and thyro-epiglottic ligament, but a short **posterior wall** formed by the mucous membrane covering the apex of the arytenoid and corniculate cartilages. The lateral walls are the aryepi-glottic folds which separate the vestibule from the piriform recesses and slope inwards towards the vestibular folds [FIG. 127]. The aryepiglottic folds enclose in their margins the slender aryepiglottic and thyro-epiglottic muscles, and the corniculate and cuneiform cartilages [FIGS. 116, 128].

Vestibular Folds

These are soft, flaccid folds of mucous membrane which extend between the thyroid and arytenoid cartilages, and contain: (1) numerous mucous glands; (2) a feeble band of fibro-elastic tissue; (3) a few muscle fibres. They lie further apart than the vocal folds, and play little or no part in the production of the voice which is unimpaired by their destruction.

The space between the two vestibular folds is the **rima vestibuli**.

Ventricle and Saccule of Larynx

The ventricle of the larynx is the narrow groove between the vestibular and vocal folds, and it partly undermines the vestibular fold. If a blunt seeker is passed along the roof of the ventricle, it enters the saccule of the larynx. This is a narrow, blind diverticulum which passes postero-superiorly between the vestibular fold and the thyroid cartilage, and may reach the upper border of the cartilage.

DISSECTION. Cut the vestibular fold away from the upper part of the arytenoid cartilage, and strip it carefully forwards from the wall of the larynx, avoiding injury to the underlying muscle (thyro-epiglotticus). Separate the fold from the thyroid cartilage, and open the saccule.

Vocal Folds

In coronal section [FIG. 127] each vocal fold is wedge-

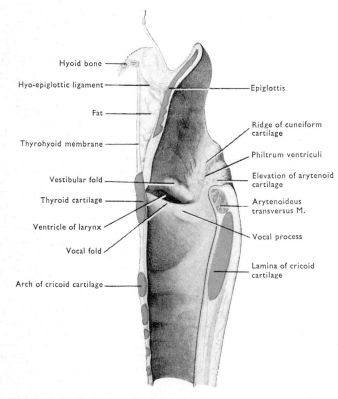

Hyoid bone

Hyo-epiglottic ligament

Fat

Thyrohyoid membrane

Vestibular fold

Thyroid cartilage

Ventricle of larynx

Vocal fold

Arch of cricoid cartilage

Epiglottis

Ridge of cuneiform cartilage

Philtrum ventriculi

Elevation of arytenoid cartilage

Arytenoideus transversus M.

Vocal process

Lamina of cricoid cartilage

FIG. 128 Median section through the larynx to show the side-wall of its right half. Cartilage blue.

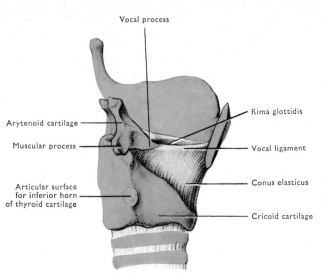

Vocal process

Rima glottidis

Arytenoid cartilage

Vocal ligament

Muscular process

Conus elasticus

Articular surface
for inferior horn
of thyroid cartilage

Cricoid cartilage

FIG. 129   Dissection to show the laryngeal fibro-elastic membrane. The right lamina of the thyroid cartilage has been removed. Cartilage blue.

shaped. The apex projects medially into the laryngeal cavity; the base lies against the lamina of the thyroid cartilage; the inferior surface slopes inferolaterally to the superior border of the cricoid cartilage, and the superior surface forms the inferior wall of the ventricle. Each vocal fold consists of the conus elasticus, the vocal ligament, and muscle fibres, all covered with mucous membrane.

Conus Elasticus and Vocal Ligament. The inferior surface of the vocal fold consists of a thin layer of fibro-elastic tissue (conus elasticus) separated from the laryngeal cavity by mucous membrane only. The conus elasticus is attached inferiorly to the upper border of the cricoid cartilage, and slopes superomedially to end in the free edge of the vocal fold as a thickened elastic band, the vocal ligament. Anteriorly, the conus elasticus is attached to the deep surface of the crico-thyroid ligament and the posterior surface of the thyroid cartilage; posteriorly, it extends to the vocal process and medial side of the arytenoid cartilage. The vocal ligament is the free edge of the conus elasticus [FIG. 129] and thus is attached from the posterior surface of

the thyroid cartilage (close to the midline and the opposite vocal ligament) to the vocal process of the arytenoid cartilage. The mucous membrane covering the vocal ligament is tightly bound to it, and is of the stratified squamous type, unlike the ciliated columnar epithelium found in most of the remainder of the larynx. This change in the epithelium at the free margin of the vocal fold gives it a whitish appearance in life, and allows it to withstand the stresses applied to this vibrating margin.

The muscle fibres in the vocal fold lie between the conus elasticus and the lamina of the thyroid cartilage. They arise from the thyroid cartilage, and most of them pass horizontally backwards to the arytenoid cartilage (**thyro-arytenoideus**). The most medial fibres arise from the vocal ligament (**vocalis muscle**) and the lateral fibres sweep superiorly into the epiglottis (**thyro-epiglotticus**).

DISSECTION. Strip the mucous membrane from the inferior surface of the vocal fold and expose the conus elasticus and vocal ligament. Separate the conus from the superior border of the cricoid cartilage and turn it superiorly, dissecting it away from the muscle which lies lateral to it [Fig. 130] but leave the vocal ligament intact. Strip the mucous membrane from the superior surface of the vocal fold, thus exposing the upper surface of the thyro-arytenoid muscle and its continuity with the thyro-epiglotticus which was exposed when the vestibular fold was removed.

Rima Glottidis

The rima glottidis is the elongated, horizontal fissure bounded on each side by a vocal fold and by the vocal process and medial aspect of the arytenoid cartilage. It is the narrowest part of the laryngeal cavity, and lies a little below its middle.

The **shape** of the rima glottidis is continually varying [FIG. 131] due to the movements of the

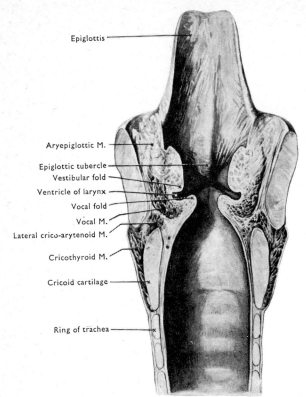

Epiglottis

Aryepiglottic M.

Epiglottic tubercle
Vestibular fold
Ventricle of larynx
Vocal fold
Vocal M.
Lateral crico-arytenoid M.
Cricothyroid M.
Cricoid cartilage

Ring of trachea

FIG. 130   Coronal section of the larynx to show the position of the muscles.

the cricoid, the posterior part of the rima is widened, and this can be accentuated by rotation of the arytenoid cartilages so that their vocal processes turn laterally [FIG. 131]. If, in addition, the lamina of the cricoid is tilted forwards, the vocal ligaments are slackened and the opening can be widened further to allow the free passage of air in forced respiration. On the contrary, if the arytenoid cartilages are drawn together and rotated so that their vocal processes are in apposition, the rima glottidis is closed. In addition, if the lamina of the cricoid is tilted posteriorly, the vocal ligaments are tightened and the passage of air is effectively prevented. This position is taken up as a preliminary to the explosive discharge of air in coughing, the tension in the vocal folds being suddenly released after the intrathoracic pressure has been built up by contraction of the expiratory muscles.

Because of the shape of the vocal folds, attempts to draw air into the thorax when the rima glottidis is closed tend to press the vocal folds together and prevent inspiration, a situation which arises in laryngeal spasm.

Delicate variations (1) in the tension and length of the vocal folds, (2) in the width of the rima, and (3) in the intensity of the expira-

arytenoid cartilages on the cricoid, and of the cricoid and arytenoid cartilages together relative to the thyroid cartilage. When the arytenoid cartilages are displaced laterally on

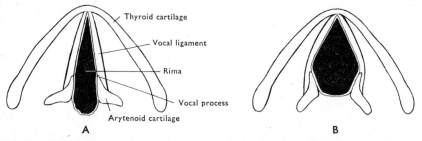

Thyroid cartilage

Vocal ligament

Rima

Vocal process

Arytenoid cartilage

A   B

FIG. 131   Two diagrams to show the movements of the arytenoid cartilages by which the rima glottidis is opened and closed.   A. Position during quiet breathing.   B. Position during forced respiration.

174

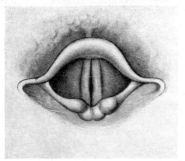

Fig. 132 Laryngoscopic view of the cavity of the larynx during phonation. The rima glottidis is closed by approximation of the vocal folds.

tory effort are together responsible for producing the changes in pitch of the voice. The lower range of pitch in the male voice is due to the greater length of the vocal folds (approximately 2·5 cm.) as compared with those in the female (approximately 1·7 cm.).

Infraglottic Part of Larynx

Superiorly this part is compressed laterally, but it widens to become circular opposite the cricoid cartilage, and is continuous with the trachea inferiorly. The walls are smooth.

Mucous Membrane of Larynx

Over most of the larynx the mucous membrane is loosely adherent to the walls except on the posterior surface of the epiglottis and

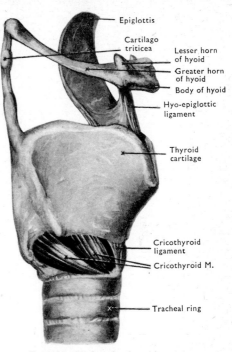

Fig. 134 Right cricothyroid muscle.

over the vocal folds. In the latter position it is so tightly bound to the vocal ligament that inflammatory swelling of the vestibular mucosa is unable to spread across this region.

On the vocal folds, the superior parts of the epiglottis, and the aryepiglottic folds the epithelium is stratified squamous in type, but elsewhere is columnar ciliated. Taste buds are found on the lateral parts of the posterior surface of the epiglottis, on the aryepiglottic folds, and on the arytenoid cartilages.

MUSCLES OF LARYNX

Intrinsic Muscles

These small muscles move the parts of the larynx on each other, and are particu-

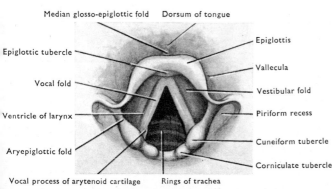

Fig. 133 Laryngoscopic view of the cavity of the larynx during moderate respiration. The rima glottidis is widely open.

175

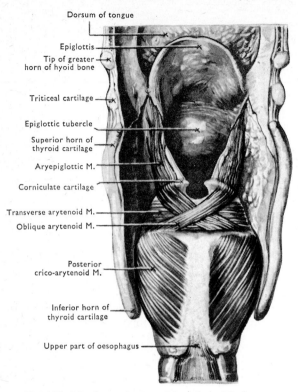

Dorsum of tongue

Epiglottis

Tip of greater
horn of hyoid bone

Triticeal cartilage

Epiglottic tubercle

Superior horn of
thyroid cartilage

Aryepiglottic M.

Corniculate cartilage

Transverse arytenoid M.

Oblique arytenoid M.

Posterior
crico-arytenoid M.

Inferior horn of
thyroid cartilage

Upper part of oesophagus

Fig. 135   Muscles on the posterior surface of the larynx.

DISSECTION.   Identify the recurrent laryngeal nerve entering the larynx deep to the inferior constrictor muscle. Strip the mucous membrane from the posterior surfaces of the arytenoid and cricoid cartilages. Note the attachment of the longitudinal oesophageal muscle fibres by a tendon to the median part of the cricoid lamina, and identify [Fig. 135] the posterior crico-arytenoid, transverse arytenoid, and oblique arytenoid muscles. The latter two have been divided in the midline, but the oblique arytenoid can be followed into continuity with the aryepiglottic muscle by stripping the mucous membrane from the margin of the aryepiglottic fold.

Posterior Crico-arytenoid. This muscle arises from the posterior surface of the lamina of the cricoid, and converges on the laterally directed muscular process of the arytenoid cartilage. Nerve supply: this and all the other intrinsic muscles of the larynx (except cricothyroid) are supplied by the recurrent laryngeal nerve. Action: the upper fibres rotate the arytenoid so that its vocal process swings laterally, opening the rima glottidis; the lower fibres pull the arytenoid laterally, further increasing the size of the rima.

Transverse and Oblique Arytenoid Muscles. They cross between the arytenoid cartilages and draw them together, closing the rima glottidis. The continuity of the oblique and aryepiglottic muscles ensures that the arytenoid cartilages are drawn together at the same time as the epiglottis is pulled down towards the arytenoid cartilages in swallowing. Thus in two ways the airway is closed during the passage of food through the pharynx.

DISSECTION.   Remove the cricothyroid muscle and, on one side, the lateral part of the lamina and the inferior horn of the thyroid cartilage, thus opening the cricothyroid joint. Take care not to injure the continuation of the recurrent laryngeal nerve (inferior laryngeal nerve) which lies deep to the posterior part of the thyroid cartilage. A sheet of muscle in the base of the

larly concerned with alterations in the length and tension of the vocal folds in the production of the voice, and in changing the size of the rima glottidis to facilitate the passage of air to the lungs.

Cricothyroid. This muscle arises from the anterolateral part of the cricoid cartilage, and fans posterosuperiorly to be attached to the inferior margin and lower part of the deep surface of the lamina, and to the inferior horn of the thyroid cartilage. Nerve supply: external branch of the superior laryngeal nerve. Action: it draws the arch of the cricoid posterosuperiorly, rotating the whole cartilage around the cricothyroid joints, so that the lamina is tilted posteriorly, the vocal ligaments are elongated and tightened, and the pitch of the voice is raised.

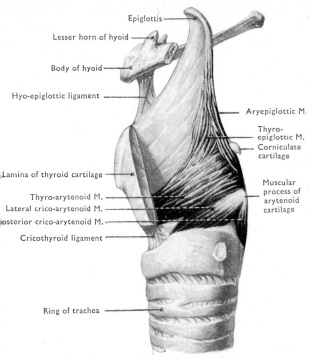

Epiglottis

Lesser horn of hyoid

Body of hyoid

Hyo-epiglottic ligament

Aryepiglottic M.

Thyro-epiglottic M.

Corniculate cartilage

Lamina of thyroid cartilage

Muscular process of arytenoid cartilage

Thyro-arytenoid M.

Lateral crico-arytenoid M.

Posterior crico-arytenoid M.

Cricothyroid ligament

Ring of trachea

FIG. 136   Muscles in the lateral wall of the larynx.

ocal fold is now exposed [Fig. 136] with the lateral rico-arytenoid muscle inferior to it.

Lateral Crico-arytenoid Muscle. It passes rom the superior border of the posterior part of the arch to the cricoid to the muscular process of the arytenoid muscle. Action: it pulls the muscular process anteriorly, rotating he arytenoid so that its vocal process swings medially and closes the rima glottidis.

Thyro-arytenoid. This muscle arises from he posterior surface of the thyroid cartilage close to the midline, and is attached to the anterolateral surface of the arytenoid cartilage. Some of the deeper fibres arise from the vocal igament and pass to the vocal process of the arytenoid, the **vocalis muscle.** The upper, lateral fibres sweep superiorly into the epiglottis, the **thyro-epiglottic muscle.** Action: he main mass pulls the arytenoid anteriorly, slackening the vocal ligament. The vocalis

tends to tighten the anterior part of the ligament while slackening the posterior part—a position taken up by the vocal cords in whispering. The thyro-epiglottic muscle aids the aryepiglottic muscle in swallowing.

Extrinsic Muscles [pp. 85, 124, 155].

Thyrohyoid acts on the fixed hyoid bone, and assisted by stylopharyngeus and palato-pharyngeus, raises the larynx under the posterior part of the tongue. This compresses the laryngeal orifice against the posterior surface of the epiglottis, which is tipped posteriorly by the tongue and the action of aryepiglotticus and thyro-epiglotticus, thus effectively closing the laryngeal orifice. In the last stage of swallowing, the **sternothyroid** draws the larynx down to its original position.

NERVES AND VESSELS OF LARYNX

Superior Laryngeal Nerve. This branch of the vagus divides into internal and external [p. 128] branches. The internal branch (sensory and autonomic) pierces the thyrohyoid membrane with the superior laryngeal artery, and breaks up into several branches in the wall of the piriform recess, which it supplies. Some branches pass in the aryepiglottic fold to the base of the tongue and epiglottis; others descend to supply the mucous membrane of the internal surface of the larynx as far as the vocal folds, and the mucous membrane covering the posterior surfaces of the arytenoid and cricoid cartilages. One branch descends deep to the thyroid cartilage to join a similar branch from the recurrent laryngeal nerve.

Recurrent Laryngeal Nerve. It ascends in the groove between the trachea and oesophagus, and enters the larynx by passing deep to the lower border of the inferior constrictor. It supplies all the intrinsic muscles of the larynx, except cricothyroid, and the mucous membrane below the rima glottidis, and it communicates with the internal branch of the superior laryngeal nerve. It is accompanied by the inferior laryngeal artery, a branch of the inferior thyroid artery, and runs posterior to the cricothyroid joint.

THE TONGUE

The tongue is a mobile organ which bulges upwards from the floor of the mouth, and its posterior part forms the anterior wall of the oral part of the pharynx. It is covered by stratified squamous epithelium, and consists of a mass of striated muscle interspersed with a little fat and numerous glands, especially in the posterior part.

It is separated from the teeth by a deep alveololingual sulcus which is filled in by the palatoglossal fold posterior to the last molar tooth. The sulcus partly undermines the lateral margins of the tongue, and extends beneath its free anterior third. In the depths of the sulcus, the mucous membrane passes from the root of the tongue across the floor of the mouth on to the internal aspect of the mandible and becomes continuous superiorly with that on the gum. Internal to the sulcus, the root of the tongue contains the muscles which connect the tongue to the hyoid bone and mandible, and transmits the nerves and vessels which supply it.

DORSUM OF TONGUE

The dorsum of the tongue extends from the tip to the anterior surface of the epiglottis. It is separated into palatine and pharyngeal parts

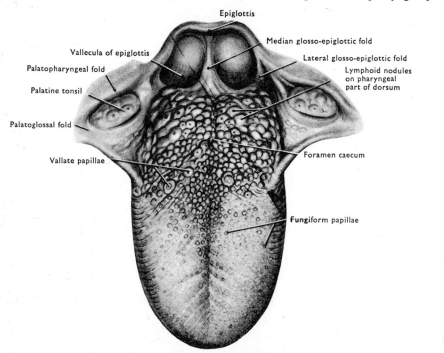

Epiglottis

Vallecula of epiglottis

Palatopharyngeal fold

Palatine tonsil

Palatoglossal fold

Vallate papillae

Median glosso-epiglottic fold

Lateral glosso-epiglottic fold

Lymphoid nodules on pharyngeal part of dorsum

Foramen caecum

Fungiform papillae

FIG. 137   The dorsum of the tongue, epiglottis, and palatine tonsils.

y a V-shaped **sulcus terminalis,** the apex of
which faces posteriorly and is marked by a pit,
the **foramen caecum** [Fig. 137]. A shallow
median groove extends from the tip of the
tongue to the foramen caecum.

The thick mucous membrane of the palatine
part is roughened by the presence of papillae.
In the pharyngeal part it is smooth, thinner,
and finely nodular in appearance, due to the
presence of small **lymphatic follicles** in the submucosa. Each of these has a small, central
epithelial pit. Posteriorly the lingual mucous
membrane is continuous with that on the
anterior surface of the epiglottis over the
median and lateral glosso-epiglottic folds and
the valleculae of the epiglottis between them.

Lingual Papillae

The **vallate papillae,** seven to twelve in
number, are the largest, and lie immediately
anterior to the sulcus terminalis. Each has the
shape of a short cylinder sunk into the surface
of the tongue, with a deep trench around it.
The opposing walls of the trench are studded
with taste buds.

Fungiform papillae, smaller and more
numerous, are the bright red spots seen
principally on the tip and margins of the living
tongue, but scattered over the remainder of
the dorsum also. Each is attached
by a narrow base, and expands into
a rounded knob-like free extremity.
Most of them carry taste buds.

Filiform papillae are very numerous,
minute, pointed projections which
cover all of the palatine part of the
dorsum and the margins of the
tongue. They are arranged in rows
which are more or less parallel to the
sulcus terminalis posteriorly, but
become more transverse anteriorly.
Their apices are cornified and may be
broken up into thread-like processes.

INFERIOR SURFACE AND SIDES

The inferior surface and sides of
the tongue are covered with smooth,
thin mucous membrane. In the
midline anteriorly the mucosa is

raised into a sharp fold which joins the inferior surface of the tongue to the floor of the
mouth **(frenulum linguae,** FIG. 109). On each
side of the frenulum, the deep lingual vein
may be seen through the mucous membrane in
the living subject, and lateral to this is a delicate, fringed fold of mucous membrane which
sweeps posterolaterally, the **fimbriated fold.**
On each side of the attachment of the frenulum
to the floor of the mouth, is the opening of the
duct of the submandibular gland on the **sublingual papilla.** Passing posterolaterally from
this, in the floor of the mouth, is the rounded
sublingual fold which is produced by the submandibular duct, and on which open a number
of the ductules of the sublingual gland.

On the sides of the tongue, anterior to the
lingual attachment of the palatoglossal arch,
are five short, vertical folds of mucous membrane **(folia linguae).** These carry taste buds
and are much better developed in some
animals, *e.g.,* the hare and rabbit.

MUSCLES OF TONGUE

The tongue is divided into halves by a
median fibrous septum, and the muscles of
each half consist of an extrinsic and an intrinsic
group:

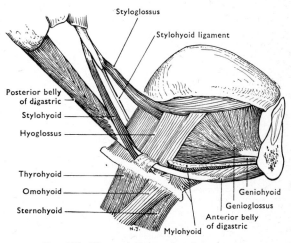

FIG. 138   The extrinsic muscles of the tongue.

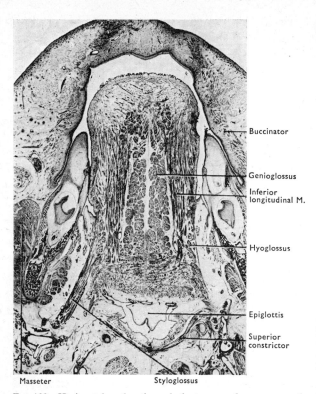

Buccinator

Genioglossus

Inferior
longitudinal M.

Hyoglossus

Epiglottis

Superior
constrictor

Masseter   Styloglossus

FIG. 139   Horizontal section through the tongue of a seven-month
human foetus.

EXTRINSIC	INTRINSIC
Genioglossus [p. 107].	Superior longitudinal.
Hyoglossus [p. 104].	Inferior longitudinal.
Styloglossus [p. 104].	Vertical.
Palatoglossus [p. 155].	Transverse.

The extrinsic muscles take origin from parts
outside the tongue, and can therefore move the
tongue as well as alter its shape. The intrinsic
muscles, being wholly inside the tongue, can
only produce changes of shape.

DISSECTION. On the cut surface of the tongue,
identify genioglossus and geniohyoid, and confirm their
attachments and position [Fig. 113]. On the right side,
separate the buccinator, pterygomandibular raphe, and
superior constrictor from their attachments to the
mandible, and turn the remainder of the body of the
mandible downwards to expose the lateral surface of

the tongue.   Avoid injury to the lingual
nerve and the palatoglossus muscle. Remove the remainder of the mucous membrane from the lateral surface of the
tongue, and follow the various extrinsic
muscles into its substance. When removing the mucous membrane from the inferior surface of the tongue near the tip,
identify a small, oval glandular mass,
the anterior lingual gland.

Movements of Tongue

The hyoid bone forms a movable
platform to which the posterior
part of the tongue is attached and
with which it moves.

The **hyoglossus** and **genioglossus**
muscles enter the tongue from
below, the former vertically along
its side and the latter in a paramedian position. Thus they depress the lateral and median parts
of the tongue respectively. In
addition, the fan-shaped genioglossus is inserted from the tip to
the level of the hyoid, hence its
posterior fibres pull the tongue forwards and help to protrude it (an
action assisted by geniohyoid) while
the anterior fibres depress and retract the tip.

The **palatoglossus** and **styloglossus** enter the lateral part of the tongue from
above. The palatoglossus passes almost transversely and is continuous with the intrinsic
transverse fibres; the styloglossus runs anteriorly along the lateral margin. Both muscles
elevate the posterior part of the tongue, the
styloglossus also retracts it, and the palatoglossus draws the palate down on to the tongue,
their combined action tending to close off the
mouth from the oral part of the pharynx.

The **superior longitudinal muscle** forms a
layer on the dorsum of the tongue; it curls the
tip upwards and rolls it posteriorly. The
inferior longitudinal muscles lie in the lower
part of the tongue, one on each side lateral to
genioglossus. They curl the tip of the tongue
inferiorly, and, acting with the superior
muscle, retract and widen the tongue.

180

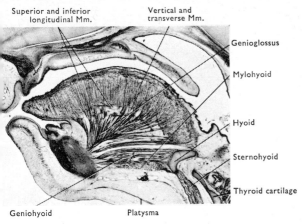

Superior and inferior longitudinal Mm.

Vertical and transverse Mm.

Genioglossus

Mylohyoid

Hyoid

Sternohyoid

Thyroid cartilage

Geniohyoid

Platysma

FIG. 140 Paramedian section through the tongue of a fourteen-week human foetus.

The **transverse muscle fibres** lie inferior to the superior longitudinal muscle, and run from the septum to the margins between the vertical fibres of genioglossus, hyoglossus, and the vertical muscle. They narrow the tongue and increase its height.

The **vertical muscle fibres** run inferolaterally from the dorsum. They flatten the dorsum, increase the transverse diameter, and tend to roll up the margins. Acting with the transverse muscles, they increase the length of the tongue.

It should be appreciated that the various muscles are used in complex combinations and that the actions given above represent only a few of the possible movements. The tongue is bilaterally symmetrical, and unilateral action of any muscle or group of muscles will cause the tongue to deviate from the midline. Thus in protrusion of the tongue with one side paralysed, the tip deviates towards the paralysed side because that side fails to act, and, lagging behind, swings the active side towards it.

Septum of Tongue

The septum is best seen in a transverse section through the tongue. It is a median fibrous partition, which is strongest posteriorly where it is attached to the hyoid bone. It does not reach the mucous membrane of the dorsum, but is separated from it by the superior longitudinal muscle.

Glands of Tongue

Small serous and mucous glands lie between the muscle fibres deep to the mucous membrane of the pharyngeal surface, tip, and margins. Small serous glands lie near the vallate papillae and open into their trenches. The anterior lingual gland consists of mucous and serous alveoli, and it lies on the inferior surface of the tongue near to its tip.

NERVES OF TONGUE

The mucous membrane and muscles of the tongue have entirely separate nerve supplies. The supply to the mucous membrane is complex and consists of: (1) the **lingual** (including taste fibres from the chorda tympani) to the anterior two-thirds; (2) the **glossopharyngeal** (including taste fibres) to the posterior third; (3) twigs of the internal branch of the **superior laryngeal** nerve to a small area adjacent to the epiglottis. The glossopharyngeal nerve supplies the vallate papillae. The nerves also carry parasympathetic secretomotor fibres to the glands buried in the substance of the tongue. The supply to the muscles of the tongue is from the **hypoglossal nerve** which innervates all the intrinsic and extrinsic muscles except palatoglossus.

The reason for this difference in the innervation is that the mucous membrane is derived from the floor of the embryonic pharynx, while the muscle originates from the occipital region, and is in series with the infrahyoid muscles which act with it. The latter are innervated by the first three cervical nerves which communicate with the hypoglossal nerve and are in series with it.

VESSELS OF TONGUE

The chief **arteries** are branches of the lingual [p. 108]; the deep artery of the tongue to the

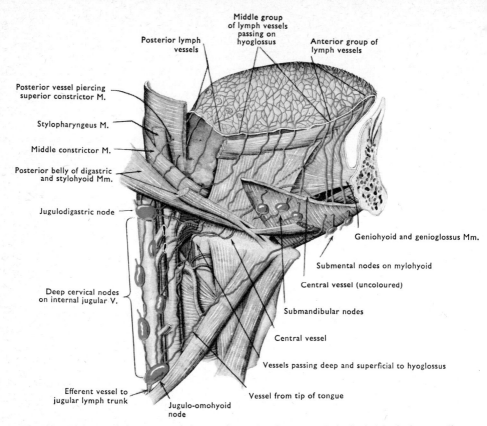

Posterior lymph vessels

Middle group of lymph vessels passing on hyoglossus

Anterior group of lymph vessels

Posterior vessel piercing superior constrictor M.

Stylopharyngeus M.

Middle constrictor M.

Posterior belly of digastric and stylohyoid Mm.

Jugulodigastric node

Geniohyoid and genioglossus Mm.

Submental nodes on mylohyoid

Central vessel (uncoloured)

Deep cervical nodes on internal jugular V.

Submandibular nodes

Central vessel

Vessels passing deep and superficial to hyoglossus

Efferent vessel to jugular lymph trunk

Jugulo-omohyoid node

Vessel from tip of tongue

FIG. 141   Diagram of the course of the lymph vessels of tongue. It is doubtful whether any lingual lymphatics reach the submental nodes which mostly drain the lower lip and symphysis region of the jaw. Lymph vessels may cross the median plane to reach the opposite deep cervical lymph nodes.

anterior part; the dorsales linguae arteries to the posterior part. Trace the deep artery to the tip, where it forms an anastomotic loop with its fellow. This is the only significant anastomosis across the midline of the tongue. The **veins** are described on page 108.

Lymph Vessels of Tongue [FIG. 141]

These vessels cannot be dissected, but they are important because of the common involvement of the tongue in cancer and its spread by these channels.

There is a rich lymphatic capillary plexus in the mucous membrane which has been de-scribed as draining by a number of separate routes. There is no doubt, however, that the great majority of the lymphatics from the mucous membrane of the tongue drain along the route of the vessels which supply it. They therefore pass posteriorly, either deep or super-ficial to hyoglossus, and running superior to the hyoid bone reach the upper deep cervical nodes in the carotid triangle close to the angle of the mandible, especially the jugulodigastric node. Drainage either to the submental or to the submandibular nodes, or direct drainage to the lower deep cervical nodes (jugulo-omohyoid, FIG. 141) is rare as a primary vent in cancer of the tongue. Nevertheless they may be implicated because adjacent superficial lymphatic plexuses communicate freely, and thus blockage of the drainage route from one area can lead to drainage through an abnormal pathway with the involvement of unusual groups of lymph nodes.

The same principle of drainage along the blood vessels applies in the case of the submental and submandibular nodes: the former receive lymph from the territory supplied by the submental artery (anterior part of floor of mouth) while the latter drain lymph from the territory of the facial artery, particularly the lips and cheek and the posterior part of the floor of the mouth.

There is no separation of the superficial lymph plexus on the right and left sides of the tongue, and the paramedian areas may drain equally to both sides.

THE ORGANS OF HEARING AND EQUILIBRATION

The 'ear' consists of the auditory apparatus and the organs concerned with balance which record both rotary movements of the head and the direction of the gravitational field acting on it. It is readily divisible into three parts; the external ear, the middle ear, and the internal ear.

The **external ear** consists of the auricle and the external acoustic meatus. The auricle collects the sound waves, and the external acoustic meatus transmits them medially to the tympanic membrane, which separates the external ear from the middle ear. The **middle**

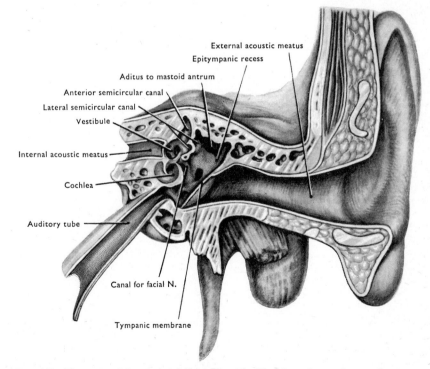

External acoustic meatus
Epitympanic recess
Aditus to mastoid antrum
Anterior semicircular canal
Lateral semicircular canal
Vestibule
Internal acoustic meatus
Cochlea
Auditory tube
Canal for facial N.
Tympanic membrane

Fig. 142   The parts of the ear (semi-diagrammatic). The blue colour represents the mucous membrane lining the middle ear and auditory tube.

ear is a narrow chamber whose cavity (the tympanic cavity) lies between the tympanic membrane and the lateral wall of the internal ear, and communicates with the nasal part of the pharynx through the auditory tube. Three small auditory ossicles lie in the middle ear, and stretch across it from the tympanic membrane to the lateral wall of the internal ear to transmit the vibrations of the tympanic membrane to the internal ear. The **internal ear** consists of a complex system of communicating cavities (the bony labyrinth) situated in the densest part of the petrous temporal bone. It contains a similarly shaped, but narrower complex of membranous tubes and sacs which constitutes the membranous labyrinth, and on which the sensory nerve fibres of the vestibulo-cochlear nerve end.

THE EXTERNAL EAR

The auricle has been examined already [pp. 1, 6].

DISSECTION. Cut away the tragus of the auricle to expose the orifice of the external meatus. Remove the anterior wall of the cartilaginous part of the meatus with knife or scissors. Pass a probe into the bony part of the meatus to determine its length, and using the probe as a guide, cut away the anterior wall of the bony part of the meatus (tympanic bone) taking care not to injure the tympanic membrane.

EXTERNAL ACOUSTIC MEATUS

The external meatus runs medially with a slight anterior inclination. It is almost exactly in line with the internal acoustic meatus, and their shadows are superimposed in a true lateral radiograph of the skull [FIG. 146]. The external meatus is approximately 24 mm. long, of which two-thirds is the bony part, but, because the tympanic membrane is placed obliquely the anterior wall and floor are longer than the posterior wall and roof. The diameter is not uniform; the narrowest point, the **isthmus,** is about 5 mm. from the tympanic membrane. The

vertical diameter is greatest at the lateral end whilst the anteroposterior diameter is greatest at the medial end, and the meatus is slightly curved with an upward convexity. All these points should be remembered when attempting to remove foreign bodies from the meatus, and in addition the fact that the bony part of the meatus is absent in the newborn and the tympanic membrane is considerably more oblique than in the adult.

The skin of the cartilaginous portion contains many **ceruminous glands** and hairs. The latter are directed laterally and prevent the entry of small objects. In the bony part of the canal the skin is thin and tightly adherent to the periosteum. It has no hairs, few if any glands, and is continued, as a very delicate layer, over the lateral surface of the tympanic membrane.

Tympanic Membrane

This is an elliptical disc which is stretched across the medial end of the external acoustic meatus, and forms the greater part of the lateral wall of the middle ear cavity. It slopes obliquely downwards, forwards, and medially, and its lateral surface is deeply concave. The medial surface is correspondingly convex, and the point of maximum convexity is called the **umbo,** which is maintained by a bar of bone, the **handle of the malleus,** the lower end of

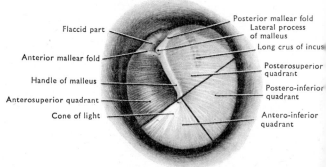

Flaccid part

Anterior mallear fold

Handle of malleus

Anterosuperior quadrant

Cone of light

Posterior mallear fold
Lateral process of malleus
Long crus of incus

Posterosuperior quadrant

Postero-inferior quadrant

Antero-inferior quadrant

FIG. 143 Left tympanic membrane as seen from the lateral side. The four arbitrary quadrants are indicated by solid lines and by the handle of the malleus.

hich reaches the umbo. The handle is part
f the most lateral of the three auditory
ssicles, and it can be seen through the tym-
anic membrane. It extends superiorly to-
ards the upper edge of the membrane, near
hich it is continuous with the **lateral process**
f the malleus which bulges the membrane into
he meatus. The small part of the membrane
uperior to the lateral process is less tense
han the remainder and forms the **flaccid
art.**

The tympanic membrane, composed of a
ense fibrous layer with the handle of the
malleus attached to its internal aspect, is
overed externally by the thin skin of the
meatus and internally by the mucous mem-
rane of the middle ear. The margin of the
ibrous part is thickened and inserted into a
istinct **tympanic groove** in a ring-like ridge of
he tympanic bone at the medial end of the
meatus. The ring and groove are replaced,
bove the lateral process of the malleus, by a
hallow depression, the **tympanic notch,** and
ere the thickened edge of the membrane
eaves the bone and passes to the lateral process
f the malleus, thus forming the anterior and

posterior **mallear folds** [FIG. 144]. Between
these folds and the margin of the tympanic
notch lies the flaccid part of the membrane,
which differs from the rest in not having a well-
defined fibrous layer.

When the living tympanic membrane is
examined, its surface appears highly polished,
and a cone of light extends antero-inferiorly
from the tip of the handle of the malleus. The
mallear folds can be seen as two striae out-
lining the flaccid part, and the long process of
the incus (the intermediate auditory ossicle)
can be seen dimly through the membrane,
parallel and posterior to the handle of the
malleus [FIG. 143].

DISSECTION. Strip the dura mater and endocranium from the floor of the middle cranial fossa as
far anteriorly as the mandibular nerve. The greater
petrosal nerve will be found emerging from the anterior
surface of the petrous temporal bone and running
anteromedially inferior to the trigeminal ganglion.

The cavity of the middle ear is separated from the
middle cranial fossa by a thin layer of bone (tegmen
tympani) and lies parallel and slightly lateral to the
greater petrosal nerve. Force a small aperture in the
tegmen with the point of a rigid knife or seeker, and
slipping a strong seeker through the
aperture under the tegmen, lever it
up and break it away, first in
an anteromedial and then in a
posterolateral direction towards
the junction of the transverse and
sigmoid sinuses. Keep the seeker
close to the tegmen to avoid damage
to the contents of the middle ear.
Clean away the broken edges of the
tegmen and expose the cavity of
the middle ear, avoiding injury to
the parts of the auditory ossicles
which extend superiorly towards
the tegmen.

Pass a blunt seeker into the anteromedial part of the cavity, and
slide it anteromedially till it appears
through the pharyngeal opening of
the auditory tube. Posteriorly the
cavity of the middle ear is a deep
trench which extends inferomedially. Immediately posterior to the
auditory ossicles its posterior (mastoid) wall rises abruptly, and the
cavity becomes continuous with the

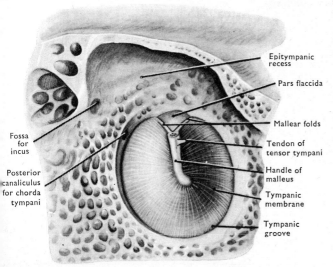

Epitympanic
recess

Pars flaccida

Mallear folds

Tendon of
tensor tympani

Handle of
malleus

Tympanic
membrane

Tympanic
groove

Fossa
for
incus

Posterior
canaliculus
for chorda
tympani

FIG. 144   View of the left tympanic membrane and epitympanic recess from
the medial side.   The head and neck of the malleus have been removed.

mastoid air cells, through the mastoid antrum, superior to the posterior wall.

Identify the rounded head of the malleus articulating with the incus, the short crus of which passes posteriorly towards the superior surface of the posterior wall of the cavity. Inferior to the head of the malleus note the sloping tympanic membrane and the handle of the malleus lying in it. A slender, tough strand passes from the malleus to the medial wall of the middle ear; this is the tendon of tensor tympani which turns through an angle of nearly 90° at the medial wall to become continuous with the muscle belly. The muscle runs in a semicanal superomedial to the auditory tube. Break through the thin wall of this canal and expose the muscle. Immediately superior to the attachment of the tendon to the malleus, the chorda tympani nerve [Fig. 148] runs over the medial surface of that bone as it traverses the tympanic membrane and it is seen as a narrow ridge. Look for the long crus of the incus which passes inferiorly to the stapes, which is not visible at this stage.

THE MIDDLE EAR, MASTOID ANTRUM, AND AUDITORY TUBE

MIDDLE EAR

The narrow middle ear cavity together with the tympanic membrane is known as the tympanum. It is lined with mucous membrane, and is filled with air. It communicates, anteriorly, with the nasal part of the pharynx through the auditory tube [FIG. 151], and, posteriorly, through the mastoid antrum [FIG. 147] with the mastoid air cells, which are small, air-filled cavities in the mastoid process.

The middle ear also contains: (1) the auditory ossicles; malleus, incus, and stapes; (2) the stapedius and tensor tympani muscles; (3) the chorda tympani nerve and the tympanic plexus of nerves.

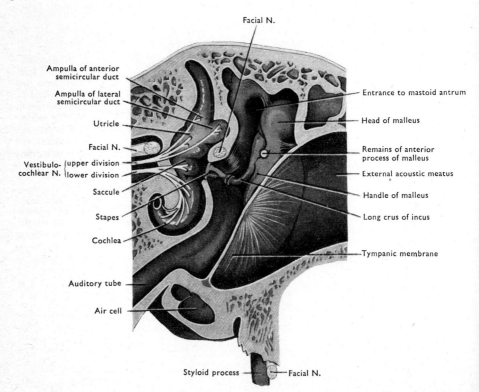

Facial N.

Ampulla of anterior semicircular duct

Ampulla of lateral semicircular duct

Utricle

Facial N.

Vestibulo- {upper division
cochlear N. {lower division

Saccule

Stapes

Cochlea

Auditory tube

Air cell

Entrance to mastoid antrum

Head of malleus

Remains of anterior process of malleus

External acoustic meatus

Handle of malleus

Long crus of incus

Tympanic membrane

Styloid process — Facial N.

FIG. 145 Coronal section through the left tympanic cavity viewed from the front (semi-diagrammatic).

186

The vertical and anteroposterior diameters are each approximately 15 mm.; the width varies from 6 mm. above to 4 mm. below, and is even less centrally where the medial and lateral walls bulge into the cavity.

The part of the cavity superior to the tympanic membrane is called the **epitympanic recess** [FIGS. 142, 148].

The **roof** or **tegmental wall** is the thin tegmen tympani, which separates the cavity from the middle cranial fossa. Chronic inflammatory conditions of the middle ear may spread through the tegmen to the meninges of the brain.

The **floor** or **jugular wall** is narrow. It is formed by a thin bony lamina which separates the cavity from the jugular fossa and its contained bulb of the jugular vein. Extension of an inflammatory condition of the middle ear through this bone may involve the vein, and may lead to thrombosis (clotting) of the blood in the vein and to the spread of infection via the blood stream.

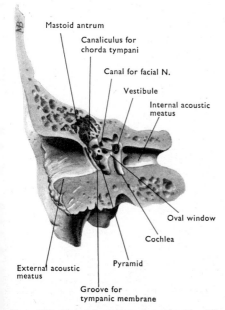

Mastoid antrum

Canaliculus for
chorda tympani

Canal for facial N.

Vestibule

Internal acoustic
meatus

Oval window

Cochlea

Pyramid

External acoustic
meatus

Groove for
tympanic membrane

FIG. 146 Coronal section through the right temporal bone seen from in front.

The **posterior** or **mastoid wall** [FIG. 146] has a series of openings in it: (1) in its upper part is the opening **(aditus)** which leads from the epitympanic recess into the mastoid antrum; (2) inferiorly, close to the medial wall, is a small aperture on the apex of a hollow, conical projection called the **pyramid** [FIG. 148]. This lodges the stapedius muscle, the delicate tendon of which enters the middle ear through the aperture on the summit, and passes to the stapes; (3) lateral to the pyramid, the opening through which the chorda tympani nerve enters the middle ear from the facial nerve posteriorly.

The **anterior** or **carotid wall** is narrow, because the medial and lateral walls converge anteriorly. It consists of three parts: (1) superiorly, the opening of the semicanal for tensor tympani; (2) the orifice of the auditory tube is intermediate; (3) inferiorly, a lamina of bone which separates the cavity from the carotid canal [FIG. 151]. The bony septum between the semicanals for the tensor tympani and the auditory tube is continued posteriorly on the medial wall of the middle ear as a shelf **(processus cochleariformis)**. The posterior end of this forms a pulley around which the tendon of tensor tympani turns laterally through 90° to run to the malleus.

The **medial** or **labyrinthine wall** separates the middle ear from the internal ear, and is entirely bony except for two small apertures [FIG. 147]: (1) the **fenestra vestibuli** (oval window) which is filled by the base of the stapes [FIG. 145] mounted in an elastic ring; (2) the **fenestra cochleae** (round window) which is closed by the delicate secondary tympanic membrane. These two apertures lead into the cavity of the internal ear, and movements of the stapes are transmitted in the form of pressure waves to the fluid which fills that cavity. Since the fluid is incompressible, movements of the stapes are allowed by corresponding movements of the secondary tympanic membrane, which thus prevents damping of the stapedial oscillations. FIGURE 147 shows the principal features, the cochlea of the internal ear forming the promontory anteriorly, while the facial nerve and the lateral semicircular canal, en-

187

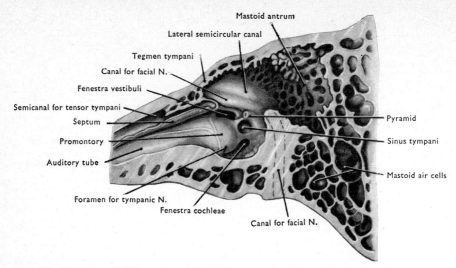

FIG. 147 Vertical section through the left middle ear and auditory tube to expose the medial or labyrinthine wall of the middle ear. The auditory ossicles have been removed.

closed in the bone, produce parallel bulges (superiorly) which extend posteriorly into the mastoid antrum.

Mucous Membrane of Middle Ear Cavity. This is a thin delicate lining, but the cavity is so narrow that it may be blocked when the mucous membrane swells during inflammation. The mucous membrane lines the walls of the cavity and covers the auditory ossicles. It is continuous with the linings of the auditory tube, mastoid antrum, and mastoid air cells, and its epithelium is a simple cuboidal layer.

Auditory Ossicles [FIG. 148]

These little bones extend in a chain from the tympanic membrane to the fenestra vestibuli, the malleus and stapes being attached to these

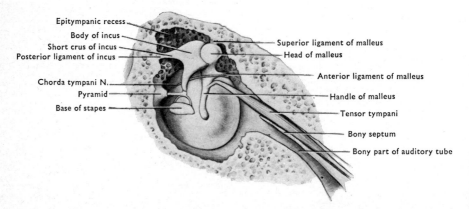

FIG. 148 Left tympanic membrane and auditory ossicles seen from the medial side. Note the auditory tube, and superior to it, tensor tympani and its semicanal.

two parts respectively with the incus slung between them.

Malleus. The **head** is the rounded superior part that lies in the epitympanic recess; the slender **manubrium** or handle is attached to the tympanic membrane.

Incus. The **body** of the incus lies in the epitympanic recess and articulates with the head of the malleus. It sends its **long crus** inferiorly to articulate with the head of the stapes, and a **short crus,** posteriorly, to be attached to the floor of the aditus by a ligament.

Stapes. It is shaped like a stirrup, and its foot piece or **base** fits into the fenestra vestibuli

on the medial wall of the middle ear.

When the tympanic membrane and the handle of the malleus move, the head imparts a rotatory movement to the incus around the axis of its short crus, the long crus swinging mediolaterally and imparting a similar movement to the stapes in the fenestra vestibuli.

Tympanic Muscles

Stapedius. It occupies the interior of the pyramid and the canal which curves inferiorly from it. Its tendon enters the middle ear through the summit of the pyramid, and is inserted into the posterior surface of the neck

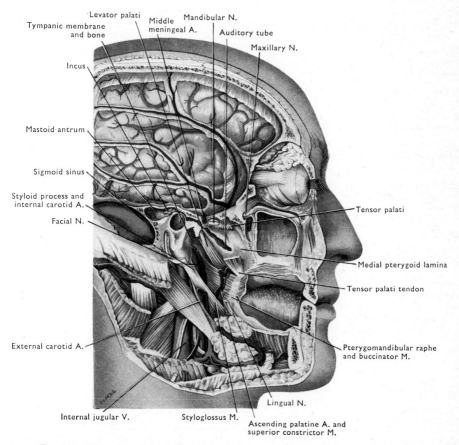

FIG. 149   Dissection of the auditory tube and mastoid antrum from the lateral side.

of the stapes. Nerve supply: the facial nerve. Action: it damps the movement of the stapes, and paralysis of it is associated with excessive acuteness of hearing (hyperacusia) owing to the uninhibited movement of the stapes.

Tensor Tympani. It arises from the superior surface of the cartilaginous part of the auditory tube and from the adjacent parts of the greater wing of the sphenoid and petrous temporal bone. It passes posterolaterally in the semicanal superior to the bony part of the auditory tube, and turns at 90° round the processus cochleariformis in the middle ear cavity, to run laterally to the superior part of the handle of the malleus. Nerve supply: the mandibular nerve, through fibres which traverse the otic ganglion. Action: it tenses the tympanic membrane, increases its medial convexity, and restricts its freedom of movement. Thus it prevents wide excursions of the ear ossicles and potential damage to the inner ear when exposed to loud sounds.

Chorda Tympani Nerve

The chorda tympani is a branch of the facial nerve; it is distributed via the lingual nerve as taste fibres to the anterior two-thirds of the tongue, and it also contains preganglionic parasympathetic fibres which pass to the submandibular ganglion. The latter synapse with cells in the ganglion which innervate the submandibular and sublingual salivary glands and the glands buried in the anterior two-thirds of the tongue [p. 107].

It arises in the canal for the facial nerve in the temporal bone, a short distance above the stylomastoid foramen [FIG. 152]. It ascends in a narrow tunnel to the posterior wall of the middle ear, and passes forwards across the medial aspect of the upper part of the tympanic membrane and the neck of the malleus, outside the mucous membrane. At the superior part of the anterior wall of the middle ear, it enters another canaliculus through which it descends to the medial end of the squamo tympanic fissure (petrotympanic part) on the base of the skull. Thence it runs antero-inferiorly, grooving the medial side of the spine of the sphenoid, and joins the lingual nerve a short distance inferior to the skull.

MASTOID ANTRUM
[FIG. 147]

This air-filled extension from the middle ear cavity lies posterior to the epitympanic recess and communicates with it through an opening

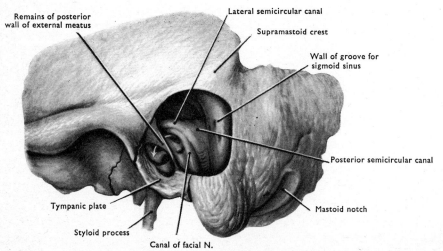

FIG. 150 Dissection of the mastoid antrum and petromastoid part of temporal bone from the lateral side. The arrow passes from the mastoid antrum into the tympanic cavity through the aditus.

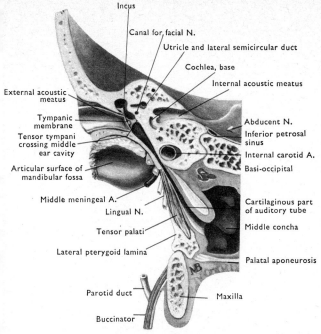

Labels on figure:
Incus
Canal for facial N.
Utricle and lateral semicircular duct
Cochlea, base
Internal acoustic meatus
External acoustic meatus
Tympanic membrane
Tensor tympani crossing middle ear cavity
Articular surface of mandibular fossa
Middle meningeal A.
Lingual N.
Tensor palati
Lateral pterygoid lamina
Parotid duct
Buccinator
Abducent N.
Inferior petrosal sinus
Internal carotid A.
Basi-occipital
Cartilaginous part of auditory tube
Middle concha
Palatal aponeurosis
Maxilla

FIG. 151 An oblique coronal section passing downwards and forwards along the line of the auditory tube, viewed from behind. The mandible and muscles of mastication have been removed leaving the branches of the mandibular nerve on the lateral aspect of tensor palati.

form an abscess in the cerebellum. The **medial wall** is the petrous temporal bone, and part of the ridge produced by the underlying lateral semicircular canal extends posteriorly into it from the aditus [FIG. 150].

The ridge on the medial wall of the middle ear, which is produced by the **facial nerve** in its bony canal, does not reach the antrum, but turns inferiorly (at the aditus) into the wall of bone which separates the middle ear cavity from the mastoid air cells and the inferior part of the antrum. In this bone the facial nerve runs vertically downwards to emerge at the stylomastoid foramen [FIG. 147].

AUDITORY TUBE

This pharyngotympanic tube consists of bony and cartilaginous parts. The cartilaginous part, approximately 2·5 cm. long, is described on page 158.

The **bony part**, approximately 1·5 cm. long, is widest at its junction with the middle ear cavity, and narrowest where it joins the cartilaginous part on the base of the skull posteromedial to the spine of the sphenoid. The bony part lies between the petrous and tympanic parts of the temporal bone, below the semicanal for the tensor tympani, and lateral to the internal carotid artery in the carotid canal [FIG. 151].

DISSECTION. Remove all the soft parts, including periosteum, from the lateral surface of the mastoid temporal bone, and identify the suprameatal triangle and the supramastoid crest. Begin by exposing the mastoid air cells and the mastoid antrum, without injuring the external meatus or entering the sigmoid sinus. With a fine chisel, remove the cortical bone from the suprameatal triangle, and extend the bony removal anteromedially, parallel with the posterior wall of the

called the **aditus ad antrum.** The antrum lies 1·5 cm. medial to the suprameatal triangle (the small triangular area on the surface the of skull immediately posterosuperior to the bony external acoustic meatus) in the adult, but is more superficial in the child. Through this lateral wall a surgical approach to the antrum may be made.

The walls of the antrum are formed by parts of the temporal bone. The tegmen tympani forms the **roof.** The **floor** and **posterior wall** are the mastoid process, and these have the openings of the mastoid air cells in them. The sigmoid venous sinus lies close to the posterior wall and may only be separated from it by a thin plate of bone [FIG. 149], while the jugular bulb may have the same close relation to the floor. Infections of the antrum may involve both veins in septic thrombosis, and this may sometimes spread along their tributaries to

external acoustic meatus, until the mastoid antrum is opened. Remove the spongy bone from the mastoid area until the compact bone posterior and medial to it is exposed. The extent of the mastoid air cells and antrum is variable.

Identify the structures which cause projections of the bony walls of the aditus and antrum; particularly the canal for the facial nerve, the sigmoid sinus, and the lateral semicircular canal [Fig. 150].

Cut away the posterior and superior walls of the external acoustic meatus up to the level of the roof of the mastoid antrum. Remove the tympanic membrane (try to identify the chorda tympani nerve at its postero-superior margin) and the handle of the malleus, to obtain a clear view of the long crus of the incus and the position of the stapes and the stapedius tendon. Review the medial wall of the middle ear [Figs. 145, 147].

INTRAPETROUS PARTS OF FACIAL AND VESTIBULOCOCHLEAR NERVES

The facial and vestibulocochlear nerves have already been traced to the internal acoustic meatus [p. 65]. These nerves should now be followed into the petrous temporal bone; the vestibulocochlear ends in the internal ear, medial to the middle ear; the facial nerve follows an angulated course through dense bone to emerge at the stylomastoid foramen on the inferior surface of the temporal bone.

DISSECTION. Identify the arcuate eminence on the anterior surface of the petrous temporal bone; it marks the position of the anterior semicircular canal. On the posterior surface of the petrous temporal bone, identify the internal acoustic meatus and the nerves entering it. Place a chisel horizontally across the upper part of the internal acoustic meatus, and, with a sharp tap from a mallet, attempt to break off the superior part of the petrous temporal bone. Frequently it fractures along the canal for the facial nerve, passes through parts of the anterior and lateral semicircular canals, and removes the roof of the internal acoustic meatus. Chip away any extra pieces of bone to expose the facial nerve as far as the aditus.

Note the sharp bend (geniculum) on the facial nerve, and the swelling on it at this point (genicular ganglion) where it turns posteriorly into the medial wall of the middle ear, and gives off the greater petrosal nerve. Follow the facial nerve posteriorly above the fenestra vestibuli till it turns inferiorly in the medial wall of the aditus.

Turn to the inferior surface and identify the facial nerve at the stylomastoid foramen. Place the edge of a chisel across the lateral margin of the foramen, and attempt to split the bone along the line of the vertical part of the facial nerve with a sharp tap. If it splits satisfactorily, the posterior canaliculus for the chorda tympani and the whole length of the canal for the facial nerve will be exposed; if not, complete the exposure with bone forceps. Note the position of the

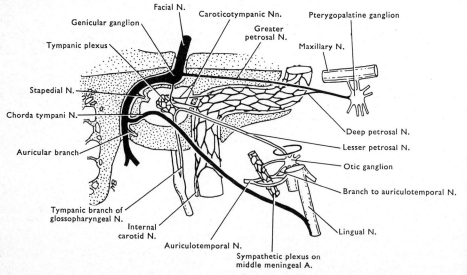

Fig. 152   Diagram of the intrapetrous part of the facial nerve and its connexions.

ertical part of the facial nerve relative to the middle
ear cavity and the mastoid air cells and antrum.
Finally break away one wall of the pyramid and expose stapedius.

Facial Nerve [FIG. 152]

This nerve runs laterally through the internal acoustic meatus anterosuperior to the
vestibulocochlear nerve, and is joined by the
nervus intermedius. At the lateral extremity of
the meatus, it enters its canal in the bone, and
continues laterally for a short distance, above
the vestibule of the internal ear, to reach the
genicular ganglion. At the ganglion, it gives
off the **greater petrosal nerve** [p. 63] and sends
a branch to the lesser petrosal nerve.

The nerve turns abruptly backwards at the
ganglion, and running posteriorly in the bone
of the upper part of the medial wall of the
middle ear cavity, swings inferiorly at the
aditus, to run vertically through the bone between the middle ear cavity, anteriorly, and
the mastoid antrum and air cells, posteriorly.
In the vertical part of its course it gives off:
(1) the nerve to stapedius; (2) the chorda
tympani; (3) twigs to the auricular branch of
the vagus.

Clinically it is possible to differentiate between injuries to the facial nerve at, or distal
to, the stylomastoid foramen, from those at the
brain or in the internal meatus. This is because
the latter are associated with loss of taste on
the anterior two-thirds of the corresponding half of the tongue (chorda tympani) and
hyperacusia (nerve to stapedius) in addition
to the paralysis of the facial muscles, while the
former are not.

Vestibulocochlear Nerve

In the internal acoustic meatus this nerve is
postero-inferior to the facial nerve. It is a
compound nerve which splits, at the lateral end
of the meatus, into its two parts, cochlear and
vestibular. Each of these subdivides further to
pass through the appropriate foramina in the
lateral end of the meatus, and supply the
various parts of the membranous labyrinth of
the internal ear [FIG. 145].

THE INTERNAL EAR

The internal ear consists of a series of communicating bony spaces (the **bony labyrinth**) in
the petrous temporal bone, and a series of
membranous tubes and sacs, the **membranous
labyrinth,** contained within it. The cochlear
portion is concerned with hearing, the remainder with equilibration, for it records the
direction of gravity acting on the head, and
rotational movements of the head. The membranous labyrinth is filled with a clear fluid
(**endolymph**) and is separated from the surrounding bone by a considerable space which
contains a similar fluid (**perilymph**) and some
delicate connective tissue.

**DISSECTION. Free the facial nerve from its canal
as far as the aditus, but retain its continuity with the
greater petrosal nerve. Using the chisel in the same
way as before, cut more bone from the superior surface
of the petrous temporal, till the level of the middle of the
internal acoustic meatus is reached. The bone should be
cracked by sharp taps from a mallet so as to avoid driving
the chisel into the middle ear cavity and the ear ossicles.
As each flake of bone is removed, examine the holes in
the bone produced by the semicircular canals, and note
the semicircular ducts of the membranous labyrinth
lying free within them. Note also the branches of the
vestibulocochlear nerve entering the bone at the lateral
end of the meatus. As the level of the middle of the
meatus is reached, the vestibule and cochlea will be
broken into. The vestibule is the cavity lying immediately lateral to the internal meatus, and separating
it from the medial wall of the middle ear; the cochlea
lies anterolateral to the lateral end of the meatus.**

**The above procedure shows the main features of the
bony labyrinth, and it is desirable at each stage to
establish the continuity of its various parts by passing
a fine wire through each foramen that is exposed. If
time permits, a better dissection may be obtained by
decalcifying an intact temporal bone in dilute acid for
several weeks, and then dissecting it carefully with a
sharp knife.**

BONY LABYRINTH

The bony labyrinth is divided into three
parts: (1) a small chamber called the **vestibule;**
(2) a coiled tube, the **cochlea,** anterior to the
vestibule; (3) three **semicircular canals** posterior to the vestibule. The cochlea and canals
communicate freely with the vestibule, and are
lined throughout by a delicate endosteum.

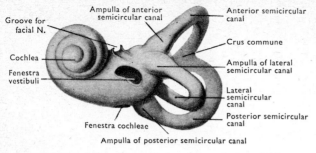

FIG. 153 Left bony labyrinth viewed from the lateral side.

Vestibule [FIGS. 146, 153, 154]

This is a small, ovoid, bony chamber about 5 mm. in length, placed between the lateral end of the internal acoustic meatus and the medial wall of the middle ear. The three semicircular canals open into its posterior part; whilst, on the lateral wall, is the **fenestra vestibuli** which is closed by the base of the stapes and the endosteal lining. When these parts are removed, the vestibule communicates with the middle ear cavity. On the antero-inferior wall of the vestibule is the opening of the **scala vestibuli,** one of the two perilymph tubes which pass into the coiled cochlea. In the posterior part of the medial wall is the mouth of a small canal (**aqueduct of the vestibule**) which passes to the posterior surface of the petrous temporal bone, where it opens between the bone and the dura mater.

Semicircular Canals

Each of the three semicircular canals (anterior, posterior, and lateral) forms considerably more than half a circle, and has a swelling (**ampulla**) at one end. They lie in planes such that each forms one of three adjacent faces of an obliquely set cube. The anterior and posterior canals lie in approximately vertical planes, and their adjoining ends meet in a common limb (**crus commune,** [FIG. 154]) which runs along the edge of the cube to the vestibule. Thus the three canals have five

points of entry to the vestibule.

The **anterior canal** is at right angles to the long axis of the petrous temporal bone, and produces the **arcuate eminence** on the anterior surface of that bone. The **posterior canal** is postero-inferior to the superior canal, and lies almost parallel to the posterior surface of the petrous temporal bone, deep to the slit for the aqueduct of the vestibule. The **lateral canal** is nearly horizontal, but slopes a little antero-superiorly in the angle between the attached ends of the other two. Its most lateral part makes a bulge in the medial wall of the mastoid antrum.

The **ampullae** lie at the anterior ends of the anterior and lateral canals, while that on the posterior canal lies at its posterior opening into the vestibule.

The semicircular canals of one inner ear are mirror images of those in the other ear. Thus, the two lateral canals lie in the same plane, and the anterior canal of one side is parallel with the posterior canal of the other. In any parallel pair, the ampullae are so arranged that endolymph in the semicircular ducts (flowing in the same direction in both as a result of rotation of the head in the plane of that pair) moves towards the ampulla in one canal and away from the ampulla in the other.

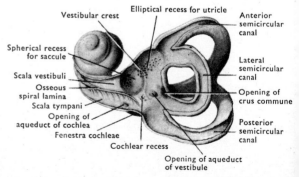

FIG. 154 Interior of the left bony labyrinth viewed from the lateral side.

194

Cochlea

The cochlea is a tapering tube coiled spirally, for two and one-half turns, around a central pillar, the modiolus. It has the appearance of a spiral shell laid on its side. The cochlea lies anterior to the vestibule, with its base directed towards the lateral end of the internal acoustic meatus, and the modiolus pointing antero-laterally towards its apex, which lies medial to the canal for the tensor tympani muscle.

The bony cochlear tube rapidly diminishes in diameter as it is traced towards its apex; the large first turn producing the bulge of the **promontory** on the medial wall of the middle ear cavity [FIGS. 147, 153].

The **modiolus** is thick at its base where it abuts on the internal meatus, but it rapidly tapers towards the apex, forming the internal wall of the cochlear tube. Winding spirally round the modiolus, like the thread of a screw, is a thin, narrow plate of bone (the **spiral lamina**) which partially divides the cochlear tube into two canals.

The modiolus is traversed by a number of minute, longitudinal canals which turn outwards towards the spiral lamina and enter the **spiral canal** of the modiolus. This canal runs in the base of the spiral lamina and lodges the sensory, **spiral ganglion** of the cochlea. The cells of the ganglion send their peripheral processes through minute canals in the spiral lamina to the sensory organ of the cochlea, and their central processes run in the canals of the modiolus, to emerge from its base in the internal acoustic meatus as the cochlear part of the vestibulocochlear nerve.

The **duct of the cochlea** is a spiral, tubular extension of the membranous labyrinth, which passes into the bony cochlear tube. It occupies the central part of the cochlear tube, lying between the spiral lamina and the lateral wall; the remainder of the space on each side of it being filled by the **scala tympani** and **scala vestibuli.** These two perilymph tubes run parallel to and on either side of the cochlear duct, and meet end to end at the apex of the cochlea **(helicotrema)** around the blind end of the cochlear duct.

The scala vestibuli is continuous with the perilymph cavity of the vestibule at the base of the cochlea, while the scala tympani ends on the secondary tympanic membrane which fills the round window (fenestra cochleae). Thus pressure waves generated in the vestibular perilymph by movements of the stapes are transferred through the scala vestibuli and the scala tympani to the secondary tympanic membrane, and its corresponding oscillations allow the free passage of the waves through these perilymph tubes, and hence through the cochlear duct and its sensory organ sandwiched between them.

The scala tympani is also continuous with the perilymphatic duct which passes through the **cochlear canaliculus** [FIG. 154] to appear immediately superior to the jugular foramen, in close association with the glossopharyngeal nerve. This duct is said to be continuous with the subarachnoid space, but it probably ends blindly on the dura mater.

MEMBRANOUS LABYRINTH

The chief parts of the membranous labyrinth are: (1) the duct of the cochlea; (2) the utricle and saccule, two small membranous sacs which lie in the vestibule, and are joined by a narrow tube through the root of the **endolymphatic duct.** The saccule is continuous with the base of the cochlear duct through the **ductus reuniens,** and the utricle has the membranous semicircular ducts arising from it. (3) Three membranous tubes, the semicircular ducts, which lie in the semicircular canals [FIGS. 145, 155].

The **semicircular ducts** are considerably narrower than the canals, and lie against the peripheral bony walls of the canals. They open into the utricle and have ampullae in the same position as the ampullae of the canals. The **ampullae** of the ducts contain a fold of their lining (crista ampullaris) which extends transversely across the ampulla and is the sensory organ of the duct. It records movements of the endolymph in the ampulla which result from rotation of the head in the plane of the duct, and which may be simulated by convection currents produced by introducing hot or cold water into the external acoustic

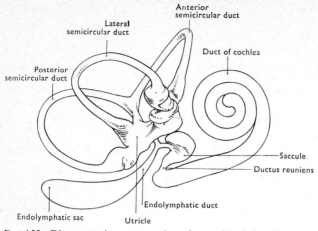

FIG. 155 Diagrammatic representation of a model of the right membranous labyrinth.

Labels in figure: Anterior semicircular duct, Lateral semicircular duct, Duct of cochlea, Posterior semicircular duct, Saccule, Ductus reuniens, Endolymphatic sac, Utricle, Endolymphatic duct.

meatus. It is innervated by the vestibular part of the vestibulocochlear nerve, which ends on the hair cells of the epithelium of the crista.

The **utricle** occupies a depression in the superior wall of the vestibule. The smaller **saccule** lies antero-inferior to it, and the endolymphatic duct (which unites them) passes through the bony aqueduct of the vestibule, to end as a dilated **saccus endolymphaticus** external to the dura mater. The utricle and saccule each have a small area of thickened epithelium in their wall, with hair cells on which lie a number of concretions of calcium salts **(statoconia).** These maculae record the direction of the gravitational field relative to the head, the macula of the utricle lying in a horizontal plane, that of the saccule in a vertical plane. Both are innervated by the vestibular part of the vestibulocochlear nerve.

THE EYEBALL

The eyeball lies in the anterior part of the orbit, enclosed in a fascial sheath which separates it from the orbital muscles and fat, and in which it rotates.

The eyeball is about 2·5 cm. in diameter, but is not perfectly spherical, for the anterior, clear part (the cornea) has a smaller radius of curvature than the rest of the globe, and protrudes from the anterior surface of the eyeball.

It is rarely possible to make a satisfactory dissection of the eyeball of a cadaver, as good results can only be achieved either with the fresh eye, or with a fresh one which has been hardened for a few days in 4 per cent. formaldehyde. The student is therefore advised to procure a number of fresh eyes from pig, sheep, or ox, and store them in formaldehyde solution, except for one which is best laid aside for a day or two to demonstrate the vitreous body.

DISSECTION. Clean the loose tissue off the surface of the eyeball. Pick up the conjunctiva and fascial sheath close to the corneal margin, and cut through these layers around the margin of the cornea. Proceed to strip all these soft parts from the surface of the white part of the eye (the sclera) working steadily backwards towards the entry of the optic nerve. The venae vorticosae will be found piercing the sclera a little posterior to the equator, and the posterior ciliary arteries and ciliary nerves will be seen entering the sclera around the attachment of the optic nerve.

To obtain a general idea of the parts which form the eyeball, make sections through hardened specimens in different planes: (1) through the equator; (2) a sagittal section through two specimens, removing the vitreous body [Fig. 156] from one. Place the sections in formaldehyde solution and keep for reference during dissection.

GENERAL STRUCTURE OF THE EYEBALL

The eyeball consists of three concentric coats, which enclose a cavity filled with three separate light-refracting media.

The coats are: (1) An external fibrous coat, the posterior five-sixths of which is the white, opaque **sclera**; while the transparent, anterior

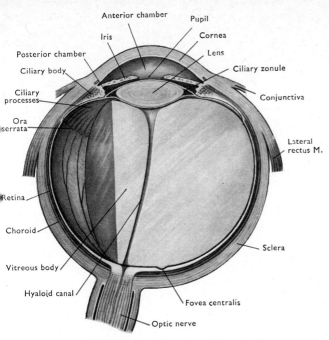

Anterior chamber
Pupil
Iris
Cornea
Posterior chamber
Lens
Ciliary body
Ciliary zonule
Ciliary processes
Conjunctiva
Ora serrata
Lateral rectus M.
Retina
Choroid
Sclera
Vitreous body
Hyaloid canal
Fovea centralis
Optic nerve

FIG. 156   Diagrammatic section of the eyeball.

between the air and the cornea, its curved surface plays a very important part in the optical system, and changes in its shape, from whatever cause, markedly interfere with the ability of the eye to focus an image on the retina.

DISSECTION. With a sharp knife, make an incision through the sclera at the equator, stopping as soon as the black choroid appears. Introduce one blade of a blunt ended pair of scissors through the cut and extend the incision through the sclera around the equator, taking care to separate the choroid from its deep surface as you proceed. Raise the anterior and posterior parts of the divided sclera from the choroid, and by careful, blunt dissection turn these parts anteriorly and posteriorly, stripping them from the choroid. Some resistance will be encountered with the anterior part close to the cornea, due to the attachment of the ciliary muscle to the deep surface of the sclera. As this attachment is broken down by continued blunt dissection, the aqueous humour will escape. The posterior part can finally be removed by dividing the optic nerve fibres where they enter the deep surface of the sclera.

The eyeball, denuded of its fibrous coat, should be placed in water for further investigation.

one-sixth is the more highly curved **cornea.** (2) A middle coat which is vascular and muscular. It consists of the **iris** anteriorly, the **choroid** posteriorly, and the thickest part, the **ciliary body,** which is intermediate in position. (3) The internal, nervous coat, the **retina,** which contains the light sensitive elements (rods and cones) and from which the nerve fibres of the optic nerve arise.

The **refracting media** are: (1) the cornea; (2) the aqueous humour, a watery medium which lies between the cornea and the lens, and fills the **anterior chamber** (between the cornea and the iris) and the **posterior chamber** (between the iris and the lens) of the eye. These two chambers are directly continuous through the aperture in the middle of the iris, the **pupil.** (3) The lens, which separates the posterior chamber from (4) the vitreous body, which occupies the largest part of the cavity of the eyeball, the **vitreous chamber.** Because the greatest change in refractive index is

FIBROUS COAT

Sclera [FIG. 156]

The sclera is a dense, collagenous coat, which covers the posterior five-sixths of the eyeball, and is loosely attached to the choroid by some delicate, pigmented areolar tissue, but firmly adherent to the ciliary body.

The point where the optic nerve pierces the sclera is approximately 3 mm. to the nasal side of the posterior pole, and slightly inferior to the horizontal meridian. Where the optic nerve pierces the sclera, the bundles of optic nerve fibres with the blood vessels to the retina among them, pass through a number of holes in the sclera, and the sheath of the optic nerve, consisting of all three meninges of the brain, fuses with the sclera; the subdural and subarachnoid spaces end at this point.

The sclera is pierced by numerous blood vessels and nerves, which supply the fibrous and vascular coats. The long and short **posterior ciliary arteries** and the **ciliary nerves** pierce it around the optic nerve. Four to five **venae vorticosae** emerge a short distance posterior to the equator, more or less equally spaced around the eyeball. The **anterior ciliary arteries** pierce it near the corneal margin [FIG. 159].

The sclera is directly continuous with the cornea, and close to their junction, a minute canal in the internal part of the sclera **(sinus venosus sclerae)** encircles the margin of the cornea, and drains the aqueous humour [FIG. 161].

Cornea

The cornea is the transparent one-sixth of the fibrous coat of the eyeball, and it is separated from the iris by the aqueous humour in the anterior chamber.

The anterior surface of the cornea is covered with a layer of epithelium which is firmly bound to it, and is continuous with the conjunctiva at the margin of the cornea. On the posterior surface of the cornea is the **posterior limiting lamina**; an elastic glassy layer which becomes wrinkled when the tension in the cornea is released, and may be torn away in shreds from the proper corneal tissue.

Pectinate Ligament of Iris. At the margin of the cornea, the posterior limiting lamina breaks up into bundles of fibres. Some of these pass posteriorly into the choroid and sclera; others arch medially into the iris (pectinate ligament of the iris) crossing the angle between the cornea and the iris in the form of a number of separate bundles, with the minute **spaces of the iridocorneal angle** between them. These spaces seem to form a communication between the anterior chamber of the eyeball and the sinus venosus sclerae through which aqueous humour can filter away into the venous system. Blockage of this system is associated with a serious condition in which the intra-ocular tension is greatly increased (glaucoma) [FIG. 157].

MIDDLE COAT

Choroid

The choroid is the largest part of the middle coat, and lies between the sclera and the retina. It is thickest posteriorly, where it is pierced by the optic nerve, and becomes thinner as it approaches the ciliary body. It is connected with the sclera by some delicate, pigmented areolar tissue and also by the blood vessels and nerves which pass between them. The deep surface of the choroid is moulded on the retina and is in contact with a layer of deeply pigmented cells which belong to the retina, but which normally adhere to the choroid, since a potential space exists between this pigmented layer

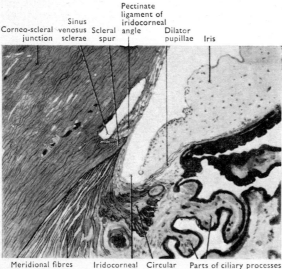

Corneo-scleral junction — Sinus venosus sclerae — Scleral spur — Pectinate ligament of iridocorneal angle — Dilator pupillae — Iris

Meridional fibres of ciliary M. — Iridocorneal angle — Circular fibres of ciliary M. — Parts of ciliary processes

FIG. 157   Section of iridocorneal angle.

f the retina and the retina proper (the rem-
ant of the cavity in the optic outgrowth of
ie embryo).

The choroid consists mainly of blood vessels
hich are arranged in two layers: (1) a deep,
ose-meshed capillary net; (2) a more super-
cial venous layer from which the venae
orticosae arise. The short posterior ciliary
teries run between these layers.

The eyeball, from which the fibrous coat has
een removed, should be gently brushed under
ater with a camel hair brush, to remove the
igment and expose the curved tributaries of
ie venae vorticosae, which appear as white
nes.

iliary Body

This region of the middle coat is divisible
ito (1) an external part, the ciliary muscle, and
) an internal part consisting of a number
f radial ridges, the ciliary processes [FIG.
58].

Ciliary Muscle. It is composed of involun-
iry muscle fibres which are arranged in two
roups, radiating and circular, which are only
isible in microscopic preparations [FIG. 157].

The **radiating fibres** arise from the deep sur-
ice of the sclera close to the cornea, and
idiate posteriorly into the ciliary processes.
he **circular fibres** are arranged in two or three
undles that lie on the deep surface of the
idiating fibres, and form a muscular ring close
> the peripheral margin of the iris. Nerve
ipply: through the short ciliary nerves by
ostganglionic parasympathetic nerve fibres
/hich originate in the ciliary ganglion; the
reganglionic fibres reach the ganglion through
ie oculomotor nerve. Action: see page 203.

DISSECTION. Expose the ciliary processes by
aaking a coronal section through an eyeball anterior
) the equator, and remove the vitreous body from the
nterior segment. Then wash out the pigment from the
nterior part of the middle coat to expose the ciliary
rocesses more fully.

Alternatively, remove the cornea by cutting round the
orneoscleral junction, and examine the exposed iris.
Iake a number of radial cuts into the anterior part of
ie sclera, and fold each segment of sclera outwards,
tripping it from the ciliary body. Remove the iris.

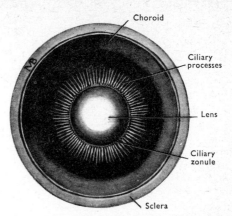

FIG. 158 Anterior half of the interior of the eyeball
viewed from behind after removal of the vitreous.

Ciliary Processes. These lie deep to the
ciliary muscle, and are continuous, anteriorly,
with the iris, and, posteriorly, with the
choroid. There are approximately seventy
processes, each of which extends anteriorly
from the anterior margin of the choroid, to
end as bulbous nodules in the space between
the peripheral margin of the iris and the
margin of the lens. They form the peripheral
boundary of the posterior chamber of the eyeball. The deep surfaces of the processes are
applied to the vitreous membrane, the outer
condensed part of the vitreous body, and also
to the peripheral part of the ciliary zonule
[p. 203] to which they are attached.

Iris

The iris lies anterior to the lens and the
posterior chamber. It is separated from the
cornea by the anterior chamber, and is bathed
by aqueous humour on both surfaces. Its cir-
cumference is continuous with the ciliary body,
and is connected to the cornea by the pectinate
ligament.

The iris varies greatly in colour. It is circular in outline and surrounds a central aperture, the **pupil**. Its anterior surface shows a
faint radial striation: its posterior surface is
deeply pigmented and is formed from the
same epithelial layer as the retina. The pupil is
circular in Man, but may be slit-like in other

199

mammals, either in the horizontal or the vertical plane. Its diameter is constantly varying to control the amount of light reaching the retina, and this is achieved by the presence of two sets of involuntary muscle fibres in the iris. The pupil is decreased in size by the circular fibres of the **sphincter pupillae** (which lie in the pupillary margin of the iris) and dilated by the radial fibres, which pass from the sphincter towards the periphery of the iris and form the **dilator pupillae.** Nerve supply: postganglionic parasympathetic fibres from the ciliary ganglion pass to the sphincter via the short ciliary nerves. The dilator is supplied by postganglionic sympathetic fibres which originate in the carotid plexus, and reach it through the nasociliary and long ciliary nerves.

Ciliary Nerves [Fig. 159]

The **short ciliary nerves** arise from the cells of the ciliary ganglion and pierce the sclera around the optic nerve as twelve or more fine filaments. They run anteriorly, grooving the internal aspect of the sclera, and break up into fine, plexiform terminal branches in the ciliary region. These supply the ciliary muscle, the iris, and the cornea. The short ciliary nerves contain: (1) postganglionic parasympathetic fibres from the cells of the ciliary ganglion for the supply of the ciliary muscle and the sphincter of the pupil; (2) postganglionic sympathetic fibres which supply the vessels of the eyeball; (3) sensory fibres from the nasociliary nerve. The latter two groups pass through the ciliary ganglion without any functional relation to its cells.

The **long ciliary nerves** arise from the nasociliary nerve and pierce the sclera close to the optic nerve. They contain sensory and sympathetic nerve fibres. The latter originate in the superior cervical ganglion, and some of them supply the dilator pupillae.

Ciliary Arteries [Figs. 159, 160]

The **short posterior ciliary arteries** are branches of the ophthalmic artery which pierce the sclera close to the optic nerve and end in the choroid.

The **long posterior ciliary arteries** are two branches of the ophthalmic artery which pierce the sclera some distance from the optic nerve. They run anteriorly, between sclera and choroid, on opposite sides of the eyeball, and branching in the ciliary region, anastomose with the anterior ciliary arteries to form the **greater arterial circle** at the periphery of the iris [Fig. 160]. This circle supplies the iris, the ciliary muscle, and the ciliary processes.

The **anterior ciliary arteries** are minute twigs which arise from the arteries to the rectus muscles. They pierce the sclera close to the cornea, and take part in the formation of the greater arterial circle.

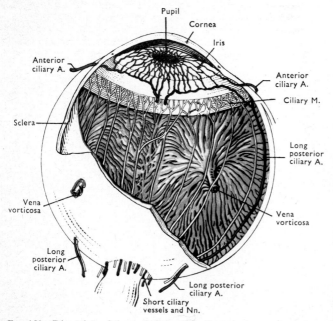

Fig. 159   Dissection of the eyeball to show the vascular coat and the arrangement of ciliary nerves and vessels.

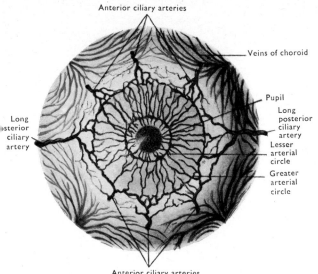

Anterior ciliary arteries

Veins of choroid

Pupil

Long
posterior
ciliary
artery

Lesser
arterial
circle

Greater
arterial
circle

Long
posterior
ciliary
artery

Anterior ciliary arteries

FIG. 160 Blood vessels of the iris and the anterior part of the choroid
viewed from in front.

The **lesser arterial circle** is a small anastomotic ring in the iris at the external border of the sphincter pupillae.

Venae Vorticosae [FIG. 159]

A large vein arises from each venous vortex in the choroid, and pierces the sclera immediately posterior to the equator. Four to five of these veins drain into the ophthalmic veins.

DISSECTION. Remove the vitreous body and retina from the posterior segment of the specimen used to show the ciliary processes. Using a stream of water, raise the choroid from the sclera and expose the venae vorticosae entering the sclera. Cut these veins, and continue to strip the choroid from the sclera until the short ciliary nerves are exposed.

In the specimen from which the sclera and cornea have been removed, strip off the iris, ciliary processes, and choroid, piecemeal, under water. This exposes the external surface of the retina.

Retina

The retina consists of: (1) a thin, outer **pigmented layer** which is adherent to the

choroid and is removed with it; (2) the delicate, internal, **nervous layer.** This is applied to the surface of the vitreous body, and is only attached to it and to the external layers where the optic nerve pierces the sclera. The pigmented layer absorbs the light which has passed through the nervous layer, and thus prevents it from being reflected back through that layer as scattered rays which would reduce the resolving power of the retina. In many nocturnal animals, the pigment is missing and the choroid forms a reflecting layer, to ensure the passage of low intensities of light twice through the retina and thereby increase its sensitivity.

The optic part of the retina ends, anteriorly, at a wavy margin, the **ora serrata,** close to the posterior margin of the ciliary body. The two layers are continued anterior to this as a very thin layer (consisting of two single layers of cells) over the ciliary processes (pars ciliaris retinae) and the posterior surface of the iris (pars iridica retinae).

During life the optic part of the retina is transparent, but soon becomes opaque after death. It consists of three layers of cells, the outermost are the light-sensitive **rods** and **cones,** and the innermost are the nerve **(ganglion)** cells that give rise to the nerve fibres which pass to the brain in the optic nerve. These nerve fibres course over the internal surface of the retina and converge on the end of the optic nerve. Opposite this they build up into a circular elevation, which is slightly hollowed out in the centre, the **optic disc.** This is situated approximately 3 mm. to the nasal side of the anteroposterior axis of the eyeball, and is the site where the nerve fibres turn posteriorly into the optic nerve and become white in colour, owing to the development of myelin sheaths on their surfaces. At the optic

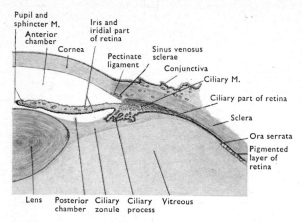

FIG. 161 Meridional section through the ciliary region of human eyeball. (After Schaffer.)

Labels in figure: Pupil and sphincter M. / Anterior chamber / Iris and iridial part of retina / Cornea / Pectinate ligament / Sinus venosus sclerae / Conjunctiva / Ciliary M. / Ciliary part of retina / Sclera / Ora serrata / Pigmented layer of retina / Lens / Posterior chamber / Ciliary zonule / Ciliary process / Vitreous

from the optic disc skirt the macul[...]

Retinal Arteries and Veins. T[...] **arteria centralis retinae** reaches t[...] retina from the ophthalmic artery [...] piercing the dural, arachnoid, an[...] pial sheaths of the optic nerve an[...] entering its substance. Thus it ap[...] pears in the eyeball at the optic dis[...] and divides into superior and inferi[...] branches, each of which divides in[...] a large temporal and a smaller nas[...] arteriole [FIG. 162]. The vario[...] branches of these arterioles run on t[...] retina to the ora serrata, but the[...] neither anastomose with each othe[...] nor with any of the other arteri[...] of the eyeball.

The **retinal veins** converge on t[...] optic disc, and enter the optic nerve [...] two small trunks which soon unite to form t[...] central vein of the retina. The latter vein drai[...] into the superior ophthalmic vein, but it mu[...] pierce the meningeal sheaths of the optic ner[...] and the contained sleeve of subarachnoid spa[...] to reach it. Increased pressure in the subarac[...] noid space tends to compress the vein an[...] cause distension of its tributaries in the retin[...] a feature which can be seen with t[...] ophthalmoscope.

The retina is the one situation where bloo[...] vessels can be examined in the living, and sig[...] of vascular pathology observed at first han[...] The student should take every opportunity [...]

disc there are no sensory retinal elements, but only the nerve fibres and the retinal blood vessels which enter through the optic nerve. At this point the nerve fibres tie down the retina to the sclera, though elsewhere there is a potential space between the nervous and pigmented layers of the retina, and no blood vessels enter the nervous layer except through the optic disc. The middle layer of the retina consists of **bipolar cells** which connect the rods and cones to the ganglion cells.

Exactly in the centre of the human retina, and lying in the visual axis, is a small yellowish spot, the **macula lutea,** which has a slight depression at its centre, the **fovea centralis.** At the fovea, the inner two layers of the nervous layer of the retina are swept aside so that the cones come to lie on the internal surface. This allows light to fall directly on these elements without the distortion which can result from passing through the other layers, and so improves the quality of the image on the cones in this tiny area. At this point also the resolving power of the retina is at its maximum, for here the sensory elements (cones) are slender and very tightly packed. The nerve fibres and blood vessels which pass to and

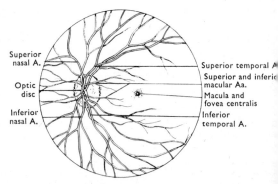

Labels in figure: Superior nasal A. / Optic disc / Inferior nasal A. / Superior temporal A[...] / Superior and inferio[...] macular Aa. / Macula and fovea centralis / Inferior temporal A.

FIG. 162 Retinal blood vessels as seen through the ophtha[...] moscope.

202

using an ophthalmoscope and seeing the normal retina and blood vessels of his fellows.

DISSECTION. **Take the eye which was put aside to lose its freshness and divide the coats around the equator. Strip the coats gently from the underlying vitreous and lens. It is advisable to place the vitreous and lens in a strong solution of picrocarmine for a few minutes, and then wash well in water. This stains the vitreous membrane, the capsule of the lens, and the ciliary zonule red, and makes their connexions readily visible.**

Vitreous Body

This is a soft, transparent, jelly-like body which fills the posterior four-fifths of the eyeball. It abuts on the retina, the ciliary processes, and the lens which forms a deep concavity on the anterior surface of the vitreous, the **hyaloid fossa.**

The vitreous body is condensed superficially to form a transparent envelope, the **vitreous membrane.** A minute canal runs through it from the optic disc to the posterior surface of the lens, and represents the remains of a branch of the central artery of the retina (**hyaloid artery**) which supplied the developing lens in the foetus, but which subsequently disappeared. This **hyaloid canal** cannot be seen in an ordinary dissection, but may be visualized in the living with a slit lamp. The minute remnant of the hyaloid artery attaches the vitreous body to the optic disc, though elsewhere it is entirely free from the retina.

Ciliary Zonule [FIG. 161]

This is a thickened part of the vitreous membrane which is fitted to the posterior surfaces of the ciliary processes. At the medial margin of the ciliary processes it splits into two layers. The posterior layer is an extremely thin membrane which lines the hyaloid fossa. The anterior layer is thicker (**suspensory ligament of the lens**) and is attached principally to the anterior surface of the capsule of the lens a short distance from its margin, but it is also attached to the margin of the lens and the posterior surface close to the margin.

The suspensory ligament holds the lens firmly in the hyaloid fossa, and maintains a degree of tension on the lens when the eye is

at rest, thus drawing it out radially, flattening it, and maintaining it at a long focal length. When the ciliary muscle contracts, it pulls the ciliary processes and zonule anteriorly, relaxes the suspensory ligament, and allows the elastic lens to round up and thus shorten its focal length. This is the mechanism of focusing on near objects (accommodation) which is intimately linked with convergence of the eyes and with constriction of the pupil in the accommodation-convergence reflex.

The **zonular spaces** are enclosed in the suspensory ligament at its multiple attachments to the lens, and form a multilocular lymph space around the margin of the lens.

DISSECTION. **Remove the lens by cutting through the suspensory ligament with scissors.**

Lens

This is a biconvex, transparent, elastic solid which lies between the iris and the vitreous body, and is enclosed in a glassy, elastic capsule. It contains no blood vessels.

The **anterior surface** is less highly curved than the posterior surface. Its central part is opposite the pupil, and lateral to this the margin of the iris is in contact with the lens, though further laterally the lens and iris are separated by aqueous humour in the posterior chamber. The **posterior surface** fits into the hyaloid fossa, and the equator is a blunt margin that forms one boundary of the zonular spaces.

DISSECTION. **Incise the anterior surface of the lens with a sharp knife, and apply a little pressure to the margin between finger and thumb. This will extrude the body of the lens and allow the capsule to be studied separately.**

Compress the body of the lens between finger and thumb, and note that the central part (nucleus) is firmer than the remainder. The lens is formed of a number of concentric laminae, a fact which may easily be proved after the lens has been hardened in alcohol.

The lens becomes tougher and less elastic with age, and this accounts for the decreasing ability to focus on near objects. It also becomes less transparent, and several varieties of opacities may form in it (cataract).

THE BRAIN

INTRODUCTION

The central nervous system consists of two types of cells: (1) the nerve cells proper; (2) the connective tissue of the central nervous system (neuroglia). The latter is a special series of cells which is intimately connected with the nerve cells, both structurally and functionally, and includes the ciliated columnar ependymal cells which line the cavities of the central nervous system.

In addition to these two types, there are the cells of the meninges which cover the central nervous system, and the blood vessels which enter its substance.

Nerve cells are very variable in size and shape, but all of them have cytoplasmic processes, and some of these extend for considerable distances from the cell body. These processes are of two types, axons and dendrites. The **dendrites** are the processes which receive stimuli from the axons of other nerve cells that end on the dendrites. They are very variable from cell to cell, but are commonly branched in a complicated fashion and restricted to the vicinity of the cell body. The **axons** are often thinner than the dendrites, and are responsible for transmitting impulses from the cell body either to other nerve cells, or to peripheral organs through the peripheral nerves. They are of considerable length (up to 1 m.) in some cases, and are capable of extensive branching so that the impulses they carry can be widely disseminated, but they may also pass to strictly circumscribed regions of the central nervous system.

Most of the axons in the central nervous system are covered with a fatty **myelin sheath.** This is in the form of a series of discontinuous segments separated by **nodes** (where the myelin is absent) and is white in colour, in contrast to the grey colour of the fresh cell bodies and dendrites which have no covering of myelin. The axon together with its myelin sheath is known as a **nerve fibre,** but the same term is applied to the thinnest axons which do not possess a myelin sheath, but are nevertheless enclosed in the same type of cells (oligodendroglia) whose processes form the myelin sheaths on the thicker axons.

Throughout most of the central nervous system, the axons are segregated into particular parts, and thus form bundles **(tracts),** while the cell bodies with their associated dendrites form clusters or **nuclei.** Because of their difference in colour in the fresh state, the tracts form the **white matter** of the central nervous system, while the nuclei make up the **grey matter.**

In the spinal medulla and in most of the brain stem (which are continuous with each other through the foramen magnum) the grey matter lies internally, and is covered by a superficial layer of white matter, which consists of longitudinally running nerve fibres.

In the cerebellum, the cerebral hemispheres, and certain other situations, there is an additional layer of nerve cells on the external surface. This rind or **cortex** of grey matter greatly increases the number of nerve cells and hence the complexity of their interactions.

Functionally the central nervous system is concerned with the receipt and integration of sensory information from all parts of the body, and with producing responses which are appropriate to the sum of the sensory information reaching it at any moment, in the light of past experience. This extremely complicated activity is achieved by the passage of impulses through the interconnected networks of cells in the central nervous system. Each cellular unit is linked into the system by junctions (**synapses**) at which the surfaces of the nerve cells come together and a mechanism exists for the transfer of activity from one cell to another. Whether the activity passes from cell to cell or dies out at the synapse depends on a number of complex factors, but it is the discontinuity at the synapses and the ability to facilitate or inhibit the passage of impulses across them in different circumstances which allows for the extreme variability of response; a variability which is also dependent on the total number of cells and synapses involved.

It is not possible to give more than the most rudimentary analysis of this complex system, but a knowledge of the arrangement of its parts and of the major tracts by which they are interrelated is an essential prerequisite to an understanding of its functions. In the following pages the gross anatomy of the central nervous system is dealt with, and some of the details of its finer structure are indicated briefly. Further details should be sought in the larger textbooks and in original publications.

The brain is that part of the central nervous system which lies within the cranial cavity. It is surrounded by the same three membranes (meninges) as the spinal medulla (dura mater, arachnoid mater, and pia mater) and they are continuous with their spinal counterparts through the foramen magnum. In the skull the dura mater is fused with the periosteum lining the cranial cavity (endocranium) so that, when the brain is removed, the arachnoid separates from the dura at the subdural space [p. 49] and the pia and arachnoid come away with the brain.

The main blood vessels of the brain and their principal branches lie in the subarachnoid space between the arachnoid and pia mater, and the smaller vessels ramify on the pia mater before sinking into the substance of the brain.

The first stage in the dissection of the brain is the examination of the arachnoid mater and the pia mater (leptomeninges) and the blood vessels which lie between them. The student must have some knowledge of the main parts of the brain before proceeding, and the following introduction, together with the information obtained when the brain was removed from the skull [p. 50] is intended to meet this need.

The student should avoid damage to the meninges during this preliminary examination, and will be greatly helped by having a brain from which the meninges and blood vessels have been removed [FIG. 163].

The fresh brain is extremely soft and unsuitable for dissection, and the specimens used are hardened in formalin so that they retain their shape. Avoid drying of the brain during dissection by storing it in a suitable preservative which will inhibit the growth of moulds.

Parts of Brain

				Cavity
FOREBRAIN	Cerebrum			Right and left lateral ventricles
	Diencephalon	Thalamus		Third ventricle
		Hypothalamus		
MIDBRAIN				Cerebral aqueduct
HINDBRAIN	Pons		Brain Stem	Fourth ventricle and central canal
	Medulla oblongata			
	Cerebellum			

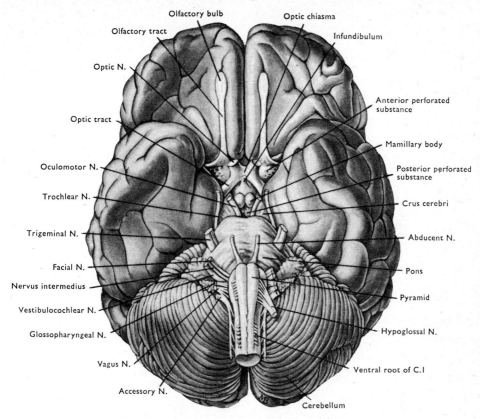

Olfactory bulb

Optic chiasma

Olfactory tract

Infundibulum

Optic N.

Anterior perforated
substance

Optic tract

Mamillary body

Oculomotor N.

Posterior perforated
substance

Trochlear N.

Crus cerebri

Trigeminal N.

Abducent N.

Facial N.

Pons

Nervus intermedius

Pyramid

Vestibulocochlear N.

Glossopharyngeal N.

Hypoglossal N.

Vagus N.

Ventral root of C.I

Accessory N.

Cerebellum

Fig. 163   The base of the brain and the cranial nerves.

With the assistance of Figures 163 and 207, identify the major parts of the brain; the details of each part will be dealt with later when they are studied individually. A macerated skull should be available to confirm the relations of the parts of the brain to the skull.

The **cerebrum** is by far the largest part. It is composed of the two cerebral hemispheres which are partially separated by the falx cerebri lying in the longitudinal fissure. The hemispheres cover the other parts of the brain so that these can only be seen on the inferior surface [Fig. 163]. The surface of each hemisphere is increased in area by extensive folding. It thus presents a number of grooves **(sulci)** between which are blunt ridges **(gyri).**

These sulci and gyri cannot be seen clearly until the meninges are removed, but it should be noted that the arrangement of these folds is never quite alike in any two brains, and even the right and left hemispheres of one brain show marked differences.

Each hemisphere has three surfaces: (1) the convex superolateral surface; (2) the medial surface, partly in contact with the falx cerebri; (3) the inferior surface, which consists of orbital and tentorial parts. The orbital part lies on the floor of the anterior cranial fossa which separates it from the orbit. The orbital part is separated from the tentorial part, which lies on a more inferior plane, by a deep horizontal fissure (stem of the lateral sulcus)

207

into which the lesser wing of the sphenoid fits. Posteriorly, the tentorial surface rests on the tentorium and slopes inferolaterally; anteriorly, it lies on the floor of the middle cranial fossa, and ends in the temporal pole which extends forwards below the lesser wing of the sphenoid into the anterior extremity of the middle cranial fossa. Posteriorly, the tentorial surface ends in the occipital pole, which fits into the fossa on the occipital bone in the angle between the grooves for the superior sagittal and transverse sinuses.

The **diencephalon** is almost entirely hidden from view by the cerebral hemispheres. It consists of a dorsal **thalamus** and a ventral **hypothalamus**, and only the floor of the latter is visible on the base of the brain. Here it appears as the small area bounded by the optic chiasma and optic tracts, anteriorly and antero-laterally, and the crura cerebri posterolaterally [FIG. 163]. It lies superior to the sella turcica and dorsum sellae of the sphenoid bone, and forms the roof of the **interpeduncular fossa**. This is a deep median hollow on the inferior surface of the brain, which lies between the temporal lobes of the brain laterally, the optic chiasma anteriorly, and the pons posteriorly. If the meninges are intact, the interpeduncular fossa is hidden by a layer of arachnoid which spans it, and forms its floor. If the arachnoid is torn, the tuber cinereum and mamillary bodies can be seen on the inferior surface of the hypothalamus [FIG. 163] in the fossa.

The **midbrain** is the narrow neck which joins the forebrain to the hindbrain, and passes through the tentorial notch. Only the anterior surface of the midbrain can be seen at this stage, and this consists of the **crura cerebri** (two broad bundles of nerve fibres, one of which issues from each cerebral hemisphere, while both enter the pons inferiorly) with the posterior part of the interpeduncular fossa between them. The posterior surface **(tectum)** of the midbrain consists of four small swellings (the **colliculi**) but is deeply buried between the cerebellum and the cerebral hemispheres, and no attempt should be made to expose it at this juncture as this may lead to the midbrain being torn across. Between the tectum and the crura cerebri lie the **tegmentum** and the **substantia**

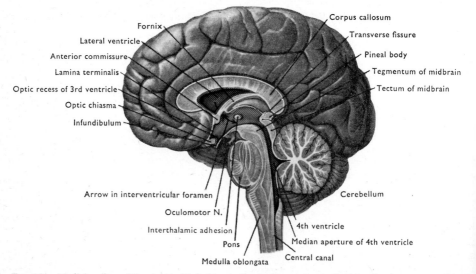

FIG. 164   Medial surface of the right half of a bisected brain. The septum pellucidum has been removed to expose the lateral ventricle.   The arrow passes through the interventricular foramen from the lateral to the third ventricle, and lies in the hypothalamic sulcus. Ependymal lining of ventricles, blue.

nigra of the midbrain [FIG. 194] only a small part of which can be seen in the interpeduncular fossa between the crura cerebri. In each half of the midbrain, the crus cerebri, substantia nigra, and tegmentum together constitute a **cerebral peduncle.** The oculomotor (third cranial) nerves emerge from the anterior surface of the midbrain, medial to the crura cerebri.

The **cerebellum** is the second largest mass of nervous tissue. It lies in the posterior cranial fossa, inferior to the tentorium cerebelli, and overlaps the posterior surfaces of the midbrain, pons, and medulla oblongata. It is easily recognized by the large number of closely set transverse fissures which cross its surface. The major parts of the cerebellum may be identified with the help of FIGURES 185 and 186, but it is sufficient, at this stage, to note that it consists of two hemispheres, and a median portion (the **vermis**) which, on the inferior surface, is deeply set between the hemispheres in a median groove, the **vallecula cerebelli.** The vallecula is partly filled by the falx cerebelli, a blunt dural fold which lies vertically between the fossae on the occipital bone for the cerebellar hemispheres.

The **pons** is the white, bulging bridge which arches across the anterior aspect of the hindbrain between the two halves of the cerebellum. Posteriorly, on each side, the pons narrows to form the rounded **middle cerebellar peduncle** which extends posteriorly into the cerebellum. The dividing mark between the pons and the peduncle is the thick trigeminal (fifth cranial) nerve, the only nerve which issues through the substance of the pons [FIG. 163].

The **medulla oblongata** is the conical, white body which extends inferiorly from the pons to join the spinal medulla at the foramen magnum. A median fissure divides the ventral surface into right and left halves, and a longitudinal ridge, on each side of the fissure, is known as the **pyramid** because it tapers to a point inferiorly. Posterolateral to the pyramid is an oval swelling, the **olive** [FIGS. 175–177].

The sixth to twelfth cranial nerves are attached to the medulla oblongata. The sixth and twelfth arise ventrally, between the pyramid and the olive; the remaining nerves are attached to the lateral surface, posterior to the olive. The seventh and eighth emerge at the lower border of the pons, and, inferior to this, the ninth, tenth, and eleventh form a linear series of rootlets, the most inferior of which extend to the level of the fifth cervical segment of the spinal medulla.

The **brain stem.** This term is usually applied to the midbrain, pons, and medulla oblongata, and is used in this sense here, though it is sometimes considered to include the diencephalon.

THE MEMBRANES OF THE BRAIN (MENINGES)

DURA MATER

This has been studied during the dissection of the head [pp. 48–54] but its parts should be reviewed in relation to the brain.

ARACHNOID MATER

This is an exceedingly thin, almost transparent membrane, which is separated from the dura mater by a capillary interval, the **subdural space.** This has many of the features of a bursa, including the presence of a film of moistening fluid, and forms a sliding plane where movement is possible between the dura and the deeper structures. The arachnoid is adherent to the dura only at the points where structures enter or leave the brain (e.g., nerves and blood vessels) and where the arachnoid granulations (q.v.) pierce the dura mater.

The **pia mater** is a close-fitting sheath which follows the contours of the brain and dips into all the irregularities of its surface. The arachnoid is closely applied to the dura and has the same smooth contours as that membrane; it therefore lies near the pia mater only where the brain and dura mater are closely fitted, but

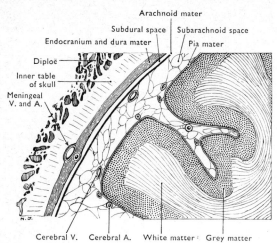

Arachnoid mater
Subdural space | Subarachnoid space
Endocranium and dura mater | Pia mater
Diploë
Inner table of skull
Meningeal V. and A.

Cerebral V.   Cerebral A.   White matter   Grey matter

FIG. 165   Diagrammatic section to show the relation of the meninges to the skull and brain.   Note that the meningeal arteries are in the endocranium, while the cerebral blood vessels lie in the subarachnoid space.

is separated from it where they are widely separated. Thus the arachnoid bridges over the irregularities of the surface of the brain, including such structures as the interpeduncular fossa, the vallecula cerebelli, and the sulci, leaving spaces (**cisterns**) of variable depth between it and the pia mater.

The arachnoid passes with the dura between the major parts of the brain, and thus covers the internal surfaces of the falx cerebri and tentorium cerebelli, and, like the dura, it is pierced by structures entering or leaving the brain.

SUBARACHNOID SPACE

This is the name given to the space between the arachnoid and pia mater. It is filled with **cerebrospinal fluid** which enters it from the cavities (ventricles) of the brain, and which acts as a mobile buffer to distribute and equalize pressures within the skull.

The subarachnoid space is broken up by a fine mesh of filaments and trabeculae which connects the arachnoid to the pia, and which may be dense in some situations (*e.g.*, over the surfaces of the cerebral hemispheres). Here it forms a kind of fluid-filled sponge which may

help to protect the surface of the brain from damage against the skull and the dural folds—the falx and tentorium. Where the pia and arachnoid are close together they are so tightly bound by the trabeculae that they cannot be separated, but in other situations (*e.g.*, over the sulci and the cisterns) the mesh is less dense and the cerebrospinal fluid can flow more freely. The larger arteries and veins of the brain traverse the subarachnoid space, and in some situations (*e.g.*, the stem of the lateral sulcus) the space forms a sleeve around the artery, and its pulsations help to force the cerebrospinal fluid along the sleeve. Prolongations of the subarachnoid space surround the branches of vessels which enter the brain substance, but these **perivascular spaces** accompany the vessels for a short distance only.

Subarachnoid Cisterns [FIG. 166]

These deep pools of cerebrospinal fluid are found where the brain does not fit closely to the dura mater, and the arachnoid and pia lie some distance apart. They are principally situated around the brain stem, on the base of the brain, around the free margin of the tentorium cerebelli, and in association with the major blood vessels.

The **cerebellomedullary cistern** lies in the angle between the cerebellum, medulla oblongata, and the occipital bone. It is directly continuous, inferiorly, with the posterior part of the spinal subarachnoid space [FIG. 166] and is accessible to a needle introduced anterosuperiorly through the posterior atlantooccipital membrane, between the posterior arch of the atlas and the posterior margin of the foramen magnum (cisternal puncture; cf., lumbar puncture, page 34).

The **cisterna pontis** lies anterior to the pons and medulla oblongata, and contains the vertebral and basilar arteries. It is continuous: (1) posteriorly, around the medulla oblongata with the cerebellomedullary cistern; (2) inferiorly, with the spinal subarachnoid space; (3) superiorly, with the interpeduncular cistern.

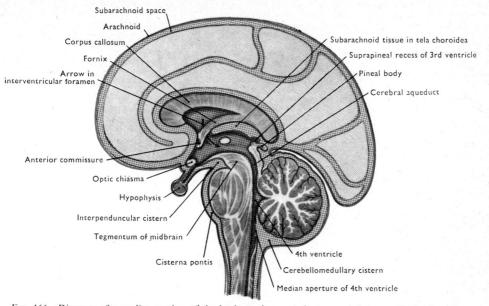

Subarachnoid space
Arachnoid
Corpus callosum
Fornix
Arrow in interventricular foramen

Subarachnoid tissue in tela choroidea
Suprapineal recess of 3rd ventricle
Pineal body
Cerebral aqueduct

Anterior commissure
Optic chiasma
Hypophysis
Interpenduncular cistern
Tegmentum of midbrain
Cisterna pontis

4th ventricle
Cerebellomedullary cistern
Median aperture of 4th ventricle

FIG. 166 Diagram of a median section of the brain to show membranes and cisterns. Red, pia mater ; blue stipple, subarachnoid space and ventricles ; blue, arachnoid ; pink, surface view of shallow subarachnoid space. The lines of blue stipple running over the pink area indicate the places where the subarachnoid space is deeper around the branches of the anterior and posterior cerebral arteries.

The **interpenduncular cistern** fills the interpeduncular fossa. At the superior border of the pons, the arachnoid turns anteriorly above the sella turcica and is stretched between the temporal lobes of the hemispheres. Here it forms the floor of the interpenduncular fossa and cistern. This cistern contains the circulus arteriosus [FIG. 169] and is continuous, laterally, with the subarachnoid spaces surrounding the middle and posterior cerebral arteries, and anteriorly (around the anterior cerebral arteries) with the cisterna chiasmatis. It seems certain that the pulsations of these arteries help to force cerebrospinal fluid from the cistern on to the surfaces of the hemispheres. That which passes along the middle cerebral artery finds its way to the cistern of the lateral fissure of the cerebrum, while, along the posterior cerebral arteries, it runs around the sides of the midbrain, close to the margin of the tentorium cerebelli, to meet on the dorsal surface of the midbrain, the cisterna ambiens. The various cisterns communicate freely,

but there is no direct communication with the subdural space, and the only communications between the cavities of the brain and the subarachnoid space are through three small openings in the roof of the ventricle of the hindbrain (fourth ventricle).

Arachnoid Villi and Granulations

The arachnoid villi are minute protrusions of the arachnoid which pass through fenestrae in the dura mater and project into the venous sinuses of the dura mater, especially the superior sagittal sinus. They contain subarachnoid tissue and fluid, and a number of minute tubules which pass through the middle of each villus and become continuous with the cavity of the venous sinus at the apex of the villus. The tubules and the cerebrospinal fluid in the mesh of arachnoid trabeculae which fills the remainder of the villus are both continuous with the subarachnoid space at the base of the villus. When the pressure of the cerebrospinal fluid exceeds that in the venous

211

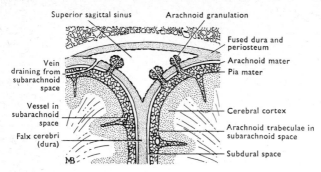

Superior sagittal sinus   Arachnoid granulation

Fused dura and periosteum
Arachnoid mater
Pia mater

Vein draining from subarachnoid space

Vessel in subarachnoid space

Cerebral cortex

Falx cerebri (dura)

Arachnoid trabeculae in subarachnoid space

Subdural space

MB   B

FIG. [167   Diagrammatic transverse section through the superior sagittal sinus and surrounding structures. Note the arrangement of the arachnoid granulations.

sinus, the trabecular spaces of the villi fill with cerebrospinal fluid, the villi bulge into the sinus, and the central tubules become patent, allowing the escape of cerebrospinal fluid into the venous sinus. If the venous pressure exceeds that of the cerebrospinal fluid, the villi collapse and the tubules are effectively closed, thus preventing the reflux of blood into the subarachnoid space.

With increasing age, the size of the villi increases till they become readily visible to the unaided eye, and form the arachnoid granulations. These may become sufficiently large to indent the overlying bone of the skull [p. 48].

DISSECTION. Divide the arachnoid along the anterior aspect of the medulla oblongata and pons. Turn the flaps aside and expose the vertebral and basilar arteries, noting the nature of the arachnoid trabeculae.

Cut posteriorly through each flap into the cerebello-medullary cistern, and identify the posterior inferior cerebellar branch of the vertebral artery, which winds posteriorly around the medulla oblongata into the cistern, on its way to the cerebellum. Identify the apertures in the roof of the fourth ventricle, by the tuft of finely granular material (choroid plexus) which protrudes through each. The median aperture can be seen in the depth of the cerebellomedullary cistern by gently lifting the cerebellum away from the medulla [Fig. 188]. The lateral apertures face anteriorly, and lie immediately posterior to the corresponding glossopharyngeal nerve. Pick up the tuft of choroid plexus protruding through the lateral aperture and pull it posteriorly: the aperture will be seen immediately anterior to the choroid plexus at the end of a sleeve-like extension of

the thin roof of the fourth ventricle [Figs. 175, 188].

Extend the median incision into the interpeduncular fossa. Note the blood vessels in the interpeduncular cistern, and the fact that its floor is perforated, posteriorly by the oculomotor nerves, and anteriorly by the internal carotid arteries and the infundibulum.

PIA MATER OF THE BRAIN

The pia mater is the immediate investment of the brain. It is thick over the medulla oblongata and spinal medulla, but more delicate elsewhere. It follows the surface of the brain accurately, passing into each sulcus, though it does not form a well defined layer in the smaller fissures of the cerebellum.

The blood vessels of the brain run on the pia mater in the subarachnoid space, and break up into fine branches which anastomose on the pia mater before passing into the substance of the brain. As they enter the brain, the small vessels carry a sleeve of pia mater and subarachnoid space (perivascular space) with them for a short distance, and the vessels do not anastomose within the brain substance. Thus if a small piece of pia mater is stripped from the surface of the brain, its deep surface is covered with a number of minute processes which are the small blood vessels entering the brain substance. If this manoeuvre is carried out on a living animal, the piece of brain lying under the excised pia mater will degenerate from lack of blood supply, because of the lack of any adequate anastomoses with vessels in the adjacent brain tissue.

In certain situations the walls of the cavities of the brain (ventricles) are thin, and consist of a layer of the lining epithelium (ependyma) only. In these regions the pia mater on the external surface is invaginated into the cavities as a series of vascular tufts which carry the ependyma before them, and thus form the choroid plexuses of the ventricles. The pial element of this complex is known as the tela choroidea. The choroid plexuses are responsible for the formation of cerebrospinal fluid within the ventricles, whence it escapes into the subarachnoid space through the apertures in the roof of the fourth ventricle. The cerebrospinal fluid circulates slowly in the subarachnoid space, assisted partly by the pulsations of the arteries in the subarachnoid space, and partly by the fact that it is removed from the space through the arachnoid granulations and villi, and is passed into lymphatics and veins associated with the extradural parts of the spinal and cranial nerves. It is probable that the cerebrospinal fluid formed by the choroid plexuses is supplemented by additions from the ependyma which lines the remainder of the cavities of the brain as well as covering the choroid plexuses, and by fluid produced in the subarachnoid space itself.

THE BLOOD VESSELS OF THE BRAIN

All the intracranial vessels, with the exception of the venous sinuses [pp. 55, 62, 65] which are enclosed in the thick dura mater, have much thinner walls than extracranial vessels of comparable size; for they are enclosed in and supported by the surrounding cranium. The walls of all but the largest veins are so thin that they are virtually invisible unless filled with blood, and thus some of them are difficult to identify. The veins are capable of considerable distention, and if the venous drainage is partially blocked by pressure on the internal jugular veins, the pooling of blood in the intracranial veins produces a marked rise in intracranial pressure, and this may be measured by means of a manometer attached to a hollow needle introduced into the subarachnoid space by lumbar or cisternal puncture. This feature may be used to confirm the continuity of the cranial and lumbar subarachnoid spaces in clinical investigations (Queckenstedt's test).

VEINS OF THE CEREBRAL HEMISPHERES

Most of these veins lie on the surfaces of the hemisphere in the subarachnoid space, and they drain into the venous sinuses of the dura mater by crossing the subarachnoid and subdural spaces, and piercing the arachnoid and dura.

Veins of Superolateral Surface

The **superior cerebral veins** [FIG. 168] converge on the superior sagittal sinus, the anterior and posterior veins entering the sinus obliquely from in front and behind, and all passing inferior to the lateral lacunae of the sinus. Most of the **inferior cerebral veins** converge on the superficial middle cerebral vein, but those of the occipital lobe run inferiorly into the transverse sinus.

The **superficial middle cerebral vein** runs anteriorly in the mouth of the posterior ramus of the lateral sulcus [FIG. 207] and curving medially into the stem of that sulcus, ends in the cavernous sinus. Its cut end will be found piercing the arachnoid near the medial end of the stem of the lateral sulcus. Posteriorly, the superficial middle cerebral vein is frequently connected to the superior sagittal sinus by a wide **superior anastomotic vein,** and commonly to the transverse sinus by the **inferior anastomotic vein** [FIG. 168]. These anastomotic veins may become important if the cavernous sinus is blocked, but there are also smaller connexions between the superficial veins and the veins in the interior and on the base of the hemisphere by perforating veins which pass through the substance of the hemisphere.

Veins of Inferior Surface of Hemisphere

These drain in a number of directions: (1) anteriorly, to the anterior and superficial middle cerebral veins; (2) posteriorly, to the basal vein (q.v.); and (3) directly to the superior petrosal, straight, and transverse sinuses.

Veins of Medial Surface of Hemisphere

These veins will be seen later when the hemispheres are separated, but parts of this

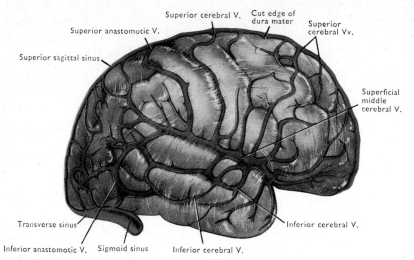

Fig. 168 Veins of the superolateral surface of the hemisphere, seen through the arachnoid mater.

system can be seen now, so a brief description is given.

The main vein on the medial aspect is the **great cerebral vein.** It emerges from beneath the posterior end (splenium) of the corpus callosum (the mass of white matter which passes between the two hemispheres, FIGURE 164), and curves superiorly around the splenium to join the inferior sagittal sinus and form the straight sinus [FIG. 35]. If the occipital lobes of the hemispheres are gently separated, the cut end of the great cerebral vein will be seen close to the splenium.

The great cerebral vein is joined by a number of symmetrical tributaries from the midbrain and cerebellum inferior to it, and by the basal veins which curve round the sides of the midbrain to reach it from the inferior surface of the brain.

Each **basal vein** is formed deep in the medial part of the stem of the lateral sulcus by the confluence of: (1) the **anterior cerebral vein,** which runs with the corresponding artery and enters the basal vein from in front; (2) the **deep middle cerebral vein** which lies in the depths of the lateral sulcus on the insula; (3) the **striate vein** or veins which descend through

the substance of the brain and emerge close to the formation of the basal vein through the anterior perforated substance [FIG. 163].

DISSECTION. Divide the arachnoid over the stem of the lateral sulcus and depress the temporal pole so as to expose the beginning of the middle cerebral artery, the deep middle cerebral vein, the striate veins, and the origin of the basal vein. If the latter is filled with blood it will be seen passing posteriorly close to the optic tract [Fig. 163] and should be traced as far as possible towards the great cerebral vein.

The veins of the brain stem and cerebellum mainly drain in a posterior direction to reach the basal and great cerebral veins, and the adjacent venous sinuses. The veins of the medulla oblongata communicate with those of the spinal medulla.

ARTERIES OF THE BRAIN

Two internal carotid and two vertebral arteries carry the total blood supply of the brain. The vertebral arteries enter the skull through the foramen magnum. Each internal carotid reaches the brain by traversing the carotid canal and the superior part of the foramen lacerum. It then takes a sinuous course through the cavernous sinus, and

214

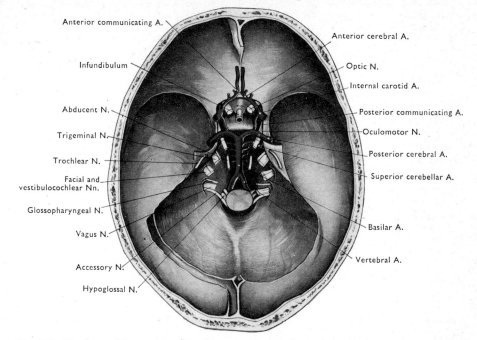

FIG. 169   The floor of the cranial cavity after removal of the brain, but with the arteries at the base of the brain *in situ*.

piercing the dural roof of the sinus, ends immediately lateral to the optic chiasma, inferior to the anterior perforated substance [FIG. 163], by dividing into its terminal branches.

Vertebral Arteries

Each vertebral artery enters the subarachnoid space in the upper part of the vertebral canal by piercing the lateral aspect of the dura mater and arachnoid. It ascends anterosuperiorly through the foramen magnum, and curves round the ventrolateral aspect of the medulla oblongata, close to the rootlets of the hypoglossal nerve, to unite with its fellow at the lower border of the pons and form the median basilar artery. The two vertebral arteries are often of very different calibre.

Intracranial Branches. (1) The **posterior spinal artery** is the first intracranial branch. It passes inferiorly on the spinal medulla among the dorsal rootlets of the spinal nerves [p. 36], and it may arise from the posterior inferior cerebellar artery. (2) The **posterior inferior cerebellar artery** is the largest branch, and it arises soon after the vertebral artery pierces the meninges. It pursues a very tortuous course posteriorly on the side of the medulla oblongata, and passes among the rootlets of the hypoglossal, vagus, and glossopharyngeal nerves. Here it supplies branches to the lateral part of the medulla oblongata, occasionally as far cranially as the inferior border of the pons. It then runs on to the posterior surface of the medulla oblongata, between the thin roof of its cavity (the fourth ventricle) and the cerebellum, and supplying the choroid plexus of that ventricle, turns downwards on to the surface of the cerebellum, and divides into branches to supply it. In size it varies inversely with the anterior inferior cerebellar artery, but it is usually much larger than the latter vessel. (3) The **anterior spinal**

artery arises near the inferior border of the pons, and runs inferomedially to join its fellow on the ventral surface of the medulla oblongata. It sends branches into the median part of the medulla oblongata, and continues inferiorly throughout the length of the spinal medulla. It gives branches into the anterior median fissure of the spinal medulla which supply the grey matter, and surface branches which pass round the lateral aspect of the spinal medulla to anastomose with the posterior spinal artery, and supply the superficial parts of the white matter of the anterior and lateral columns. The anterior spinal artery receives a variable number of tributaries from the arteries on the ventral roots of the spinal nerves. One of these usually enters on one of the most inferior thoracic ventral roots (commonly the tenth) and is responsible for supplying most of the arterial blood to the lumbosacral region of the spinal medulla.

Basilar Artery

This artery is formed at the inferior border of the pons by the junction of the two vertebral arteries, and it terminates at the superior border of the pons by dividing into the two posterior cerebral arteries. It lies on the median groove of the pons in the cisterna pontis, and is supported anteriorly by the basilar part of the occipital bone and the dorsum sellae of the sphenoid [FIG. 169].

Branches [FIG. 170]. (1) The **pontine** branches are numerous slender twigs which pierce the substance of the pons. Some pass directly into the pons, while others run laterally over its surface and enter it further laterally. (2) The **artery of the labyrinth** is a slender branch which arises at the inferior border of the pons, and accompanies the vestibulocochlear nerve to the internal ear. It may arise from the anterior inferior cerebellar artery. (3) The **anterior inferior cerebellar artery** arises close to the labyrinthine artery, and runs laterally along the inferior border of the pons, passing superficial to and supplying the sixth, seventh, and eighth cranial nerves. It then loops around the flocculus and supplies the anterior part of the inferior cerebellar surface. (4) The **superior cerebellar artery** is a large branch which arises close to the superior border of the pons. It winds posteriorly along the superior border of the pons, and, supplying it and the lateral aspect of the inferior part of the midbrain (which lies immediately superior to the pons) sends branches to the superior surface of the cerebellum, inferior to the tentorium cerebelli. (5) The **posterior cerebral arteries** are two large vessels which diverge at the superior border of the pons, and curve round the lateral aspect of the superior part of the midbrain, deep to the cerebral hemisphere. Posteriorly, each artery runs on to the corresponding hemisphere, and, passing towards the occipital pole, divides into two main terminal branches which are distributed as shown in FIGURE 197. Since the posterior cerebral and superior cerebellar arteries curve

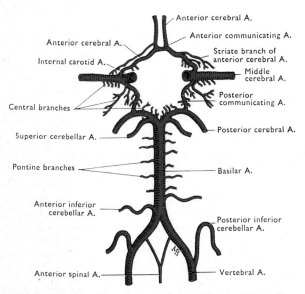

FIG. 170   Diagram of the arteries on the base of the brain including the circulus arteriosus.

Anterior cerebral A.

Anterior cerebral A.

Internal carotid A.

Central branches

Superior cerebellar A.

Pontine branches

Anterior inferior cerebellar A.

Anterior spinal A.

Anterior communicating A.

Striate branch of anterior cerebral A.

Middle cerebral A.

Posterior communicating A.

Posterior cerebral A.

Basilar A.

Posterior inferior cerebellar A.

Vertebral A.

around the superior and inferior parts of the midbrain respectively, the nerves arising from the midbrain (third and fourth cranial) pass anteriorly between these two branches of the basilar artery.

Branches of the Posterior Cerebral Artery. (1) Small **central branches** run medially to pierce the anterior surface of the midbrain between the crura cerebri, and form the perforations in the **posterior perforated substance** [FIGS. 163, 170]. Others enter the lateral aspect of the midbrain. (2) The **posterior choroid artery** (frequently multiple) arises on the lateral aspect of the midbrain, and passes laterally to supply the greater part of the choroid plexus in the cavity of the hemisphere (lateral ventricle) and the choroid plexus and part of the

wall of the cavity of the diencephalon (the third ventricle). (3) The branches to the cerebral cortex will be seen when the medial aspect of the hemisphere is exposed.

On the anterior surface of the midbrain, each posterior cerebral artery receives a slender posterior communicating branch from the corresponding internal carotid artery. This forms part of the arterial circle in the interpeduncular fossa.

Internal Carotid Arteries

The cut end of each internal carotid artery can be seen immediately lateral to the optic chiasma. It is passing into a shallow pit (the vallecula) immediately inferior to the anterior perforated substance [FIG. 163]. Here the

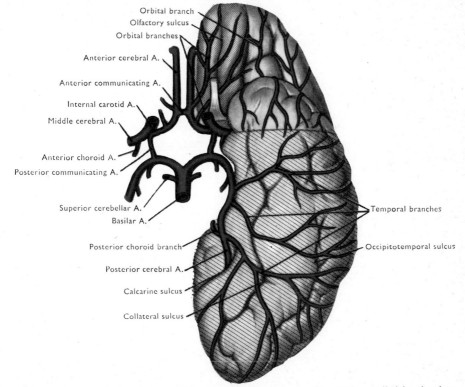

Orbital branch
Olfactory sulcus
Orbital branches
Anterior cerebral A.
Anterior communicating A.
Internal carotid A.
Middle cerebral A.
Anterior choroid A.
Posterior communicating A.
Superior cerebellar A.
Basilar A.
Posterior choroid branch
Posterior cerebral A.
Calcarine sulcus
Collateral sulcus
Temporal branches
Occipitotemporal sulcus

FIG. 171 Arteries of the inferior surface of the left hemisphere. The areas supplied by the three arteries are indicated by: red stipple, anterior cerebral artery; red cross-hatching, posterior cerebral artery; no colour, middle cerebral artery.

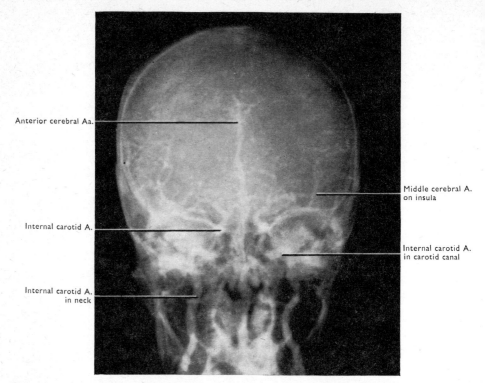

Anterior cerebral Aa.

Middle cerebral A.
on insula

Internal carotid A.

Internal carotid A.
in carotid canal

Internal carotid A.
in neck

FIG. 172   Anteroposterior radiograph of the skull showing both internal carotid arteries injected with an X-ray opaque medium. This has been carried by the circulating blood into the middle and anterior cerebral arteries.

artery gives off two small branches, and divides into the middle and anterior cerebral arteries. The small branches are:

(1) The **posterior communicating artery** passes posteriorly, across the crus cerebri to join the posterior cerebral artery. It gives off minute branches to the crus, optic tract, and hypothalamus. It is usually a slender vessel, but it may be large on one or both sides, and form the major route for blood passing to the posterior cerebral artery. In such cases, occlusion of the internal carotid may produce profound damage in the territory of the posterior cerebral artery. (2) The **anterior choroid artery** arises superior to (1), and passes posterolaterally, close to the optic tract. It gives branches into the crus cerebri, and turns later-

ally, superior to the medial aspect of the temporal lobe (uncus, FIGS. 209, 224) to enter the choroid plexus of the inferior horn of the lateral ventricle which lies in the temporal lobe.

Anterior Cerebral Artery. Only a small part of this artery can be seen before the medial aspect of the hemisphere is exposed. This part runs horizontally in an anteromedial direction above the optic chiasma [FIGS. 171, 197]. It then bends sharply upwards into the longitudinal fissure, and is connected to its fellow of the opposite side by the short **anterior communicating artery** [FIG. 170] which lies anterosuperior to the optic chiasma. Beyond this it runs on the medial surface of the hemisphere, curving upwards and backwards, close

218

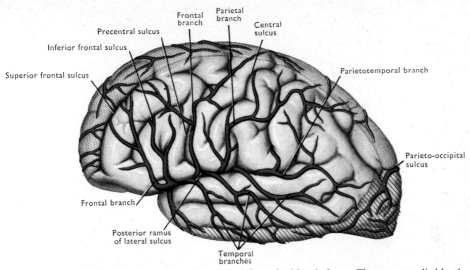

Frontal branch
Parietal branch
Precentral sulcus
Central sulcus
Inferior frontal sulcus
Superior frontal sulcus
Parietotemporal branch
Parieto-occipital sulcus
Frontal branch
Posterior ramus of lateral sulcus
Temporal branches

FIG. 173   Arteries of the superolateral surface of the left cerebral hemisphere. The areas supplied by the three arteries are indicated by: red stipple, anterior cerebral artery; no colour, middle cerebral artery; red cross-hatching, posterior cerebral artery.

to its fellow, but separated from it by arachnoid and the falx cerebri towards the end of its course [FIG. 197].

Branches. (1) Several slender branches pierce the brain anterior to the optic chiasma and enter the anterior hypothalamus. (2) Branches pass to the optic chiasma and the optic nerve. (3) One or more larger branches arise in the region of the anterior communicating artery and take a recurrent course to the medial part of the anterior perforated substance. Here they send a number of perforating branches into the brain substance. (4) The cortical branches will be seen later.

Middle Cerebral Artery. This large branch lies in line with the internal carotid artery, and thus particulate matter passing through that artery enters the middle cerebral artery more frequently than the anterior cerebral. The middle cerebral artery runs laterally in the stem of the lateral sulcus, and breaks up into a number of branches on the **insula** (a buried part of the cerebral cortex which may be seen by opening the posterior ramus of the lateral sulcus [FIG. 198] and separating the temporal lobe from the frontal and parietal lobes [FIG.

233]. These branches emerge on to the superolateral surface of the hemisphere between the lips of the lateral sulcus, and supply most of that surface [FIG. 173] and also the adjacent parts of the orbital and tentorial surfaces, including the temporal pole [FIG. 171]. This area includes most of the 'motor' and 'sensory' areas and all of the 'auditory' area of the cerebral cortex.

The **central branches** are numerous small **striate arteries** that pass superiorly through the anterior perforated substance (principally its lateral part) to supply the deep nuclei of the hemisphere, chiefly the corpus striatum (q.v.).

Circulus Arteriosus [FIG. 170]

This arterial circle extends from the superior border of the pons to the longitudinal fissure, and it lies principally in the interpeduncular fossa. It is composed of the posterior cerebral, posterior communicating, anterior cerebral, and anterior communicating arteries. It forms a route through which blood entering by either internal carotid artery or the basilar artery may be distributed to any part of the cerebral hemispheres. Because of variations in the

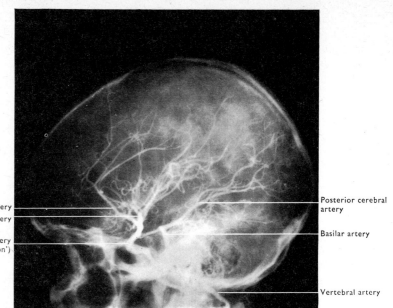

Anterior cerebral artery

Middle cerebral artery

Internal carotid artery ('carotid siphon')

Posterior cerebral artery

Basilar artery

Vertebral artery

FIG. 174 Lateral radiograph of the skull of a patient taken immediately after the injection of X-ray opaque material into one internal carotid and one vertebral artery. The distribution of these two arteries is outlined. Note the posterior communicating artery apparently joining the superior end of the basilar artery to the internal carotid artery.

calibre of the vessels which form the circulus, it is important, before tying off a carotid artery for any reason, to determine the nature of the circle by carotid or vertebral angiography [FIG. 174], combined with compression of one or more of the feeding vessels to determine the efficacy of the parts of the circle.

Two types of branches arise from the circle and its major branches; these are arbitrarily divided into cortical and central, and they differ from each other in the extent of their anastomoses. The **central branches** are very numerous and slender, they tend to arise in groups and immediately pierce the surface of the brain to supply its internal parts. The largest collections of these pass through the anterior and posterior perforated substances. They do not anastomose to a significant extent within the brain substance. The **cortical branches** ramify over the surface of the cortex and anastomose fairly freely on the pia mater.

They give rise to numerous small branches which enter the cortex at right angles and, like the central branches, do not anastomose in it. It follows that blockage of an artery on the pia mater may produce little if any damage to the brain, but damage to branches entering the substance of the brain leads to the destruction of brain tissue.

The arteries of the brain are liberally supplied with **sympathetic nerves** which run on to them from the carotid and vertebral plexuses. They are extremely sensitive to injury and readily react by passing into prolonged spasm, and this of itself may be sufficient to cause damage to brain tissue since even the least sensitive of neurons cannot withstand absolute loss of blood supply for a period exceeding seven minutes.

DISSECTION. Remove the blood vessels and the remains of the arachnoid and pia mater from the base of

220

le brain, cutting the cerebral arteries as they leave the interpeduncular cistern. Do not attempt to remove he pia mater from the brain stem as this will result in removal of the cranial nerves. Note the points of entry of the medial central branches of the posterior cerebral arteries, and avoid pulling the central branches of the middle cerebral arteries out of the brain, rather cut them at their origin and leave them for later dissection.

THE BASE OF THE BRAIN

Interpeduncular Fossa

This is the rhomboidal space bounded by the pons, the crura cerebri, and the optic tracts and chiasma. The crura cerebri [FIG. 163] emerge from the cerebral hemispheres, and are crossed by the optic tracts, which are immediately applied to their lateral surfaces. Inferiorly, the crura converge as they descend to enter the pons, and form the most anterior part of the midbrain.

Structures in Interpeduncular Fossa. These are: (1) The **oculomotor nerves,** each of which emerges immediately dorsomedial to the corresponding crus. (2) The **posterior perforated substance,** which is a layer of grey matter lying in the angle between the crura cerebri, and pierced by the central branches of the posterior cerebral arteries which arise close to the origin of these vessels. (3) The **mamillary bodies** are a pair of small, white, spherical bodies which protrude, side by side, from the ventral surface of the hypothalamus immediately anterior to the posterior perforated substance. (4) The **uber cinereum** is a slightly raised area of grey matter between the mamillary bodies and the optic chiasma. The **infundibulum** arises from the tuber cinereum immediately posterior to the optic chiasma; it is the narrow stalk which connects the hypothalamus to the hypophysis (pituitary gland) but it was cut when the brain was removed.

Anterior Perforated Substance

This small area of grey matter forms the roof of the vallecula of the cerebrum, and is pierced by the central branches of the middle and anterior cerebral arteries. It is continuous, laterally, with the roof of the stem of the lateral sulcus. Anteriorly, it is bounded by the diverging striae of the olfactory tract; medially, by the optic tract; posteriorly, by

the uncus [FIGS. 163, 208]. The anterior perforated substance is directly continuous, superiorly, with the corpus striatum in the interior of the hemisphere.

Lamina Terminalis

This thin, grey membrane extends superiorly from the optic chiasma, and forms the anterior wall of the third ventricle, the median cavity which separates the two halves of the diencephalon. The lamina terminalis may be seen by bending the optic chiasma gently downwards, when the continuity of the lamina terminalis with the anterior perforated substance may be confirmed on both sides [FIG. 208].

SUPERFICIAL ATTACHMENTS OF THE CRANIAL NERVES

Twelve pairs of cranial nerves are attached to the brain, but of these, the second is not a true nerve as it is developed from an outgrowth of the full thickness of the brain tube, and not by the outgrowth of axons either from cells situated within the central nervous system or within ganglia closely associated with it. The nerve fibres which it contains are, therefore, more akin to a tract than to a peripheral nerve. The twelve pairs of nerves are:

1. Olfactory.	7. Facial.
2. Optic.	8. Vestibulocochlear.
3. Oculomotor.	9. Glossopharyngeal.
4. Trochlear.	10. Vagus.
5. Trigeminal.	11. Accessory.
6. Abducent.	12. Hypoglossal.

A minute bundle of nerve fibres attached to the cerebrum posterior to the striae of the olfactory tract has been described as a thirteenth pair (the nervi terminales). They accompany the corresponding olfactory tract

221

anteriorly, and are distributed with it to the nose, but their function is unknown.

Each cranial nerve enters or leaves the brain surface at its **superficial attachment,** and the fibres which it contains either arise from (efferent or motor fibres) or terminate on (afferent or sensory fibres) nuclei within the brain. These constitute respectively the **deep origins** and the **deep terminations** of the cranial nerves.

The first two pairs are attached to the forebrain; the third and fourth to the midbrain; the fifth to the pons; the remainder to the medulla oblongata, and, in the case of the eleventh, to the cervical spinal medulla also.

The cranial nerves fall naturally into three groups according to the position of their super-ficial attachment to the brain, which may either be ventral, or lateral, or dorsal.

Cranial Nerves with Ventral Attachments

Olfactory Nerves. Approximately twenty of these on each side pass through the cribriform plate of the ethmoid, and end in the olfactory bulb. They are unusual in that they consist of bundles of minute, non-myelinated nerve fibres which arise in the olfactory cells of the nasal mucous membrane, and are so delicate that no trace of them will be seen on the olfactory bulb [FIG. 163].

Optic Nerve. This is a thick, cylindrical nerve. It is composed of myelinated nerve fibres which arise in the retina, and it joins the anterolateral angle of the optic chiasma.

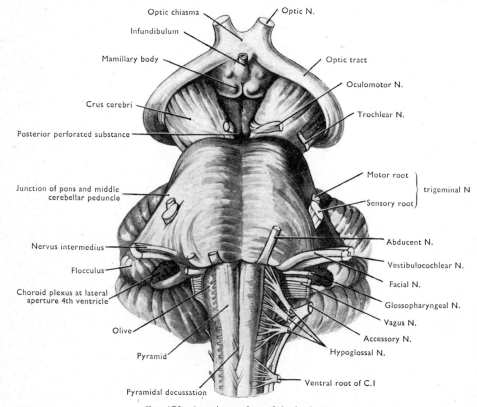

Optic chiasma — Optic N. — Infundibulum — Mamillary body — Optic tract — Crus cerebri — Oculomotor N. — Trochlear N. — Posterior perforated substance — Motor root — trigeminal N — Junction of pons and middle cerebellar peduncle — Sensory root — Nervus intermedius — Abducent N. — Flocculus — Vestibulocochlear N. — Choroid plexus at lateral aperture 4th ventricle — Facial N. — Glossopharyngeal N. — Olive — Vagus N. — Accessory N. — Pyramid — Hypoglossal N. — Pyramidal decussation — Ventral root of C.1

FIG. 175 Anterior surface of the brain stem.

Oculomotor Nerve. It arises as a compact bundle of rootlets from the groove on the medial aspect of the cerebral peduncle in the posterior part of the interpeduncular fossa.

Abducent Nerve. It emerges from the groove between the inferior border of the pons and the lateral surface of the pyramid [FIG. 175].

Hypoglossal Nerve. It is formed by a row of rootlets which arise from the anterior aspect of the medulla oblongata in the groove between the pyramid and the olive [FIG. 175]. They are directly in line with the ventral rootlets of the first cervical nerve.

Cranial Nerves with Lateral Attachments

Trigeminal Nerve. This is the largest of the cranial nerves. It is attached to the lateral aspect of the pons, and consists of two roots: a larger, posterolateral, sensory root, consisting of loosely packed nerve bundles, and a smaller, anterosuperior, motor root which is compact and applied to the sensory root.

Facial and Vestibulocochlear Nerves. These two nerves, with the small **nervus intermedius** between, emerge around the inferior border of the pons, posterior to the olive, and in the same vertical line as the other laterally attached cranial nerves.

The facial nerve is motor, while the nervus intermedius [FIG. 175] carries its sensory and parasympathetic fibres. It lies anterior to the larger vestibulocochlear nerve which splits into a posterior (cochlear) part and an anterior (vestibular) part around a white ridge on the posterolateral part of the medulla oblongata, the inferior cerebellar peduncle [FIGS. 177, 192].

Glossopharyngeal, Vagus, and Accessory Nerves. These nerves arise as a vertical series of rootlets from a groove posterior to the olive in the medulla oblongata, and, in the same line, from the lateral aspect of the spinal medulla as far inferiorly as the fifth cervical spinal segment. The rootlets which form the glossopharyngeal nerves can only be differentiated from the others because they pierce the dura mater separately at the jugular foramen. A part of the accessory nerve may still be attached to the brain, and, if a portion of the spinal medulla is present, its spinal and cranial roots may be seen; the latter more widely spaced than the former [FIG. 175].

Cranial Nerve with a Dorsal Attachment

Trochlear Nerve. This slender nerve arises from the dorsal surface of the brain stem immediately inferior to the midbrain, after having crossed from the opposite side within the substance of the brain. It will be seen later when the anterior lobe of the cerebellum is removed, but it may be found winding round the lateral aspect of the midbrain towards the interpeduncular region, immediately superior to the pons [FIGS. 38, 190].

DISSECTION. When the attachments of the nerves have been identified, clean the surface of the pons and medulla oblongata, but leave the nerve roots in position as far as possible.

THE HINDBRAIN

THE MEDULLA OBLONGATA

This conical part of the brain extends from the pons to the spinal medulla, which it joins at the foramen magnum. It is approximately 2·5 cm. long, and was once known as the bulb, a term which is occasionally used in some clinical conditions, *e.g.*, bulbar paralysis.

The anterior surface of the medulla oblongata lies against the basilar part of the occipital bone, while the posterior surface is lodged in a groove on the anterior surface of the cerebellum, the vallecula cerebelli. The inferior half is tunnelled by the narrow central canal, which ascends through it from the spinal medulla, and opens out into the fourth ventricle on the posterior surface of its superior half.

The medulla oblongata is partially divided by an **anterior median fissure** which is continuous with that of the spinal medulla, but is interrupted in the lower medulla oblongata, where bundles of fibres from the pyramids cross the midline through it, interdigitating with each other (**decussation of the pyramids,** FIG. 176).

The **posterior median sulcus** of the spinal medulla extends upwards to the inferior angle of the fourth ventricle, separating the uppermost parts of the fasciculi gracilis and the tubercles of the nuclei gracilis at their superior extremities [FIGS. 188, 192].

SURFACE FEATURES

Pyramid

On the anterior surface note the two pyramids separated by the anterior median fissure, except at the decussation. The pyramids are bundles of nerve fibres which originate from cells in the cerebral cortex, principally in the precentral gyrus [FIG. 198], and descend through the hemispheres, the crura cerebri, and the pons to form the pyra-

mid in the medulla oblongata. Most of the fibres cross in the decussation to form the **lateral corticospinal tract** in the lateral funiculus of the spinal medulla [FIG. 25]; the remainder descend (without crossing) in the anterior funiculus, the **anterior corticospinal tract.** Because these fibres pass through the pyramid, the tracts they form are commonly called the pyramidal tracts. The lateral corticospinal tract extends throughout the length of the spinal medulla, and contributes fibres to every level of it. The anterior corticospinal tract terminates in the thoracic region of the spinal medulla, some of its fibres crossing at every level superior to this to end in the grey matter of the opposite side. The size of the pyramidal decussation, and hence the size of the anterior corticospinal tracts, varies considerably, but the termination of the fibres appears to be the same irrespective of the number that cross in the decussation.

Olive

Posterolateral to the pyramid, and separated from it by the rootlets of the hypoglossal nerve, is the oval elevation of the olive [FIG. 177]. It is produced by the olivary nucleus, which has the shape of a crumpled bag of grey matter with its open mouth facing medially, and from which issue its efferent fibres passing to the opposite half of the cerebellum via the inferior cerebellar peduncle [FIG. 180]. The surface of the olive is often traversed by a number of bundles of nerve fibres passing posteriorly from the region of the anteromedian fissure towards the inferior cerebellar peduncle. These are the **anterior external arcuate fibres,** and they arise in the arcuate nucleus which lies on the pyramid. This nucleus and the fibres represent an inferior extension of the pontine nuclei and the pontocerebellar fibres which arise from them. Similar fibres arise in the arcuate nucleus [FIG. 181], pass posteriorly through the midline of the medulla oblongata, and run across the floor of the fourth ventricle to the cerebellum forming the **striae medullares** of the fourth ventricle, which will be seen later [FIG. 192].

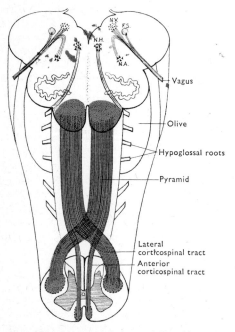

N.V.
F.S.
N.H.
N.A.
Vagus
Olive
Hypoglossal roots
Pyramid
Lateral corticospinal tract
Anterior corticospinal tract

FIG. 176 Diagram of the medulla oblongata and spinal medulla to show the decussation of the pyramids (corticospinal tracts).

Inferior Cerebellar Peduncle

Posterolateral to the olive, and separated from it by a shallow groove in which the rootlets of the ninth, tenth, and eleventh cranial nerves are attached, is a thick bundle of fibres on the posterolateral margin of the medulla oblongata, the inferior cerebellar peduncle. It begins about half way up the medulla oblongata, passes upwards and slightly laterally to the inferior border of the pons, where it is covered by the cochlear part of the vestibulocochlear nerve (a narrow grey ridge composed of the dorsal and ventral cochlear nuclei), and disappears medial to the middle cerebellar peduncle to pass posteriorly into the cerebellum. This peduncle forms a route of communication from the medulla oblongata and the spinal medulla to the cerebellum.

Spinal Tract of the Trigeminal Nerve [Fig. 177]

Immediately anterior to the inferior cerebellar peduncle is a poorly defined longitudinal ridge, through which the rootlets of the ninth and tenth cranial nerves emerge. This descending spinal tract of the trigeminal nerve is a bundle of the sensory fibres of that nerve, and it descends through the pons and medulla oblongata into the superior part of the spinal medulla. Here it is directly continuous with the **dorsolateral tract** [Fig. 248]; a similar bundle formed from the dorsal rootlets of the spinal nerves, which also consists principally of fibres conveying impulses from pain and thermal sensory endings. The ridge formed by the spinal tract is often poorly defined in its intermediate part, because a bundle of fibres from the lateral funiculus of the spinal

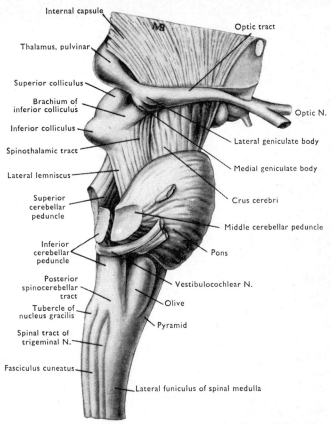

Internal capsule

Optic tract

Thalamus, pulvinar

Optic N.

Superior colliculus

Brachium of inferior colliculus

Lateral geniculate body

Inferior colliculus

Spinothalamic tract

Medial geniculate body

Lateral lemniscus

Superior cerebellar peduncle

Crus cerebri

Middle cerebellar peduncle

Inferior cerebellar peduncle

Pons

Posterior spinocerebellar tract

Vestibulocochlear N.

Tubercle of nucleus gracilis

Olive

Spinal tract of trigeminal N.

Pyramid

Fasciculus cuneatus

Lateral funiculus of spinal medulla

FIG. 177   Lateral view of the brain stem.   See also FIGS. 175 and 192.

medulla (**posterior spinocerebellar tract**) crosses it obliquely to enter the inferior cerebellar peduncle. The spinal tract carries sensory fibres from the trigeminal area into the reflex zone of the neck muscles, so that the head may be moved rapidly away from a painful stimulus applied to the trigeminal area.

Gracile and Cuneate Fasciculi

On the posterior surface of the inferior half of the medulla oblongata, note the fasciculus gracilis adjacent to the posterior median sulcus, and the **gracile tubercle** in which it ends superiorly. The fasciculus cuneatus is immediately lateral to the fasciculus gracilis, and it

225

ends at a slightly higher level in a poorly defined eminence, the **cuneate tubercle** [FIGS. 188, 192].

These fasciculi are composed of nerve fibres which originate in the cells of the dorsal root ganglia of the spinal nerves of the same side, and ascend without interruption to the groups of nerve cells at their superior extremities (nuclei gracilis and cuneatus) which produce the corresponding tubercles. The fibres in the fasciculus gracilis originate in the inferior half of the body, those in the fasciculus cuneatus arise in the superior half.

The **gracile and cuneate nuclei** lie at the lower end of the inferior cerebellar peduncle, and their cells, which receive impulses from the fibres of the fasciculi through synapses, give rise to: (1) the **internal arcuate fibres** which sweep anteriorly from the nuclei through the substance of the medulla oblongata, and, crossing the midline anterior to the central canal as the great sensory **decussation of the lemnisci** [FIG. 179], ascend as the **medial lemniscus** [FIG. 248] to the thalamus. In the medulla oblongata, the medial lemnisci are in the form of flat bands adjacent to the midline and dorsal to the corresponding pyramid [FIG. 180] but they diverge laterally in the pons and midbrain, reaching the lateral surface of the midbrain. This pathway from the dorsal root ganglia to the thalamus, conveys impulses which originate from sensory endings in tendons, and joints, from pressure and touch endings in the skin, and is concerned with the conscious appreciation of these senses, for the thalamus relays the impulses to the cerebral cortex. (2) **Posterior external arcuate fibres** arise from the accessory cuneate nucleus on the lateral aspect of the main cuneate nucleus, and pass superiorly into the inferior cerebellar peduncle. The accessory cuneate nucleus receives collaterals (branches) from the fibres in the fasciculus cuneatus. Thus this nucleus transmits ascending impulses to the cerebellum from the upper half of the body on the same side [FIG. 179].

Spinocerebellar Tracts [FIGS. 177, 189]

These are two other pathways which connect the spinal medulla with the cerebellum. The **posterior spinocerebellar tract** arises from the cells of the thoracic nucleus (FIG. 25; between the first thoracic and the second lumbar segments of the spinal medulla) which receive impulses through branches of the fibres in the fasciculus gracilis. The axons of the tract ascend in the most posterolateral part of the lateral funiculus of the same side, and entering the medulla oblongata anterior to the spinal tract of the trigeminal nerve, pass posteriorly over its lateral surface to enter the inferior cerebellar peduncle [FIG. 179]. This tract transmits impulses from the inferior half of the body to the cerebellum.

The **anterior spinocerebellar tract** ascends in the lateral funiculus immediately anterior to the posterior spinocerebellar tract. Its exact origin in the spinal medulla is unknown, but it passes through the medulla oblongata and pons, anterior to the spinal tract of the trigeminal nerve, and turns posteriorly into the cerebellum over the superior cerebellar peduncle [FIG. 177] above the level of entry of the trigeminal nerve.

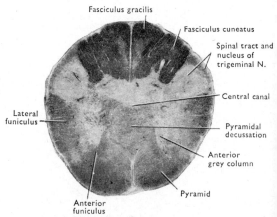

FIG. 178 Transverse section through the lowest part of the medulla oblongata. Grey matter, white; white matter, grey to black depending on density of myelinated fibres.

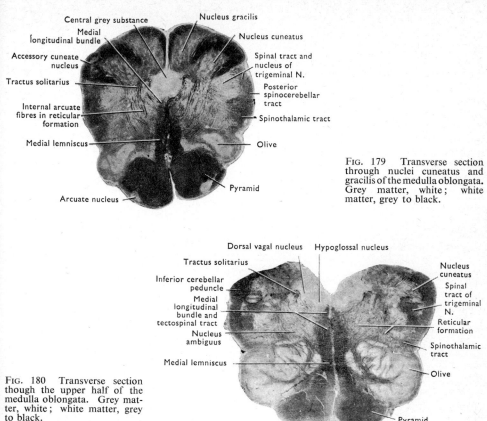

Central grey substance

Medial longitudinal bundle

Accessory cuneate nucleus

Tractus solitarius

Internal arcuate fibres in reticular formation

Medial lemniscus

Arcuate nucleus

Nucleus gracilis

Nucleus cuneatus

Spinal tract and nucleus of trigeminal N.

Posterior spinocerebellar tract

Spinothalamic tract

Olive

Pyramid

Fig. 179   Transverse section through nuclei cuneatus and gracilis of the medulla oblongata. Grey matter, white; white matter, grey to black.

Dorsal vagal nucleus   Hypoglossal nucleus

Tractus solitarius

Inferior cerebellar peduncle

Medial longitudinal bundle and tectospinal tract

Nucleus ambiguus

Medial lemniscus

Nucleus cuneatus

Spinal tract of trigeminal N.

Reticular formation

Spinothalamic tract

Olive

Pyramid

Fig. 180   Transverse section though the upper half of the medulla oblongata. Grey matter, white; white matter, grey to black.

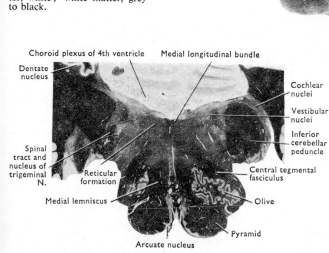

Choroid plexus of 4th ventricle   Medial longitudinal bundle

Dentate nucleus

Spinal tract and nucleus of trigeminal N.

Reticular formation

Medial lemniscus

Arcuate nucleus

Cochlear nuclei

Vestibular nuclei

Inferior cerebellar peduncle

Central tegmental fasciculus

Olive

Pyramid

Fig. 181   Transverse section through the uppermost part of the medulla oblongata. Grey matter, white; white matter, grey to black.

227

Spinothalamic Tract [FIGS. 180, 248]

This tract arises from cells in the posterior horn throughout the length of the spinal medulla. The fibres cross in the white commissure, ascend in a position anterior to the anterior spinocerebellar tract, and passing through the medulla oblongata posterior to the olive, join the medial lemniscus in the pons and run with it to the thalamus. This tract conveys impulses which evoke the conscious sensations of pain, temperature, and touch. The spinothalamic tract and medial lemniscus carry impulses which have to do with the conscious appreciation of various sensations, while fibres which pass to the cerebellum have nothing to do with this function, although they transmit the same information.

Grey and White Matter of Medulla Oblongata

The above tracts form a large part of the white matter of the medulla oblongata and lie on or near its surface. In the interior there is a scattered mixture of grey and white matter (the **reticular formation**), certain deeply placed tracts, and a number of well defined nuclei. In the inferior part, a compact sleeve of grey matter surrounds the narrow central canal. At the middle of the medulla oblongata, the central canal opens into the inferior angle of the fourth-ventricle (a diamond-shaped cavity which lies on the posterior surfaces of the medulla oblongata and pons) and its surrounding grey matter becomes continuous with the grey matter in the floor of the fourth ventricle. Most of the nuclei of the cranial nerves lie in this grey matter.

For the following sections it is advisable to have available microscopic sections of representative regions of the brain stem which have been stained to show the myelin of the nerve fibres. If this is not possible, FIGURES 178–181, 182–184, 193–196, are photographs of such sections designed to show the main features. They should be used in conjunction with FIGURES 189, 239, 248–249, which are diagrams based on these sections.

CRANIAL NERVES WITH NUCLEI IN THE MEDULLA OBLONGATA

Trigeminal Nerve. The fibres of the spinal tract of the trigeminal nerve extend throughout the length of the medulla oblongata, and terminate at all levels in the spinal nucleus which lies on its medial side [FIGS. 178–181]. The fibres which end in the nucleus caudal to the fourth ventricle are principally concerned with the sensations of pain and temperature from the trigeminal area, but the spinal tract and nucleus also receives fibres of general sensation from the other cranial nerves entering the medulla oblongata through it; notably the ninth, tenth, and eleventh. The spinal nucleus gives rise to nerve fibres which cross the midline to join the spinothalamic tract.

Facial Nerve. The motor nuclei of the facial nerve lie in the inferior part of the pons. Its sensory fibres enter the tractus solitarius [FIGS. 180, 248] and terminate on the nucleus of that tract in the medulla oblongata. These fibres are concerned with the sense of taste.

Vestibulocochlear Nerve. Sensory fibres from the cochlea have already been seen passing into the **cochlear nuclei** which overlie the superior part of the inferior cerebellar peduncle in the medulla oblongata. The vestibular fibres pass anterior to the same peduncle and fan out into the **vestibular nuclei** in the floor of the fourth ventricle. These nuclei underlie the vestibular area [FIG. 192] which is partly in the pons also [FIGS. 181, 189, 249].

Glossopharyngeal, Vagus, and Cranial Part of Accessory. The preganglionic parasympathetic fibres in these nerves arise in the cells of the **dorsal nucleus of the vagus** [FIG. 180] the superior extremity of which is known as the **inferior salivatory nucleus** and sends fibres into the glossopharyngeal nerve for distribution to the otic ganglion. Efferent nerve fibres to pharyngeal and laryngeal muscles arise in the **nucleus ambiguus** [FIGS. 180, 249] and pass into all three nerves. Visceral sensory nerve fibres, including taste fibres in the ninth and tenth nerves, enter the **tractus solitarius** and end in its nucleus, which surrounds the tractus solitarius. General sensory fibres enter the spinal tract of the trigeminal (see above) and this respect correspond with the arrangement of dorsal spinal roots, all of which send fibres into the dorsolateral tract for termination in the posterior horn of the spinal medulla.

Hypoglossal Nerve. This pure motor nerve arises from a single, paramedian nucleus [FIG. 180] which extends throughout the greater part of the medulla oblongata, and gives rise to the long row of hypoglossal rootlets [FIG. 149].

THE PONS
[FIG. 175]

This is the superior part of the hindbrain, and it is characterized by the presence of a marked ridge covering its anterior and lateral aspects. This ridge (convex in all directions) is composed of transverse bundles of nerve fibres which arise from the **pontine nuclei** buried in its substance [FIG. 183], and converge posteriorly, on each side, to form the **middle cerebellar peduncle** where the trigeminal nerve pierces it. The fibres in the peduncle pass to the cerebellar cortex. Anterior to the trigeminal nerves, the ridge forms the **basilar part of the pons,** which receives the crura cerebri at its superior margin, and emits the pyramid at its inferior margin. The fibres of the crura cerebri split up into the **longitudinal bundles of the pons,** and most of them end in the pontine nuclei (corticopontine fibres), the greater part of the remainder emerges as the pyramids (corticospinal fibres) and a few cross to the region of the motor cranial nerve nuclei of the opposite half of the pons (corticonuclear fibres). Anteriorly, the basilar part of the pons is grooved by the **basilar sulcus** (which lodges the basilar artery) and it lies adjacent to the basiocciput and dorsum sellae of the skull.

The **dorsal part of the pons** separates the basilar part from the floor of the superior half of the fourth ventricle [FIGS. 183, 187], and cannot be seen at present. It is continuous superiorly with the tegmentum of the midbrain and, inferiorly, with the medulla oblongata. Structures such as the medial lemniscus and spinothalamic tract, which are continued into the pons from the medulla oblongata, pass

into the dorsal part of the pons, with the exception of (1) the pyramid (which extends inferiorly from the basilar part) and (2) the inferior cerebellar peduncle (which passes dorsally into the cerebellum). In addition the dorsal part contains the superior extension of the reticular formation of the medulla oblongata and several discrete nuclei, including the nuclei of certain cranial nerves.

CRANIAL NERVES WITH NUCLEI IN PONS

Trigeminal Nerve [FIGS. 183, 249]. Parts of all four nuclei of the trigeminal nerve lie in the pons. Immediately after piercing the junction of the basilar part of the pons and the middle peduncle of the cerebellum, the nerve enters the lateral edge of the dorsal part of the pons, and becomes continuous with two nuclei which lie side by side. The medial of these is the **motor nucleus** which gives rise to the nerve fibres which innervate the muscles of mastication etc.; the lateral nucleus is the **superior sensory nucleus of the trigeminal nerve,** which probably receives fibres concerned with tactile information from the trigeminal area. The **spinal tract and nucleus** extend inferiorly from the point of entry of the trigeminal nerve, and are found at the lateral margin of the dorsal part of the pons in its inferior half. A small bundle of fibres passes dorsally from the trigeminal nerve, between the motor and superior sensory nuclei, to the lateral margin of the floor of the fourth ventricle, and turns superiorly to traverse the midbrain. This is the mesencephalic tract of the trigeminal nerve [FIG. 248], and it contains the proprioceptive sensory fibres from that nerve. It differs from all other peripheral sensory neurons in that its cells of origin lie scattered along the tract and are not situated in the trigeminal ganglion.

Abducent Nerve. This small nucleus lies immediately anterior to the floor of the fourth ventricle, in the most inferior part of the pons, close to the midline. It raises a small protuberance on the floor of the ventricle which is called the **facial colliculus** [FIG. 192] because the facial nerve is closely associated with this nucleus [FIGS. 182, 249].

229

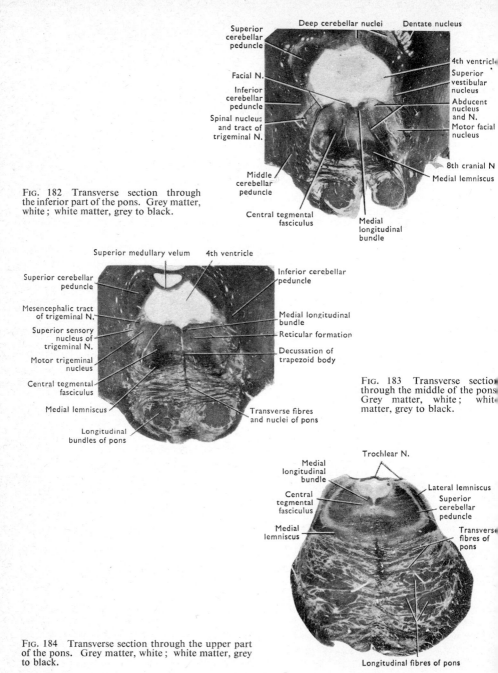

Superior cerebellar peduncle

Deep cerebellar nuclei   Dentate nucleus

4th ventricle

Facial N.

Superior vestibular nucleus

Inferior cerebellar peduncle

Abducent nucleus and N.

Spinal nucleus and tract of trigeminal N.

Motor facial nucleus

8th cranial N.

Medial lemniscus

Middle cerebellar peduncle

Central tegmental fasciculus

Medial longitudinal bundle

FIG. 182 Transverse section through the inferior part of the pons. Grey matter, white; white matter, grey to black.

Superior medullary velum   4th ventricle

Superior cerebellar peduncle

Inferior cerebellar peduncle

Mesencephalic tract of trigeminal N.

Medial longitudinal bundle

Superior sensory nucleus of trigeminal N.

Reticular formation

Motor trigeminal nucleus

Decussation of trapezoid body

Central tegmental fasciculus

Medial lemniscus

Transverse fibres and nuclei of pons

Longitudinal bundles of pons

FIG. 183 Transverse section through the middle of the pons. Grey matter, white; white matter, grey to black.

Trochlear N.

Medial longitudinal bundle

Lateral lemniscus

Central tegmental fasciculus

Superior cerebellar peduncle

Medial lemniscus

Transverse fibres of pons

Longitudinal fibres of pons

FIG. 184 Transverse section through the upper part of the pons. Grey matter, white; white matter, grey to black.

230

Facial Nerve. The motor nuclei of the facial nerve lie in the most inferior part of the pons. (1) The nucleus which supplies the muscles of facial expression etc., lies immediately anteromedial to the spinal nucleus of the trigeminal nerve [Fig. 182]. The axons which arise in the nucleus pass posteromedially towards the abducent nucleus, and running superiorly on its medial side, hook round its superior margin (**genu of facial nerve**) and descend anterolaterally to emerge at the inferior border of the pons, immediately lateral to their nucleus of origin. (2) In its course through the pons the facial nerve is joined by preganglionic parasympathetic fibres from the **superior salivatory nucleus,** which lies in the inferior part of the pons, superior to the inferior salivatory nucleus. These parasympathetic fibres pass peripherally through the greater petrosal and chorda tympani nerves to the pterygopalatine and submandibular ganglia respectively.

Vestibulocochlear Nerve. The superior part of the vestibular area extends into the inferior part of the pons, between the floor and lateral wall of the fourth ventricle [Fig. 182]. In this area lie parts of the vestibular nuclei on which fibres of the vestibular division terminate.

DISSECTION. Clean the meninges from the superior and posterior surfaces of the cerebellum, but avoid depressing the cerebellum too strongly to expose all of its superior surface. With the assistance of figures 185–188 identify its main parts, including the fissura prima, horizontal fissure, the superior and inferior vermis, and the hemispheres and flocculus.

THE CEREBELLUM

The cerebellum consists of a median part, the **vermis,** which is only clearly separated from the lateral parts, **hemispheres,** on the inferior surface. The cerebellum is wrapped around the posterior surface of the brain stem, which is lodged in a wide groove on its anterior surface. Postero-inferiorly it is deeply notched by the falx cerebelli.

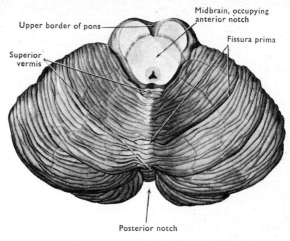

FIG. 185 Superior surface of the cerebellum.

The **superior vermis** is the median ridge on the superior surface. It lies inferior to the line of junction of the tentorium cerebelli with the falx cerebri. Here it is separated from the straight sinus by pia, arachnoid, and the inferior dural layer of the tentorium.

The **inferior vermis** bulges into a deep median hollow on the inferior surface of the cerebellum (the vallecula cerebelli) and though it is clearly demarcated from the hemispheres by deep furrows, each part of it is continuous with a part of the hemispheres. Thus the nodule [Fig. 186] is continuous with the flocculus, and forms the flocculonodular lobe; the uvula is continuous with the tonsil, and so on, in the same way as the superior vermis is more clearly continuous with the corresponding parts of the hemispheres. The cerebellum is divided by a number of transversely placed fissures of considerable depth, and between these the surface is folded in a complex manner which gives rise to the multiple fine fissures running transversely over its exposed surface and even within the major fissures.

The great complexity of the cerebellum was no doubt responsible for the number of highly fanciful names which have been applied to its various parts. It is inadvisable for the student to burden his memory with all of these terms, and only those which have a functional or descriptive value are used here.

FISSURES OF THE CEREBELLUM

The general arrangement of the cerebellum can most easily be understood if it is appreciated that it develops from a ridge of tissue which lies transversely in the thin roof of the fourth ventricle opposite the pontine part of the brain stem. This ridge expands posteriorly to an enormous degree but does not increase its area of attachment to the brain stem to a corresponding extent. Thus the superior and inferior margins of the original ridge remain close together in the roof of the fourth ventricle, while the intermediate part expands superiorly over the posterior surface of the midbrain, and inferiorly over the medulla oblongata, hiding both from view posteriorly. Because of this method of growth, the cerebellum becomes greatly folded, and the roof of the fourth ventricle is drawn posteriorly into the centre of the cerebellum in a tent-like recess [FIG. 187]. As a result the parts of the thin roof of the fourth ventricle superior and inferior to the attachment of the cerebellum sweep anterosuperiorly and antero-inferiorly from the recess to form the superior and inferior medullary vela [FIGS. 187, 188]. Of

the great number of fissures formed in the cerebellum, three are of particular importance

1. **Fissura Prima** [FIGS. 185, 187]. This deep fissure cuts across the superior surface of the cerebellum and separates the anterior and posterior lobes.

2. **Horizontal Fissure** [FIG. 186]. This fissure extends from one middle cerebellar peduncle to the other, and lies close to the junction of the superior and inferior surfaces of the cerebellum.

3. **Posterolateral Fissure.** This fissure lies on the inferior surface of the cerebellum, and separates the nodule and flocculus from the remainder of the cerebellum. It is the first fissure to appear in development, and it marks a functional separation of the **flocculonodular lobe** (which has connexions with the vestibular apparatus and is therefore primarily concerned with equilibration) from the remainder of the cerebellum. Disease of this part of the cerebellum manifests itself in disturbances of balance, while disease of the remainder is primarily associated with disturbances of muscle tone and coordination.

CEREBELLAR CORTEX

The surface of the cerebellum is a thin layer of grey matter which overlies the deeper white matter. This cerebellar cortex is uniform in structure throughout, and consists of three layers: (1) The deepest layer of small granule cells on which the incoming fibres end. (2) The middle layer; a single row of large cell bodies of the **Purkinje cells** which send their axons deeply into the white matter and their branching dendrites superficially into the third layer where they spread out in a plane at right angles to the fissures and to the ridges between them (the folia). (3) A surface layer into which the axons of the granule cells pass, and running parallel to the folia, synapse with the dendrites of the Pur

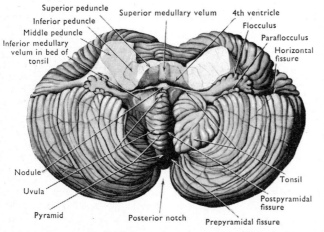

Superior peduncle
Inferior peduncle
Middle peduncle
Inferior medullary velum in bed of tonsil
Superior medullary velum
4th ventricle
Flocculus
Paraflocculus
Horizontal fissure
Nodule
Uvula
Pyramid
Tonsil
Postpyramidal fissure
Posterior notch
Prepyramidal fissure

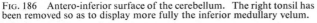

FIG. 186   Antero-inferior surface of the cerebellum. The right tonsil has been removed so as to display more fully the inferior medullary velum.

inje cells. The structure of the cortex is uni-
orm throughout, but the distribution of the
fferent fibres is not. Vestibular fibres pass to
he flocculonodular lobe; spinocerebellar fibres
ass to the vermis and paravermal regions of
he anterior lobe, to adjacent parts of the pos-
erior lobe, and to the pyramid and uvula [FIG.
87] of the posterior lobe. The hemispheres
redominantly receive fibres from the pons via
he middle cerebellar peduncle, and also from
he olive via the inferior peduncle. The fibres
rom the pons relay impulses which arise in the
erebral cortex and reach the pons through the
rura cerebri. The very large size of the hemi-
pheres of the cerebellum in Man is related to
he increased size of the cerebral cortex. In
ther mammals where the cerebral cortex is less
vell developed, there is a corresponding reduc-
ion in the size of the hemispheres, the vermis
orming a proportionately greater part of the
erebellum.

DISSECTION. Split the cerebellum into two equal
arts by means of a median sagittal section through
e vermis. Make this incision carefully, separating
e two parts as the incision is deepened. Approxi-
ately half way between the superior and inferior

margins of the cerebellum, a narrow slit will be opened
into; this is the cerebellar (fastigial) recess of the fourth
ventricle. Superior and inferior to this recess, progress
with care to avoid cutting through the superior and
inferior medullary vela [Fig. 187].

Remove the posterior part of the right half of the
cerebellum by means of a cut through it at right angles
to the middle cerebellar peduncle, more or less parallel
to the medulla oblongata. Place the edge of the knife
against the middle cerebellar peduncle just posterior
to the flocculus [Fig. 186] and its tip in the lateral end
of the fissura prima. Cut medially along the line of the
fissura prima to meet the median section, the inferior
part of the edge of the knife passing immediately
posterior to the tonsil [Fig. 186]. This section exposes:
(1) the folded grey matter of the cortex and the white
matter deep to it, which forms a delicate branched
arrangement close to the cortex, the arbor vitae
cerebelli; (2) a crinkled bag of grey matter buried in
the central mass of white matter relatively close to the
midline and to the cerebellar recess of the fourth
ventricle. This is the dentate nucleus, the largest of
the deep nuclei of the cerebellum, which extend laterally from the midline along the posterior margin of the
cerebellar recess of the fourth ventricle [Fig. 191].

Identify the superior cerebellar artery running along
the superior margin of the cerebellum and sending
branches into the inferior part of the midbrain and
the superior part of the cerebellum. Cut its branches

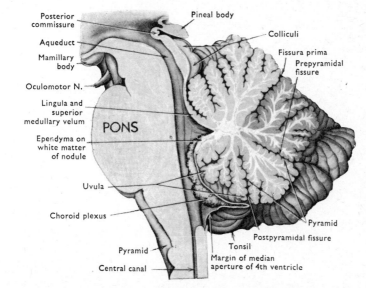

FIG. 187   Median section through the brain stem and cerebellum.

to the cerebellum, and the veins passing superiorly from the cerebellum to the great cerebral vein, the cut end of which may be seen posterior to the superior part of the midbrain. Carefully pull the anterior lobe of the cerebellum postero-inferiorly, and identify the trochlear nerve under cover of its margin. Strip the anterior lobe away from the remainder of the cerebellum, tearing its connexions with the white matter, but avoiding damage to the trochlear nerve. This exposes the superior surface of the middle cerebellar peduncle, the superior cerebellar peduncle passing superiorly into the midbrain [Figs. 190, 192] and medial to this peduncle, a thin tongue-like strip of cerebellar cortex (the lingula) passes upwards fused to a delicate white sheet, the superior medullary velum.

Superior Medullary Velum

This velum extends transversely between the two superior cerebellar peduncles, roofs over the superior part of the fourth ventricle (into which it may be depressed by light pressure from a blunt seeker) and becomes continuous above with the roof of the midbrain. Here a median ridge of white matter (frenulum veli) descends on to it from the groove between th inferior colliculi [FIG. 192], and the fourth cranial nerves emerge, one on each side, afte having crossed in the most superior part c the velum [FIG. 184].

DISSECTION. With a blunt seeker, lift the surfac layer of neuroglia from the superior cerebellar pedunc and expose its fibres running superiorly. Note that as plunges into the midbrain, its lateral aspect is covere by a low ridge of white matter (the lateral lemniscus passing posteriorly over it into the inferior colliculu Split the superior medullary velum in the midline an confirm the presence of the fourth ventricle deep to it

Turn to the inferior surface of the cerebellum an gently lift the right tonsil out of its bed [Figs. 18 188]. Avoid damage to the thin roof of the inferior par of the fourth ventricle (inferior medullary velum) b dividing the branches of the posterior inferior cerebella artery which pass into the tonsil from the main stem c the artery on the inferior medullary velum. As th tonsil lifts away from the inferior medullary velum, pul

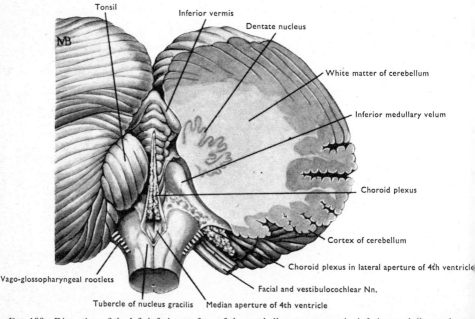

FIG. 188   Dissection of the left inferior surface of the cerebellum to expose the inferior medullary velum and the median and lateral apertures of the fourth ventricle. The medulla oblongata has been displaced anteriorly so as to open up the median aperture. Note the choroid plexus which is visible at both apertures and can also be seen through the thin roof of the fourth ventricle.

234

the remainder of the posterior lobe of the cerebellum away with it, but leave the flocculus and nodule intact, and the posterior inferior cerebellar artery on the velum.

If the inferior medullary velum is intact, find the median aperture of the fourth ventricle [Fig. 188] and pass a blunt seeker through it to define the extent of the velum and the cavity of the fourth ventricle. Pass the tip of the seeker along the lateral recess of the fourth ventricle to the lateral aperture, and then posteriorly, superior to the nodule, into the cerebellar recess.

Follow this recess to its lateral extremity, noting the extent of the inferior medullary velum, and push the tip of the seeker into the cerebellar substance at the posterior apex of the recess; the tip will appear through the substance of the dentate nucleus which lies immediately posterior to the lateral part of the recess [Fig. 188].

Note the presence of choroid plexus on the ventricular surface of the inferior medullary velum, and follow it from the median aperture of the fourth ventricle to the lateral recess. The part of the velum to which it is attached is little more than a layer of ependyma and does not appear white like the superior part.

Pull the flocculus away from the middle cerebellar peduncle in a medial direction. A thin strip of white matter will tear away with it (peduncle of the flocculus) and this has the inferior medullary velum attached to it [Fig. 186]. Cut through the velum in the midline and turn it downwards to expose the choroid plexus on its anterior aspect, and the lateral recess of the fourth ventricle. Lift the left half of the cerebellum gently backwards and look into the opposite lateral recess from the ventricular aspect.

Inferior Medullary Velum

This velum stretches inferiorly from the nodule and peduncle of the flocculus to (1) the inferior cerebellar peduncles, inferolaterally; (2) the lateral aperture of the fourth ventricle, laterally; (3) the median aperture, inferiorly. The greater part of it forms the bed of the tonsil of the cerebellum (a rounded hollow which contains the posterior inferior cerebellar artery). Its median part lies in contact with the nodule and uvula of the inferior vermis, and curves posteriorly on to the inferior surface of the uvula

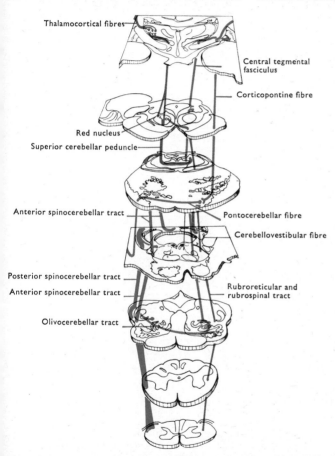

Thalamocortical fibres

Central tegmental fasciculus

Corticopontine fibre

Red nucleus

Superior cerebellar peduncle

Anterior spinocerebellar tract

Pontocerebellar fibre

Cerebellovestibular fibre

Posterior spinocerebellar tract

Anterior spinocerebellar tract

Rubroreticular and rubrospinal tract

Olivocerebellar tract

FIG. 189   An outline diagram to show the main afferent (blue) and efferent (red) connexions of the cerebellum. Note the afferent pontocerebellar, olivocerebellar, and spinocerebellar pathways, and the efferent pathway to the red nucleus and thalamus. The efferent connexion to the red nucleus links the cerebellum with the brain stem and spinal medulla; the connexion with the thalamus links it with the cerebral cortex. The outline drawings are not to scale, but correspond with the illustrations of transverse sections of the brain stem, FIGS. 178–184, and 193–196.

[FIG. 187] in such a way that the median aperture of the fourth ventricle is a V-shaped orifice, which faces inferiorly [FIG. 188]. Thus air introduced into the lumbar subarachnoid space ascends to the cerebellomedullary cistern, and some of it finds its way directly into the fourth ventricle, whence it rises through the cerebral aqueduct to the other ventricles of the brain [FIG. 187].

DISSECTION. Identify the inferior cerebellar peduncle [Fig. 177] on the posterolateral aspect of the medulla oblongata, and note a grey ridge which extends across its posterior aspect from the eighth cranial nerve. This is formed by the cochlear nuclei. Strip away these nuclei and expose the upper part of the peduncle. Push a blunt seeker superiorly along the line of the inferior peduncle between that peduncle and the middle peduncle, and pull it posteriorly through the white matter, thus separating these peduncles. Repeat the same process on the medial side of the inferior peduncle, and separate the inferior and superior peduncles. This will show the fibres of the inferior peduncle curving medially over the posterior aspect of the superior peduncle and dentate nucleus. When the inferior peduncle has been completely freed, grasp the dentate nucleus between finger and thumb and lift it posteriorly; the superior peduncle will be raised from its bed owing to the fact that the majority of its fibres arise in the dentate nucleus.

CEREBELLAR PEDUNCLES

These are three compact bundles of nerve fibres on each side, which connect the cerebellum with the brain stem [FIG. 189].

Middle Penducle

This is the largest and most lateral of the three. It is formed of fibres which arise in the opposite half of the basilar part of the pons, and pass to the cerebellar cortex. They transmit impulses which reach the pons from the cerebral cortex via the crura cerebri.

236

The peduncle enters the cerebellum through the anterior end of the horizontal fissure.

Inferior Peduncle [FIGS. 190, 192]

This peduncle forms on the posterolateral surface of the medulla oblongata, and ascending between the other two peduncles, sweeps posteromedially towards the vermis of the cerebellum, though some of its fibres enter the hemispheres. It consists mainly of afferent fibres to the cerebellum from the spinal medulla, the olive, the reticular formation of the medulla oblongata, and the vestibular nuclei and nerve. It also transmits efferent cerebellar fibres to the medulla oblongata, principally to the vestibular nuclei and the reticular formation.

Superior Peduncle

This is the principal efferent pathway from the cerebellum, and its fibres arise mainly in the dentate nucleus. Each of these peduncles begins in the roof of the fourth ventricle, but

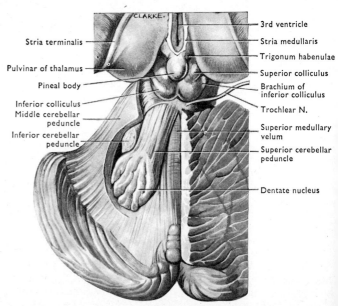

Stria terminalis
Pulvinar of thalamus
Pineal body
Inferior colliculus
Middle cerebellar peduncle
Inferior cerebellar peduncle

CLARKE.

3rd ventricle
Stria medullaris
Trigonum habenulae
Superior colliculus
Brachium of inferior colliculus
Trochlear N.
Superior medullary velum
Superior cerebellar peduncle
Dentate nucleus

FIG. 190 Dissection to show the dentate nucleus, cerebellar peduncles, tectum of the midbrain, and superior surface of the diencephalon.

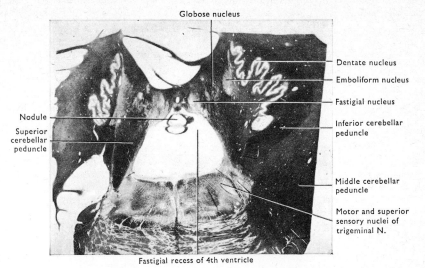

Globose nucleus

Nodule

Superior
cerebellar
peduncle

Dentate nucleus

Emboliform nucleus

Fastigial nucleus

Inferior cerebellar
peduncle

Middle cerebellar
peduncle

Motor and superior
sensory nuclei of
trigeminal N.

Fastigial recess of 4th ventricle

FIG. 191   Oblique transverse section, parallel to the cerebellar recess of the fourth ventricle, to show the cerebellar nuclei.

passes anteriorly as it ascends, forming the lateral wall of the superior part of the fourth ventricle, and passing towards the opposite peduncle as it enters the midbrain. The two peduncles meet and intermingle in the inferior part of the midbrain, anterior to the cerebral aqueduct. Here the fibres of each superior peduncle pass to the opposite side (decussate) the majority running superiorly to the red nucleus in the upper midbrain, while a small number descend into the dorsal part of the pons as the **descending limb** of the superior cerebellar peduncle [FIGS. 182–184, 192–194].

Dentate Nucleus

This is the largest and the most lateral of a group of four nuclei which lie deep in the white matter of each half of the cerebellum, close to the cerebellar recess of the fourth ventricle. It has the shape of a thin, crinkled lamina of grey matter, which is very similar in appearance to the olive in section, and, like it, has a wide mouth or hilus which faces anteromedially, and through which the axons of its cells emerge to form the superior cerebellar peduncle. It receives nerve fibres which converge on it from the greater part of the cerebellar

cortex, except the vermis, and which originate in the Purkinje cells of the middle layer.

The other three deep nuclei (globose, emboliform, and fastigial) of each half of the cerebellum lie between the dentate nucleus and the midline, and receive nerve fibres from the Purkinje cells of the vermal and paravermal regions of the cerebellar cortex. Most of their efferent fibres leave the cerebellum through the superior peduncle, except for those of the fastigial nucleus which hook over the superior peduncle and descend in the inferior cerebellar peduncle to the vestibular nuclei and the reticular formation of the medulla oblongata.

`THE FOURTH VENTRICLE

This is the diamond-shaped cavity of the hindbrain which extends from the superior border of the pons to the middle of the medulla oblongata, and lies behind these structures, and in front of the cerebellum and the medullary vela. Superiorly, it narrows to become continuous with the cerebral aqueduct in the midbrain, and, inferiorly, the tiny central canal of the inferior half of the medulla oblongata and spinal medulla opens into it.

237

The ventricle is widest at the level of the junction of the pons with the medulla oblongata, and here it extends laterally on each side, to form a tubular **lateral recess,** which curves over the posterior aspect of the inferior cerebellar peduncle. This recess passes as far as the tip of the flocculus, where it opens into the subarachnoid space through the **lateral aperture** of the fourth ventricle, posterior to the ninth and tenth cranial nerves. The deepest part of the ventricle is opposite the inferior part of the pons where the tent-like cerebellar recess extends posteriorly almost to the level of the dentate nuclei. Immediately inferior to this, the inferior medullary velum passes anteriorly and the ventricle becomes a shallow slit, though its depth again increases towards the inferior angle as the velum curves posteriorly on the anterior surface of the uvula of the cerebellum to the margin of the **median aperture** of the fourth ventricle.

ROOF OF THE FOURTH VENTRICLE

Superior to the cerebellar recess, the superior medullary velum with the lingula of the cerebellum fused to its posterior surface, forms the greater part of the roof. The superior medullary velum extends between the superior cerebellar peduncles, and gradually narrows to meet the inferior part of the tectum of the midbrain. Inferior to the cerebellar recess, the thin inferior medullary velum forms a U-shaped structure in the midline where it extends from its cerebellar attachment around the anterior surfaces of the nodule and uvula to end at the margin of the median aperture. Laterally, it is attached to the posterior surface of the medulla oblongata, and these attachments converge towards the median aperture inferiorly, but superiorly they pass laterally over the posterior surface of the inferior cerebellar peduncle to form the inferior limit of the lateral recess [FIG. 188].

Tela Choroidea and Choroid Plexuses of Fourth Ventricle

The pia mater which covers the surface of the brain passes superiorly between the roof of the fourth ventricle and the cerebellum, and has the posterior inferior cerebellar artery on it. This pia mater is the tela choroidea. On each side of the midline, a tufted, vascular fold of pia mater invaginates the ependyma of the roof of the fourth ventricle from the margin of the median aperture to a point opposite the lateral recess. Here each choroid plexus (vascular pia mater or tela choroidea covered with ependyma) turns laterally towards the corresponding lateral recess and extends into its roof. It passes to the lateral aperture, through which some of its tufts extend as a miniature cauliflower-like excrescence immediately inferior to the flocculus of the cerebellum. Thus each half of the choroid plexus is L-shaped, and the extremities of the L can be seen in the intact brain at the median and lateral apertures of the fourth ventricle [FIGS. 175, 188].

FLOOR OF THE FOURTH VENTRICLE
[FIG. 192]

The floor is diamond-shaped and consists of a layer of grey matter which contains the nuclei of various cranial nerves and is separated from the ventricle by a layer of ependyma. The floor is formed by the posterior surfaces of the pons and the superior half of the medulla oblongata. Between the aqueduct superiorly, and the central canal inferiorly, its lateral boundaries are the superior cerebellar peduncle, the inferior cerebellar peduncle, the cuneate and the gracile tubercles.

The floor is divided into right and left halves by a median groove, and a ridge on each side of this is known as the **eminentia medialis.** A slight swelling in each ridge opposite the inferior part of the pons is the **facial colliculus.** This is produced by the nucleus of the abducent nerve with the facial nerve looping round it in the horizontal plane.

About the middle of each half of the floor a few fine bundles of fibres can be seen through the ependyma. They emerge from the median groove and pass laterally towards the inferior cerebellar peduncle. These are the **medullary striae,** and they are composed of aberrant

238

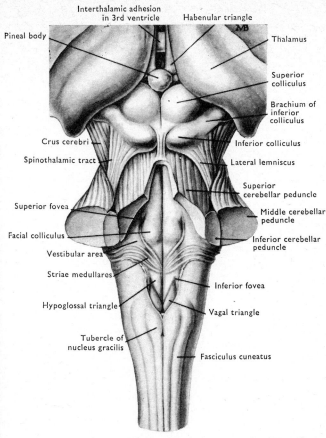

Interthalamic adhesion in 3rd ventricle
Habenular triangle
Pineal body
Thalamus
Superior colliculus
Brachium of inferior colliculus
Crus cerebri
Inferior colliculus
Spinothalamic tract
Lateral lemniscus
Superior cerebellar peduncle
Superior fovea
Middle cerebellar peduncle
Facial colliculus
Inferior cerebellar peduncle
Vestibular area
Striae medullares
Inferior fovea
Hypoglossal triangle
Vagal triangle
Tubercle of nucleus gracilis
Fasciculus cuneatus

FIG. 192   Posterior view of the brain stem. See also FIGS. 175 and 177.

glossopharyngeal complex, and is known as the **vagal triangle.** The lateral area is the inferior part of the **vestibular area** which forms a poorly defined swelling in the lateral part of the floor of the ventricle, and extends superiorly into the inferior part of the pons. It is formed by the **vestibular nuclei,** the termination of the vestibular fibres of the vestibulocochlear nerve. The slight groove medial to the vestibular area represents the remains of the sulcus limitans of the developing neural tube, and is slightly accentuated by an ill-defined angular depression in the inferior part of the pons, opposite the facial colliculus, the **superior fovea.** Above the superior fovea, the small area of floor, lateral to the eminentia medialis, has a dark tinge (the locus ceruleus) produced by pigmented cells beneath the ependyma, the substantia ferruginea.

pontocerebellar fibres which arise in the arcuate nuclei [p. 224] and pass by this route to the cerebellum, thus dividing the floor of the ventricle into pontine and medullary parts. The size and number of these striae is very variable.

In each half of the medullary part, there is a V-shaped depression (the **inferior fovea**) which divides the floor into three triangular areas. The medial area, part of the eminentia medialis, overlies the superior part of the hypoglossal nucleus and is known as the **hypoglossal triangle.** The intermediate part overlies the dorsal nucleus of the vago-

DISSECTION. If a satisfactory dissection of the peduncles of the cerebellum has not been obtained on the right half, place your fingers in the medial part of the horizontal fissure of the left half of the cerebellum, and tear off the upper part of this half. This exposes the superior peduncle and parts of the other two. With blunt forceps, pick up thin layers of the white matter near the posterior border of the cerebellum and strip them forwards. In this way the surface of the dentate nucleus is exposed, and its continuity with the superior peduncle can be confirmed.

Remove the remains of the membranes from the surface of the midbrain, avoiding, if possible, damage to the trochlear nerves. Identify the pineal body between the superior colliculi [Fig. 190] and note that it is attached to the dorsal surface of the brain at the junction of the midbrain and diencephalon, inferior to the splenium of the corpus callosum.

THE MIDBRAIN

The midbrain is the short, thick stalk which connects the hindbrain, in the posterior cranial fossa, with the cerebrum superior to the tentorium cerebelli. It traverses the tentorial notch, and is about 2·5 cm. long and slightly more in width. The narrow tubular cavity which traverses it (the cerebral aqueduct, FIGURE 166) joins the fourth ventricle inferiorly to the third ventricle superiorly. Identify the inferior end of the aqueduct, and pass a fine probe through it. The smaller part of the midbrain, which is posterior to the aqueduct is the tectum, and it consists of the four colliculi. The larger part, anterior to the aqueduct, is partly subdivided into its two halves, the cerebral peduncles. In the undissected brain, the tectum is overlapped by the anterior lobe of the cerebellum and by the splenium of the corpus callosum, but the anterior parts of the cerebral peduncles, the crura cerebri, can be seen on the base of the brain, where they form the boundaries of the posterior part of the interpeduncular fossa.

TECTUM
Colliculi

These are four small swellings visible on the posterior surface of the tectum. They consist of mounds of grey matter with many laminae in the superior pair. Inferiorly, the superior cerebellar peduncles enter the substance of the midbrain anterior to the inferior colliculi. Each peduncle is crossed obliquely by a ridge of white matter (the **lateral lemniscus,** FIGS. 177, 184) which emerges from the superior border of the pons, posterior to the crus cerebri, and passes posterosuperiorly into the **inferior colliculus.** This bundle of nerve fibres arises in the cochlear nuclei, and transmits auditory impulses to the inferior colliculus, one of the groups of nerve cells concerned with auditory reflexes. On the side of the midbrain, note a similar ridge (**brachium of the inferior colliculus,** FIGS. 177, 194) passing anterosuperiorly from the inferior colliculus to a small, rounded protuberance

(**medial geniculate body**) lodged between the superior part of the lateral wall of the midbrain and the posterior surface of the crus cerebri. The brachium transmits auditory impulses to the geniculate body, a thalamic nucleus which relays the impulses to the cerebral cortex where they are consciously appreciated.

Note the trochlear nerves emerging from the dorsal surface of the brain stem immediately inferior to the inferior colliculi. The pineal body lies between the two **superior colliculi** [FIG. 192], each of which is connected to the thalamus of the forebrain at its superolateral margin by a slight ridge (**brachium of the superior colliculus,** FIG. 230). This consists of a bundle of nerve fibres from the optic tract which runs over the postero-inferior surface of the thalamus to the colliculus and to the region between it and the root of the pineal body (the **pretectal region**). These parts are concerned with visual reflexes, and the colliculus is connected to the cranial nerve nuclei and to the motor cells of the spinal medulla through the **tectospinal tract** [FIGS. 180, 239]. It is through this pathway that the reflex turning of the head and eyes towards a source of light is achieved.

CEREBRAL PEDUNCLES

Each cerebral peduncle consists of: (1) the crus cerebri, anteriorly; (2) the tegmentum, posteriorly; (3) a thin pigmented layer of cells between these, the substantia nigra [FIG. 194, 195].

Crus Cerebri

This is a broad bundle of nerve fibres which has the superficial appearance of a rope because of the spirally arranged grooves and ridges on its surface. The nerve fibres of each crus arise in the cerebral cortex of the corresponding hemisphere, pierce the hemisphere, and converge on its inferior surface, to emerge as the crus where the optic tract crosses their lateral surface. The posterior cerebral artery, the basal vein, and the trochlear nerve also cross the lateral surface of the crus. The two crura are separated by the posterior part of the interpeduncular fossa, which contains the oculomotor nerves and the central branches of the posterior cerebral artery passing into the posterior perforated substance. Posteriorly, it is separated from the tegmentum of the midbrain by the substantia nigra, and laterally by a shallow groove (the lateral sulcus of the midbrain) in the superior part of which the medial geniculate body is lodged [FIG. 177].

The nerve fibres in the crus arise from all parts of the cerebral cortex, and converge radially on the crus, so that those from the frontal region lie in its anteromedial part, while those from the occipital and temporal regions lie in its posterolateral part. The great majority of its fibres end in the nuclei of the basilar part of the pons and constitute the **cortico-pontine fibres.** A smaller number traverse the pons and emerge as the pyramid on the medulla oblongata, thus forming the **cortico-spinal fibres.** A still smaller number leave the crus to cross towards the motor cranial nerve nuclei of the opposite side. These are the **corticonuclear fibres,** and they correspond to the corticospinal fibres but they end in the brain stem and not on the cells of the spinal medulla. It should be noted that the great majority of the corticospinal fibres, like the corticonuclear fibres, cross to the opposite side before their termination. Since most of the corticospinal and the corticonuclear fibres arise in the posterior part of the frontal lobe (*i.e.*, near the middle) of the hemisphere, these fibres lie in the intermediate part of the crus ; and of these the corticonuclear fibres are the most medial, while those passing to the lumbo-sacral part of the spinal medulla are the most lateral.

In the section which follows, most of the details are not visible in the gross specimen, but refer to stained sections of the brain stem. It is desirable for the student to have these available for study, but, failing this, FIGURES 193, 194, and 195 show the points which are mentioned, and should be consulted.

Substantia Nigra [FIGS. 194, 195]

This curved plate of grey matter lies between the crus cerebri and the tegmentum, and contains many large nerve cells with a considerable amount of black pigment in their cytoplasm. These cells have connexions with the tegmentum of the midbrain and with the corpus striatum in the centre of the corresponding hemisphere, and are believed to play an important part in the control of muscle tone and activity, but their exact role is not clear. The substantia nigra extends from the superior border of the pons into the infero-lateral part of the hypothalamus, superior to the midbrain.

Tegmentum

This is a thick column of mixed grey and white matter, which is continuous inferiorly with the dorsal part of the pons, and superiorly with the hypothalamus. It is only visible on the surface of the midbrain in the interpeduncular fossa and on the lateral surface where it is crossed by the brachia of the colliculi and the lateral lemniscus [FIG. 177]. Posteriorly, it is directly continuous with the tectum at the level of the cerebral aqueduct, which is surrounded by a thick tube of grey matter (the **central grey substance**) in which lie the nuclei of the oculomotor and trochlear nerves and the mesencephalic nucleus of the trigeminal nerve [FIGS. 193, 194]. The tegmentum contains a number of important nuclei and tracts:

1. The **red nucleus** is a rounded rod of reddish grey matter which lies in the medial part of each half of the tegmentum at the level of the superior colliculus, and extends into the hypothalamus above. It is the most obvious structure in a transverse section through the superior part of the midbrain, but is surprisingly white in the fresh tissue because of the mass of fibres from the **superior cerebellar peduncle** which traverse and form a capsule for it. These fibres decussate in the tegmentum at the level of the inferior colliculus, and ascend to the red nucleus where most of them end though a few pass directly on to the thalamus. In Man the majority of the cells of the red nucleus send their axons to that part of the

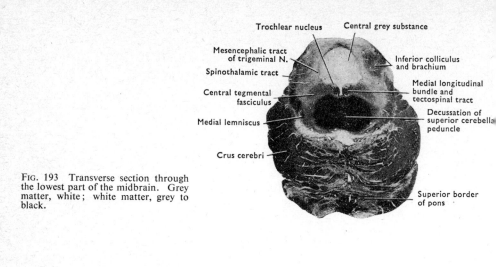

FIG. 193 Transverse section through the lowest part of the midbrain. Grey matter, white; white matter, grey to black.

Trochlear nucleus

Central grey substance

Mesencephalic tract of trigeminal N.

Spinothalamic tract

Central tegmental fasciculus

Medial lemniscus

Crus cerebri

Inferior colliculus and brachium

Medial longitudinal bundle and tectospinal tract

Decussation of superior cerebellar peduncle

Superior border of pons

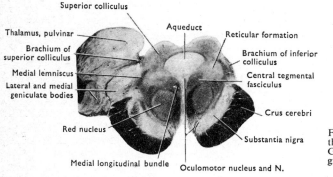

Superior colliculus

Thalamus, pulvinar

Brachium of superior colliculus

Medial lemniscus

Lateral and medial geniculate bodies

Red nucleus

Medial longitudinal bundle

Aqueduct

Reticular formation

Brachium of inferior colliculus

Central tegmental fasciculus

Crus cerebri

Substantia nigra

Oculomotor nucleus and N.

FIG. 194 Transverse section through the upper part of the midbrain. Grey matter, white; white matter, grey to black.

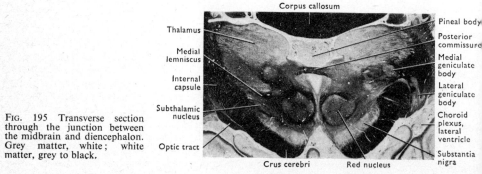

Corpus callosum

Thalamus

Medial lemniscus

Internal capsule

Subthalamic nucleus

Optic tract

Crus cerebri

Red nucleus

Pineal body

Posterior commissure

Medial geniculate body

Lateral geniculate body

Choroid plexus, lateral ventricle

Substantia nigra

FIG. 195 Transverse section through the junction between the midbrain and diencephalon. Grey matter, white; white matter, grey to black.

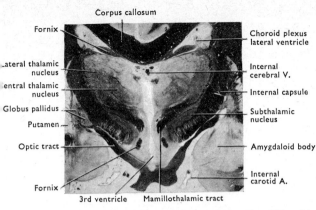

Corpus callosum

Fornix

Lateral thalamic nucleus

Ventral thalamic nucleus

Globus pallidus

Putamen

Optic tract

Fornix

Choroid plexus lateral ventricle

Internal cerebral V.

Internal capsule

Subthalamic nucleus

Amygdaloid body

Internal carotid A.

3rd ventricle   Mamillothalamic tract

FIG. 196   Section through the diencephalon parallel to FIG. 195 and to optic tract.   Grey matter, white ; white matter, grey to black.

thalamus which relays these impulses to the posterior part of the frontal lobe of the cerebral hemisphere, the part from which corticospinal and corticonuclear fibres arise. A small number of cells in the caudal part of the red nucleus give rise to fibres (**rubroreticular and rubrospinal tracts**) which decussate in the ventral part of the tegmentum (**ventral tegmental decussation**), and descend through the dorsal part of the pons to the lateral part of the medulla oblongata and upper spinal medulla.

2. The **medial longitudinal fasciculus** is a small, compact bundle which extends from the upper part of the midbrain into the spinal medulla. It lies adjacent to the midline and the nuclei of the oculomotor and trochlear nerves, and maintains this position through the brain stem. It is an intersegmental bundle which connects the various levels of the brain stem, and receives its major single contribution from the vestibular nuclei. In the spinal medulla it is continuous with the anterior intersegmental tract or fasciculus proprius [FIGS. 179, 180, 184, 193, 194].

3. The **dorsal longitudinal fasciculus** lies posterior to the nuclei of the third and fourth cranial nerves in the central grey matter. It connects the hypothalamus with the midbrain and pons.

4. The **medial lemniscus** and **spinothalamic tracts** [FIGS. 193, 194, 195] ascend through the tegmentum from the dorsal part of the pons, and pass further laterally as they ascend (the spinothalamic dorsolateral to the medial lemniscus) so that they come to underlie the brachium of the inferior colliculus in the upper midbrain. At this level the spinothalamic tract gives off fibres to the superior colliculus, the **spinotectal tract**. In addition to the fibres which these tracts contain in the medulla oblongata, trigeminal fibres have joined them when they reach the midbrain level.

5. The **tectospinal tract** consists of fibres which arise in the deeper layer of the superior colliculus. They sweep around the margin of the central grey substance, decussate (the **dorsal tegmental decussation**) anterior to the medial longitudinal fasciculus, and descend through the dorsal part of the pons, the medulla oblongata, and spinal medulla anterior to the fasciculus. Fibres of this tract end in the reticular formation of the brain stem and in the spinal medulla, and produce reflex movements in relation to visual stimuli reaching the superior colliculus; *e.g.*, turning of head and eyes towards a sudden flash of light [FIG. 239].

6. The **central tegmental tract** is a large diffuse bundle of fibres, dorsolateral to the red nucleus. It can be traced [FIGS. 181, 183, 189, 194] from the upper midbrain, through the dorsal part of the pons to end in the capsule of the olive. It probably transmits a number of different fibres, but it almost certainly forms a pathway between the corpus striatum and the olive, through which the former is connected with the cerebellum by the olivocerebellar fibres.

7. The fibres of the **oculomotor nerve** can be seen in section [FIGS. 194, 249] sweeping ventrally through the medial part of the red nucleus in the superior part of the midbrain.

They emerge through the sulcus medial to the crus cerebri into the interpeduncular fossa.

8. In the inferior part of the midbrain, the fibres of the **trochlear nerve** may be seen running postero-inferiorly around the central grey substance, to meet and decussate in the most superior part of the superior medullary velum, and emerge posterior to the superior cerebellar peduncle [FIGS. 184, 193, 249].

9. The **reticular formation** of the midbrain occupies the lateral parts of the tegmentum between the central grey substance and th medial lemniscus and spinothalamic tract. is directly continuous with the reticular form: tion of the dorsal part of the pons and wit the lateral part of the hypothalamus. probably intimately concerned with the genes of complicated reflexes of the righting variet; which may be stimulated by afferent impuls from the vestibular apparatus or from th proprioceptors of the body.

The lateral lemniscus and the auditory path way has been described already [p. 240].

THE CEREBRUM

The dissectors should begin by reviewing the relation between the skull and brain with the assistance of a dried skull, and should note the relation of the parts of the brain to the folds of dura mater (the falx cerebri and the tentorium cerebelli) if a partially dissected head is available. Reference should also be made to the short account of craniocerebral topography and to FIGURE 252.

The **longitudinal fissure** is the narrow cleft between the two hemispheres. It is occupied by: (1) the falx cerebri; (2) the fold of arachnoid which follows the surface of the falx; (3) the pia mater covering the medial surfaces of the hemispheres; (4) the arteries and veins which lie in the subarachnoid space between the arachnoid and the pia. The falx was removed when the brain was taken from the skull, but the other structures are still *in situ*.

DISSECTION. Separate the two hemispheres at the longitudinal fissure, and expose the mass of white matter which joins them deep in the fissure. This is the corpus callosum, the posterior part of which (splenium) has already been seen as a thick, rounded mass superior to the pineal body. Identify it in this position and note a large vein issuing from the brain between the pineal and the splenium of the corpus callosum, the great cerebral vein. Clean this vein and identify as many of its tributaries as may be seen filled with blood. These include superior cerebellar veins and the basal veins passing posteriorly around the side of the midbrain to join the great cerebral vein.

Turn to the superior surface of the hemispheres, and, drawing them apart, divide the corpus callosum in the median plane, starting at the splenium. Proceed care fully, noting that the corpus callosum is much thinne immediately anterior to the splenium, and that a thi layer of pia mater extends anteriorly, inferior to th corpus callosum. When about 3 cm. of the corpu callosum has been divided, examine the pia mater dee to it and identify two small veins which run posterior! in it and unite to form the great cerebral vein; thes are the internal cerebral veins [Fig. 226]. The shee of pia mater in which they lie separates the corpu callosum from the roof of the third ventricle and extend laterally to the choroid plexus of the lateral ventricle within the hemispheres. It is therefore the tela choroide of the third and lateral ventricles. Divide the pia mate in the midline, between the internal cerebral veins, an open into the vertical, slit-like cavity of the thir ventricle immediately beneath.

Continue the division of the corpus callosum. Kee; strictly to the midline and avoid extending the incisio beyond its inferior margin. As the incision is carrie forwards and the hemispheres are allowed to fall apart a bridge of tissue will be seen crossing the third ven tricle (the interthalamic adhesion, Fig. 229). Attache to the inferior surface of the corpus callosum furthe anteriorly are two thin, vertical sheets of white matte (the laminae of the septum pellucidum) and these may be pushed apart by gentle blunt dissection to expose a space between them, the cavum septi pellucidi [Fig 219]. As the anterior end of the corpus callosum i reached, it will be seen to turn inferiorly and then posteriorly to form the bend or genu of the corpus callosum, which thins out inferiorly to form the rostrun [Fig. 202]. Divide the genu and rostrum between the laminae of the septum pellucidum, and separate the two arches (fornices) of white matter, one of which is attached to the inferior margin of each lamina of the septum pellucidum. As this is done, the anterior extremity of the third ventricle will be opened and a round bundle will be seen crossing the midline immediately anterior to the columns of the fornix as they turn vertically downwards. This is the anterior commissure [Figs. 213, 229]. Divide it as it lies at the superior margin of the lamina terminalis (the anterior wall of the third ventricle) and cut vertically through the thin lamina terminalis.

Turn to the inferior surface of the brain and identify the optic chiasma. Pull it inferiorly and note the divided lamina terminalis above it. Divide the optic chiasma in the midline, and carry the median incision posteriorly through the floor of the third ventricle, dividing the infundibulum and separating the mamillary bodies. Do not carry the incision any further than this, but divide the right posterior cerebral artery close to its origin from the basilar artery. Turn to the right side of the brain and make a transverse cut through the upper part of the right half of the midbrain so as to join the two ends of the median cut. Now lift away the right hemisphere and examine its medial aspect.

Most of the features of the medial aspect will be examined later, but the dissectors should take this opportunity to pass a fine probe through the cerebral aqueduct from the posterosuperior part of the third ventricle to the fourth ventricle.

Anterior Cerebral Artery [FIG. 197]

The beginning of this vessel has been examined already [p. 218], but it can now be followed from the anterior communicating artery over the superior surface of the corpus callosum to supply the medial surface and the adjacent margin of the superolateral surface as far posteriorly as the splenium of the corpus callosum.

Posterior Cerebral Artery

This vessel supplies the remainder of the medial surface of the hemisphere and the greater part of the tentorial surface. Its main branches on the medial surface run in the calcarine and parieto-occipital sulci [FIG. 203].

Follow the branches of these arteries, noting in particular the posterior choroidal branches of the posterior cerebral artery. These arise as it runs round the lateral aspect of the midbrain, close to the superior surface of the margin of the tentorium, and they pass deep to the cortical margin. In its first part the posterior cerebral artery lies on the hippocampal margin of the hemisphere, and this

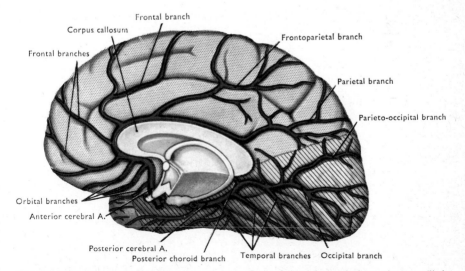

Frontal branch
Corpus callosum
Frontal branches
Frontoparietal branch
Parietal branch
Parieto-occipital branch
Orbital branches
Anterior cerebral A.
Posterior cerebral A.
Posterior choroid branch
Temporal branches
Occipital branch

FIG. 197 The arteries of the medial and tentorial surfaces of the right hemisphere. Area supplied by the anterior cerebral artery, red stipple; by the posterior cerebral artery, red cross-hatching; and by the middle cerebral artery, no colour.

ends anteriorly in a rounded swelling, the **uncus,** which tends to be thrust through the tentorial notch when the supratentorial pressure exceeds that in the infratentorial compartment [FIG. 209].

General Features of Surface of Hemisphere

The **frontal pole** lies opposite the root of the nose and the medial part of the superciliary arch.

The **occipital pole** is more pointed than the frontal. It lies a short distance superolateral to the external occipital protuberance, and its medial aspect may be grooved by the superior sagittal sinus turning into the transverse sinus.

The **temporal pole** fits into the anterior part of the middle cranial fossa, and is overhung by the lesser wing of the sphenoid. The various **borders of the hemisphere** are named: the superomedial, inferolateral, superciliary, medial orbital, medial occipital, and hippocampal [p. 255] borders. The superciliary border is at the junction of the superolateral and orbital surfaces; the medial orbital lies at the junction

of the medial and orbital surfaces; the medial occipital border is at the junction of the medial and tentorial surfaces. The superomedial border is self-explanatory. The inferolateral border (at the junction of the superolateral and tentorial surfaces) lies immediately superior to the transverse sinus in its posterior part and exhibits a notch **(preoccipital notch)** about 3 cm. from the occipital pole, where the inferior anastomotic vein enters the transverse sinus. This notch is used as one landmark which artificially separates the occipital and temporal lobes of the brain [FIG. 207].

DISSECTION. Review the vessels on the surface of the hemisphere, and then proceed to strip the meninges from its surface. On the superolateral surface, strip the meninges towards the lateral sulcus [FIG. 198] pulling them off along the line of the other sulci. Note the large branches of the middle cerebral artery which issue from the lateral sulcus.

CEREBRAL SULCI AND GYRI

In studying the sulci and gyri of the hemisphere, it should be clear that there are great

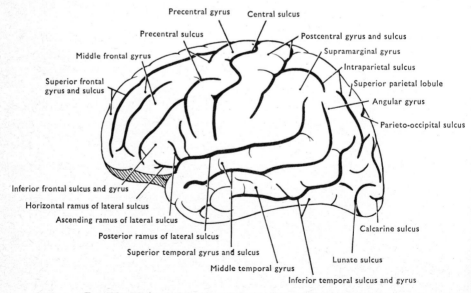

FIG. 198 Diagram of the superolateral surface of the left hemisphere.

individual variations in the details of their arrangement, and that it is inadvisable to try to learn the details of the cerebral configuration, though it is important to know the position of the major sulci and gyri. These can be identified with the help of FIGURES 198, 199, 203, 205, and 209. From these it will become apparent that the majority of the sulci run longitudinally in the hemisphere with the exception of the central, precentral, postcentral, and parieto-occipital which are more or less transverse to the long axis of the hemisphere.

The following account deals only with some of the important features of the sulci and gyri, and does not attempt to mention all of them. The student should confirm the position of all those mentioned in the above figures, and should be conversant with their position.

The **sulci** vary in depth from slight grooves to deep fissures, and some of them (calcarine and collateral, FIGURES 203 and 209) are sufficiently deep to indent the wall of the lateral ventricle in the depths of the hemisphere.

The **gyri** consist of a central core of white matter (nerve fibres running to and from the overlying cortex) covered by a layer of grey matter, the **cerebral cortex.** The cortex extends as an uninterrupted sheet over the whole surface of the hemisphere, and consists of nerve cells which are arranged in six layers parallel to the surface. These layers are differentiated from each other by their different content of cells, but they are difficult to separate in many situations, and tend to be arranged in such a manner that certain areas of the cortex can be recognized easily in a microscopic section, while others can not. Any special features of the different regions of the

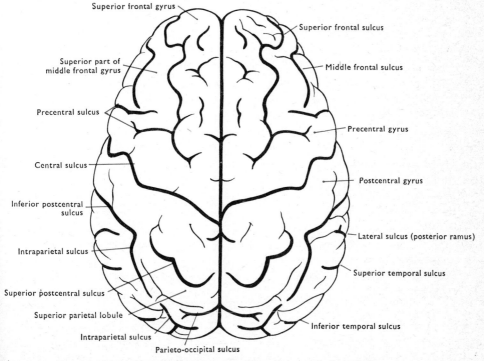

FIG. 199   Diagram of the superior surface of the cerebral hemispheres.

cortex which are discussed will be mentioned briefly, but the student should refer to the larger textbooks for details of the microscopic structure of the cerebral cortex. It is a great advantage if the student can have microscopic preparations to study, for only very few of the features of the structure of the cerebral cortex are visible to the unaided eye. In general, the cerebral cortex varies both in thickness and microscopic structure in its various parts, but the correlation between structure and function is, as yet, in its infancy. The cortex is thicker on the summits of the gyri than in the depths of the sulci, and is much thicker in the posterior part of the frontal lobe than in the adjacent anterior part of the parietal lobe on the opposite wall of the central sulcus [FIG. 198].

Lateral Sulcus [FIGS. 198, 209]

The various parts of this deep and complex sulcus are formed by the meeting of folds of the surrounding cortex which overgrow a portion of the surface adherent to the solid central part of the hemisphere (corpus striatum) in such a manner that, during development, it becomes a buried island of cerebral cortex, **the insula.**

The stem of the sulcus begins in the vallecula and runs laterally between the temporal pole and the posterior part of the orbital surface of the hemisphere. It transmits the middle cerebral artery. The stem ends on the superolateral surface by dividing into anterior, ascending, and posterior rami [FIG. 198]. The first two cut into the inferior frontal gyrus, while the horizontal part of the posterior ramus separates the frontal and parietal lobes of the brain superiorly, from the temporal lobe inferiorly. If the lips of this sulcus are pulled apart, the insula is exposed, and the main branches of the middle cerebral artery can be seen running over it before emerging from

the sulcus on to the superolateral surface of the hemisphere.

Central Sulcus [FIGS. 198, 203]

This important sulcus is often difficult to identify. It begins superiorly on the medial surface approximately midway between the frontal and occipital poles, and passes anteroinferiorly to end just superior to the posterior ramus of the lateral sulcus, 2–3 cm. posterior to the origin of that sulcus. The central sulcus separates the frontal and parietal lobes of the hemisphere, but it is of especial importance because it separates the main 'motor' and 'sensory' areas of the cerebral cortex [FIG. 200]. The **'motor' area** lies in the anterior wall of the central sulcus and the adjacent part of the precentral gyrus, while the 'sensory' area lies in the corresponding region immediately posterior to this. The 'motor' area is the region from which most of the corticospinal and corticonuclear nerve fibres arise, and the region where low intensity stimulation most readily elicits movements of the contralateral side of the body. The **'sensory' area** is the region to which the impulses ascending in the medial lemniscus and spinothalamic tracts are transmitted. Within these areas

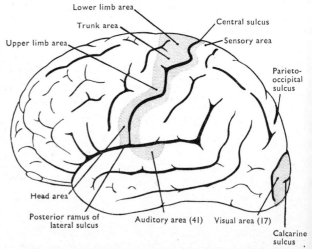

FIG. 200   Diagram of the superolateral surface of the left hemisphere, to show 'motor' (red) and 'sensory' areas (blue).

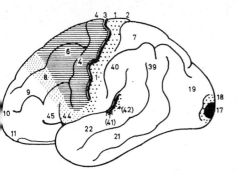

FIG. 201 Diagram of the superolateral surface of the left hemisphere to indicate the position of some of the areas which can be differentiated on the basis of their histological structure. The numbers indicate some of the areas described by Brodmann though the extent of these areas is not shown. Black, koniocortex of the primary receptive areas; large dots, parakoniocortex; small dots, frontal dysgranular cortex; cross-hatching, frontal agranular cortex.

here is a further functional subdivision, for movements of the opposite side of the head nd neck are most easily elicited by stimula-ion of the inferior precentral region, the

upper limb, trunk, and lower limb following in sequence superiorly. An exactly similar arrange-ment of the sensory fibres is found in the post-central region; those from the opposite side of the head reaching the inferior postcentral region, with the other regions of the body represented in sequence superiorly.

In the endocranium, the frontal branch of the **middle meningeal artery** runs parallel to, and a short distance anterior to, the central sulcus [FIG. 252]. Thus haemorrhage from this artery is likely to press on this region of the brain and interfere with the voluntary pro-duction of movements in the opposite half of the body.

If a small wedge of cortex is cut out across the central sulcus, the greater thickness of the precentral cortex as compared with the post-central cortex is immediately obvious. This difference in thickness is associated with a marked difference in microscopic structure. The 'sensory' cortex, like the other areas of the cortex to which sensory fibres pass, is composed almost exclusively of small cells,

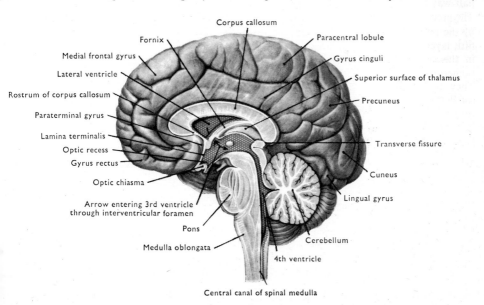

FIG. 202 Medial surface of the right half of bisected brain. The septum pellucidum has been removed to expose the lateral ventricle. The arrow passes through the interventricular foramen from the lateral to the third ventricle, and lies in the hypothalamic sulcus. Ependymal lining of ventricles, blue.

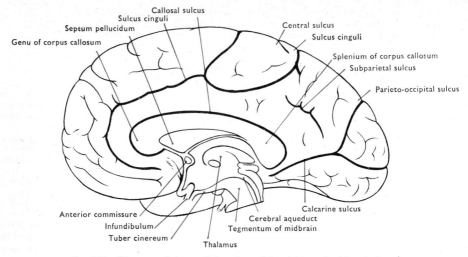

Fig. 203 Diagram of the medial surface of the right cerebral hemisphere.

has poorly marked lamination, and a moderately well-defined white line (nerve fibres) which is sometimes visible to the naked eye, running through its fourth layer, i.e., virtually half way through the thickness of the cortex. The precentral, 'motor' cortex is characterized by the presence of giant pyramidal cells in its fifth layer. These are among the largest cells in the cerebral cortex, and are particularly numerous in the superior part of the area. They are known as the **giant pyramidal cells** (of Betz) and they give rise to a small proportion of the corticospinal fibres. This cortex does not show a white stria such as that in the postcentral cortex, and contains many medium-sized pyramidal-shaped cells in its other layers. Throughout the greater part of the cerebral cortex, the fourth layer is composed of small cells, and has a granular appearance under the low power of the microscope. This granular layer is absent in the posterior part of the frontal lobe, which is, therefore, known as the **frontal agranular cortex,** another feature which differentiates it from the parietal lobe.

Parieto-occipital and Calcarine Sulci [FIG. 203]

These sulci form a Y-shaped arrangement on the medial aspect of the posterior part of

the hemisphere. Both are very deep sulc The superior end of the parieto-occipital sulcu reaches the superolateral surface, and th posterior end of the calcarine may exten round the occipital pole on to the superolatera surface. In the latter case the end of the ca carine sulcus is surrounded by the **luna**

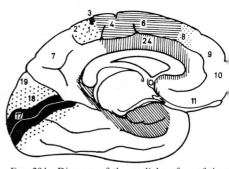

Fig. 204 Diagram of the medial surface of the left hemisphere to indicate the position of some of the areas which can be differentiated on the basis of their histological structure. The numbers indicate some of the areas described by Brodmann though the extent of these areas is not shown. Black, koniocortex of the primary receptive areas; large dots, parakoniocortex; small dots, frontal dysgranular cortex; horizontal cross-hatching, frontal agranular cortex; oblique cross-hatching, allocortex (rhinencephalon); vertical cross-hatching, cingulate agranular cortex.

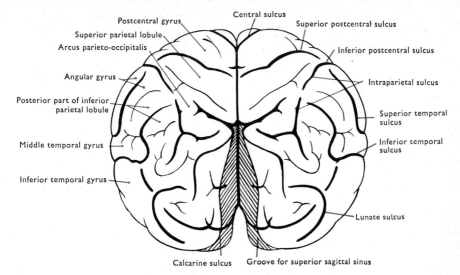

Central sulcus
Postcentral gyrus
Superior postcentral sulcus
Superior parietal lobule
Inferior postcentral sulcus
Arcus parieto-occipitalis
Angular gyrus
Intraparietal sulcus
Posterior part of inferior parietal lobule
Superior temporal sulcus
Inferior temporal sulcus
Middle temporal gyrus
Inferior temporal gyrus
Lunate sulcus
Calcarine sulcus
Groove for superior sagittal sinus

FIG. 205   Diagram of posterior view of the cerebral hemispheres.

ulcus [FIG. 205]. An imaginary line joining he superior end of the parieto-occipital sulcus ɔ the pre-occipital notch separates the

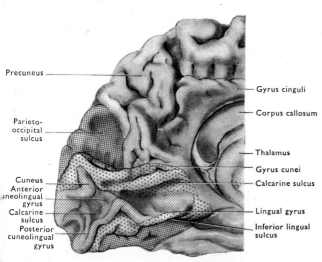

Precuneus
Gyrus cinguli
Corpus callosum
Parieto-occipital sulcus
Thalamus
Gyrus cunei
Cuneus
Calcarine sulcus
Anterior cuneolingual gyrus
Calcarine sulcus
Lingual gyrus
Inferior lingual sulcus
Posterior cuneolingual gyrus

IG. 206   Posterior part of the medial surface of the left hemisphere. The ɪlcarine sulcus has been forced open to expose the cortex lying in its epths. Fine blue dots, visual receptive area (area 17); coarse blue dots, ɪe area immediately surrounding area 17 to which it sends fibres (area 8); upper and lower dark blue areas (area 19) have long association ɔnnexions with other parts of the cortex.

occipital lobe from the parietal and temporal lobes [FIG. 207].

The **calcarine sulcus** is of considerable functional significance, for it is in the cortex which lines its walls and spills over on to the medial surface for a few millimetres that the nerve fibres conveying visual impulses to the cerebral cortex end [FIGS. 204, 206]. This visual cortex is one of the few regions which can be recognized with the unaided eye. This is because it has a very well defined white stria running through it parallel to the surface of the cortex. This is equivalent to the stria seen in the postcentral cortex, but is much more marked, and is readily visible in a cross-section cut through the calcarine sulcus. The presence of this stria has led to the name **striate cortex** being applied to the visual area in the walls of the calcarine sulcus. At the

251

margin of the visual area the cortex changes its structure abruptly, and the stria ceases to be visible. It is, therefore, possible to map out the visual area with moderate accuracy by cutting a series of thin slices through the occipital lobe, and following the extent of the visual stria in these slices.

DISSECTION. Cut a slice through the calcarine sulcus, posterior to its junction with the parieto-occipital sulcus, and examine the cortex for the presence of the stria.

The nerve impulses that reach one calcarine sulcus arise as a result of light stimuli in the opposite half of the field of vision. The arrangement of the nerve fibres carrying these impulses is such that impulses arising as a result of stimuli in the lower half of the field of vision, end in the superior wall of the sulcus, and vice versa, while those from the periphery end far forwards in the sulcus, and those from the centre end posteriorly. The position of small injuries to this region of the·brain is, therefore, relatively easy to localize accurately

from the defects which they produce in the opposite half of the field of vision.

The arbitrary division of the superolateral surface of the hemisphere into **lobes** is completed by extending the horizontal part of the posterior ramus of the lateral sulcus posteriorly to meet the line joining the parieto-occipital sulcus and the pre-occipital notch, thus separating the parietal and temporal lobes. Although the central sulcus, which separates the frontal and parietal lobes, also separates parts of the cerebral cortex which are functionally very different from each other, the other lines separating the lobes of the hemisphere should not be assumed to be equally important; their purpose is purely descriptive, and they are depicted in FIGURE 207.

Other important features of the surface of the hemispheres are mentioned below.

The '**motor speech area**' lies in the region of the anterior and ascending rami of the lateral sulcus [FIG. 198]. This region is intimately connected with the control of movements of the larynx and tongue through the motor area immediately posterior to it, but the common

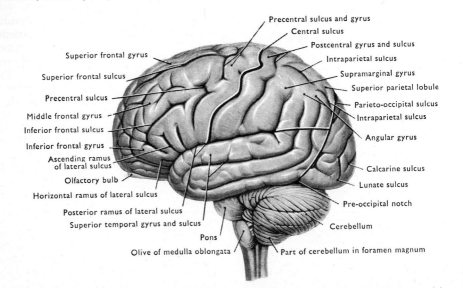

Precentral sulcus and gyrus
Central sulcus
Postcentral gyrus and sulcus
Intraparietal sulcus
Supramarginal gyrus
Superior parietal lobule
Parieto-occipital sulcus
Intraparietal sulcus
Angular gyrus
Calcarine sulcus
Lunate sulcus
Pre-occipital notch
Cerebellum
Part of cerebellum in foramen magnum

Superior frontal gyrus
Superior frontal sulcus
Precentral sulcus
Middle frontal gyrus
Inferior frontal sulcus
Inferior frontal gyrus
Ascending ramus of lateral sulcus
Olfactory bulb
Horizontal ramus of lateral sulcus
Posterior ramus of lateral sulcus
Superior temporal gyrus and sulcus
Pons
Olive of medulla oblongata

FIG. 207 Lateral surface of the left half of the brain (semi-diagrammatic) to show the main sulci and gyri, and the division of the superolateral surface into lobes by means of the central sulcus and two arbitrary lines shown in black and white.

statement that this 'centre' is present in the left hemisphere of right-handed individuals, and vice versa, is based on insufficient evidence, and the complex mechanism which subserves speech involves many other regions of the brain.

The **auditory area,** the cortical area to which auditory impulses are primarily relayed, lies on the middle of the superior surface of the superior temporal gyrus and, to a small extent, on the lateral surface of that gyrus, inferior to the postcentral gyrus [FIG. 200]. If the superior temporal gyrus is pulled inferiorly, a transverse gyrus will be seen running across its superior surface. This is the region of the auditory area.

The **inferior parietal lobule** is the part of the parietal lobe inferior to the intraparietal sulcus. The posterior ramus of the lateral sulcus and the superior and inferior temporal sulci sweep superiorly into it and divide it into three parts arranged around the ends of these sulci [FIG. 198]. The two anterior parts are known as the **supramarginal** and **angular gyri** and are believed to be important in the recognition of structures and symbols, and in an extension of this, the recognition of the body image. The part which this region of the brain plays in this activity is not understood, but there are considerable differences in lesions of this region in the dominant (usually the left) and the non-dominant hemisphere.

The **olfactory bulb and tract** lie in the **olfactory sulcus** close to the medial margin of the orbital surface of the frontal lobe. The olfactory bulb is a narrow, oval body which lies on the dura mater and endocranium immediately above the cribriform plate of the ethmoid, and these structures alone separate it from the nasal mucous membrane. Lateral

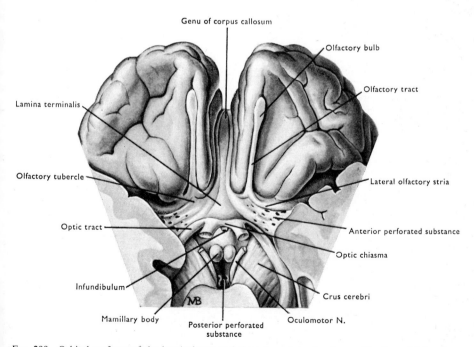

Genu of corpus callosum

Olfactory bulb

Olfactory tract

Lamina terminalis

Olfactory tubercle

Lateral olfactory stria

Optic tract

Anterior perforated substance

Optic chiasma

Infundibulum

Crus cerebri

MB

Oculomotor N.

Mamillary body

Posterior perforated substance

FIG. 208 Orbital surfaces of the hemispheres and the interpeduncular fossa. The frontal lobes have been separated slightly to show the genu of the corpus callosum, and the optic chiasma has been pulled inferiorly to uncover the lamina terminalis.

to this the orbital surface lies on the orbital part of the frontal bone. Fractures of the anterior cranial fossa are, therefore, liable to damage the olfactory bulb and to lead to blood and cerebrospinal fluid leaking into the nose and the orbit. In the former case a route for infection of the meninges may be opened through such a fracture into the nose, and in those cases where the frontal air sinus invades the orbital part of the frontal bone, infection may extend from the sinus to the subarachnoid space.

Follow the olfactory tract posteriorly [FIG. 208]. It appears to split into a **medial** and a **lateral stria** at the anterior margin of the anterior perforated substance where it joins a small grey elevation, the **olfactory trigone**. The medial stria curves round the posterior end of the gyrus rectus to the medial side of

the hemisphere, and disappears in the region of the **paraterminal gyrus** [FIG. 202]. The lateral stria runs posterolaterally on the margin of the anterior perforated substance, curves round the stem of the lateral sulcus and enters the uncus. Grey matter extends from the olfactory trigone to the uncus along the lateral olfactory stria, and these parts, trigone, uncus, and the grey matter of the stria, constitute the **piriform area** in which the olfactory fibres end.

The **uncus** is the raised area on the medial surface of the temporal lobe, and it is separated from the remainder of the temporal lobe by the **rhinal sulcus** [FIG. 209]. The posterior surface of the uncus is notched by the anterior extremity of the **hippocampal sulcus** (giving it a hook-like appearance) and it is continuous with the **parahippocampal gyrus**

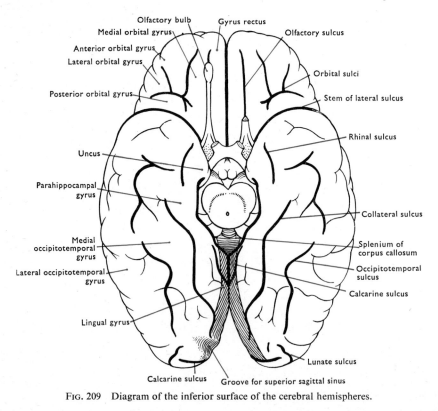

Olfactory bulb
Medial orbital gyrus
Anterior orbital gyrus
Lateral orbital gyrus
Posterior orbital gyrus
Uncus
Parahippocampal gyrus
Medial occipitotemporal gyrus
Lateral occipitotemporal gyrus
Lingual gyrus
Gyrus rectus
Olfactory sulcus
Orbital sulci
Stem of lateral sulcus
Rhinal sulcus
Collateral sulcus
Splenium of corpus callosum
Occipitotemporal sulcus
Calcarine sulcus
Lunate sulcus
Calcarine sulcus
Groove for superior sagittal sinus

FIG. 209   Diagram of the inferior surface of the cerebral hemispheres.

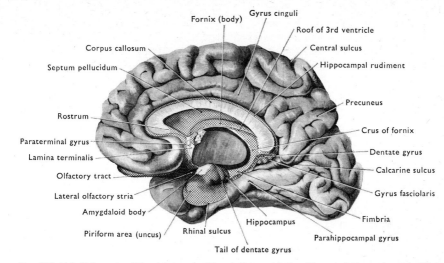

Fornix (body)

Gyrus cinguli

Roof of 3rd ventricle

Corpus callosum

Central sulcus

Septum pellucidum

Hippocampal rudiment

Precuneus

Rostrum

Paraterminal gyrus

Crus of fornix

Lamina terminalis

Dentate gyrus

Olfactory tract

Calcarine sulcus

Lateral olfactory stria

Gyrus fasciolaris

Amygdaloid body

Fimbria

Hippocampus

Piriform area (uncus)

Rhinal sulcus

Parahippocampal gyrus

Tail of dentate gyrus

Fig. 210 Medial aspect of the right cerebral hemisphere with the rhinencephalon coloured. The olfactory bulb, tract, and lateral stria, the uncus, and the dentate gyrus are shown in red. The hippocampus, supracallosal hippocampal vestige (indusium griseum), paraterminal gyrus, septum pellucidum and medial olfactory stria are shown in blue.

which is separated from the remainder of the temporal lobe by the collateral sulcus, with which the rhinal sulcus is often continuous. The uncus and parahippocampal gyrus form the **hippocampal border** of the hemisphere which lies close to the free margin of the tentorium.

Open the hippocampal sulcus on the right hemisphere and find the **dentate gyrus** in its depths. This gyrus is a minute structure, transversely ridged, which is continuous anteriorly with the uncus. Posteriorly, it sweeps upwards towards the splenium of the corpus callosum on the inferior surface of which it becomes continuous with a small ridge of grey matter, the **gyrus fasciolaris.** This gyrus is continuous with a thin layer of grey matter on the superior surface of the corpus callosum **(indusium griseum)** which can be followed over it, in the callosal sulcus, to reach the paraterminal gyrus inferior to the rostrum of the corpus callosum [Fig. 210]. The indusium griseum is continuous with the cortex of the gyrus cinguli in the depths of the callosal sulcus, and contains two delicate,

longitudinal bands of fibres buried in it, the medial and lateral **longitudinal striae.** These run from the hippocampus posteriorly, to the paraterminal gyrus anteriorly.

The olfactory bulb, tract, trigone and striae, together with the uncus, dentate gyrus, hippocampus—which will be seen later—indusium griseum, septum pellucidum, and paraterminal gyrus were called the **rhinencephalon** in the mistaken belief that they were all concerned with olfaction. Only the olfactory trigone and the anterior piriform area are known to receive olfactory fibres direct from the olfactory bulb, but the name is still applied to this ring of cortex on the medial aspect of the hemisphere.

THE WHITE MATTER OF THE CEREBRUM

The white matter of the cerebrum consists of the nerve fibres which lie deep to the cerebral cortex and connect the various parts of the cortex with each other and with the other parts of the central nervous system. In this enormous mass of nerve fibres three different groups may be recognized because of their different connexions. These are: (1) Association fibres, which connect the various parts of the cerebral cortex of one hemisphere with each other. (2) Commissural fibres, which cross the midline and connect the parts of the two hemispheres with each other. (3) Projection fibres, which connect the cerebral cortex with other regions of the central nervous system. All three types pass in both directions, (*i.e.*, to and from the cerebral cortex) and all are intermingled in the centre of the hemisphere to form the mass of white matter which underlies the sulci and gyri, but in certain situations each group forms bundles of fibres which may be dissected separately for part of their course.

ASSOCIATION FIBRES

These fibres are of all lengths. **Short association fibres** pass from one part of a gyrus to another part of the same gyrus, or they may loop round a sulcus to an adjacent gyrus. Other association fibres run for long distances (*e.g.*, between the frontal and occipital lobes) and it is these long association fibres that form the bundles which can be demonstrated and which will be exposed during the dissection; they are: (1) the

cingulum on the medial aspect; (2) the superior longitudinal bundle on the superolateral aspect; (3) the fasciculus uncinatus on the superolateral and orbital aspects; (4) the inferior longitudinal bundle on the tentorial aspect [FIGS. 211, 234].

Cingulum

This is the only association bundle which can be displayed at this stage; the others, together with the projection fibres will be seen later.

DISSECTION. **On the right hemisphere, scrape away the grey matter of the gyrus cinguli [Fig. 210] and expose a rounded bundle of white matter lying longitudinally within it. It is simplest to determine the edge of this bundle (the cingulum) by removing the cortex between it and the superior surface of the corpus callosum, and then to clean superiorly. The superior surface of the cingulum cannot be defined because nerve fibres enter this surface from the surrounding cortex of the medial aspect of the hemisphere and run in it for variable distances. Clean the medial and inferior surface of the cingulum throughout the length of the corpus callosum and then follow it, anteriorly, towards the anterior perforated substance, and, posteriorly, around the splenium of the corpus callosum and through the length of the parahippocampal gyrus as far as the uncus. In this latter part, the cingulum has a twisted, rope-like appearance. Lift off a portion of the fibres of the**

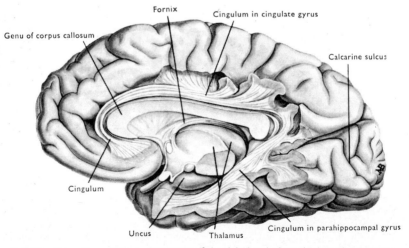

FIG. 211   Dissection of the medial aspect of the right hemisphere to show the cingulum.

256

cingulum by pushing a blunt instrument between its fibres, and demonstrate its longitudinal nature by tearing these away from the remainder. In this way its continuity into the surrounding cortex will be demonstrated though it is not possible to determine any detailed connexions by this means.

The cingulum is a thick bundle of long association fibres which pass longitudinally between the various parts of the cerebral cortex on the medial aspect of the hemisphere. The cingulum extends from the region of the paraterminal gyrus to the uncus, and thus forms almost a complete circle (cingulum means a girdle) which is capable of connecting all parts of the medial surface of the hemisphere together [FIGS. 211, 212].

COMMISSURAL FIBRES

The greatest number of commissural fibres is found in the corpus callosum, though other commissures of the forebrain are present: (1) the anterior commissure; (2) the optic chiasma; (3) the posterior and habenular commissures in the midbrain-diencephalic junction, at the root of the pineal body.

Corpus Callosum

This great commissure is formed by nerve fibres which converge on it from the greater part of the cerebral cortex, and then fan out into the opposite hemisphere. The various fibres do not mix with each other, but retain the same relation to the surrounding fibres throughout their course, and are transmitted to the part of the opposite hemisphere which corresponds to that from which they arose. Thus fibres from the medial surface of the hemisphere form U-shaped bundles hooking through the superficial part of the commissure, while fibres from the lateral aspect of the hemisphere lie more deeply and run a more horizontal course.

DISSECTION. On the right hemisphere, lever out the remains of the cingulum from the gyrus cinguli, and pull it away from the remainder of the cortex. This will expose the superficial fibres of the corpus callosum curving into the medial aspect of the hemisphere, and forming, with the corresponding fibres in the opposite hemisphere, two-thirds of a circle, the forceps minor. Immediately posterior to the splenium is the deep parieto-occipital sulcus, around which fibres of the splenium have to pass to reach the cuneus [Fig. 202] on the medial aspect of the hemisphere. These fibres should be followed around the parieto-occipital sulcus which forces them further laterally than elsewhere so that they form the forceps major. Note that the calcarine sulcus lies immediately inferior to the forceps major, and that it is possible to enter the posterior horn of the lateral ventricle by lifting the cortex of the upper wall of the calcarine sulcus away from the forceps major, for the sulcus and the forceps both indent the medial wall of the posterior horn of the ventricle [Fig. 222]. Make a coronal section through the right occipital lobe immediately posterior to the splenium and confirm the relation of these parts to the lateral ventricle. On the cut surface, a white layer of fibres about 2 mm. thick can be seen crossing the roof of the posterior horn of the lateral ventricle and turning down to form its immediate lateral wall. This is the tapetum, and it appears whiter than the white matter immediately lateral to it because it is cut parallel to the fibres it contains, while the other has been cut transversely. The tapetum consists of those fibres of the splenium which turn inferiorly, as a separate sheet, to pass to the inferior parts of the occipital lobe and to the temporal lobe. Thus the fibres of the splenium which form the forceps major and the tapetum virtually surround the posterior horn of the lateral ventricle [Fig. 212].

Turn to the genu of the corpus callosum [Fig. 203], push the handle of a knife into its fibres, parallel to the surface, and lift up a strip of its superficial fibres. Tear these laterally and, if the result is satisfactory, they will be seen to separate from another group of fibres which are passing vertically towards the cerebral cortex, the corona radiata. This appearance is due to the fact that the fibres of the corpus callosum passing horizontally towards the superolateral surface of the hemisphere intersect with the vertically placed fibres of the corona radiata [Fig. 212].

The corpus callosum unites the medial surfaces of the two cerebral hemispheres for nearly half their anteroposterior length, and lies nearer the anterior than the posterior ends of the hemispheres.

The upper surface of the corpus callosum forms the floor of the middle part of the longitudinal fissure. The anterior cerebral vessels lie on the pia mater covering it, and the falx cerebri touches it posteriorly, but does not reach it further forwards where the falx

257

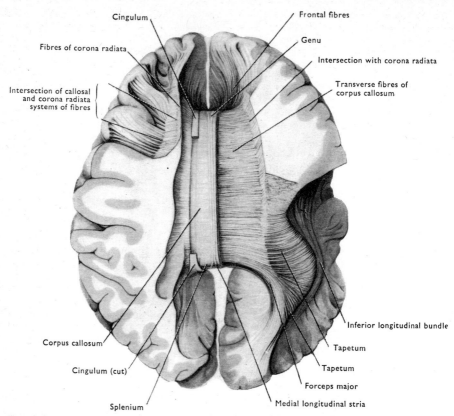

Cingulum

Frontal fibres

Fibres of corona radiata

Genu

Intersection with corona radiata

Intersection of callosal and corona radiata systems of fibres

Transverse fibres of corpus callosum

Corpus callosum

Cingulum (cut)

Splenium

Inferior longitudinal bundle

Tapetum

Tapetum

Forceps major

Medial longitudinal stria

FIG. 212 The corpus callosum exposed from above, with the right half dissected to show the course of some of its fibres.

becomes progressively less deep. It is covered on each side by the gyrus cinguli.

The main part or **trunk** of the corpus callosum is thinner than the extremities [FIG. 211]. The posterior end or **splenium** is full and rounded because of the large number of fibres which it transmits from the occipital and temporal lobes. It overlies the upper part of the midbrain, and extends posteriorly to the highest part of the cerebellum. Anteriorly the corpus callosum is folded back on itself to form the **genu**; the lower, recurved portion, which thins rapidly as it passes posteriorly, is the **rostrum.** The tip of the rostrum is usually connected by neuroglia to the superior extremity of the lamina terminalis anterior to the

anterior commissure [FIG. 202] but occasionally the cavum septi pellucidi is open anteriorly between these two structures.

Every part of the corpus callosum radiates out into the section of the hemisphere which lies opposite it; the rostrum extends inferiorly to the orbital surface; the genu passes to the anterior part of the frontal lobe; the trunk contains fibres to the remainder of the frontal lobe and to the parietal lobe; the splenium carries fibres to the posterior parts of the parietal lobe and to the occipital and temporal lobes. Most of these fibres intermingle with other groups shortly after leaving the corpus callosum and cannot be dissected out separately, but it is possible to define the fibres of the forceps major and minor and of the tapetum [FIG. 212, and p. 257] which remain separate. It is also possible to follow the fibres of the rostrum to the medial and orbital surfaces inferior to it [FIG. 241].

The **forceps major** consists of those fibres of the splenium of corpus callosum which arch laterally around the parieto-occipital sulcus to reach the cuneus posterior to that sulcus. The fibres of the forceps major lie in the medial wall of the posterior horn of the lateral ventricle, and they connect the cortex superior to the calcarine sulcus with the corresponding cortex of the opposite hemisphere.

The **tapetum** consists of a separate layer of fibres which pass through the splenium of the corpus callosum, spread out over the roof of the posterior horn of the lateral ventricle, and, turning downwards, sweep over the lateral wall of both posterior and inferior horns of the lateral ventricle [FIG. 212] to reach the temporal lobe and the inferior parts of the occipital lobe. Some of these fibres sweep round the inferior surface of the posterior horn of the lateral ventricle to the lingual gyrus [FIG. 202] on the medial aspect of the occipital lobe, and these fibres connect the cortex inferior to the calcarine sulcus with the corresponding cortex of the opposite hemisphere.

Attached to the inferior surface of the corpus callosum is the septum pellucidum with the fornix attached to its inferior margin. These two structures form the medial wall of the body of the lateral ventricle, while the corpus callosum forms the roof of this part of the alaterl ventricle. These parts will be seen when the lateral ventricle is dissected.

In the midline the corpus callosum overlies the thin roof. of the median, slit-like third ventricle, but is separated from it by a thin sheet of pia mater, the **tela choroidea of the third ventricle.** This sheet of pia mater extends anteriorly between the splenium of the corpus callosum and the dorsal surface of midbrain and pineal body. It contains the posterior choroidal branches of the posterior cerebral arteries, which supply the choroid plexus in the roof of the third ventricle and in the body of the lateral ventricle, and the internal cerebral

veins which unite to form the great cerebral vein inferior to the splenium [FIG. 226].

Anterior Commissure

This is a round bundle which crosses the median plane in the superior part of the lamina terminalis, immediately anterior to the column of the fornix and the interventricular foramen [FIG. 213]. The fibres in this commissure arise mainly in the temporal lobe and will be seen later in the dissection.

Posterior Commissure [FIGS. 213, 229]

This is a slender bundle which crosses the median plane immediately dorsal to the upper part of the aqueduct and inferior to the root of the pineal body. It is composed mainly of fibres which arise in the midbrain, and it carries fibres from the superior colliculi, the medial longitudinal bundle, and a number of nuclei associated with that bundle in the superior part of the midbrain.

Habenular Commissure

It lies at the root of the pineal body, and is separated from the posterior commissure by the small recess of the third ventricle which extends into the pineal, the **pineal recess.** It passes between the habenular nuclei in the habenular triangle [FIG. 229] and it has the posterior margin of the thin roof of the third ventricle attached to it [FIG. 213].

PINEAL BODY

This is a small glandular structure which lies between the superior colliculi and is attached to the habenular and posterior commissures by its stalk. It is invaded by the pineal recess of the third ventricle, while the thin roof of that ventricle is folded posteriorly over its superior surface to form the **suprapineal recess** of the third ventricle [FIG. 213]. The anterior part of the stalk of the pineal divides into right and left habenulae which pass anteriorly along the medial aspect of the corresponding habenular triangle to become continuous with a narrow, white ridge lying at the junction of the medial and superior surfaces of the thalamus, the **stria medullaris**

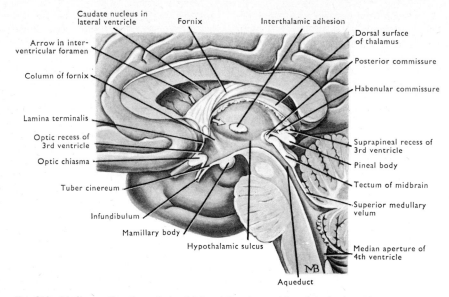

Caudate nucleus in lateral ventricle

Fornix

Interthalamic adhesion

Arrow in inter-ventricular foramen

Column of fornix

Lamina terminalis

Optic recess of 3rd ventricle

Optic chiasma

Tuber cinereum

Infundibulum

Mamillary body

Hypothalamic sulcus

Dorsal surface of thalamus

Posterior commissure

Habenular commissure

Suprapineal recess of 3rd ventricle

Pineal body

Tectum of midbrain

Superior medullary velum

Median aperture of 4th ventricle

Aqueduct

FIG. 213 Median section through the third and fourth ventricles of the brain. The septum pellu-cidum has been removed to expose the lateral ventricle.

thalami [FIG. 229]. The lateral edge of the thin roof of the third ventricle is attached to these structures.

The functions of the pineal body are not fully understood, but there is evidence that it produces pharmacologically-active substances one of which is concerned with the control of sodium metabolism by the suprarenal gland. Whatever its functions, the pineal commonly calcifies in middle age, and the ability to visualize it in radiographs may be a simple way of demonstrating a shift of the brain to one side.

The **habenular nuclei** lie in the habenular triangles. These are small triangular areas which lie between the medial aspect of the thalamus, the pineal stalk, and the superior colliculus. The nuclei receive fibres via the stria medullaris thalami, and they give rise to a small bundle of fibres (fasciculus retroflexus) which traverses the upper part of the tegmentum of the midbrain to end in the interpeduncular nucleus, a small collection of cells in the posterior perforated substance.

THE THIRD VENTRICLE
[FIG. 213]

This is the narrow, slit-like cavity which lies in the median plane between the two halves of the diencephalon, and extends from the lamina terminalis anteriorly, to the superior end of the aqueduct and root of the pineal posteriorly.

The **roof** of the ventricle consists of a layer of ependyma which is invaginated on each side by the overlying vascular pia mater to form a minute, linear choroid plexus. The roof is attached on both sides to the stria medullaris thalami, and extends from the interventricular foramen anteriorly, to the habenular commissure posteriorly, looping posteriorly over the superior surface of the pineal body to form the suprapineal recess of the ventricle.

The **floor** extends posteriorly from the **optic recess** on the superior surface of the optic chiasma into the **infundibular recess,** and then passes, above the mamillary bodies and the tegmentum of the midbrain, to the aqueduct.

The anterior commissure indents the anterior wall of the ventricle at the superior end of the lamina terminalis. Immediately posterior to this the column of the fornix forms a low ridge in the lateral wall. Posterior to the column of the fornix, and almost hidden by it, is a small, obliquely placed aperture which opens into the lateral ventricle. This is one half of the **interventricular foramen,** and it forms the only communication between the lateral ventricle and the other cavities of the brain. On each side, the narrow strip of choroid plexus in the roof of the third ventricle becomes continuous with the choroid plexus of the corresponding lateral ventricle through the interventricular foramen, and this is often so narrow that it is nearly filled by the choroid plexus. Thus any hypertrophy of the plexus at this situation easily blocks the communication between the two ventricles, causing an increase in pressure in the lateral ventricle. If this is unilateral it may be sufficient to cause compression of the opposite hemisphere and a shift of the midline structures towards that side.

The **lateral wall** of the third ventricle is traversed by a shallow groove (**hypothalamic sulcus**) from the interventricular foramen to the aqueduct. This sulcus separates the thalamus above from the hypothalamus below, and immediately above it the two thalami bulge towards each other so that they frequently meet and fuse, thus forming the **interthalamic adhesion.** This adhesion has no functional significance and is not a commissure.

THE LATERAL VENTRICLE AND THE CHOROID FISSURE

The lateral ventricle is a C-shaped cavity which extends from its anterior horn in the frontal lobe in a continuous curve posteriorly (central part), then inferiorly, and finally anteriorly, to end in the temporal lobe as the inferior horn. From its convex posterior surface a posterior horn extends backwards to a variable extent into the occipital lobe [FIG. 220]. The size and shape of this ventricle is very variable. In the young, the walls lie almost in apposition, while with increasing age and loss of neural tissue the ventricle expands and may reach a considerable size without any increase in its internal pressure. In young children an increase of pressure in the ventricles causes the brain and skull to expand if it is continued for a considerable time (hydrocephalus), but in older

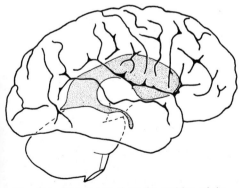

FIG. 214 Drawing to show the position of the lateral ventricle (shaded) in the hemisphere. The posterior horn in this case is particularly small.

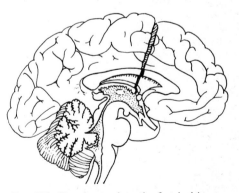

FIG. 215 Drawing to show the first incision to be made in the dissection to expose the lateral ventricle.

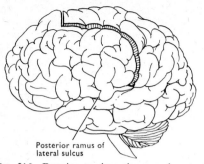

Posterior ramus of
lateral sulcus

FIG. 216 Drawing to show the second part of
the incision to be made in the dissection to expose the lateral ventricle.

children and adults no such expansion is
possible and distention of the ventricle can only
occur as a result of the loss of nervous tissue.

The lateral ventricle may be demonstrated
radiologically in the living by the introduction
of a contrast medium, and this is most easily
achieved by introducing air into the lumbar
subarachnoid space, whence it rises to the
cerebellomedullary cistern, and a considerable
amount enters the median aperture of the
fourth ventricle, which faces inferiorly. From
the fourth ventricle the air rises through the
aqueduct to the third ventricle, and passes into
the lateral ventricles through the interventricular foramen, which is in the highest part of
the third ventricle and lies between the column
of the fornix and the anterior part of the
thalamus [FIG. 213].

The following dissection is illustrated in
FIGURES 215, 216, 217, and 218. It has
the advantage that it exposes the complete
extent of the ventricle by dividing the brain
into two parts which may readily be fitted
together again so that the form and position
of the ventricle and the choroid fissure may be
appreciated without doing significant damage
to any of the deep structures of the hemisphere. In addition the brain stem remains in
continuity with the anterior portion, which
greatly facilitates the further dissection of the
cropus striatum and the internal capsule. The
dissection is, however, difficult and the student
should seek the assistance of an experienced
demonstrator.

DISSECTION. On the left hemisphere, place the
point of a knife in the interventricular foramen and
make a vertical cut through the fornix, septum pellucidum, and medial aspect of the hemisphere as shown in
Figure 215. Open the cut as it is made, and carry the
point of the knife as far as the lateral edge of the
lateral ventricle, but avoid cutting into its floor. Now
turn the knife so that its edge faces posteriorly and cut
backwards and then downwards, keeping the point of
the knife in the lateral edge of the lateral ventricle and
following its curve as far as the posterior ramus of the

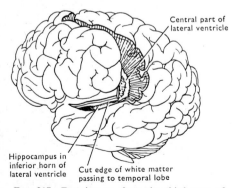

Central part of
lateral ventricle

Hippocampus in
inferior horn of
lateral ventricle

Cut edge of white matter
passing to temporal lobe

FIG. 217 Drawing to show the third part of
the incision used to expose the lateral ventricle.

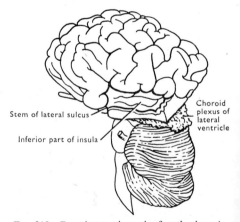

Stem of lateral sulcus

Inferior part of insula

Choroid
plexus of
lateral
ventricle

FIG. 218 Drawing to show the fourth phase in
the dissection of the lateral ventricle. The third
incision has been extended through the uncus into
the inferior part of the choroid fissure, and the
occipitotemporal part of the brain removed, leaving the choroid plexus of the lateral ventricle
attached to the 'frontal' part.

lateral sulcus [Fig. 216]. Note the ridge of the choroid plexus protruding into the ventricle from its floor [Fig. 219].

Depress the temporal lobe strongly, exposing the inferior part of the insula. Place the tip of the knife in the ventricle, and holding it as nearly vertical as possible, cut forwards through the medial part of the transverse temporal gyri on the superior surface of the temporal lobe, and enter the sulcus (circular sulcus) which separates the insula from the temporal lobe. This cut divides the white matter passing horizontally into the temporal lobe and opens into the roof of the inferior horn of the lateral ventricle. Carry the cut anteriorly along the circular sulcus to the stem of the lateral sulcus [Fig. 217] opening the cut and confirming that it enters the inferior horn of the lateral ventricle as you proceed.

Withdraw the knife, and holding the brain with the frontal pole upwards, separate the temporal lobe from the frontal lobe, thus opening the stem of the lateral sulcus. Place the knife in the anterior part of the previous incision, and make a horizontal cut medially through the temporal lobe in the inferior part of the stem of the lateral sulcus, following the anterior edge of the inferior horn of the lateral ventricle. Open this cut as it is made and note the choroid plexus protruding into the inferior horn of the lateral ventricle from its

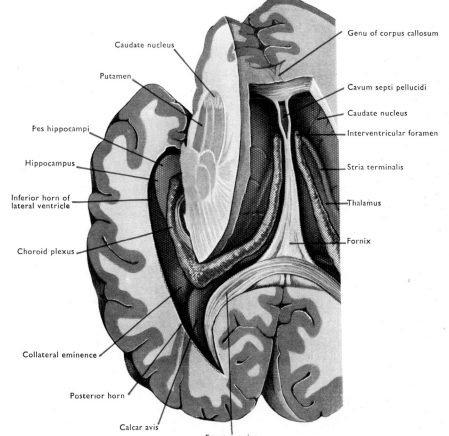

FIG. 219 Dissection from above to show the lateral ventricle. Ependyma, blue; choroid plexus, red. It should be appreciated that the choroid plexus is covered with ependyma on its ventricular aspect, but this is not shown.

medial wall approximately 1·5 cm. from its tip. Cut through the medial wall of the ventricle to the anterior extremity of the choroid plexus in the inferior horn.

The hemisphere is now separated into two parts which are held together by the ependyma which passes over the choroid plexus between them. The two parts are: (1) a 'frontal' part with the brain stem attached to it; (2) an 'occipitotemporal' part which carries the medial parts of the frontal and parietal lobes, the arch of the fornix, fimbria, hippocampus, and the trunk and splenium of the corpus callosum in one piece.

Turn to the medial side, and lifting the fornix away from the superior surface of the thalamus, separate the choroid plexus from the fornix and leave it attached to the thalamus. Slowly separate the occipitotemporal part from the frontal part along this line of the choroid fissure, between the fornix and the thalamus, and note the posterior choroidal branches of the posterior cerebral artery passing to the choroid plexus from the artery as it lies on the hippocampal margin. Divide these to prevent them pulling the choroid plexus from the surface of the thalamus.

When the two parts have been separated, they may be replaced as often as necessary to relate the internal appearances to the surface structures.

CHOROID FISSURE
[p. 228]

This is the fissure through which the two parts of the dissected brain were torn apart. It is the line along which a vascular sheet of pia mater is tucked into the lateral ventricle

and carries the wall of the ventricle in front of it to form the choroid plexus of the lateral ventricle. In this part of the ventricular wall no nervous tissue is developed, so that the vascular pia mater is applied directly to the ependymal lining. The choroid fissure lies in the concavity of the curve of the fimbria and fornix [FIG. 224] and is placed between the fornix and the thalamus in the central part of the ventricle, and between the fimbria and the roof of the inferior horn of the ventricle in the inferior horn. The choroid fissure is sometimes confused with the **transverse fissure** [FIG. 202], which is the horizontal slit below the splenium of the corpus callosum through which the pia mater (tela choroidea) from which the choroid plexuses spring, is continuous with the pia mater over the surface of the brain.

Before studying the lateral ventricle in detail note the position of the choroid plexus and follow it from the interventricular foramen to the inferior horn of the lateral ventricle. It lies at the lateral extremity of a sheet of pia mater which covers the dorsal surface of the thalamus between the roof of the third ventricle and the root of the choroid plexus, and which widens posteriorly as the lateral ventricle and choroid plexus move progressively further from the median plane. It is continuous with the pia mater around the midbrain which also forms tela choroidea where the hippocampal margin of the hemisphere lies against it and the choroid fissure sweeps antero-inferiorly around the side of the upper midbrain

LATERAL VENTRICLE

The **anterior horn** of the lateral ventricle curves inferiorly into the frontal lobe and is triangular in cross section. The narrow floor is formed by the rostrum of the corpus callosum; the roof and anterior wall by the trunk and genu

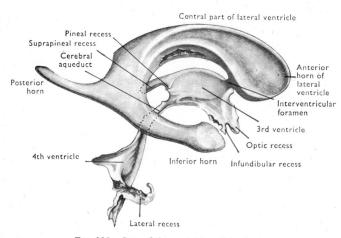

Central part of lateral ventricle

Pineal recess
Suprapineal recess
Cerebral aqueduct
Posterior horn
4th ventricle
Lateral recess
Inferior horn
Infundibular recess
Optic recess
3rd ventricle
Interventricular foramen
Anterior horn of lateral ventricle

FIG. 220   Cast of the ventricles of the brain.

264

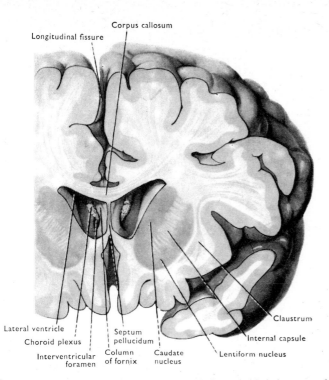

Corpus callosum

Longitudinal fissure

Lateral ventricle

Choroid plexus

Interventricular foramen

Column of fornix

Septum pellucidum

Caudate nucleus

Claustrum

Internal capsule

Lentiform nucleus

FIG. 221   Coronal section through the hemispheres behind the genu of the corpus callosum, seen from in front. Cf. FIGS. 222, 241.

interventricular foramen. A number of tributaries enter it from the centre of the hemisphere by running across the caudate nucleus outside the ependyma of the ventricle. (3) The **stria terminalis** runs with the thalamostriate vein and is a slender bundle of fibres which passes with fibres of the fornix to the grey matter around the anterior commissure. It arises in the amygdaloid body. (4) A narrow strip of the dorsal surface of the thalamus. (5) The choroid plexus. (6) The **fornix**. Anteriorly this is a rounded bundle, but posteriorly it becomes progressively flattened and extends laterally into the floor of the lateral ventricle. The choroid plexus is attached to the lateral margin of the fornix, and the torn ependyma can be seen on this edge in the occipito-temporal part of the brain.

of the corpus callosum; the vertical medial wall by the septum pellucidum, and the lateral wall by the bulging head of the caudate nucleus [FIG. 241].

The **central part** of the ventricle is roofed by the trunk of the corpus callosum. The medial wall is formed by the fornix and septum pellucidum anteriorly, and by the fornix posteriorly, and becomes less extensive as it is followed posteriorly [FIGS. 243, 245].

The floor consists from lateral to medial of the following structures: (1) The **caudate nucleus** which lies in the angle between the floor and the roof, and narrows rapidly as it is traced posteriorly. (2) The **thalamostriate vein** runs anteriorly in the groove between thalamus and caudate nucleus, and passes medially beneath the ependyma to join the internal cerebral vein just posterior to the

The **posterior horn** begins at the splenium of the corpus callosum, and extends posteriorly into the occipital lobe, tapering to a point. The roof, lateral wall, and floor are formed by a sheet of fibres (tapetum) from the splenium of the corpus callosum which arches over it and passes inferiorly to the lower parts of the occipital lobe [FIG. 222]. The inferomedial wall is invaginated by two ridges; the upper of these **(bulb of the posterior horn)** is formed by the fibres of the forceps major. The lower ridge **(calcar avis)** is produced by the calcarine sulcus which extends deeply into the medial surface of the occipital lobe.

The **inferior horn** is the direct continuation of the ventricular cavity into the temporal lobe. It runs inferiorly, posterior to the thalamus, and then passes anteriorly, curving medially to end at the uncus. The lateral wall

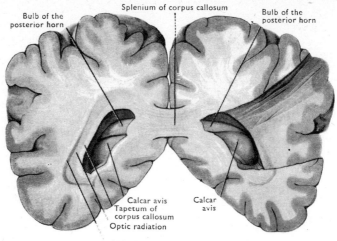

Bulb of the posterior horn

Splenium of corpus callosum

Bulb of the posterior horn

Calcar avis
Tapetum of corpus callosum
Optic radiation

Calcar avis

Inferior longitudinal bundle

FIG. 222 Coronal section through the posterior horns of the lateral ventricals.

is formed by the tapetum of the corpus callosum. The roof, which can be seen on the inferior surface of the 'frontal' part of the brain, consists of the stria terminalis and the tail of the caudate nucleus applied to the white matter passing laterally into the temporal lobe. Both these structures can be followed from the floor of the central part of the ventricle, and both become continuous with the amygdaloid body at the tip of the inferior horn. The

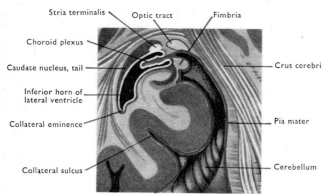

Stria terminalis
Optic tract
Fimbria
Choroid plexus
Caudate nucleus, tail
Inferior horn of lateral ventricle
Collateral eminence
Collateral sulcus
Crus cerebri
Pia mater
Cerebellum

FIG. 223 Coronal section through the inferior horn of the lateral ventricle.

amygdaloid body is an oval mass of grey matter which overlies the tip of the inferior horn of the ventricle, and is continuous medially with the cortex of the temporal lobe [Fig 242]. The floor is broad posteriorly where the inferior and posterior horns meet, and is often raised **(collateral triangle)** by the collateral sulcus. Anteriorly the floor narrows and its medial part is formed by a convex ridge produced by the hippocampus, but covered by a layer of nerve fibres (the **alveus**) which passes medially from the hippocampus to a ridge on the medial border of the hippocampus (the **fimbria of the hippocampus**).

Hippocampus

Traced anteriorly the hippocampus turns medially near the tip of the inferior horn of the lateral ventricle and becomes continuous with the uncus. This part of the hippocampus is ridged and known as the **pes hippocampi** [FIG. 224]. Traced posteri

266

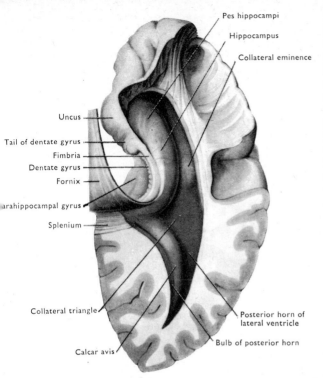

Pes hippocampi
Hippocampus
Collateral eminence
Uncus
Tail of dentate gyrus
Fimbria
Dentate gyrus
Fornix
arahippocampal gyrus
Splenium
Collateral triangle
Posterior horn of lateral ventricle
Bulb of posterior horn
Calcar avis

Fɪɢ. 224   Dissection to show the posterior and inferior horns of the right lateral ventricle, viewed from above.

orly the hippocampus virtually disappears at the splenium of the corpus callosum, but is continuous with a small ridge which curves round the inferior surface of the splenium, the **gyrus fasciolaris** [Fɪɢ. 210].

Fimbria of Hippocampus. This narrow strip of white matter on the medial margin of the hippocampus is formed by the fibres of the alveus which arise in the hippocampus. The medial margin of the fimbria is sharp and has the ependyma reflected off the choroid plexus attached to it, thus forming one margin of the choroid fissure. Anteriorly it is continuous with the recurved tip of the uncus, but posteriorly it becomes continuous with the crus of the fornix [Fɪɢ. 224]. The alveus, fimbria, and fornix form the efferent pathway for the cells of the hippocampus, but they also contain

fibres which pass from the cells in the region of the anterior commissure (septal nuclei) to the hippocampus. The fibres leaving the hippocampus pass: (1) To the opposite hippocampus through the **commissure of the fornix,** which is situated where the crura of the fornix meet inferior to the corpus callosum [Fɪɢs. 219, 226]. (2) To the septal and anterior hypothalamic region. (3) To the mamillary body. In addition, a few of its fibres may pass direct to the anterior nuclei of the thalamus.

Dentate Gyrus

This is a narrow ribbon of grey matter which lies in the medial concavity of the hippocampus, inferior to the fimbria of the hippocampus. It is readily recognized by the transverse notches which divide it into a number of 'teeth'. Posteriorly it is continuous with the gyrus fasciolaris, and through it with the thin layer of grey matter on the superior surface of the corpus callosum, the **indusium griseum.** Anteriorly the dentate gyrus passes into the cleft of the uncus, reappearing as the narrow **tail of the dentate gyrus** which fades out as it passes superiorly over the recurved portion of the uncus [Fɪɢ. 224].

RHINENCEPHALON

The hippocampus, dentate gyrus, indusium griseum, and septum pellucidum were long thought to be part of the rhinencephalon or 'smell brain'. Certainly the uncus receives olfactory fibres, but it is clear that the hippocampus has many other connexions, and its considerable development in Man with a poorly developed sense of smell, and in the Cetacea which have no olfactory bulbs, makes it clear that it is concerned with other functions, at least in these animals.

Septum Pellucidum

This thin, vertical partition consists of two parallel laminae, each of which connects the fornix to the corpus callosum and fills the interval in the concavity of its genu. It varies directly in depth and length with the size of the lateral ventricle, and may extend as far posteriorly as the splenium of the corpus callosum or only for a short distance beyond the interventricular foramen. It lies between the anterior horns and central parts of the two lateral ventricles, and its two laminae may be separated by the **cavity of the septum pellucidum.** In lower mammals it is thicker and contains a number of septal nuclei which are found around the anterior commissure ventral to the septum in Man.

Fornix

The fornix is a paired structure, one of which is present in each hemisphere, but the two are so closely fused beneath the middle of the trunk of the corpus callosum that they are usually described as a single structure. Each half of the fornix is composed of fibres which enter it from the fimbria, and together with that structure the fornix forms almost one complete turn of a spiral. The **fimbria** begins close to the uncus and runs posterosuperiorly to enter the **crus of the fornix,** a flattened strip which arches upwards, medially, and forwards under the splenium of the corpus callosum to become continuous with the body of the fornix. The body is formed where the two crura fuse, but anteriorly they become more cylindrical and separate to form the **columns of the fornix.** These sweep inferiorly between the anterior commissure and the interventricular foramen, and curving posteriorly through the anterior hypothalamus, end in the mamillary body close to the midline and medial to the beginning of the fimbria. This spiral bundle of fibres forms the outer margin of the **choroid fissure** between the beginning of the fimbria and the interventricular foramen. It therefore has the ependyma of the choroid plexus attached to its sharp lateral margin throughout this length, and it is separated from the inner margin of the choroid fissure (mainly thalamus) by the tela choroidea passing laterally into the choroid plexus.

The crura and body of the fornix groove the posterior and superior surfaces of the thalamus respectively, and they lie in the medial part of the floor of the lateral ventricle. The columns of the fornix form slight ridges on the lateral wall of the third ventricle inferior to the interventricular foramen.

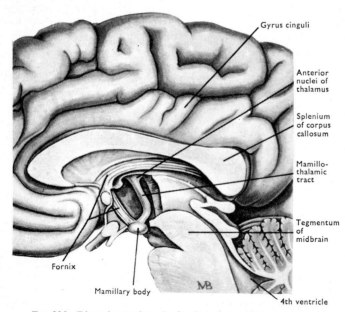

Gyrus cinguli

Anterior nuclei of thalamus

Splenium of corpus callosum

Mamillo-thalamic tract

Tegmentum of midbrain

Fornix

Mamillary body

MB

4th ventricle

FIG. 225   Dissection to show the fornix and mamillothalamic tract.

DISSECTION. Make two parallel cuts through the epen-

268

dyma of the lateral wall of the third ventricle, one on each side of the column of the fornix between the interventricular foramen and the mamillary body, in the 'frontal' part of the left hemisphere. Remove the ependyma between these, and scrape away sufficient of the underlying grey matter to expose the column of the fornix and follow it to the mamillary body.

At the mamillary body avoid injury to another bundle which appears to arise from the anteromedial part of the mamillary body and pass laterally across the fornix into the wall of the third ventricle. Cut through the ependyma on each side of this mamillothalamic tract, and follow it first laterally and then superiorly to the anterior tubercle of the thalamus, which contains the anterior nuclei of the thalamus.

Mamillothalamic Tract [Fig. 225]

If the mamillary body is dissected free from the floor of the third ventricle and only the column of the fornix and the mamillothalamic tract are left connected to it, it gives the appearance of being a loop on the fornix through which it becomes continuous with the mamillothalamic tract. In fact the fibres of the column of the fornix end in the nuclei of the mamillary body, and new fibres arise from its cells to form the mamillothalamic tract. The mamillothalamic tract is a compact bundle which passes laterally and then superiorly to the anterior nuclei of the thalamus. On the way its fibres branch to give rise to a diffuse bundle passing inferiorly to the tegmentum of the midbrain (the **mamillo-tegmental tract**) and they spread out as they approach the anterior nuclei of the thalamus.

The impulses discharged by the hippocampus into the fimbria and fornix reach the nuclei of the thalamus which project to the gyrus cinguli through the mamillothalamic tract, and can also have an effect on the brain stem mechanisms by way of the mamillotegmental tract. It is of some interest that fibres which arise in the gyrus cinguli enter the cingulum and pass through it to the parahippocampal gyrus and the hippocampus, thus producing a feed-back to the hippocampus.

Tela Choroidea and Internal Cerebral Veins

The tela choroidea is a fold of pia mater which extends anteriorly through the transverse fissure [Fig. 164] below the splenium of the corpus callosum. It passes forwards inferior to the fornix and superior to the roof of the third ventricle and the dorsal surface of the thalamus. The fold contains the internal cerebral veins and the posterior choroidal branch of the posterior cerebral artery [Fig. 226]. These vessels supply the vascular choroid plexuses of the

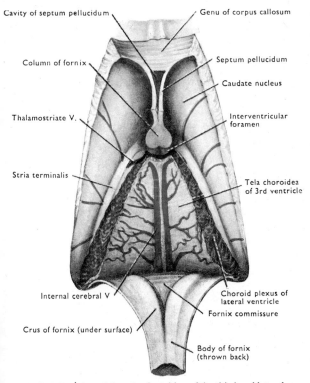

Cavity of septum pellucidum
Genu of corpus callosum
Column of fornix
Septum pellucidum
Caudate nucleus
Thalamostriate V.
Interventricular foramen
Stria terminalis
Tela choroidea of 3rd ventricle
Internal cerebral V
Choroid plexus of lateral ventricle
Fornix commissure
Crus of fornix (under surface)
Body of fornix (thrown back)

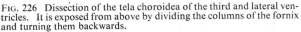

Fig. 226   Dissection of the tela choroidea of the third and lateral ventricles. It is exposed from above by dividing the columns of the fornix and turning them backwards.

269

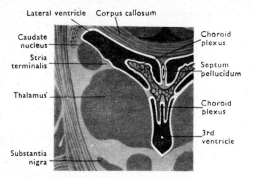

Fig. 227 Coronal section through the thalamus and associated structures just posterior to the interventricular foramen. Note the choroid plexuses of the third and lateral ventricles.

the tela, with the corresponding narrow strip of choroid plexus in the roof of the third ventricle. These two strips lie side by side on the inferior surface of the tela choroidea close to the midline, and are supplied by its contained blood vessels.

Each **internal cerebral vein** receives a number of tributaries from the choroid plexuses of the third and lateral ventricles and the corresponding thalamostriate vein and begins at the apex of the tela choroidea. The two internal cerebral veins run posteriorly, side by side, in the roof of the third ventricle, and unite to form the great cerebral vein inferior to the splenium of the corpus callosum. This vein emerges through the transverse fissure, and joins the inferior sagittal sinus to form the straight sinus by sweeping superiorly over the splenium with the superior layer of the tela choroidea of the third ventricle which becomes continuous with the pia mater on the superior surface of the corpus callosum. The inferior layer of the tela choroidea becomes continuous with the pia mater covering the surface of the midbrain, and it forms a sheath for the pineal body.

central parts of the lateral ventricles, into which the lateral margins of the tela are invaginated beyond the lateral edges of the fornix. Thus the tela choroidea narrows anteriorly as the two lateral ventricles and their choroid plexuses approach one another, and it ends in an apex at the interventricular foramen where the choroid plexuses of the lateral ventricles each become continuous around the anterior extremity of

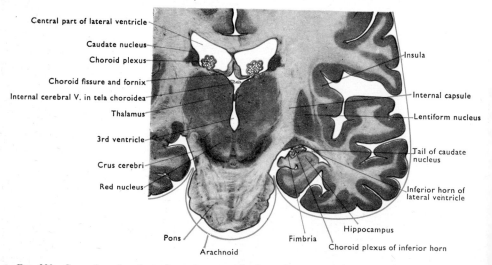

Fig. 228 Coronal section through cerebrum, midbrain, and pons to show the arrangement of the pia mater, and the choroid plexuses of the lateral ventricle in semi-diagrammatic form. Pia mater, red; arachnoid mater, ependyma, and internal cerebral veins, blue.

DISSECTION. On the 'frontal' part of the left hemisphere, remove the tela choroidea of the third ventricle by dividing the thalamostriate vein where it joins the internal cerebral vein, and pulling the tela posteriorly. Note that the epen-dyma covering the choroid plexus has a linear attach-ment to the superior surface of the thalamus, and identify again its torn margin on the lateral edge of the fornix in the 'occipitotemporal' part of the left hemisphere.

THE THALAMI AND THE OPTIC TRACTS

THALAMUS

The thalamus is a large mass of grey matter which lies obliquely across the path of the cerebral peduncle as it ascends into the hemi-sphere. It is the great sensory relay station for the cerebral cortex, and some of its cells trans-mit ascending sensory impulses to the sensory receptive areas of the cortex. In addition it has reciprocal connexions with most parts of the cerebral cortex and a number of sub-cortical masses of grey matter.

The **anterior two-thirds** of the medial surfaces of the two thalami are covered with ependyma and form the lateral walls of the third ventricle

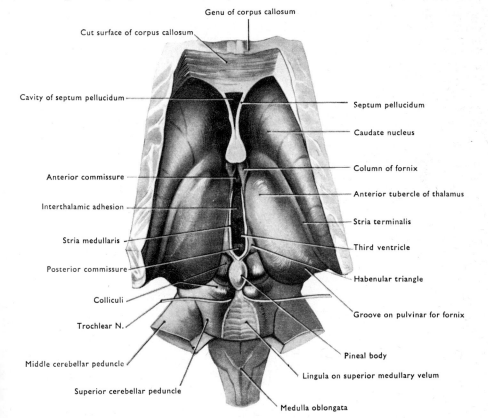

Genu of corpus callosum

Cut surface of corpus callosum

Cavity of septum pellucidum

Anterior commissure

Interthalamic adhesion

Stria medullaris

Posterior commissure

Colliculi

Trochlear N.

Middle cerebellar peduncle

Superior cerebellar peduncle

Septum pellucidum

Caudate nucleus

Column of fornix

Anterior tubercle of thalamus

Stria terminalis

Third ventricle

Habenular triangle

Groove on pulvinar for fornix

Pineal body

Lingula on superior medullary velum

Medulla oblongata

FIG. 229   The thalami and third ventricle seen from above after removal of the overlying tela.   Cf. FIG. 226.

271

superior to the hypothalamic sulcus [Fig. 213]. In this part they frequently fuse across the cavity of the ventricle to form the **interthalamic adhesion.** The posterior thirds are more widely separated by the superior part of the midbrain and the pineal body [Fig. 229] and are not covered with ependyma.

The **posterior end** of the thalamus (the **pulvinar**) is wide and overhangs the superior part of the midbrain. Laterally it is grooved by the crus of the fornix, and beyond that it forms a small part of the floor of the lateral ventricle. It is limited laterally by a slender ridge of white matter (the **stria terminalis**) which courses round the lateral margin of the thalamus from the amygdaloid body to the septal nuclei in company with the thalamostriate vein. Lateral to these is the caudate nucleus which forms a ridge in the lateral part of the floor of the lateral ventricle.

The **superior surface** is limited laterally by the stria terminalis and thalamostriate vein, and it tapers anteriorly to end in the rounded **anterior tubercle** of the thalamus just posterior to the interventricular foramen and the column of the fornix. The tubercle is formed by the **anterior nuclei** of the thalamus which receive the mamillothalamic tract and project to the cingulate gyrus of the cerebral cortex. The groove for the fornix courses obliquely across the superior surface of the thalamus, and the area of this surface lateral to the groove is covered with the ependyma of the floor of the lateral ventricle, while the groove and the area medial to it are covered by the tela choroidea of the third ventricle. Where the superior and medial surfaces meet there is a delicate ridge of white matter coursing anteroposteriorly across the thalamus to end in the **habenular triangle** [Fig. 229]. This is the **stria medullaris thalami,** and it also arises in the septal nuclei and has the thin roof of the third ventricle attached to its medial margin.

The **lateral surface** of the thalamus is hidden at present, but it lies in contact with the internal capsule [Figs. 244, 245].

The **inferior surface** is mostly hidden for it rests on the hypothalamus. The posterior part of this surface is free and exhibits two swellings, the medial and lateral geniculate bodies [Fig. 230].

Medial Geniculate Body [Figs. 177, 194]

This is a well defined, oval mass which lies in the angle between the inferior surface of the thalamus, the lateral aspect of the midbrain, and the dorsal surface of the crus cerebri. It is the thalamic nucleus which receives the **brachium of the inferior colliculus.** This is a well defined ridge which passes obliquely across the lateral surface of the midbrain from the inferior colliculus to the medial geniculate body, and conveys auditory impulses to the geniculate body for transmission to the superior temporal gyrus of the cerebral cortex.

Lateral Geniculate Body [Figs. 177, 245]

This is a less well defined swelling approximately 1 cm. lateral to the medial geniculate body. It is directly continuous with the lateral part of the optic tract, and the majority of the fibres in this tract end in it. It thus forms the thalamic termination of the optic fibres, and it gives rise to the fibres of the **optic radiation** which convey the impulses it receives to the occipital lobe of the cerebral cortex. Some of the fibres in the optic tract bypass the lateral geniculate body, and running between the two geniculate bodies over the inferior surface of the thalamus, enter the superolateral margin of the superior colliculus. These fibres form the **brachium of the superior colliculus** and are concerned with the production of visual reflexes such as the turning of the head and eyes towards a sudden flash of light and the constriction of the pupil when the retina is exposed to light. This brachium differs from the brachium of the inferior colliculus in that it is solely concerned with reflexes, is not part of the pathway concerned with vision, but conducts from the optic tract to the midbrain.

The geniculate bodies are, therefore, the thalamic nuclei concerned with the auditory

272

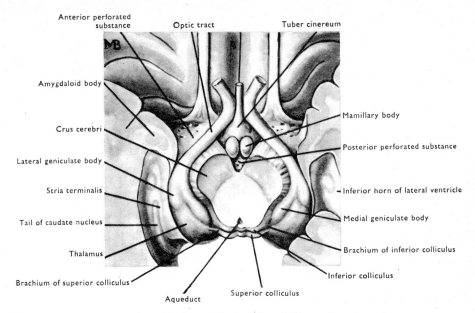

Anterior perforated substance

Optic tract

Tuber cinereum

Amygdaloid body

Crus cerebri

Lateral geniculate body

Stria terminalis

Tail of caudate nucleus

Thalamus

Brachium of superior colliculus

Aqueduct

Superior colliculus

Mamillary body

Posterior perforated substance

Inferior horn of lateral ventricle

Medial geniculate body

Brachium of inferior colliculus

Inferior colliculus

FIG. 230   Dissection of the base of the brain from below to show the optic tracts.

and visual pathways, and are essential in the transfer of the corresponding impulses to the cerebral cortex. The colliculi, on the other hand, are concerned with reflex activities triggered by the auditory (inferior colliculus) and visual (superior colliculus) impulses.

OPTIC TRACTS

Each optic tract begins at the posterolateral corner of the optic chiasma, and passing posterolaterally between the anterior perforated substance and the tuber cinereum, runs superior to the medial aspect of the temporal lobe and over the crus cerebri. The optic tract crosses the junction of the crus cerebri with the mass of fibres within the hemisphere with which it is continuous, the internal capsule. As it lies lateral to the crus, the optic tract is close to the choroid fissure [FIG. 223] of the inferior horn of the lateral ventricle, and is crossed by the anterior choroid branch [FIG. 171] of the internal carotid artery on its way to the fissure, and by the basal vein pass-

ing around the midbrain to the great cerebral vein.

Each optic tract appears to divide posteriorly into medial and lateral roots; the medial root passes towards the medial geniculate body, but actually ends in the medial part of the lateral geniculate body which lies adjacent to the medial geniculate body. The lateral root enters the surface swelling formed by the lateral part of the lateral geniculate body [FIG. 245]. The groove between the two roots is the hilus of the lateral geniculate body, and some of the fibres overlying the hilus continue as the brachium of the superior colliculus [FIG. 239].

Each optic tract contains nerve fibres which originate from the temporal half of the ipsilateral retina and the nasal half of the contralateral retina (the fibres from the nasal parts of the retinae crossing in the chiasma). These are the parts of the retinae which receive light from the opposite half of the field of vision. Hence division of one optic tract is followed by blindness in the opposite half of the field of vision, an homonymous hemianopia, and any partial lesions of the optic pathway between the chiasma and the visual cortex in the occipital lobe lead to visual defects which involve the corresponding part of the field of vision of both eyes. Division of the optic nerve, on the other hand, produces blindness in the affected eye only.

For blood supply, see FIGURES 173 and 197.

Before proceeding to the deep dissection of the hemisphere, the areas of the cerebral cortex should be reviewed with special reference to those regions in which particular functions have been localized [pp. 246–255, and FIGS. 200, 201, 206, 210].

THE DEEP DISSECTION OF THE HEMISPHERE

The following dissections are carried out on the left hemisphere on which the lateral ventricle has already been exposed; the right hemisphere is retained so that sections of it can be cut at a later phase. The use of the left hemisphere for these dissections facilitates the exposure of certain structures, but makes it difficult to see the entire extent of certain of the association bundles and of the corona radiata. This can be overcome by placing the two parts of the hemisphere together and continuing the dissection from the 'frontal' part into the 'occipitotemporal' part of the divided left hemisphere.

INSULA

DISSECTION. The inferior part of the insula is already exposed on the 'frontal' part of the left hemisphere. To complete its exposure lift up the frontoparietal operculum, which covers the posterosuperior part of the insula, and tear the operculum upwards and backwards away from the rest of the brain. This exposes the greater part of the insula and the posterior part of the superior longitudinal bundle [Fig. 231]. Tear away the parts of the frontal lobe which still cover the anterior parts of the insula and uncover the anterior part of the superior longitudinal bundle. This part is less clearly shown than the posterior part because it is traversed by many fibres of the corona radiata passing laterally through it.

The insula is that part of the cerebral cortex which is submerged in the lateral sulcus. It is roughly triangular in outline, and its margin is formed by the **circular sulcus** of the insula, where the cortex covering the surface of the insula becomes continuous with the cortex on the deep surfaces of the folds of the hemisphere (**opercula**) which hide the insula from

view. The surface of the insula is marked by a number of sulci and gyri radiating superiorly from the stem of the lateral sulcus, which lies at the apex of the insula known as the **limen insulae** [FIG. 232]. Note that the middle cerebral artery lies on the limen insulae as it passes laterally on to the surface of the insula in the stem of the lateral sulcus. Medial to the limen insulae is the **anterior perforated substance** through which the striate branches of the middle cerebral artery pass into the substance of the brain.

The function of the insula is unknown, but there is evidence that a secondary sensory area extends over the parietal operculum on to the superior surface of the insula, and a secondary auditory area may also extend over the tem-

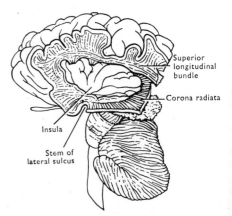

Superior longitudinal bundle

Corona radiata

Insula

Stem of lateral sulcus

FIG. 231   First phase in the dissection of the 'frontal' part of the brain. The frontal and parietal parts of the operculum have been torn off and the insula and superior longitudinal bundle exposed.

274

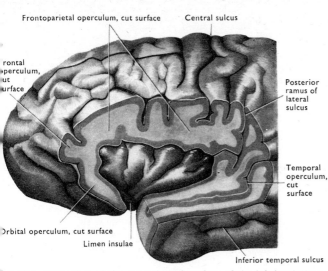

Frontoparietal operculum, cut surface   Central sulcus

Frontal operculum, cut surface

Posterior ramus of lateral sulcus

Temporal operculum, cut surface

Orbital operculum, cut surface

Limen insulae

Inferior temporal sulcus

FIG. 232   Dissection of the superolateral surface of the left hemisphere to display the insula.

oral operculum on to its inferior part. Stimulation of the insula also produces alterations in gastric motility and a number of other actions which may be mediated either through the subjacent lentiform nucleus or by way of intracortical connexions.

DISSECTION. With a blunt instrument, such as the handle of a knife, raise up the lower border of the insula, which will strip away from the subjacent structures through a thin layer of grey matter which lies deep to the white matter of the insula. This grey matter is the claustrum. Lift the whole of the insula away from the rest of the 'frontal' part of the left hemisphere, turning the insula superiorly towards the superior longitudinal bundle. When completely removed it will expose a part of the claustrum overlying a rounded, smooth zone of white matter (the external capsule) and superior to that, a fan-shaped layer of white matter radiating outwards towards the superior longitudinal bundle. This is part of the corona radiata.

Using the handle of the knife, scrape away the remains of the claustrum from the external capsule, and note that it passes deep to a ridge of white matter just superior to the stem of the lateral sulcus. This is a fronto-temporal association bundle, the fasciculus uncinatus, the inferior margin of which hooks round the stem of the lateral sulcus deep to the limen insulae to pass between the frontal lobe and the temporal pole. The

superior margin of the fasciculus uncinatus is straight and passes postero-inferiorly towards the temporal lobe from the frontal lobe, fanning out in both the temporal and the frontal lobes [Fig. 233].

Pass the handle of the knife downwards between the external capsule and the fasciculus uncinatus towards the lateral margin of the anterior perforated substance. This will free the narrow middle part of the fasciculus from the external capsule, and if the fasciculus is lifted away from its bed its fibres will be seen fanning out into the adjacent parts of the frontal and temporal lobes.

Fasciculus Uncinatus [FIG. 234]

This thick bundle of association fibres passes between the frontal and temporal lobes of the brain, and its inferior fibres hook round the stem of the lateral sulcus into the anterior part of the temporal lobe, while its superior fibres pass directly backwards and downwards towards the posterior part of the temporal lobe. At both ends it fans out, but is narrow

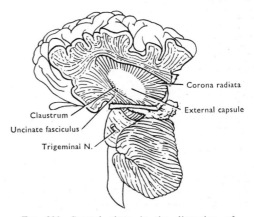

Corona radiata

External capsule

Claustrum

Uncinate fasciculus

Trigeminal N.

FIG. 233   Second phase in the dissection of the 'frontal' part of the brain. The insula has been removed and the external capsule, claustrum, and fasciculus uncinatus uncovered.

275

in the middle, thus giving it the shape of a sheaf bent inferiorly.

DISSECTION. Place the 'occipitotemporal' part of the left hemisphere in position on the 'frontal' part, and note where the superior longitudinal bundle on the 'frontal' part abuts on the white matter of the 'occipitotemporal' part. Insert the blunt handle of a knife into the white matter of the 'occipitotemporal' part immediately superficial to the point where the superior longitudinal bundle abuts on it, and lever up the surface, tearing it away from the subjacent tissue. This will demonstrate the posterior end of the superior longitudinal bundle turning inferiorly and fanning out into the occipital and temporal lobes, superficial to the fibres of the corona radiata.

Superior Longitudinal Bundle [FIG. 234]

This is a thick bundle of longitudinal association fibres which lies immediately external to the circular sulcus of the insula. It extends around the insula from the frontal pole to the tip of the temporal pole, and is thickest superior to the posterior half of the insula. Fibres enter and leave its external surface throughout its length, and it occupies approximately the same position on the lateral surface of the brain as the cingulum [FIG. 211] does on

the medial surface, thus connecting the various parts of the cerebral cortex on the superolateral surface of the hemisphere.

DISSECTION. Turn to the inferior surface of the temporal lobe and insert the handle of the knife obliquely upwards and forwards into its inferior surface close to the occipital pole. Tear the inferior part away from the remainder, and expose a bundle of fibres which runs horizontally forwards into the temporal lobe. This is the inferior longitudinal bundle.

Inferior Longitudinal Bundle

This is a bundle of association fibres which runs horizontally through the temporal and occipital lobes near their inferior surfaces. It is applied to the inferior surface of the corona radiata, and connects the various parts of the cerebral cortex on the tentorial surface of the hemisphere.

DISSECTION. Remove the external capsule from the lentiform nucleus which lies deep to it. This may be done by removing the external capsule piecemeal, but it is better to lift up a strip of the external capsule and expose the rounded grey surface of the lentiform nucleus; then introduce a blunt instrument beneath the remainder of the external capsule and separate it from

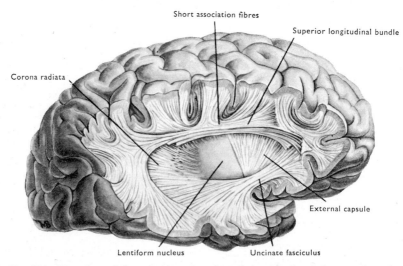

FIG. 234 Dissection of the superolateral surface of the right hemisphere to show the laterally placed association bundles.

276

the lentiform nucleus by moving the instrument gently back and forth.

As the external capsule is removed note a number of fine vessels which run in grooves over the lateral surface of the lentiform nucleus. These are the striate branches of the middle cerebral artery, and if followed inferiorly, converge on the anterior perforated substance. Follow some of them to the anterior perforated substance.

External Capsule

This is a thin layer of white matter which courses over the lateral surface of the lentiform nucleus and separates it from the claustrum and the white matter of the insula [FIG. 243]. Since the external capsule strips from the lentiform nucleus with ease it seems unlikely that many of its fibres enter the lentiform nucleus, but a certain number appear to pass to the claustrum, and some are probably association fibres passing between the temporal lobe and the frontal and parietal lobes.

DISSECTION. On the medial side of the 'frontal' part of the left hemisphere, insert the handle of a knife into the anterior horn of the lateral ventricle and pull the genu and rostrum of the corpus callosum forwards, thus separating them from the rest of the brain. This exposes the head of the caudate nucleus and its conti-

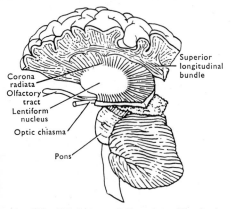

FIG. 235 Third phase of dissection. The fasciculus uncinatus, claustrum, and external capsule have been removed exposing the lentiform nucleus. The rostrum of the corpus callosum, together with the medial orbital part of the frontal lobe, have been torn away from the medial side and the antero-inferior is seen emerging medial to the anterior end of the lentiform edge of the corona radiata nucleus.

nuity with the lentiform nucleus superior to the anterior perforated substance. It also leaves the most anterior part of the corona radiata emerging from the internal capsule between the caudate and lentiform nuclei, and passes to the frontal lobe. Because of the amount of tissue which has been removed from its lateral and medial sides, the fibres of the corona which spread laterally and medially in the frontal lobe have been removed, and only the centrally placed fibres remain passing directly forwards into the frontal lobe [Fig. 235]. The whole extent of the lentiform and caudate nuclei and the corona radiata should now be explored, their position relative to each other and to the internal cover of the lentiform nucleus (the internal capsule) will be clarified by subsequent dissection and the section of the right hemisphere.

Find the anterior commissure on the medial surface of the 'frontal' part of the left hemisphere, and remove the grey matter immediately inferior to it so as to follow it laterally below the inferior part of the lentiform nucleus [Fig. 242]. It can be traced inferior to the nucleus, superior to the anterior perforated substance, to enter the shelf of white matter which extends laterally into the temporal lobe above the inferior horn of the lateral ventricle. This is the same shelf of white matter which is cut when the lateral ventricle is exposed, and into which the fibres of the fasciculus uncinatus and the sublentiform part of the corona radiata run to reach the temporal lobe. The fibres of the anterior commissure fan out into this white matter of the temporal lobe.

Anterior Commissure

This commissure is complementary to the corpus callosum, and connects the two temporal lobes. Seen from below the full extent of the commissure has the shape of a cupid's bow, but at its ends it fans out into the temporal lobe. Its fibres have a twisted appearance like a piece of string, and it crosses the midline in the superior part of the lamina terminalis immediately anterior to the columns of the fornix. Laterally it curves slightly forwards, superior to the anterior perforated substance (olfactory tubercle) and then curves posteriorly below the lentiform nucleus to enter the temporal lobe. Its fibres fan out posteriorly in the white matter of the temporal lobe.

In lower mammals the anterior commissure is said to convey a number of commissural fibres between the olfactory bulbs and other olfactory parts of the forebrain, but if such an element is present in the anterior commissure in Man it must be a very small part of it.

Striate Arteries

The lateral striate branches of the middle cerebral artery have already been seen coursing over the lateral surface of the lentiform nucleus and piercing its surface after entering the brain through the anterior perforated substance. In the dissection of the anterior commissure the more medially placed striate arteries have been seen ascending through the anterior perforated substance into the caudate and lentiform nuclei to supply them and the internal capsule which runs between them [FIG. 243]. The vessels from the lentiform nucleus also pierce the internal capsule and enter the lateral surface of the thalamus on the medial side of the internal capsule. The most medial of the striate arteries arise from the anterior cerebral artery, usually near the anterior communicating artery, and run a recurrent course to the anterior perforated substance [FIG. 170]. These pass to the caudate nucleus and to the anterior hypothalamus. The striate arteries which play a part in the supply of the internal capsule may be thrombosed or ruptured, thus interfering with the pathways to and from the cerebral cortex. This condition, known as a stroke, causes paralysis of the opposite side of the body due to the involvement of the corticospinal pathways, and frequently affects sensation because of the injury to thalamocortical fibres in the internal capsule.

CORONA RADIATA

This mass consists of the nerve fibres passing between the cerebral cortex and other parts of the central nervous system. It therefore consists of the **projection fibres** of the cerebral cortex passing inferiorly into the internal capsule, and of **corticopetal fibres,** principally from the thalamus. The fibres of the corona radiata are continuous with the internal capsule around the periphery of the lentiform nucleus, and they spread out in a fan-like fashion into the cerebral cortex both anteroposteriorly and transversely. Those which

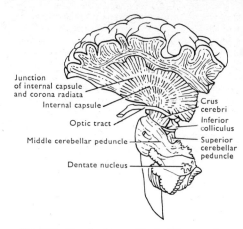

FIG. 236 Fourth phase. The lentiform nucleus has been stripped from the internal capsule to expose the continuity of that structure with the crus cerebri at the level of the optic tract. The cerebellum is also partly dissected to show the superior and middle peduncles.

emerge anterior and superior to the lentiform nucleus pass to and from the frontal and parietal lobes; those which emerge posterior to the nucleus (retrolentiform part) pass to and from the occipital lobe; while those which emerge beneath the posterior end of the lentiform nucleus (sublentiform part, between it and the tail of the caudate nucleus in the roof of the inferior horn of the lateral ventricle) pass to and from the temporal lobe.

DISSECTION. To expose the internal capsule, remove the lentiform nucleus from the lateral side of the internal capsule. The lentiform nucleus does not strip easily from the internal capsule because a large number of fibres enter the lentiform nucleus from the internal capsule. Some of these are concentrated into two sheets (the medullary laminae) which pass downwards and laterally through the lentiform nucleus and divide it into three parts. The outer, darker part of the lentiform nucleus (the putamen) is continuous with the caudate nucleus between the bundles of the internal capsule; the inner, paler segments [Figs. 243A, 244] comprise the globus pallidus. The latter segments send the efferent fibres of the lentiform nucleus (the ansa lenticularis) through and around the inferior part of the internal capsule into the hypothalamus.

Bend the corona radiata medially and run a blunt instrument round the margin of the lentiform nucleus to separate it from the base of the corona. Continue strip-

278

ing the nucleus from the internal capsule downwards owards the stem of the lateral sulcus, noting the small ranches of the striate arteries passing to the capsule. he plane of the lateral surface of the internal capsule uns inferomedially towards the lateral surface of the rus cerebri. When the nucleus is completely separated rom the capsule, note that it is still attached to the rain by a loop of fibres which curves round the inferior dge of the internal capsule to enter the hypothalamus n its medial side, the ansa lenticularis.

Remove the lentiform nucleus completely by dividing he ansa, and note the continuity of corona radiata and he internal capsule, and the optic tract running round he internal capsule at its junction with the crus cerebri Fig. 237]. Strip the optic tract from the lateral side f the internal capsule and confirm its continuity with he crus cerebri.

INTERNAL CAPSULE

Certain gross features of the internal capsule re now obvious. (1) It lies medial to the lenti-

form nucleus. (2) It is continuous superiorly with the corona radiata, and inferiorly with the crus cerebri. (3) Its fibres radiate in a fan-shaped manner so that the fibres from the frontal lobe enter its anterior part, run a long course in it, and enter the medial part of the crus cerebri. The temporal fibres enter it just superior to the optic tract, run a very short distance in it, and enter the posterolateral part of the crus with the occipital fibres. It follows from this that the position of the various groups of fibres in the internal capsule and crus is determined by their position of origin in the hemisphere, and that the fibres which arise in the precentral gyrus (**corticonuclear** and **corticospinal fibres**), near the midpoint between the frontal and occipital poles, will enter the middle region of the internal capsule and crus. (4) If the dissection has been satisfactory, the strands of grey matter passing

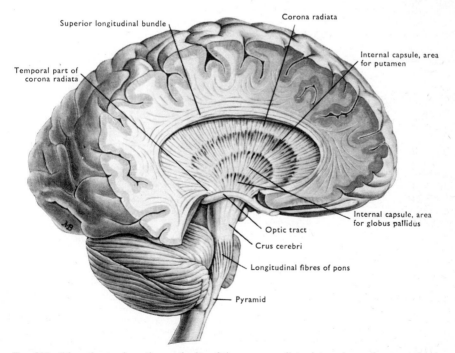

Superior longitudinal bundle

Corona radiata

Internal capsule, area for putamen

Temporal part of corona radiata

Internal capsule, area for globus pallidus

Optic tract

Crus cerebri

Longitudinal fibres of pons

Pyramid

FIG. 237 Dissection to show the continuity of the corona radiata, internal capsule, crus cerebri, longitudinal fibres of the pons, and the pyramid.

between the putamen and the caudate nucleus will be visible near the superior edge of the internal capsule. Also the torn ends of the two medullary laminae will be seen as two rough ridges on the lateral surface of the internal capsule.

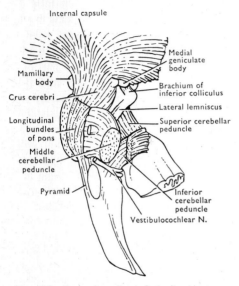

FIG. 238   Deep dissection of the brain stem. The left half of the pons has been torn away between two cuts to display the longitudinal fibres passing through it to become continuous with the pyramid in the medulla oblongata. The three cerebellar peduncles are also displayed.

DISSECTION. Make two vertical cuts through the transverse fibres of the pons, one in the midline and the other immediately anterior to the entry of the trigeminal nerve. Strip off the superficial transverse fibres of the pons between these, and expose the longitudinal fibres of the pons [Fig. 238]. These are the fibres of the crus cerebri which break up into bundles in the basilar part of the pons, and running between the transverse fibres, mainly end in the pontine nuclei. A small proportion can be followed through the pons to emerge at its inferior border as the pyramid on the anterior surface of the medulla oblongata [Fig. 247].

Clean the surface of the pyramid and follow it inferiorly. Note that it gradually tapers in the lower part of the medulla oblongata, and that opposite this the anterior median fissure of the medulla oblongata is filled with interdigitating bundles of fibres. These are

the decussating fibres of the pyramids passing toward the lateral funiculus of the spinal medulla to form the lateral corticospinal tract, which extends into the sacral spinal medulla. A variable proportion of the fibres in the pyramid continues inferiorly, without decussation, into the anterior funiculus of the spinal medulla, to form the anterior corticospinal tract. The fibres of this tract decussate before termination in the grey matter of the spinal medulla, and the tract usually terminates in the upper thoracic region.

The above dissections demonstrate that the corona radiata, internal capsule, crus cerebri

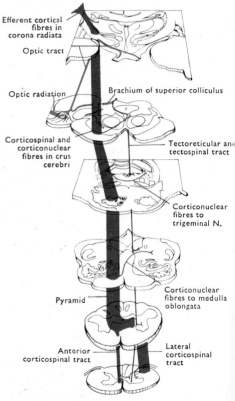

FIG. 239   A diagram to show the course of the corticonuclear and corticospinal (red) fibres (of one side) through the brain stem. In addition the fibres in one optic tract (blue) are shown passing to the lateral geniculate body and to the superior colliculus, and the descending pathway (tectospinal and tectoreticular, red) for visual reflexes from the superior colliculus. The outline drawings of brain stem sections are not to scale, but correspond to FIGS. 178–184 and 193–196.

longitudinal fibres of the basilar part of the pons, the pyramid, and the corticospinal tracts form one continuous mass of fibres [FIG. 237] and that only those fibres which enter the corticospinal tracts run through the whole extent of this pathway. It is through the latter, 'motor' pathway that the cerebral cortex can stimulate the motor cells of the spinal medulla. The majority of the descending cortical fibres end in the thalamus, lentiform and caudate nuclei, and in the pons, and almost all of the ascending fibres are found only in the internal capsule and corona radiata, since they enter this system from the thalamus.

THE BASAL NUCLEI OF THE CEREBRUM

The basal nuclei of the cerebrum are: (1) the corpus striatum, consisting of the caudate and lentiform nuclei; (2) the claustrum; and (3) the amygdaloid body. All of these masses of grey matter have been seen in the previous dissections, but their relations are best studied in sections of the hemisphere, which also help to clarify the position and gross connexions of the thalamus and hypothalamus.

Sections of the hemisphere can be carried out on the right side which is nearly intact, but it is desirable to have both horizontal and transverse sections for study. For this purpose, groups of students should combine their specimens if it is not possible to have another brain. Specially stained macroscopic sections are also of considerable assistance [see APPENDIX] but the staining masks certain features of the white matter which are visible in freshly cut slices and which help to determine the direction in which particular groups of fibres are running. Thus, when white matter is cut parallel to its fibres it appears whiter than when the section is made across the fibres, and it is possible, for example, to differentiate between the tapetum and the corona radiata in sections through the posterior part of the hemisphere [FIG. 250].

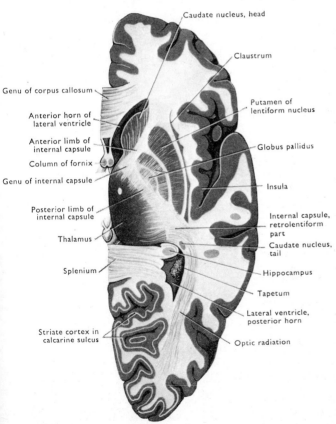

Caudate nucleus, head

Claustrum

Genu of corpus callosum

Putamen of lentiform nucleus

Anterior horn of lateral ventricle

Anterior limb of internal capsule

Globus pallidus

Column of fornix

Genu of internal capsule

Insula

Posterior limb of internal capsule

Internal capsule, retrolentiform part

Thalamus

Caudate nucleus, tail

Splenium

Hippocampus

Tapetum

Striate cortex in calcarine sulcus

Lateral ventricle, posterior horn

Optic radiation

FIG. 240   Horizontal section through the right cerebral hemisphere at the level of the interventricular foramen.

DISSECTION. Make a horizontal cut through the right hemisphere which passes through the interventricular foramen and the inferior half of the splenium of the corpus callosum. This is best carried out with a large knife pulled through the brain in a single sweep.

If a second hemisphere is not available for the transverse sections, then the horizontal section should be studied, the two parts placed together, and the transverse sections cut from the same hemisphere. This method is not ideal, and every effort should be made to obtain a separate hemisphere for the transverse sections.

The transverse sections are cut as follows: (1) through the posterior part of the genu of the corpus callosum [Fig. 241]; (2) through the anterior perforated substance [Fig. 242]; (3) immediately anterior to the infundibulum [Fig. 243]; (4) just anterior to the mamillary bodies [Fig. 244]; (5) obliquely downwards through the crus cerebri and pons (if present) [Fig. 245]; (6) through the splenium of the corpus callosum [Fig. 250].

Horizontal Section

The main features of this section are immediately visible in FIGURE 240, but certain special points should be noted:

1. The white and grey matter of the hemisphere, cortex, basal nuclei, and thalamus.

2. The buried **insula** with its white matter is lateral to: (1) the **claustrum** (a thin layer of grey matter with a slightly scalloped lateral surface); (2) the **external capsule**; and (3) the **lentiform nucleus,** the latter divided into its three parts by the medial and lateral **medullary laminae.** The outer segment is the **putamen,** the inner two are the **globus pallidus.**

3. The V-shaped **internal capsule** bent round the medial aspect of the lentiform nucleus is divisible, in this view, into anterior and posterior limbs which meet at the **genu.** Medial to the **anterior limb** is the head of the caudate nucleus in the anterior horn of the lateral ventricle, while medial to the **posterior limb** are the thalamus, and further posteriorly, the tail of the caudate nucleus still in the wall of the ventricle. Note that the posterior limb is darker in colour than the anterior limb because the fibres of the former are cut transversely, and that, similarly, the **optic radiation,** a part of the corona radiata, passing towards the occipital lobe is lighter in colour than the fibres of the **tapetum**

which separate it from the posterior horn of the lateral ventricle [c.f., FIG. 250].

4. Identify the genu and splenium of the **corpus callosum,** and note the relation of these parts to the lateral ventricle.

5. Note the position and extent of the **striate cortex.** The specimen illustrated in FIGURE 240 has an unusually extensive striate area.

6. Examine the cut surface of the lentiform nucleus and note the cut ends of the striate branches of the middle cerebral artery in it. Note also the cortical branches of the same artery on the insula.

With the assistance of FIGURES 221, and 241–245, identify the structures visible in the transverse sections, and relate their positions to those seen in the horizontal section and to the features seen in the dissection of the left hemisphere. In this manner try to build up a three-dimensional picture of the internal structure of the cerebral hemisphere. This can be achieved most readily by placing the sections together to reconstruct the hemisphere and taking them apart several times.

CORPUS STRIATUM

The corpus striatum consists of the caudate and lentiform nuclei, which are two parts of the same mass partially separated by the fibres of the internal capsule. Around its periphery the internal capsule lies between the caudate and the putamen of the lentiform but centrally it separates the lentiform nucleus from the thalamus and hypothalamus. The separation of the caudate from the putamen of the lentiform nucleus is incomplete, for the head of the caudate is fused with the putamen anteriorly, and elsewhere they are also connected between the bundles of the internal capsule by strands of grey matter.

The separation of the caudate nucleus from the putamen of the lentiform nucleus is probably of less functional significance than the separation of the putamen from the globus pallidus [FIGS. 243, 244], for the caudate and putamen have an identical histological structure and similar connexions, while the

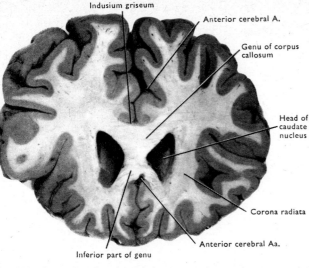

Indusium griseum

Anterior cerebral A.

Genu of corpus callosum

Head of caudate nucleus

Corona radiata

Anterior cerebral Aa.

Inferior part of genu

FIG. 241   Coronal section through the genu of the corpus callosum and the anterior horns of the lateral ventricles.

structure and connexions of the globus pallidus are very different.

Caudate Nucleus

This comma-shaped nucleus has a wide, thick **head** which lies in the lateral wall of the anterior horn of the lateral ventricle, and is fused with the anterior end of the lentiform nucleus inferior to the anterior limb of the internal capsule. Here the common mass is fused with the anterior perforated substance, and receives the striate branches of the middle and anterior cerebral arteries through it. The head tapers rapidly to the narrow **body,** which runs posteriorly in the

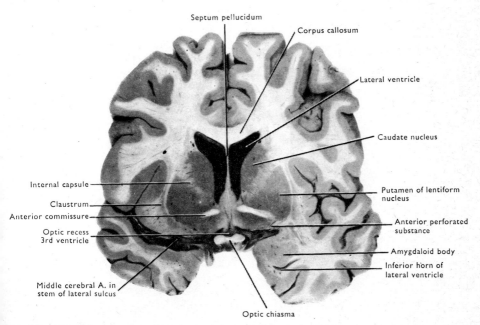

Septum pellucidum

Corpus callosum

Lateral ventricle

Caudate nucleus

Putamen of lentiform nucleus

Anterior perforated substance

Amygdaloid body

Inferior horn of lateral ventricle

Internal capsule

Claustrum

Anterior commissure

Optic recess 3rd ventricle

Middle cerebral A. in stem of lateral sulcus

Optic chiasma

FIG. 242   Coronal section through the brain at the level of the optic chiasma. On the right the section is slightly posterior to that on the left half.

lateral part of the floor of the central portion of the lateral ventricle. The **tail**—narrow and flat—turns inferiorly, and runs anteriorly in the roof of the inferior horn to end in the amygdaloid body. The tail may be discontinuous in places in the roof of the inferior horn.

The ventricular surface of the caudate nucleus is covered with ependyma. The deep surface of the head is fused with the anterior limb of the internal capsule, while the deep surfaces of the body and tail lie on the base of the corona radiata external to the peripheral margin of the lentiform nucleus. A thin strand of association fibres, the fronto-occipital bundle lies between the convexity of the caudate nucleus and the inferior surface of the corpus callosum.

Lentiform Nucleus

This large, lens-shaped nucleus lies lateral to the internal capsule, and has three surfaces.

The **lateral surface** is smooth and convex, and is grooved inferiorly by the lateral striate vessels before they sink into its substance. It is separated from the claustrum by the external capsule.

The **medial surface** is highly convex, and its apex lies opposite the interventricular foramen on the genu of the internal capsule, between the head of the caudate nucleus anteriorly and the thalamus posteriorly. Branches of the striate arteries pierce the nucleus, enter and supply the internal capsule, and continue through it to supply the caudate nucleus and the lateral part of the thalamus.

The **inferior surface** is fused anteriorly with the anterior perforated substance and through it is continuous with the amygdaloid body [FIG. 243]. In this situation the lentiform is deeply grooved by the anterior commissure [FIG. 242]. Posteriorly the lentiform nucleus lies on the white matter which passes laterally into the temporal lobe. This shelf of white matter contains the **sublentiform part of the internal capsule** (auditory radiation) and separates the lentiform nucleus from the tail of the caudate nucleus, the optic tract and the inferior horn of the lateral ventricle [FIG. 245].

The lentiform nucleus is divided by two

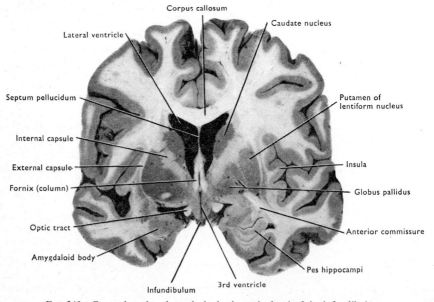

FIG. 243   Coronal section through the brain at the level of the infundibulum.

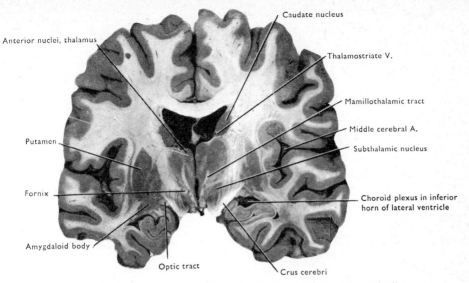

Anterior nuclei, thalamus

Putamen

Fornix

Amygdaloid body

Optic tract

Caudate nucleus

Thalamostriate V.

Mamillothalamic tract

Middle cerebral A.

Subthalamic nucleus

Choroid plexus in inferior horn of lateral ventricle

Crus cerebri

FIG. 244   Coronal section through the brain at the level of the mamillary bodies.

ertical sheets of white matter (the lateral and nedial **medullary laminae**) into three parts. The lateral, darker part is the **putamen**, the wo paler, medial segments form the **globus allidus**.

The **connexions** of the corpus striatum are omplex and not completely understood. It s clear, however, that the caudate and putamen receive a considerable number of fibres rom the cerebral cortex and thalamus. The fferent fibres of both these nuclei pass predominantly to the globus pallidus, the medial egment of which, unlike the other two nuclei, ontains a number of large nerve cells, and ;ives rise to most of the nerve fibres which eave the corpus striatum. The efferent fibres of the globus pallidus (**ansa lenticularis**) pass nedially through and around the ventral part of the internal capsule to enter the lateral part of the hypothalamus (subthalamus) [FIG. 244]. Here some fibres end on the subthalamic nucleus, while others turn caudally to reach he tegmentum of the midbrain (e.g., red ucleus and substantia nigra, FIG. 245), the emainder pass medially into the hypohalamus or turn dorsally to the thalamus,

whence the impulses they convey may be transmitted to the cerebral cortex.

The **functions** of the corpus striatum are not clear, but it appears to be concerned with the regulation of muscle tone and the control of automatic movements, as well as playing a part in the control of voluntary movements. The involvement of the corpus striatum in pathological lesions tends to lead to a state of increased muscular tone, the disappearance of associated movements (e.g., swinging the arms in walking), and the development of a tremor which is present during rest. The genesis of these symptoms is not understood, but their disappearance when the internal capsule or the thalamus is subsequently damaged seems to suggest that they may in part be due to the uncontrolled action of the cerebral cortex.

Claustrum [FIGS. 242–245]

This thin plate of grey matter which lies between the external capsule and the white matter of the insula is of unknown function, but appears to belong to the basal nuclei of the telencephalon. Antero-inferiorly the claustrum reaches its greatest thickness and is fused

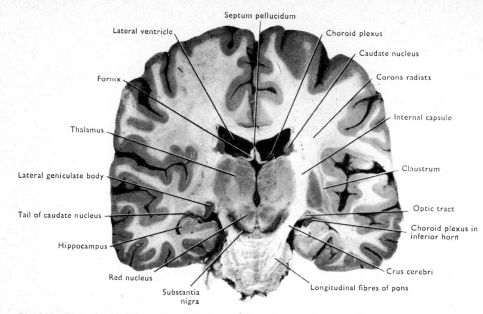

Lateral ventricle
Septum pellucidum
Choroid plexus
Caudate nucleus
Corona radiata
Fornix
Thalamus
Internal capsule
Lateral geniculate body
Claustrum
Tail of caudate nucleus
Optic tract
Choroid plexus in inferior horn
Hippocampus
Crus cerebri
Red nucleus
Longitudinal fibres of pons
Substantia nigra

FIG. 245 Coronal section through the brain passing through the basilar part of the pons. Note the division of the thalamus into anterior, medial, lateral, and central nuclei on the left.

with the anterior perforated substance and the amygdaloid body [FIG. 243]. It seems to receive nerve fibres through the external capsule, but its connexions are unknown.

Amygdaloid Body [FIG. 243]

This complex of nuclei lies over the tip of the inferior horn of the lateral ventricle and is fused with the claustrum and the anterior perforated substance. It is continuous with the tail of the caudate nucleus posteriorly, and with the cortex of the uncus medially. It probably receives afferent fibres from a considerable number of sources, some from the olfactory system. Its efferent fibres pass mainly into the stria terminalis, but some pass

by way of the diagonal band across the anterior perforated substance to much the same regions, the anterior hypothalamus and septal nuclei.

The **stria terminalis** is a delicate bundle of fibres which arises in the amygdaloid body. It passes posteriorly along the medial side of the tail of the caudate nucleus in the roof of the inferior horn of the lateral ventricle. Curving upwards with the caudate nucleus, it enters the floor of the central part of the lateral ventricle and runs forwards with the thalamostriate vein, between the thalamus and the body of the caudate nucleus. At the interventricular foramen it turns inferiorly with the fornix, and ends in the anterior hypothalamus and septal nuclei.

THE NUCLEI AND CONNEXIONS OF THE THALAMUS

If the differentiation between grey and white matter is good in the brain slices, the main subdivisions of the thalamus may be

seen, but its minor subdivisions are only visible in microscopic sections.

The thalamus is divided into a number of

separate cell groups or nuclei by the presence of two layers of white matter (medullary laminae) which run through it approximately in a sagittal plane. The **lateral medullary lamina** lies close to the internal capsule and is separated from it by a thin, broken lamina of grey matter [FIGS. 244, 245] the **reticular nucleus** of the thalamus. The **medial medullary lamina** forms a more complete layer and lies more or less midway between the lateral wall of the third ventricle and the internal capsule. It divides the thalamus into **medial** and **lateral nuclei** [FIG. 245] and ventrally it sweeps in a medial direction to separate the medial nucleus from the **ventral nuclei** which lie between the medial nucleus and the hypothalamus. There is no clear line of demarcation between the lateral nucleus and the ventral nuclei. Antero-superiorly the medial medullary lamina splits to enclose the **anterior nuclei** [FIGS. 244, 245] while posteriorly it encloses the **central nucleus** [FIG. 245] and a number of other small nuclei (the intralaminar nuclei) lie in this lamina but are not visible to the unaided eye.

Afferent Connexions

The main bundles of afferent fibres to the thalamus are: (1) The **spinothalamic tract** and **medial lemniscus,** which bring impulses arising in sensory endings in the opposite side of the body, together with some uncrossed fibres in the spinothalamic tract and ascending fibres from the reticular formation of the brain stem, which carry similar, bilateral impulses. (2) Visual fibres of the **optic tract,** which end in the lateral geniculate body. (3) **Acoustic fibres,** which pass to the medial geniculate body in the brachium of the inferior colliculus. (4) The **mamillothalamic tract,** which conveys impulses from the mamillary body through the plane of the medial medullary lamina to the anterior nucleus of the thalamus. Some of the latter impulses arise as a result of impulses which reach the mamillary body through the fornix.

In addition to these, most of the thalamic nuclei receive fibres from the cerebral cortex:

Thalamic nucleus	Area of cortex sending fibres to thalamic nucleus.
Ventral	Posterior frontal and anterior parietal lobes.
Medial	Anterior part of frontal lobe.
Lateral (including pulvinar)	Parietal and occipital lobes.
Lateral geniculate body	Striate cortex of occipital lobe.
Medial geniculate body	Superior temporal gyrus.
Anterior	Hippocampus via fornix directly, and mamillary body indirectly.
Reticular	The greater part of the cortex.

These fibres reach the thalamus via the corona radiata and internal capsule.

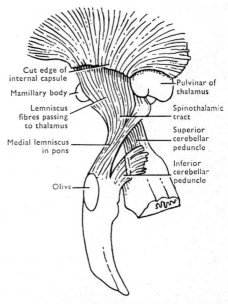

FIG. 246 Deep dissection of brain stem, see also FIG. 238. The pons, middle cerebellar peduncle, crus cerebri, and pyramid have been torn away, leaving the superior and inferior cerebellar peduncles and the lemniscus system exposed. Note the continuity of the dentate nucleus with the superior cerebellar peduncle.

Cut edge of internal capsule
Mamillary body
Lemniscus fibres passing to thalamus
Medial lemniscus in pons
Olive
Pulvinar of thalamus
Spinothalamic tract
Superior cerebellar peduncle
Inferior cerebellar peduncle

DISSECTION. To expose the ascending pathways from the brain stem and spinal medulla, make a deep median incision into the pons on the left half of the brain, and deepen the cut which was made through the left half of the pons immediately anterior to the trigeminal nerve to expose the longitudinal fibres of the pons. With the handle of a knife, free the left pyramid from the anterior surface of the medulla oblongata and pull it upwards, tearing away all the longitudinal and transverse fibres of the basilar part of the pons between the median and lateral cuts. As the superior border of the pons is reached pull the crus cerebri away with it in a superior direction as far as the inferior part of the internal capsule [Fig. 246].

The removal of this ventral mass of tissue from the brain stem exposes a horizontal sheet of fibres running longitudinally, and in the midbrain a sheet of pigmented grey matter, the substantia nigra [Fig. 245]. The longitudinal sheet of fibres in the pons and midbrain [Fig. 247] consists of the medial lemniscus, the spinothalamic tract, and the lateral lemniscus at the lateral border. Follow the lateral margin of the sheet superiorly on to the exposed lateral surface of the midbrain and note its continuity with the lateral lemniscus previously exposed there. Also note how the medial lemniscus

sweeps laterally as it ascends, and comes to lie on the lateral aspect of the midbrain at the level of the superior colliculus. Here some of the fibres of the spinothalamic tract pass into the superior colliculus (spinotectal tract). Follow the medial lemniscus superiorly till it disappears into the thalamus on the medial aspect of the internal capsule.

ASCENDING TRACTS IN THE BRAIN STEM

The sheet of fibres now exposed consists of the medial lemniscus, spinothalamic tract, and lateral lemniscus from medial to lateral.

Medial Lemniscus [FIGS. 180, 183, 193, 248]

The medial lemniscus is one of the great ascending tracts. It transmits impulses which arise in tactile and proprioceptive sensory endings. It is formed by fibres which arise in the opposite nuclei cuneatus and gracilis, and sweep across the midline to ascend through the medulla oblongata as a vertical sheet immediately posterior to the pyramid. It is the

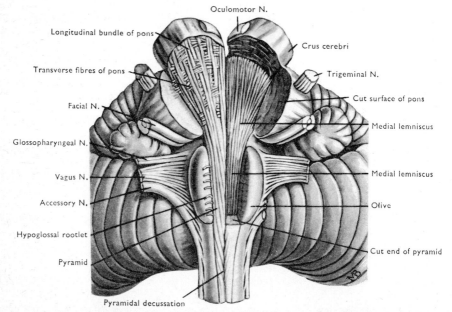

FIG. 247 Dissection of the pons and medulla oblongata. On the left of the illustration, the longitudinal fibres of the pons and pyramid have been exposed, but they have been removed on the right to expose the medial lemniscus lying posterior to them.

288

anterior surface of this mass of fibres which is exposed when the pyramid is raised out of its bed. As it enters the pons the medial lemniscus turns through a right angle and becomes a horizontal sheet of fibres which extends laterally from the midline. As it ascends, it gradually moves away from the midline and reaches the lateral aspect of the superior part of the midbrain, ascending vertically from this position to end in the thalamus. Thus the fibres of the two sides which transmit these impulses through the spinal medulla (fasciculi gracilis and cuneatus) and medulla oblongata (medial lemniscus) lie side by side adjacent to the midline, and may therefore be injured bilaterally by a single lesion in the midline. In the pons and midbrain this is no longer possible because the medial lemnisci diverge from each other.

Spinothalamic Tracts [FIGS. 180, 248]

The spinothalamic tracts which ascend through the anterolateral parts of the white matter of the spinal medulla and the lateral parts of the medulla oblongata, are widely separated from the posterior funiculi and medial lemnisci respectively in these two situations. But in the pons, the medial lemnisci extend laterally to join the spinothalamic

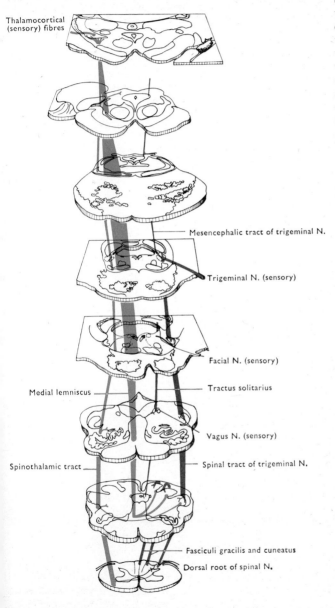

Thalamocortical (sensory) fibres

Mesencephalic tract of trigeminal N.

Trigeminal N. (sensory)

Facial N. (sensory)

Medial lemniscus

Tractus solitarius

Vagus N. (sensory)

Spinothalamic tract

Spinal tract of trigeminal N.

Fasciculi gracilis and cuneatus

Dorsal root of spinal N.

FIG. 248 An outline diagram to show the course taken by the primary sensory fibres (red) in the spinal and cranial nerves, and the secondary ascending pathways (blue) through which the impulses they carry are transmitted to the thalamus and cerebral cortex. The pathways shown are those concerned with the conscious appreciation of the various sensory impulses. The outline drawings of the brain stem slices are not to scale, but they correspond to FIGS. 178–184 and 193–195.

289

tracts, and continue superiorly fused with them. Thus the spinothalamic tracts, which are principally concerned with the transmission of impulses arising in pain, temperature, and touch endings, may be injured on one side of the spinal medulla and medulla oblongata without injury to the posterior funiculi or medial lemniscus, but in the pons and midbrain the medial lemniscus and corresponding spinothalamic tract may be injured by a single localized lesion.

Again, because the spinothalamic tracts are pierced by the ventral roots of the spinal nerves in the spinal medulla, lesions of these tracts are frequently associated with ventral root injury. The position of the spinothalamic tracts in the lateral part of the medulla oblongata places them in association with the laterally attached cranial nerves (facial, vestibulocochlear, glossopharyngeal, vagus, and cranial part of the accessory) which may be damaged in association with injuries of the spinothalamic tracts in the medulla oblongata.

Lateral Lemniscus [FIGS. 177, 184, 192, 249]

The lateral lemniscus, which is formed by fibres arising in the cochlear nuclei of the vestibulocochlear nerves of both sides, joins the lateral edge of the combined medial lemniscus and spinothalamic tracts in the pons, and together these three groups of fibres form the ascending sheet which may be exposed by removal of the basilar part of the pons. In this dissection it is possible to demonstrate the continuity of the lateral lemniscus with the cochlear nuclei by displacing the middle and inferior cerebellar peduncles laterally. The fibres of the lateral lemniscus on the lateral edge of the sheet turn posteriorly across the superior cerebellar peduncle to enter the inferior colliculus, while some of the fibres of the spinothalamic tract

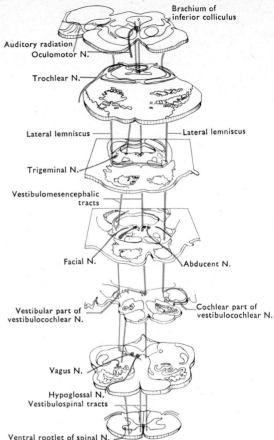

FIG. 249 An outline diagram to show the position of the motor cranial nerve nuclei and the course taken by their fibres passing through the brain stem to their points of exit (red). On the right the ascending connexions of the cochlear part of the vestibulocochlear nerve are shown (blue); on the left, the principal connexions of the vestibular part of the same nerve are indicated (blue). The outline drawings are not to scale, but correspond with FIGS. 178–184 and 193–194.

on the dorsal aspect of the medial lemniscus run posteriorly into the superior colliculus (**spinotectal tract**), the remainder passing superiorly into the thalamus.

The fibres of the lateral lemniscus reach it from the cochlear nuclei partly as decussating fibres which pass through the medial lemniscus in the pons (the trapezoid body) and partly as

290

direct fibres from the cochlear nuclei of the same side. Thus each lateral lemniscus, and the other parts of the auditory pathway superior to it, carry impulses from both ears, and damage to this pathway on one side does not prevent acoustic impulses from either ear reaching the thalamus and cerebral cortex, and hence does not cause unilateral deafness such as would arise from injury to the vestibulo-cochlear nerve on one side.

The lateral lemniscus ends in the inferior colliculus, but the impulses which it carries are transmitted to the thalamus (medial geniculate body) via the brachium of the inferior colliculus.

Thalamic Termination of Sensory Pathways

It has been seen already that the fibres of the optic tract end in the lateral geniculate body, and that the acoustic fibres in the brachium of the inferior colliculus end in the medial geniculate body. The fibres of the medial lemniscus and spinothalamic tracts terminate in the posterior part of the ventral nucleus of the thalamus.

EFFERENT FIBRES OF THE THALAMUS

The table on page 287 which shows the afferent connexions of the thalamus from the cerebral cortex is equally appropriate to show the efferent fibres from the thalamus to the cerebral cortex (with the exception of the anterior nuclear complex which projects to the cingulate gyrus) for most of these connexions are reciprocal.

In addition to these connexions the thalamus sends fibres to the hypothalamus and to the corpus striatum. In particular the medial nucleus sends fibres to the hypothalamus, and the central and intralaminar nuclei are said to project to the striatum. There is physiological evidence that the intralaminar nuclei may project diffusely to the cerebral cortex, but there is no anatomical confirmation of this.

Within the general mass of thalamocortical fibres are those which transmit the sensory information carried to the thalamus in the optic tract, the acoustic pathway, and the medial lemniscus and spinothalamic tracts. These are known as the sensory radiations, and they reach the cerebral cortex through the internal capsule and corona radiata in the

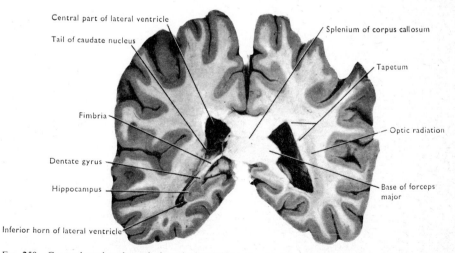

FIG. 250 Coronal section through the splenium of the corpus callosum to show the continuity of the central part and inferior horn of the lateral ventricle. Note how the fibres of the splenium and its tapetum virtually surround the posterior part of the lateral ventricle, as the fibres of the genu surround the anterior horn. Cf. FIG. 241.

same fashion as all the other thalamocortical fibres.

Optic Radiation

The fibres of this radiation arise in the cells of the lateral geniculate body, and sweep forwards into the retrolentiform part of the internal capsule. As they do so, they spread out into a broad sheet which turns around the concave surface of the lateral ventricle, and passes posteriorly between the tail of the caudate nucleus and the lentiform nucleus, to cross the lateral aspect of the tapetum [FIG. 250] and continue towards the occipital pole on the lateral aspect of the posterior horn of the lateral ventricle [FIG. 240]. As the optic radiation passes posteriorly, the fibres at its superior and inferior margins hook over the corresponding margins of the posterior horn of the lateral ventricle to reach the **striate cortex** in the superior and inferior walls of the **calcarine sulcus** on the medial aspect of the ventricle. The fibres of the inferior half of the radiation end in its inferior wall, those from the superior half end in its superior wall. Since the fibres in the most peripheral parts of the optic radiation (which carry impulses from the peripheral parts of the retinae) are the first to turn over or under the posterior horn of the ventricle, they end furthest anteriorly, while those situated successively nearer the centre of the radiation turn around the posterior horn at more and more posterior levels. Thus the central fibres (which carry impulses from the macular region) reach the most posterior parts of the calcarine sulcus, including the occipital pole. As the fibres of the optic radiation pass around the concave surface of the lateral ventricle, those lying most inferiorly tend to sweep forwards, superior to the inferior horn of the lateral ventricle, before turning posteriorly. In so doing these fibres run parallel and relatively close to the optic tract which is immediately medial to the temporal lobe of the brain. Thus lesions in this situation may injure either the optic tract, or the inferior part of the optic radiation, or both. The fibres in the inferior part of the radiation carry impulses which arise in the inferior parts of the corresponding halves of the retinae, while the fibres in the superior part of the radiation carry impulses from the superior parts of the same halves of the retinae.

In addition to the fibres passing to the cerebral cortex, the optic radiation contains fibres passing in the opposite

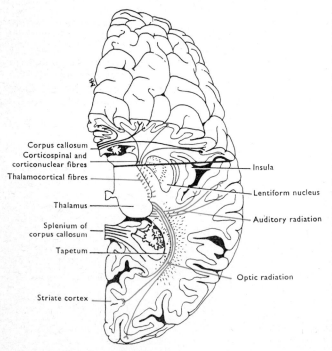

Corpus callosum
Corticospinal and corticonuclear fibres
Thalamocortical fibres
Thalamus
Splenium of corpus callosum
Tapetum
Striate cortex
Insula
Lentiform nucleus
Auditory radiation
Optic radiation

FIG. 251 Superior surface of a right hemisphere from which the upper parts of the parietal and occipital lobes have been removed. On the cut surfaces the various groups of fibres are shown diagrammatically. Red, motor fibres; blue, sensory fibres; black, commissural fibres of corpus callosum.

direction which run to the lateral geniculate body and to the superior colliculus. The latter are concerned with the production of eye movements through the descending tectal pathways.

Acoustic Radiation

The fibres of this radiation arise in the medial geniculate body and pass antero-laterally into the sublentiform part of the internal capsule, between the roof of the inferior horn of the lateral ventricle and the lentiform nucleus. They then turn superiorly to end on the superior surface of the superior temporal gyrus (transverse temporal gyrus) and to a small extent on its lateral surface [Figs. 200, 245, 251].

General Sensory Radiation

The cells of the posterior ventral nucleus of the thalamus, which receive impulses through the medial lemniscus and spinothalamic tracts, send fibres through the lateral aspect of the thalamus into the posterior limb of the internal capsule. These fibres ascend through the internal capsule and fan out to end in the posterior wall of the central sulcus and the immediately adjacent part of the postcentral gyrus [Fig. 200]. They are so arranged that fibres conveying sensory information from the head end inferiorly, and those carrying impulses from the lower limb and perineum end superiorly, even extending on to the medial surface of the hemisphere. The fibres which transmit impulses from the medial lemniscus retain the discrete point to point localization which is characteristic of that tract and of the posterior fasciculi from which it receives the impulses, and they therefore convey information which allows accurate localization of the part of the body stimulated. The spino-thalamic system does not have the same discrete point to point localization and is also partially bilateral in the information which it carries. It follows from this that lesions of this sensory radiation or of the postcentral gyrus produce profound disturbances of proprio-ception and tactile sense on the opposite side of the body, while pain and temperature sensations are only slightly affected though their localization (a function of the medial lemniscus system) is greatly disturbed.

HYPOTHALAMUS

This part of the brain forms the lateral wall of the third ventricle inferior to the hypo-thalamic sulcus, and extends laterally to the lower part of the internal capsule. It appears on the inferior surface of the brain surrounded by the optic tracts and crura cerebri, and has the mamillary bodies and infundibulum attached to this surface. In coronal section it is possible to divide the hypothalamus into lateral (subthalamus) and medial parts, only the latter appearing on the inferior surface, while the former overlies the inferior part of the internal capsule. Both parts are directly continuous inferiorly with the tegmentum of the midbrain without any line of demarcation, and the medial part (the hypothalamus of the physiologist) is particularly concerned with visceral activity.

The connexions of the hypothalamus are complex and incompletely understood, and details should be sought in larger textbooks, but a few of the major connexions are mentioned here.

Medial Part

Afferent Connexions. These reach the medial hypothalamus from: (1) the hippocampus via the fornix; (2) the thalamus, conveying impulses from many systems including the cerebral cortex; (3) the olfactory system, by fibres which pass posteriorly into the hypothalamus from the anterior perforated substance; (4) the striatum via the ansa lenticularis; (5) the brain stem by ascending fibres passing through the tegmentum of the midbrain.

Efferent Connexions. These can be divided into three main groups: (1) fibre connexions with other parts of the brain; (2) fibre connexions with the posterior lobe of the hypophysis; (3) vascular connexions with the anterior lobe of the hypophysis.

(1) The fibre connexions with other parts of the brain are numerous but the largest

single tract is the **mamillothalamic tract** which passes to the anterior nuclei of the thalamus. Thence fibres are relayed to the cingulate gyrus which has connexions with the hippocampus through the cingulum. The fibres in the mamillothalamic tract branch to give rise to a descending tract which passes into the midbrain, and a considerable number of other fibres descend into the brain stem from the lateral part of the medial hypothalamus.

(2) Certain groups of cells (principally the supra-optic, paraventricular, and tuberal nuclei) send their axons into the posterior lobe of the hypophysis. These do not innervate the posterior lobe in the usual manner, but act as ducts for the secretory materials synthesized in cells of the nuclei, and these materials are stored in the posterior lobe.

(3) The vascular connexion consists of capillaries of the hypothalamus (medial part) which form veins running inferiorly with the infundibulum. These veins break up into capillaries in the anterior lobe of the hypophysis, and are believed to carry hormones from the hypothalamus which can stimulate the anterior lobe to specific activity.

The nervous and vascular connexions with the hypophysis are concerned with the slow alterations in hormonal concentrations in the blood stream, by means of which the hypothalamus may produce slow, prolonged alterations in the activity of other organs. The connexions with the brain stem are presumably concerned with rapid, short duration alterations in visceral activity.

Lateral Part

The lateral part of the hypothalamus (subthalamus) consists of a number of groups of cells among which the **subthalamic nucleus** is the large oval structure seen in coronal sections of the brain [FIG. 244]. It lies superior to the upper extremity of the substantia nigra, and its inferior part is close to the red nucleus.

The subthalamus receives fibres from the thalamus and a considerable number of the fibres of the ansa lenticularis which enter it from the globus pallidus of the corpus striatum. Most of its efferent fibres pass inferiorly into the tegmentum of the midbrain, and it is closely associated with that part of the brain in the control of muscle tone. Lesions of the subthalamic nucleus are said to give rise to hemiballismus, a violent or writhing movement which principally affects the opposite upper limb.

CRANIOCEREBRAL TOPOGRAPHY

After the dissection of the brain is completed, the dissectors should review the relation of the brain to the skull and meninges. This is a most important topic since the effects of head injuries in different regions are dependent on the association of the parts of the brain to the skull and to the structures in or on the surfaces of the skull. Thus fractures of the base of the skull may allow blood and cerebrospinal fluid to escape into the nose, orbit, or external acoustic meatus, and fractures which cross the grooves for the middle meningeal artery may lead to extensive haemorrhage between the dura and periosteum with compression of the brain. Depressed fractures of the skull may irritate the underlying nervous tissue or interfere with its function, thus producing convulsions or paralysis if over the motor area of the cerebral cortex (precentral gyrus) and visual disturbances if the occipital pole is involved, the central area of vision being particularly affected in such a posterior injury.

Some of the main features of cranial topography have been described already [pp. 207–208] but the following points should be noted again. It should always be remembered that there are many different shapes of skull and that there is no such thing as an exact relationship between the parts of the brain and the surface features of the skull; the points mentioned below are approximate only:

1. A point two finger's breadth posterior and one finger's breadth superior to the notch on the posterior margin of the junction of the frontal and zygomatic bones (which is easily

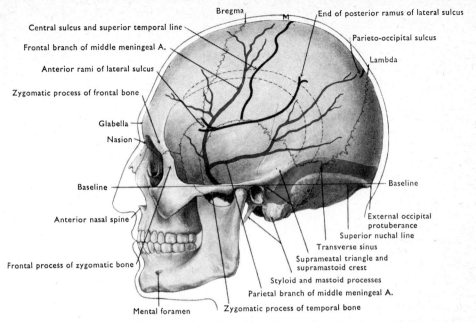

Central sulcus and superior temporal line

Frontal branch of middle meningeal A.

Anterior rami of lateral sulcus

Zygomatic process of frontal bone

Glabella

Nasion

Baseline

Anterior nasal spine

Frontal process of zygomatic bone

Mental foramen

Bregma

M

End of posterior ramus of lateral sulcus

Parieto-occipital sulcus

Lambda

Baseline

External occipital protuberance

Superior nuchal line

Transverse sinus

Suprameatal triangle and supramastoid crest

Styloid and mastoid processes

Parietal branch of middle meningeal A.

Zygomatic process of temporal bone

FIG. 252   Lateral view of the skull to show the position of certain important intracranial structures. M = midpoint between nasion and inion.

palpated) marks (a) the approximate position of the inferior end of the coronal suture, (b) the anterior end of the posterior ramus of the lateral sulcus, (c) the point where the lesser wing of the sphenoid meets the lateral wall of the skull, and (d) the situation where the frontal branch of the middle meningeal artery is frequently buried in the bone of the skull.

2. The coronal suture passes superiorly and slightly backwards from this point to its meeting with the sagittal suture at the bregma. The point of meeting of these sutures can be felt as a slight depression, and represents the position of the anterior fonticulus in the infant.

3. The frontal branch of the middle meningeal artery ascends more or less parallel to the coronal suture and frequently about a finger's breadth posterior to it.

4. The central sulcus also lies parallel to the coronal suture, but approximately two finger's breadth posterior to it. The superior extremity of this sulcus lies 1 cm. posterior to the midpoint on a median line joining the root of

the nose to the external occipital protuberance.

5. The posterior ramus of the lateral sulcus passes posteriorly and slightly superiorly. At first it lies on the line of the squamoparietal suture, but then passes deep to the parietal bone; its terminal part ascends for a short distance inferior to the parietal eminence.

6. If the line of the posterior ramus of the lateral sulcus is extended anteriorly to pass a short distance superior to the orbital margin, it marks the inferior margin of the frontal lobe.

7. A line, convex anteriorly, drawn from the point mentioned in (1) to meet the superior margin of the zygomatic arch approximately at its middle, marks the anterior extremity of the temporal lobe. The inferolateral margin of the cerebral hemisphere is indicated by the extension of the same line posteriorly along the superior margin of the zygomatic arch (immediately superior to the external acoustic meatus) and then horizontally to a point 1 cm. superolateral to the external occipital protuberance.

295

APPENDIX

MACROSCOPIC STAINING OF BRAIN SECTIONS

THE following method of increasing the contrast between white and grey matter, which may be applied to sections of any part of the brain, is based on the work of J. H. Mulligan, 'A Method of Staining the Brain for Macroscopic Study', *Journal of Anatomy* (1931) **65**, 468.

The method depends for its success on the production of a thin, relatively impervious fatty layer on the surface of the white matter by the action of warm phenol solution on the myelin. By this means, tannic acid in aqueous solution, which can pass into the grey matter, is prevented from entering the white. Treatment with a soluble iron salt then produces a purplish-black coloration of the surface of the grey matter.

1. Cut a brain, well fixed in formalin, into slices and wash thoroughly in running water. The slices may with advantage be refixed in 10 per cent. formalin for 8 hours and then washed again; but this is not essential.

2. Place the sections for 2 minutes in a large volume of the following mixture at 60°C.

Phenol	40 g. (4 per cent.)
Copper sulphate	5 g. (0·5 per cent.)
Concentrated hydro-chloric acid	1·2 ml. (0·12 per cent.)
Water to	1 litre

3. Rinse in a large volume of cold water for 1 minute.

4. Place in 2 per cent. solution of tannic acid for 1 minute.

5. Wash thoroughly (5 minutes) in running water.

6. Place in 2 per cent. solution of iron alum till the grey matter is purplish-black. This usually requires *less than 1 minute*, and the sections should be transferred rapidly to water just before the desired depth of staining is attained.

7. Wash well in running water.

Caution.—Throughout the process avoid rough handling of the sections, as the fatty layer of the stained areas may easily be rubbed off.

INDEX

INDEX

309